POLAND

U.S.S.R.

CARPATHIAN MTS.

UKRAINE

SLOVAKIA

CERNĂUTI

BUKOVINA

Dniester River

BESSARABIA

MOLDAVIA

Prut

KISHINEV

River

Tisza River

ERGOM

HUNGARY

OLD

BUDAPEST

AL

ROUMANIA

TRANSYLVANIA

MOHACS

NOVISAD

TITEL

River

BELGRADE

GALATZ

BRAILA

PLOESTI

BUCHAREST

GIURGIU

SILISTRA

RUSTCHUCK

DANUBE DELTA

CONSTANZA

DOBRUDJA

IRON GATES

BALKAN MTS.

SERBIA

SOFIA

BULGARIA

BLACK SEA

LAVIA

MONTENEGRO

GUSA

ALBANIA

SKOPLJE

MACEDONIA

TURKEY

CONSTANTINOPLE

GREECE

DARDANELLES

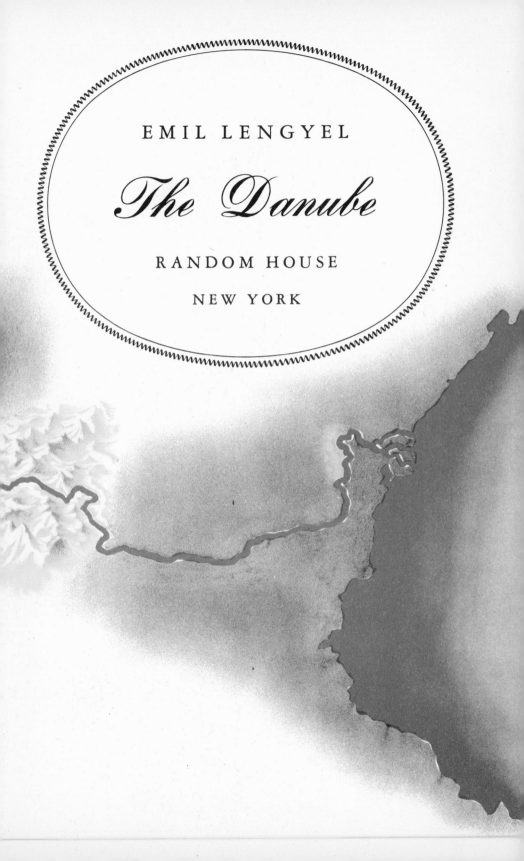

EMIL LENGYEL

The Danube

RANDOM HOUSE

NEW YORK

TO
MY WIFE

Contents

INTRODUCTION   3

I. THE BROWN DANUBE

   1. Castles, Ruins, Miracles   15

   2. Austria Yesterday—"Ostmark" Today   46

   3. Vienna—Dream and Reality   129

   4. The Danube Greets the Slav   158

II. THE GREEN DANUBE

   1. Hungary—Rural Landscape and a Conflict   211

   2. Budapest—A Hungarian Rhapsody   270

III. THE RED DANUBE

    1. The Yugoslav Kingdom—Keystone of the Balkans   297

    2. Roumania—The Danube Meets the Sea   362

    3. Bucharest—Last Outpost of Danubia   443

EPILOGUE   458

INDEX   465

Illustrations and Maps

Map of the entire Danube Basin   *End sheets*

Map of the Brown Danube   13

Klosterneuburg on the Danube   42

Genghis Khan (after a painting)   58

L'Aiglon   74

Emperor Franz Joseph I   90

Prince Ernst Ruediger von Starhemberg and
   Chancellor Engelbert Dollfuss   106

Hitler invades Austria   122

Map of the Green Danube   209

Hungarian shepherd wearing *shuba*   234

Regent Nicholas Horthy   250

Budapest from St. Gellert's   280

Map of the Red Danube   295

Ada Kaleh Island   314

Carmen Sylva   330

Nicholas Pashich   346

Stephen Radich   350

King Carol of Roumania   426

Mme. Magda Lupescu   442

Roumanian Gypsies   452

THE DANUBE

THE Danube flows through twenty thousand years. It gave protection to the Stone-Age man long before the Tiber became immortal. It was a center of culture thousands of years before Paris had become a fishing village. It saw the bowmen of Sesostris the Egyptian, the archers of Darius the Persian, the hoplites of Alexander the Macedonian, the lancers of Charlemagne the Frank, the warriors of the Hungarian conqueror Árpád, the Janizaries of Soleiman the Magnificent, the hordes of Genghis Khan the Tatar, and the Grande Armée of Napoleon the Great.

It has seen more wars than any other river. Godfrey of Bouillon's Crusaders, bound for the Holy Land, were massacred on its banks. The flower of an entire country was crushed at the battle of Mohács, five centuries later. Slaughters that horrified the world here more than justified the name of the "unspeakable Turk." Here the Holy Alliance drowned hopes of a freer day in blood.

3

The Battle of Nations against Napoleon was fought in adjacent land. The first World War broke out in the Danube valley. The clouds of the second World War are gathering there. If history bestowed names, it would long ago have called the river "The Beautiful Red Danube."

The Danube flows across several civilizations. Along its course of 1,750 miles the culture of two thousand years is revealed. At the Danube's source industrial cities produce twentieth-century machines; the fishermen in the Danube delta, where the river dies, live the life of St. Peter's contemporaries. Sailing down the Danube you sail into mankind's past.

The Danube is the river of bold ambitions and shattered dreams. Here Rome once hoped to make a stand forever. Here the Ottoman sought to conquer the world. Here the House of Habsburg built an Empire, stretching as far as the Americas. On the Danube, Napoleon made his bid for world power. Hitler, too, has heard the call to arms.

On the river bank, vastness destroyed Rome, and Islam began to crumble. There Napoleon lost a world to the Danube's Habsburgs. There man gazes into the future for signs of change.

The Danube attracts and repels, binds and dissolves. It is a river of contradictions. It attracted the seekers of pasture, was a majestic highway of trade. Its gold, copper, tin and salt fired ambition. Its valley is the burial ground of Avars, Celts, Dacians, Goths, Huns, Longobards, Vandals. Today Europe's three great races, German, Slav and Latin, are caught in its swirl.

Nature made the Danube a unifying force. There the Kingdom of Hungary stood for a thousand years, and the House of Habsburg for many centuries. Kingdom and Empire have vanished.

4

Introduction

The Danube is a frontier. There the Roman "Limes" separated light from darkness—the eternal city from the barbarians. Tidal waves of history, sweeping the East and West, flung the remnants of many races on the banks of this frontier river.

The Danube is also the river of romance. Two stars mark the place of its origin in guide books, officially attesting its beauty. The silver streak of the young Danube in the Black Forest is the tourist's delight. The ruined castles of titled cutthroats are impressive sights, reminders of the time when nobility was synonymous with murder. The Danube reached high, as shown by the spire of the Ulm Minster, said to be one of the tallest in this wide world. The *comptoirs* of old Regensburg, the beer-gardens of gay Linz, the spring-time orchards of the Wachau fascinate the tourist, enchanted by the perfume of the Vienna Woods which inspired Mozart, Beethoven and Brahms. Budapest, "the dream city," calls, and the mirage of the Magyar plains beckons.

Yet some Danubian countries could not be more obscure if they were in the heart of Africa. Books are written in the private code of specialists, as if the Danube were merely a subject for academic debate. Today the Danube and the countries in its valley can no longer be removed from public interest. History has taken permanent quarters in the Danube basin, and its record can scarcely be written fast enough. Is there any other part of the world in which changes have taken place so rapidly? In twelve months two countries were wiped out in the river valley. To-morrow may bring the loss of independence to their neighbors. Germany's giant shadow falls across the Danube. Today she and her satellites control more than two-thirds of the river. Alliances and counter-alliances are concluded. The dangerous peninsula—

5

the Balkans,—which the Danube bounds in the north, is again seeking protection.

We shall see the Danube in Old Germany, then make our first stop in ex-Austria, whose masters once ruled the world. She gave mankind a new concept of greatness and, later on, of charm. It was no mere accident that the immortals of music sang on the banks of the Danube. Former Czechoslovakia, an experiment in democracy, will next command our attention. Hungary offers a lesson and a heart-throb. No other country anywhere preserved its frontiers for a thousand years. And Hungarians have long memories.

Then we go to the Balkans, where the Danube is even more a frontier river. The name of Yugoslavia is comparatively new, but then, the name of Czechoslovakia was not much better known a short time ago. What is the "curse of the Balkans"? Why has it been the bloody peninsula so long?

Roumania is the last station, and there the river dies, to be reborn. The Danube is nowhere standardized.

In the Danube valley political volcanoes are seething. Its green-carpeted surface has never grown into a solid crust. Hissing steam escapes from every crevice. A curse weighs heavily on the beautiful blue Danube no less than on the Rhine—the Nibelungen curse. It is the curse of greed, because the river is rich and occupies strategic approaches between East and West, North and South.

Rivers have their characters. The Rhine is a frontier river, like the Danube. It separates the North from the South, the Baltic Sea from the Mediterranean, pasture from forest, wealth from poverty. Yet the Rhine connects countries of related culture; Westphalia's factories are no different from Strasbourg's. The inhabitants are of similar cultural level even though they speak German, Dutch or French, whether they live under a dictator or parliamentary democracy.

The brooding spirit of Europe's largest river, the Volga, is in harmony with the steppes. It is like a dreamy Slav, used to open spaces, unable to utilize them. The monster factories at Gorki and Stalingrad look strange on its banks, used to the sight of endless horizons filled with wheat. The river may have taught the old Russian the slow rhythm of his movements.

When man was beginning to polish his stone implements, in the neolithic age, long before the days of written history, parts of the Danubian region were inhabited. The air was warm then, the forests abundant and man unequal to the jungle's strength. The porous soil along part of the Danube enabled prehistoric shepherds to graze their herds. Remnants of Stone-Age culture have been found at Vinca, near Belgrade, capital of Yugoslavia. The earliest Danubians were in touch with the primitives of the Aegean Sea.

Culture spread up-stream, from east to west. The Hungary of today was then a land of swamps, but life-giving loess farther north enabled the men with the stone-ax to thrive. The early settlers built their huts on the banks of the Danube. The only evidences of these prehistoric shelters are irregular oval depressions filled with refuse. A primitive millionaire may have occupied a hut with a porch, a sign of Stone-Age luxury. The Danubian primitives dyed the cheeks of their dead with red ocher, probably to simulate health for the life underground. They left them bracelets, beads, stone implements and vases. Cave dwellings abound in the Danube region.

Who were the early Danubians and how did they make their living? Their eyebrow ridges and eye-sockets, experts assure us, suggest Nordics, but the available material is insufficient for final conclusions. The second part of the question is more interesting. Agriculture is suggested by primitive mills for grinding. Fragments of plowshares of later periods have also been found. The early Danubians had lean and fat years, depending upon Nature's whims, since they knew nothing about fertilization and crop-rotation. In bad times many, perhaps most, of them died. They had cattle, sheep, goats, swine, but no horses, except in the adjacent land, where Poland lies today. In the Northern parts, the population was not sedentary, as at Vinca. There was plenty of land, and they could move about freely, except for the resistance of hostile nomads. They clung to the Danube region, then a much more highly civilized river than the Rhine. From the Danube enlightenment was spreading to the west, as far as Belgium. The Rhine was colonized more slowly because there the forests were dense. Danubian peasants carried culture to France.

War was unknown among the Danubians—at least evidence is lacking that they knew about mass murder as a way of convincing neighbors that their cause was just. The symbol of fertility, Mother Goddess, was known to them in the form of clay figurines. Objects of mystic value enjoyed great vogue.

The Danubians sought new ways of self-expression, and in a later period their pottery became artistic; form and color began to play a part. Now they supported their houses with posts—no longer dug them into the soil—and the roofs were gabled. Trade became more important, and villages tended to move toward important routes. This meant wealth, which had to be protected.

Warriors appeared on the scene. Civilization came to the late Stone Age with a vengeance. The graves indicate that woman's position improved and monogamy prevailed.

A major catastrophe overtook the Danubians toward the end of the Stone Age. A migratory race swept out of the unknown, carried onward by hunger, and overwhelmed the natives. The newcomers are known as the "bell-beaker" folk because of their characteristic funeral vessels. The rims of their dishes are turned up into five peaks, which sometimes exhibit a series of horizontal slits.

The Bronze Age saw the Middle Danube region in full flower. Never before did it play a more impressive part. "Hungarian bronzes were exported far and wide," writes V. Gordon Childe, who devoted years of study to the prehistoric Danube. "A great variety of ornaments of gold or bronze were worn in Hungary, both by men and women. The neck was encircled by necklaces of beads and pendants. The arms were weighted with bracelets and armcoils of hammered metal. Rings adorned the fingers, the leather girdle was studded with metal buttons, while girdles of hammered bronze were soon to be made. Even the legs were decked with anklets and cylinders. Pins served to hold the garments in place and to adorn the hair. Rings were hung from the ears and other pendants twisted in the locks. Hungarian apparel must have had a thoroughly barbaric look; similar trappings are worn in Africa or Borneo today. But the Hungarian objects often have a distinctly esthetic merit. Hungarian warriors were now armed with battle-axes, proving that civilization definitely conquered the Danube valley.

Along the middle course of the Danube trade was brisk. Tin came from Bohemia and copper from Transylvania. The influence of the Danube began to penetrate the North, up the Dnieper river, then to the Volga, spreading across the Russian steppes. The art of the late Bronze Age of the Ukraine was founded almost entirely on Hungarian types. The barbarian North and even distant Britain received the higher civilization of the Eastern Mediterranean via the Danube for two thousand years. The Danubian culture, originating in Hungary, moved up-stream to Eastern and Central Germany, reached the Black Forest near the Rhine. From Troy the influence of the East continued to move up the Danube. The North Syrian and Cypriote type of battle-ax and the sacred ivy-leaf pendant have left their mark in the Danube valley.

The westward trend was reversed when iron revolutionized the life of man. While the Danube continued to be of vital importance, it was no longer the seat of culture. The West was forging onward, and today it dominates the East.

But the Danube continued to stir the imagination of the Mediterranean world. As well-informed a man as Aristotle thought the Danube sprang in the Pyrenees, flowed across all Europe and emptied itself with one stream in the Adriatic and the other in the Dardanelles. Lesser contemporaries, too, talked much, knew little about the Danube. The Romans represented it as a bearded river god, head declining, garments waving, resting on a sea monster. Sometimes the Danube was worshiped as a god, alone or in Jupiter's exalted company. A stone inscription near Eschingen, at the river's source, seems to establish the Danube's deity.

"Beautifully flowing" is the name Hesiod gave to the Danube, known to him as the Ister. He described it as the sister of the Nile, son of Okeanos and Tethys. To the Romans the upper river was known as Danubius or Danuvius, and the lower reaches as Ister. The separating line may have been today's Vienna, although some authorities think it was farther south. The ancient Germans called it Doene or Tona, the Slavonians, Donava. Today the Germans call it Donau, the Hungarians Duna, the Roumanians Dunarea.

The river of endless feuds, the very name of the Danube opens violent controversy. "Don, Na," means "Two Rivers" in Celtic. The ancients could not agree on the source of the Danube. Some of the early writers derived the Danube's name from Deus Abnobius, to whom a temple was dedicated near its source. The Germans say it is derived from Ton, clay, suggesting the color of the river. This does not fit into the romantic but false picture of the blue Danube. Other German scholars link up the name with Ton, sound, or Donner, thunder. One weighty authority suggests Tanne, German for fir, which is the distinctive tree of the Black Forest, where the river rises.

And it is at this source that our story begins.

The Brown Danube

1. Castles, Ruins, Miracles

$\mathcal{T}$HE Danube rises in the Black Forest," every school child recites.

A quadrangular freestone basin, measuring about eighty feet, topped by a marble slab in the courtyard of the palace of the Princes of Fuerstenberg, is the official birthplace of the Danube. The flow of water from the pool is less than a cubic inch per minute—a modest beginning for a river so mighty. "Altitude— 678 meters (2,250 feet). . . . Distance from the river delta— 2,840 kilometers (1,775 miles)," the inscription reads. This is in Donaueschingen, bailiwick of Huefingen, Grand Duchy of Baden, in the southwestern part of the German Reich, not far from Alsace.

But the source of the river in the Black Forest is subject to dispute. Geographers tell us that the source of the stream is farthest away from its mouth. The freestone basin does not meet this demand. Candidates for the honor are two mountain brooks, the Brigach and Brege, uniting a short distance beyond Eschingen with the official Danube. The Brigach rises on Sommerau ridge, which Nature seems to have created for the benefit of tourists. From this observation point they can follow the meanderings of the Rhine, which is here closest to the Danube. The Brigach cascades down nature-made terraces of moss-covered native stone, past story-book houses with large gables. The brook skirts heavy granite hills with frolicking disdain. In past centuries it carried a trickle of gold dust.

Trout fishermen love the Brege, which rushes toward the Brigach, urged onward by the mating instinct of small rivers. Climbing to the crest of one of the fir-clad peaks, we cannot see France to the southeast, but we know that she is not far off. This is the same serene air, the same hard-working yet contented life. Red-roofed peasant houses are protected by clumps of trees. The blue of the hillsides is dotted with toy-like villages. The procession of hay-wagons on the country roads moves slowly. The steeples of the churches are very high, because the travelers needed definite directions when the countryside was more densely wooded.

The farmers here are well-to-do and they show it by throwing their legs wide apart like so many minor Colossi bestriding their little world. The high crown of their Sunday hats was the latest Paris fashion when the exiled Duke of Orleans held his court in these parts during the Revolution. This was a haven for aristocratic refugees from France. It recalled the beauties of the country they had been forced to flee. The farmers of this section of Baden are as aristocratic in some ways as were the titled émigrés. They consider "strangers" those whose families have tilled the soil only for a few generations. They speak the dialect of Baden, austere and guttural, but mellowed by Latin memories.

This is the country of clock masterpieces, inspired by fairy tales. Nimble fingers have carved diminutive verandas of tiny mansions to embellish the clocks. They have fashioned exuberant cathedrals and peasant chests, which find ready markets in all parts of the world. Nature is so good to these people, and so free of excesses, that their life is sunny, their music lithe, their tales gay. It would take more years than any dictator can live to make them the clocklike instruments strong men love.

The saga of this land of castles and mirages begins at the birthplace of the Danube. A young aristocrat of the fourteenth century, who was as beautiful as fancy makes dead youth, strayed into a peasant house and lost his heart to a wench even more beautiful than he. She was to marry a young man of the village, but the young aristocrat's passion was inflamed. Strong-willed herself and in love with the other man, she resisted his advances. He bought the entire town, to exercise the master's right of the first night, *jus primae noctis.* She was summoned to the castle on the night of her wedding to the peasant boy. In her nuptial garment she concealed a dagger, meant either for herself or for the young aristocrat. In the vestibule she sank on her knees in front of the white marble statue of the Virgin, imploring her protection. The weapon fell to the ground. The impassioned lover came to his senses, and all ended well.

The spirit of France hovers over the birthplace of the Danube. Even today intolerance encounters resistance. Along the Danube valley, Napoleon's Grande Armée started its epic march. The young Corsican had a dream. The boldness of the dream itself was almost immortal. The audacious sleep-walker soared beyond the bounds set for earthbound creatures. Could fate be forced to yield to magnificent unreason? The Danube was to yield the answer.

Napoleon captured the birthplace of the Danube, and without wasting time, swept on. In the imperial city of Vienna a blind soothsayer foretold doom, and a few days later the Conqueror's soldiers trod its uneven cobblestones. He faced the rising sun with a challenge. The Danube country was swept by the hope of peace in a World Empire. The eternal feminine in man gloried in submission to the born ruler. He was to worship at the feet of the ruthless Corsican. Before long the birthplace of the Danube saw Napoleon's retreat.

In the wake of defeat came reaction. The World Empire was no more. It was shattered into small nations. The Danube was to remain the river of a dozen national dreams. The Grand Duchy of Baden remained, and so did the Kingdom of Bavaria, but the German Reich was born. Eschingen slept on, a small provincial town of Southern Germany. Its princely palace now displays the swastika. But its archives still contain documentary evidence against intolerance. It has some first editions of Rousseau and Voltaire, also some valuable "Danubiana," forgotten books on the Danube, the most cosmopolitan of all rivers.

At every turn the country offers a surprise. Visitors from austere Northern Germany call it *niedlich,* bewitching. The villages are so placed that no stage manager could have given greater dramatic value to their locations. Down a low incline the young Danube winds its way, unconscious of its future greatness. Man likes to put rivers to work, driving water-mills, carrying ships, guarding frontiers, protecting castles; but what can one do with a stream which can be crossed in a single stride? Not even the robber barons of the Middle Ages knew how to put this part of the Danube to their use.

The rocks in the way of the Danube impede its flow and force it to twist and turn, trying to make grades which are too high. It is only at Sigmaringen, some forty miles down-stream, that it begins to look more like a river. And it is there that the first "beer-terraces" appear.

Since the days of old, Germany has sought consolation in the golden brew. While ancient Greeks and Romans regarded beer as the drink of barbarians, the Germans considered it the nectar of the gods. As early as the first century of our era Tacitus wrote in his *Germania:* "The beverage of the German is a liquor from barley or from wheat, and, like the juice of the grape, it is fermented to a spirit. . . . They do not drink it merely to quench their thirst. If you indulge their love of liquor to the excess they require, you need not employ the terror of your arms; their own vices will subdue them. . . . They hold the convivial moment the true season for business, when the mind opens itself in plain simplicity, or grows warm with bold or noble ideas."

The beer gardens on the Danube and elsewhere now blossom into Nazi festivals. While their customers consume oceans of beer and mountain ranges of sausage, their patriotic sentiments are keyed to the highest pitch by martial music and high-pressure oratory. When the band strikes up the "Horst Wessel Song," Germany's man in the street feels Siegfried's courage taking possession of his body, and with sparkling eyes and glowing cheeks he renews his allegiance to the Fuehrer. When song and speech are over, the band strikes up a tamed jazz tune and he joins the swirling crowd under the lighted sign of the swastika.

A small town floats into view, say, Immendingen. All of these towns are pretty, because this is a well-to-do part of the country and the German can live well on little. Your mind will turn back to the depressed areas of England and begin to wonder what the terms of "have" and "have-not" nations mean. Does Germany aspire to acquire the slums of rich Great Britain?

These towns are so attractive that thoughts about politics seem to be sacrilegious. The air is saturated with sunshine which is never over-strong, and the breeze is caressing. The flowers are riotously bold in their bid for the bees' attention.

As we follow the river, it suddenly drops out of sight, rushing into cavernous rocks. A chain of pools, separated by grassy promontories, and seemingly detached from the stream, comes to light farther down. Once some scientist dropped coloring material into these pools. Later these dyes found their way by subterranean passages into a small tributary of the Rhine, a few miles to the south. It seems that in an unusually magnanimous mood the Danube yields some of its substance to a rival. So strange are the river's ways in these parts that some geographers maintain that its real source is the Elta, a gay rivulet, which joins it beyond the rocks.

The visitor is surprised to find such scanty evidences of waste and pollution in Europe's most highly industrialized country. So great is the esthetic power of the Danube—and incidentally, so insignificant is she as yet as a source of power—that factories keep in the background, often disguised as mansions.

The main square of Muehlheim might fit into the "Master-singers." When will Hans Sachs make his entrance, applying himself to boots and song? When will gamboling apprentices romp down the winding street, breaking into high-pitched chant? Where is the wheel to designate the cartwright's shop? Where is the sign of the fat calf, emblem of the butcher's guild? The airplane from Berlin to Zurich appears to be a fantastic creation

20

of bewitched fancy. Surely, no such buzzards were seen in the time of Hans Sachs.

Villages now crowd the Danube banks. The river quenched thirst and was the friend of the fire-fighter. It was the cheapest— and often the only—highway of travel and trade. Man's first attempts at civilization were water-born. The Danube provided the quickest way of escape when the blazing horizon signaled the approaching foe.

Here the line of ruins begins. Their large number is a tribute to the importance of the Danube. It is pleasant to think of the castles in terms of the songs of the *Minnesaenger* of the Middle Ages. The ruins look poetic even without the setting sun. Olympian feasts, torch-light processions, inspired bards reciting epics of valor are essential to the imaginary setting. The *Minnesaenger* neglected to sing of the underground dungeons, many of which are still preserved. Nor did they sing of the hostages, whose chains alone are preserved. They did not sing about the nocturnal descents of the noble knights, to whom heralds brought news of the approach of merchant caravans.

Scattering its energies, the Danube is still a lusty infant. It assumes a character of its own only when it becomes navigable. Spry little brooks hurry to lose themselves in the river, intent upon sharing a greater fate. They scurry northward from Alpine heights, playing hide and seek with themselves in sweet-smelling meadows. They meander southward from the Swabian Raue Alp, a flawless mantle of green. The Danube zigzags northeastward, just before making up its mind to strike out for the east. It is significant that the Danube never formed a boundary of the German country it traverses, nor of any country until we reach its lower sweep. The boundaries were formed by much smaller rivers. This again is a tribute to the Danube's importance as an artery of travel. The migratory tribes of the East used it for their forays into the West, spreading their rule on both banks. After the War, the Danube was for twenty years the frontier between Hungary and Czechoslovakia. It was a strategical boundary, as the Czechs, who demanded it at the Peace Conference, frankly admitted.

Now we have reached the town of Ulm, where the Danube becomes navigable for small boats. The famous Minster will stop the visitor, no matter how great his hurry. He will have time to reflect on the incongruity of a town with some sixty thousand inhabitants and a church so vast. It is the largest church of the entire Danube valley. Ulm could never qualify as a shipping center. Its hinterland embraced the Lutheran creed. The one-time cathedral is now the pride of the reformed church. You would be held in contempt if you attempted to leave town without scanning the horizon from the tower. It is a sight for the gods, indeed. Local patriotism says that it is the best observation point in all Germany, from which you can survey large segments of the South and North of Germany. Cloudily detached from earth, the snow-capped Tyrolean Alps seem to float in the azure sky. Against this lofty competition, the Wuerttemberg hills in the west give a good account of themselves. The Danube is a narrow ribbon of indefinite color slashing across a vaporous green.

From here on small boats assist us in gaining an inside view of the Danube, and it is no longer necessary to steal glimpses from behind jealous rocks. In half an hour an airplane could take us to the largest and most important town of the Danube of Old Germany—Regensburg. But who would want to be in such a hurry? A century ago the journey took fourteen hours by water, and contemporary observers report that the trip was not deemed too long. Hours then meant less than now. How much wiser were our fathers to take their pleasures in such leisurely way.

When Rome was the center of the Western world, this was the boundary line between North and South, barbarism and culture. The village names still ring with Latin accents. The southern bank is a treasure trove of culture; the northern bank was the emplacement of altars to the Sun-God. This was before the barbarians of the East made the Danube their highway.

Now we have reached Bavarian Germany, where we hear accents that will accompany us all the way to Vienna and beyond. Here Nature is good to its children, and they are good to Nature. If Germany had farmlands as rich as this elsewhere, she would have little cause for complaint. Hard work is carved into the peasants' cheeks, but the humorous twinkle in their eyes contradicts the belief that the peasant's life is a round of cares. Their *Lieder* inspired Brahms to set to music the joy of life. Napoleon paused here long enough to choose it as a Summer resort when Germany was France. Hitler paid frequent visits to these peasants when he began his climb to power. He showered them with compliments, and called them most typically German. Not far from here is Berchtesgaden, where he seeks solitude. There he consults his "hunches," in close contact with the Danubian country, his real home.

In the town of Lauingen a monument is dedicated to the Countess of Dillingen, a horse, and the greatest scholar of the thirteenth century. The Countess was a charitable lady, who gave most of her fortune to the church. The horse once graced a bishop's stable, and must have been the Man-o'-War of its day.

The scholar was Albert the Great, "Albertus Magnus," to whom Dante assigned a place of honor in the Sun Heaven. This famed Dominican scholar was familiar with all the secrets of the universe, spiritual as well as physical. Such erudition was less difficult than it would be today, since the science of his century was condensed in a slender book of verse. His name, "Doctor Universalis," was inscribed on the monument.

The tale of an unusual occurrence is told in the stone of the tower of the town. A shaggy Magyar pagan bullied the townsmen, treating them with contempt. None dared to accept the challenge of such an awful foe. Finally, a little bootmaker found the giant's taunts beyond endurance, seized a sword and engaged him in single combat. Hard pressed, the cobbler held his ground, then severed the pagan's head with a bold stroke. His fellow-townsmen went wild with joy, and because of him the town long enjoyed a good name. They are still proud of the bootmaker. His is the story of the little German David defeating the alien giant, Goliath.

Not far from the Danube, at Blenheim, one of the crucial battles of the world was fought in the war of Spanish Succession. It decided whether the House of Habsburg or the Bourbon dynasty was to rule over Spain. England made common cause with the Austrians because she feared that the Bourbons would try to dominate all Europe. "The angel," in Addison's words, "who passed over pale Britannia," was the Duke of Marlborough, one of those heroic but imaginative figures the English find in critical hours. The French lost forty thousand dead in a single engagement, a tremendous figure in that backward century. Compare this with the half million dead of Verdun in the World War. Although the Bourbons got the Spanish throne, they had to promise not to unite that country with France. They kept their pledge, partly because they had less training in treaty-breaking than our own contemporaries and partly because the English army was strong. The English got Gibraltar, until recently the symbol of invincible strength.

The dead of Blenheim were still unburied when victor and vanquished exchanged compliments.

"I am sorry," the Iron Duke told the commanding Marshal of the French Army, now his prisoner, "that so great a misfortune should befall one for whom as a man and soldier I entertain the most profound esteem."

"I congratulate you," the Marshal replied tartly, "on having conquered the best troops in the world."

The reputation of Donauwoerth would deserve to be as great as that of Rothenburg if nothing but merit counted in such matters. It is the perfect medieval town, except for its noisy motorcars. History throws its aura even around the head of the stone dachshund of the tobacco shop. The medieval armor of Wallenstein's soldiers would be more appropriate here than the brown shirt. The Fuggerhaus recalls the founding in this imperial town of the oldest banking dynasty in Central Europe. A bushy beard is the main feature of a statue in the main square. The inscription is "Uncle Ludwig," the elderly wearer of the beard, hugging a young wench. He is King Ludwig I of Bavaria, famed because of his love affair with the Spanish dancer, Lola Montez, and, more so, because he helped to make Munich one of the great art centers of the age. The site of his statue was one time occupied by the stake, where heretics were purified of sin. Local records tell of many victims. It was here, where the Danube is in its most romantic mood, that the horror of the Thirty Years' War was let loose upon mankind. All around, the countryside had joined the Reformation but the abbot of Donauwoerth held out. He arranged a dazzling procession, which the spectators watched in sullen silence. Then a stone crashed through the brocade of his baldachin, and this signal set the world afire. When the casualties were counted, two million Germans, half the population, were dead.

Donauwoerth was the scene of a royal tragedy. Marie, Duchess of Brabant, wife of Louis the Severe, Duke of Bavaria, was fond of playing chess with Count Henry, a devoted vassal. One evening, the young Count asked Marie for the royal favor of being addressed as "thou," instead of the formal "you." She could not comply with this request for fear of being misunderstood.

Soon afterward, the Duke and the Count marched to war against an aggressive neighbor, the Bishop of Augsburg, and the Duchess was left in the care of the castle confessor, who was in the enemy's pay. In order to weaken the Bavarian Army, he implored the Duchess to prevail upon her husband to return home and trust the campaign to his generals. When the Duke refused to comply, the spy persuaded the Duchess to let Count Henry act in her behalf. In a letter to him, she promised to grant him the favor he had asked, if he succeeded in inducing the Duke to return. The letter fell into the husband's hands, who dashed home in a rage, assuming the worst without question, and put her to death. The Duke learned of his wife's innocence, and his hair turned white overnight, although he was only twenty-seven years old. The body of the Duchess lies in the convent he built to atone for his fatal mistake. So unbearable became Donauwoerth to him that he had the capital removed to Munich, where it has been ever since.

In Castle Oberhausen lies the body of Latour d'Auvergne, *"le premier grenadier de France,"* hero of many battles. A consummate showman, Napoleon Bonaparte, First Consul, knew the dramatic value of honoring the unknown living of the French Army under his command. He made this hero the "first private" rather than "last general" of the armed forces. But the *"premier grenadier"* could not rest on his laurels, an immortal on full pension. The life of a retired hero was an anti-climax. He was to see the Danube again, and in a battle on its banks he rushed into the fray ahead of his comrades, trusting to fate, his faithful ally. Not used to looking back, he did not notice the Austrian Uhlan who dashed after him and transfixed the world's first private with his lance. Napoleon won the battle, lost a symbol, and the victors' drums were festooned with crepe for three days. Latour d'Auvergne's sword is a relic in the Invalides of Paris, near Napoleon's resting place. His heart was placed in a silver box, which the First Consul had appended to the colors of the Forty-sixth Brigade.

History is crowding in on us on both banks of the Danube. In that dreamy little town of Ingolstadt, the legendary Dr. Faustus, doctor of all sciences, frequenter of all taverns, attracted a host of students from all parts of Germany. The townspeople of his time wondered whether he was really in league with the Evil One. He is still alive to them, part of the Danube lore. Marlowe and Goethe immortalized in him the conflicting desires of the human heart.

From here all the way to the Rhine, a hundred and fifty miles away, stretches the Pfahlgraben, also known as the Devil's Ditch, the remnants of the ancient Roman fortifications. In its heyday it must have been a veritable Chinese wall, dividing the Roman Danube region from the land of the unsubdued tribes. Emperor

Probus had completed it just in time to make it witness the end of Roman glory. Waves of tribal invaders swept over it. It was gained and lost by many newcomers. Builders of feudal castles later used its watch-towers as stone quarries.

Not so long ago, Vohburg on the Danube was known as the most virtuous town of Bavaria. Certified virgins were given the equivalent of $20—50 *guldens*—at their nuptials, and the dowry was provided by the community. The stage-coach seems to have brought temptation to town, and anxious fathers' sleep was disturbed by the presence of overnight guests in the hostelry.

Nibelungen lore haunts this part of the Danube, where its banks are steep and rocky, an ideal background for royal tragedy. It was here that King Gunther's Nibelungen crossed the Danube on their way from the Rhine to the court of Attila, wrath of God, who spread terror from Pest, farther down the river. Water witches had foretold doom: only the priest of the expedition would return to the Rhine, unless his blood was offered to the pagan hosts of Valhalla. Protected by the dark rocks, Hagen, the villain, attempted to drown the priest in the Danube narrows, to save his own life. He failed, and the Nibelungen were lost.

A short distance down the Danube the Benedictine friars inform the visitor that their monastery was founded in the seventh century. Warrior missionaries guarded this vital spot, and where the cross failed to convince, the sword was the final argument. The pagans of these parts were slow to see that the crucified God with the haggard cheeks was more useful than the giants of Valhalla. The monastery stems out of a rock, its outlines reflected in the Danube. No stage manager could have found a more impressive place. A temple of Minerva, dedicated to the God-Emperor Domitian, occupied a nearby site in classical times.

28

Today it is a popular inn, frequented by motorists on the Regensburg highway.

Rocks form bold outlines, rising sheerly to six hundred feet, obscuring the sun. Castle-builders monopolized frightening ledges. The ruins of Braun, Gross-Essing and Geissenberg are perched on eyries seemingly without foundations. That elusive object of tourist search, "romance," cannot be far away. On a June night in pre-Hitler days I saw here a group of tow-headed "birds of passage," *Wandervoegel,* members of a progressive youth group. The youngsters' eager faces were turned toward the darkness, from which a voice issued. It was their leader's, a young Wotan, who decried the feudal way of life. He wound up by talking hopefully of the future. A swarm of bewildered bats began their nightly rounds.

On its way north, the Danube describes a bold curve, before turning east. It is now in the heart of Germany, flanked by elaborate turrets and gables. The "Inn of the Golden Lamb" and the "Tavern of the White Horse," of which there are many here, have their *Stammgaeste,* regular customers, day after day. Times may be bad, politics disturbing, but a jug of beer at the end of the day is a reward for the daily toil. The thick-set burghers drink it with the usual ritual. In this village they spill a few drops on the sandy floor—a libation to the devil. In another town only a special type of clay may be used for the stein. In still another place the figures on the jug have symbolic meanings.

In the village of Oberndorf we must halt to hear one of the most famous incidents of Danube history. On a June day in 1208, the Count Palatine of Bavaria, Otto of Wittelsbach, murdered the German King Philip for an imagined slight to his honor. Otto was placed under the ban of the Empire, and thus became an outcast. Haunted by his conscience, he undertook a pilgrimage to Rome; fearful of vengeance, he led a nocturnal life. He reached Kehlheim on the Danube, where he took shelter in a shed of the Ebrach monastery. His furtive looks aroused a neighbor's suspicion. An alarm was raised. Out came the Marshal of the Empire, Henry of Kalden, who had vowed revenge for the death of his liege lord. He recognized the regicide, slashed off his head and flung it into the Danube.

On the following day the head was still floating, gnashing its teeth, glaring at the spectators, refusing to sink or be carried away by the current. Then the Black Friar of Ebrach seized the miraculous cross which eagles had brought from the Mount of Calvary and, holding it firmly in both hands, addressed the dead man's head from the river bank in words still recorded in stone:

"Dus. milabundus. Dom. infernis. presto, diabolorum."

Hearing this, the head whirled around, shook its clotted locks in the Black Friar's face and sank to the bottom, while the spectators fell prostrate. That night blue flames issued from the spot where the head was last seen. The Friar fixed the cross on the river bank for seven days, until the flames were extinguished. For nine years the body of the regicide was left on the heath, blown by wind, washed by rain. The rock on which it was exposed is called the "murder stone,"

> *"Where oft ye may hear the voice of death,*
> *And oft ye may see dark Otto's form,*
> *As he rides on the silver mists of heath,*
> *And chants a ghastly dirge in the storm."*

So we reach Regensburg, one-time capital of Danubian shipping, at the intersection of the transcontinental highway and the road leading to the Brenner Pass, the highway of emperors, the road to Italy. This was the crusaders' meeting place, the gateway to the East. Today Regensburg is typical of Southern Germany. Here the Northerner is still *Sau-Preuss,* pig-Prussian. People here still cherish the classical prejudice against the land of Borealis, cold and cruel. To many of them the German North is an extension of the Slavic steppe. To them, as to Heinrich Heine, Prussian soil appears to be corroded by glacial moraines, its soil by arctic cold. These are the people of Bavaria, Wuerttemberg and Baden —a garden country. Sixteen centuries after the end of Roman rule, the North and South, subdued and unsubdued, still stand apart. The Danube belongs to the South; the North knows little about it.

Regensburg was the center of the little universe which lived its thriving life because of the Danube. Today the river no longer affects its existence the same way. But the mansions of former merchant princes still carry the traditions of old counting-houses. Much of the social life of the town takes place on the river banks. In past centuries, Regensburg boatsmen explored the Danube, the Black Sea, Constantinople. They brought back their stories to town, where they were embellished into fiction. Turkey appealed to the burghers as a land of a million marvels. Regensburg was the headquarters of Oriental lore.

Regina Castra, a fortified town, was Rome's name for this spearhead into Germania. The legions left from this salient for their Northern campaigns. They were to sweep the barbarians into the icy sea, at the end of the world. The barbarians had none of the Roman engines of war, and to the patricians they must have appeared a contemptible rabble. They had no *thermae* to bathe their bodies, no *fora* to exercise their wits. Their minds

31

were too dull for the intricacies of Roman law, and their politics were crude. They knew nothing about the gods of Olympus; they did not know how to build roads; and their country was as uncouth as their skin garments. Their eyes were blue and their beards blond; their bodies were large—all of which made them look ridiculous. Their speech was rough and their lips could not utter the smooth cadences of the Latin tongue. They never responded to the beauties of poetry, and Virgil, to them, might have been a water demon.

To the Romans, the whole world belonged to the *urbs,* the city—the whole world except the country north of Regensburg, on the other side of the Danube. The barbarians in their rugged forests were a danger. Hence Regina Castra, Regensburg, was built. Hence, too, Emperor Trajan took his legions down the Danube, all the way to the Black Sea, the end of the world in the East. Having amassed such great treasures, Rome became fearful, suspecting the blond giants who were attracted by her dazzling fame. In the beginning the world-city kept them at bay. After Rome had declined, it was the myth of her strength which the barbarians respected. Legends die hard. But greed was besieging the gates of privilege and wealth. The first push, caused by despair born of hunger, showed the barbarians that Rome was an empty shell.

The more territory the Empire gained at Regensburg on the Danube and other key positions, the more it had to defend. The farther afield the legions deployed, the more they had to depend upon native forces. The more tribesmen joined the legions, the more Rome's striking power was weakened. The larger the concentration of wealth, the more restless the proletariat became at home. The greater the trouble in the city, the less was the Em-

pire's striking power. The condition of the poor became worse
the richer Rome grew. Now the poor had a standard to judge by,
and felt injustice more acutely. The coming of a new day was
heralded. The Christian faith was to bridge the gap between
work and its reward.

Rome fell, and Regina Castra acquired new names: Ratisbon
and Ratispone, the latter suggesting a river port. Here Charlemagne launched his campaign against the Far East of his day,
Pannonia, in the middle Danube region. The ideal of a universal
Christianity was still strong, and he felt the power to make it
true. Gold bought special privileges for Regensburg from Arnold
the Bastard. The Holy Land was an answer to the prayers for
redemption to many, but to not a few among the camp-followers
it was a chance to rob and burn. Some of them began to fight
at Regensburg, and the Jew, then as now, was the ideal enemy.
The town's two score Jewish families were dead after the first
crusaders had passed.

In the thirteenth century this was a free imperial city, both
prosperous and pestilential, guarded by mercenaries, decimated
by the Black Death. "The Delight of Mankind," as Emperor
Maximilian II was called by his contemporaries, breathed here
his last during an epidemic of the plague. "It excites melancholy
regret," a French historian wrote, "that the reign of so excellent
a sovereign was limited only to twelve years, while Philip II occupied the throne for more than forty."

Ambassador Street of Regensburg was said to have been built
for a Congress of Princes, and the old Town Hall was the seat
of the Imperial Diet for a century and a half. The Germany of
those days consisted of some three hundred sovereign countries;
the Empire was a fiction. That Regensburg was chosen for the

33

honor attests her importance and that of the German Danube. The sessions of the Diet were brilliant social functions, in which Princes of the Empire sought to establish their precedence over their neighbors by extravagance. This was a magnificent setting of the Holy Roman Empire, which in Voltaire's oft-repeated words, was neither Holy, nor Roman, nor even an Empire. Napoleon, Empire-builder and Empire-wrecker, dealt a death-blow to Regensburg when he wrested the imperial crown from the unsteady hands of Emperor Franz of the House of Habsburg. Thus the warning on the Rathaus became a memory:

"Let every Senator who enters this court to sit in judgment lay aside all private affections: anger, violence, hatred, friendship and adulation. Let thy whole attention be given to public welfare; for as thou hast been equitable or unjust in passing thy judgment on others, so mayst thou expect to stand acquitted or condemned before the awful tribunal of God."

The story of the twelfth-century Regensburg bridge across the Danube is part of the river lore. The chief architect, according to legend, turned over the building of the bridge to a gifted pupil. Intoxicated with his good fortune the young man laid a bet with his master that before May Day the span would be ready. Eventually he found the term too short, and in a moment of anger called upon the devil for assistance. The friar standing next to him on the unfinished bridge revealed himself as the Evil One.

"Build me those fifteen arches by May Day," the young man commanded, "and thou shalt have the devil's fee."

"And what will it be?"

"As thou hast a particular affection for souls, I shall give thee the first two—male and female—to cross the bridge."

34

A Dog, a Cock and a Hen

The devil set to work with glee, and the bridge was finished by the first of May. The ceremonies lured a throng to the spot, eager to cross the span. A wolf-dog, a cock and a hen were also in the crowd. As the moment of opening the bridge drew nearer, the spectators' desire to be the first to cross increased.

"Jacob," the young architect instructed his foreman, "let the animals lead the way!"

The dog, the cock and the hen were shown to the front. As they crossed the bridge, a dreadful noise was heard, while the mangled remains of the animals were scattered in all directions.

"Cheated, cheated of my fee!"

The images of the dog, cock and hen are carved into the stone balustrade of the bridge.

Opposite the Town Hall of Regensburg a famous combat is celebrated in a life-size fresco. Craco the Giant challenged the boldest of the bold in single combat on the main square of the town. His appearance was so forbidding that none dared to accept his challenge. Shamed, the Emperor himself offered to meet the giant.

"God forbid," exclaimed Hans Dollinger, a burgher of small stature but stout heart, "that a faithful subject should look on with folded arms whilst his liege-lord is placed in jeopardy."

He astounded the spectators by standing his ground. At the third encounter, the lances of both warriors were broken. Baring their blades, the combatants cried, "Havoc!" Being at a greater advantage because of his longer blade, the giant saw the battle won. Brandishing his sword, he prepared to sever the challenger's head, but each time he advanced the Emperor flung the cross into his face. Hans defeated his opponent by thrusting his sword between the joints of his lower harness, hurling him to the ground. Local legend holds that the hair on the Saviour's head of the wooden cross, which the Emperor held in the heathen's face, has not ceased growing. The broken lances of the combatants were displayed for a long time. Stories such as this, variants of the David and Goliath myth, are typical of the little man's wish-dreams.

On top of Regensburg Cathedral a man of stone is in the act of throwing himself to the ground. He was the builder who, popular belief holds, made another one of those foolish bets about the completion of his work, and, finding himself unable to meet the date, committed suicide.

A tale of tragedy and heroism is told by the effigy of St. John de Nepomuc, patron saint of continental bridges. He was confessor of the wife of a tyrannical King of Bohemia, a madly jealous husband, who demanded of him to divulge the secrets of the holy confession. He refused to do so, and the King had him cast into prison, then had him taken to Prague, where he was thrown into the Moldau River, within sight of the royal castle.

The tragic life of the saint is linked with the torture chamber of the Regensburg Town Hall. It is one of the best-preserved chambers of horrors in Germany. The accused was laid on the rack, which looks like a long bedstead; his arms were fastened to a rope, which was pulled through a windlass to stretch his limbs. Another instrument of torture was the deathless gallows. The accused was raised by ropes to the top bar of a vertical frame; two heavy stones were attached to his feet. After having been raised high, he was suddenly dropped to within a few inches of the ground. The jerk of the fall usually wrenched every joint out of its socket. Behind a heavily screened wooden trellis the judges were unseen, hearing and seeing all. Thus in the name of brotherly love, suspects of heresy were made to unite with the Lord in suffering.

This is the land not merely of castles and ruins, but also of miracles. Far-famed Albertus Magnus, for instance, gave a sermon in the Regensburg Cathedral and at the very same time was seen in his Donaustauf study, twelve miles down the Danube. From his window of multi-colored rose he saw one of the oldest Benedictine abbeys, St. Emmeram, where the corpse of St. Dionysius, "the Areopagite," first bishop of Athens, is entombed. But the body of the same saint is also shown in St. Denys, where he is revered as the patron saint of France. There he was supposed to have suffered martyrdom. Stranger still, the head of the same saint is worshiped in Germany's Bamberg Cathedral, and a fourth head is enshrined in the church of the Prague Castle in Bohemia. Danubian lore purports that Regensburg purloined the body from St. Denys. The monks of the latter refused—and still refuse—to admit that the relic was not in their possession. Thereupon the Benedictines induced Pope Leo XI to ex-communicate all who doubted the authenticity of the body in their abbey.

The Danube undergoes a change beyond Regensburg, and so does Bavaria. One can see here that the river is destined to do things on a large scale. Imperceptibly, we are turning our back to the efficient West and its high-pressure industries. The breath of the East can already be felt, although it is a long way off. The village tavern *Zum Weissen Roessl* presents a more animated picture than the inns higher up the Danube. The enjoyment of life takes more time, and the peasant's movements are a trifle slower. On the fields, the tractor is still a newcomer; the horse is man's working companion. In a Regensburg church not long ago horses were given indulgence.

The peasants' houses have gradually become larger, rather than tall, so as to accommodate the many children. The costumes of the farmers' daughters are more elaborate, often riotously embroidered. The knees of the men are bare. Old customs still thrive, survivals in a practical age. At the wedding, the best man ushers the bridegroom into the sacristy, boxes his ears sharply and pulls his hair, to remind him of conjugal fidelity.

Every turn of the Danube reminds you of an epoch of history. At Castle Donaustauf, Austrians, Bohemians, Franks, Huns, Magyars, Swedes, Vandals sought to maintain their rule because here, too, important roads intersect. The South tempted the nomads with its fabulous riches, magnified by distance. The West attracted the refugees of parched lands with rain-soaked meadows.

Centuries passed, cultures came in quick succession, new social classes arose. The knights' power began to decline as land grew scarcer and populations greater. Horizons were extended, new discoveries brought exotic markets into Europe's orbit. The Orient fired the imagination of the West. The silk and spices of the East were unheard-of luxuries. One step ahead was followed by many steps; one idea entailed a chain of changes. A rich merchant class challenged the claim of the nobility to rule the Danube. The power of gold defied the power of blood. Henry the Proud was humbled because he failed to see the light. He had seized the castle of Donaustauf from the cathedral and chapter of Regensburg, its lawful masters. They appealed to the burghers for help, who found the time ripe to shame the haughty Prince and besieged him, until, driven by hunger, he was forced to yield. The pioneers of a new civilization scored over the old, for the first time in the Danube basin. But the old order was reluctant to yield its place, and the vanquished set fire to the castle.

At another turn of the Danube, we are brought face to face with modern times. On top of a hill, rising three hundred feet above the river, is the monumental Valhalla, built by King Ludwig I of Bavaria, the "uncle" with the beard, who loved the Spanish dancer. The roof is carried by gigantic demi-deities, the Valkyries. Heroes and candidates for the Hall of Fame keep here incongruous company. Although it is most impressive, you do not hear much praise for this Valhalla, probably because it is too big for the Danube and also because it cost a lot of money. The Bavarians are thrifty.

Another modern building, the *Befreiungshalle,* Hall of Liberation, rises out of a maze of rivulets. The same King had it built in memory of the fiftieth anniversary of the Battle of the Nations at Leipzig, on the threshold of the Danube valley. King Ludwig I could not conceive of a monumental structure without the Danube, largest river of his realm. He disliked the French, and this monument is certainly not complimentary to Napoleon. A score of overdeveloped and underdressed Teutonic ladies carry the burden of the walls of this structure. Dozens of goddesses crowd the interior.

A short way down the river is Straubing, which is remembered for a story, containing all the elements of a thriller, including a rash young Duke ready to forfeit power for love, a beautiful young woman of the common people, who made the throne, and a villain with a beard. If our interest is merely for the good of our bodies, the story has an unhappy ending, but if our souls

39

mean something to us, the ending is happy, because all met eventually in heaven, although—as will be seen in a minute— the company was large.

The hero was Duke Albrecht III and the villain was his father, Duke Ernest, of Bavaria. The young ruler was to marry a Countess, whom he did not even know. This marriage was ordered by his father, without the benefit of love. The young lady, however, loved another young man and she eloped with him. Word of the elopement was brought to the near-fiancé at a tournament, where he had just discovered a beauty to whom he promptly lost his heart. She was Agnes Bernauer, known as the "angel," daughter of a common bathing master, socially an outcast. Duke Albrecht married her in secret, and Duke Ernest, whose intelligence service was good, demanded that he divorce her. Incensed, the young Duke proclaimed her his wife and Duchess, and conducted her into his castle on the Danube.

Some time afterward, Albrecht went to war and his father employed his absence to accuse the young Duchess of black magic. She was tortured, condemned to death and thrown into the Danube, while the people of the town looked on and lamented. She managed to free her legs of their chains, and, shrieking for help, made for the bank. She nearly landed, when an official caught her with a hooked pole, dragged her into mid-stream and kept her under water until death came. Duke Albrecht took refuge in the castle of his father's bitterest foe. The old Duke implored the Emperor for help and promised a perpetual mass for Agnes' soul. Later the young Duke married the Duchess of Brunswick, who gave him ten children.

Straubing is also celebrated because of the picture of the

Virgin, which angels brought there from a nearby village, where Luther's doctrines had taken root. The book showing the angels in attractive sailor dresses may still be seen. The village of Sosan on the Danube attributes the presence of its Virgin to a similar incident.

As we approach Austria, references to the leaders of the Reformation are becoming less complimentary. That country was a bulwark of the Church for centuries, and Rome exerted its influence on this part of the Danube, in direct contact with Italy via the Brenner Pass. Those beasts of prey you see on the walls of the monastery of Ober-Altaich are caricatures of Luther's followers. The same monastery, a learned professor of the last century assures us, preserves some hay that fed the ass on which the Saviour rode, some crumbs from the last supper, some of St. Peter's tears, a part of the staff of a saint, which had the power of frightening away rats, provided it was waved to the four quarters of heaven.

Miracles are everyday occurrences in this region of the Danube, and one cannot even begin to enumerate them all. Take the case, for instance, of the castle of Bogenberg, reflected in the waters of a turbulent river. The master of the castle made an honest living, according to the ethics of his age, by preying upon half of Bavaria. His castle was inaccessible, but for a narrow pass on its eastern end, and it was seated upon the apex of a pyramidal rock. One day he saw the image of the Virgin floating up the Danube, drifting ashore near the little market town which rested on the bank. The Count was so struck with this miracle that he presented the castle to the nearby cloister. In a village under the shadow of the castle a tooth of St. Sebastian used to be shown, and over it water was poured into a goblet. It was asserted that whoever drank of this water need fear no infectious disease for twelve months.

The monastery of Metten, which fits into the hollow of a hill, owes its existence to a miracle no less impressive. Charlemagne, local folklore tells us, while hunting one day in the woods of this part of the Danube came across a hermit cutting wood. In deference to his exalted visitor, the hermit took his ax and hung it on a sunbeam. The great ruler asked him what he wanted, and the holy man asked him for a monastery, which was built forthwith.

The solitary rock, three hundred feet high, thrusting itself out of the smooth right bank of the Danube, seems to have been placed there by nature to give medieval man a chance to enrich our lore with another miracle. How did the rock carrying a castle of the Counts of Bogen on its top get to these plains? Geologists confess to be puzzled, but not so the rural folk. They say that the devil so hated the pious people of Deggendorf across the Danube that he brought a rock from Italy to crush the village. Flying over the monastery of Metten, he suddenly heard the bells ringing Ave Maria. Gnashing his teeth with anguish and spite, he dropped the rock.

Deggendorf was famous because of the absolution granted to all pilgrims on St. Michael's Eve. A group of Jews of the village, legend tells, bought the consecrated wafer from a woman in days gone by, scratched it with horns until it bled; then the image of the Child appeared. Undeterred, the Jews baked the wafer, hammered it upon an anvil, attempted to cram it down their throats, but the hands and feet of the vision prevented it. Then they flung it into a well, which was immediately surrounded by a nimbus. This happened on St. Michael's day, and the day after

Klosterneuburg on the Danube

all the Jews of Deggendorf were massacred. "It appears," a commentator adds, "that the Deggendorfers owed the Jews a considerable amount of money."

The Danube whips itself into a miniature rage at this point, forced into twisted channels and projecting rocks on the left bank. Popular belief, ignoring natural causes, holds that it was the Counts of Ortenburg who infuriated the river. In the fourteenth century, these Counts seized all ships that as much as grated against the bank. Should adroit boatmen steer their vessels past the danger, armed ships of the titled gangsters gave them chase until the victims were driven ashore and their craft could be claimed by right. The traveling Frenchman, Froissart, wrote apropos of these Counts and their kind: "When a German hath taken a prisoner, he putteth him into irons, and into hard prison, without any pity, to make him pay the greater ransom. . . . They are covetous people, above all other. They have no pity if they have the upper hand, and they demean themselves with cruelty to their prisoners. . . . They are people worse than Saracens or Paynims. . . ."

In this land of miracles, we must not forget the village of Kinzing, one-time Roman fort, and its St. Severinus. It happened in the fifth century, when miracles occurred more frequently than now. The saint's friend, Sylvin, died and was buried in the church. The holy man, who was greatly attached to him, brought him back to life, but Sylvin had found death sweet and wanted to die again. It was a little girl of the village who saw this miracle with her own eyes, hidden in the church. The saint saved the village from a torrential Danube by planting a cross on the river bank.

As we approach the frontiers of Old Germany, we see chains of mountains in the northeast. The ones in the hazy background

43

are parts of the Bohemian Woods, which formed part of the Reich and Czechoslovakia. The ones nearer to the traveler are the Bavarian Woods, scented hills, with trees standing in impeccable rows. The woods rise and fall in gentle rhythm. The forests close up on a group of red roofs, commanded by a bulbous tower, squatting on a whitewashed church. Here Nature is mellow and full of charm, its moods are gracious, the weather kind. Vilshofen greets us on the left bank before we reach Passau, the last station on this part of the journey. From the Danube the low hills rise, their contours sweet. So lovely a sight ought not to suggest the gruesome story to which the local monastery is said to owe its life. Henry Tuschl, a knight, caught his wife in an act of infidelity and was so enraged that he had her walled up alive in his castle, which he deeded to a religious order. *"Zwei Hund an ain Bain, Ich Tuschl bleib allain,"* he wrote on the charter, and did remain alone with his two dogs, shunning female company. The word *allain,* old-German for "alone," was written upon the houses, clothes and arms of members of this order.

A river so calm puts the traveler into a tranquil mood. It creates that atmosphere of deep peace which city people dream about, but never attain.

> *"Ne'er saw I, never felt, a calm so deep!*
> *The river glideth at his own sweet will;*
> *Dear God! The very houses seem asleep;*
> *And all that mighty heart is lying still!"*

A few miles down, the Danube again becomes the devil's cauldron. At Passau two rivers rush to meet the older stream, anxious to find a way from behind the rocks which impede its flow at every turn. It was the devil who plucked up the rocks and pitched them into the river, legend holds, so enraged was he at the crusaders' attempts to reach the Holy Land by way of the Danube.

Passau has been called "the most fascinating town of the Danube," a title none too popular in Vienna and Budapest. She also has been called the "Coblentz of the Danube," against which no protests have yet been heard. Looking at it from the *Oberhaus,* Upper House, the scene is enchanting. The rivers Inn and Ilz, which rush into the Danube, reveal entirely different characters. The one is dark and the other light. They bob up and down in their rocky beds, eager to be lost in the Danube. Before Germany swallowed Austria, the people of Passau hinted that the rivers were in such a great hurry because they wanted to reach the Danube before it crossed the boundary into Austria, a few minutes' drive away. Germany's dictator, Adolf Hitler, was born on the Austrian side of the Inn, some sixty miles to the south.

The solid green cover of hills is broken by the black of fir trees which lead the eyes to the water's edge. Cottages of the Swiss type lift their gables above the green maze. Rustic bridges over abysses call attention to torrential mountain brooks below.

The *Oberhaus* was once the residence of the Prince Bishops of Passau. More recently it became a military prison. It seems that the devil has been working overtime here, not only pitching rocks into the Danube. The choice of this site for a prison must surely have been his. *Niederhaus,* the Lower House, at the foot of the rocky hill, was a stone fortress and is now a lovers' paradise. Below Passau, castles line the Danube, which here forms a chain of what seem to be beautiful lakes, each apparently shut in by boldly carved hills. A few hundred yards farther down is the frontier of Austria.

45

$\mathscr{R}$IVERS do not change their characters when they pass frontiers.

In the month of March of 1938, Austria was absorbed by the German Reich and became known as "Ostmark," eastern marches. The very names of Upper Austria and Lower Austria, the two most populous provinces, have been replaced by the names of Upper Danube and Lower Danube. But the name of Austria is so enshrined in history that I shall use it more often than the new one.

The Inn and Ilz, the two rivers we saw from the hilltop, rush into the Danube from north and south. They created a frontier which endured for centuries. They were the boundaries of *Oesterreich*, the eastern realm or marches, and also of the hereditary domain of the House of Habsburg. Here began the realm of the dynasty which at one time ruled the entire Danube valley, all

46

Spain, the Netherlands, including today's Belgium, the best parts of Italy and the recently discovered Americas. The Habsburgs were also the Holy Roman Emperors, only a name, to be sure, but a glorious one. To the Danube, more than to anything else, the House of Austria owed its fortune. It opened the East and South to them, facilitated their empire-building in the North and West. With the two frontier rivers, the Danube assumes a strategical, as well as trade, importance. Until now it was hardly more than a setting for castles and miracles. Here it becomes a life-giving force.

To the Austrians the Danube means more than to the Germans; it is their national river and the biggest. To the German *Die Wacht am Rhein* is a symbol; the Rhine is his national river. Visitors to Germany would consider their trip incomplete without an excursion down the Rhine, but they seldom think of visiting the German Danube. Visitors to Austria, on the other hand, go into ecstasies over the "beautiful blue Danube."

Although the two whimsical rivers we saw at Passau formed the boundary between Austria and the German Reich for many centuries, the difference between the two countries is hardly perceptible. The German Danube is crowded with the exciting romance of war and civil strife. The feudal lords fought the enemy and their own neighbors. They stamped their individualism on the river banks.

Along the Austrian Danube monasteries dominate the scene. There the religious wars never led to the split that rent the Germanies asunder. The Austrian Danube is more Catholic than the German. But the Austrian Danube has not its proportionate share of castles and ruins. The dynasty of the Habsburgs ruled there for seven centuries and tolerated no petty tyrants. A strong

47

central authority was the blight of strongholds that are laws unto themselves. As in France when the Sun King began to dominate the national sky, in Austria the central authority was strong. The "color" of the country was concentrated in the imperial capital of Vienna, whose court attracted wealth, title and distinction. Even before miraculous Versailles was ever heard of, Vienna was the sun of its own universe.

The leisurely rhythm of life in rural Bavaria becomes slightly slower in Austria. The silence is deeper on the banks of the Danube and factory chimneys are less numerous. The village girls are more eager to wave your boat a joyous welcome. The art of enjoying life has been more highly developed in Austria than in Bavaria. This is the classical land of *Gemuetlichkeit,* joviality. Through the Habsburg dynasty, the Austrians benefited from a world dominion so long that they could not help acquiring the art of smiling. Life was good to them, until the catastrophe robbed them of their joy.

The unaided eye sees little difference between the Bavarian and the Austrian, especially in the neighborhood of the former frontier. Both are predominantly blond and tall, with heavy bones. On either side of the frontier good shots abound, largely because their forests were at one time well stocked with game. Men who like *petites* find women of this frontier-land overdeveloped. They seem to be made for work rather than show, except in Vienna, which produced a highly attractive type. The Bavarians and Austrians speak the same dialect, showing the influence of the South and Italy; it is melodious and soft. The hard language of the Prussian is out of favor here. The German of the Austrian and Bavarian is as different in vocabulary from the Northern German as English is from "American."

Valley of Enchantment

The Austrian Danube is about 230 miles long, from Passau to the so-called Hungarian Gate. *Unsere Donau,* the Austrians boasted, our Danube. The city of Linz beckons, even though it cannot stop us for long. She was the capital of Upper Austria until Germany took her. That tomb in the Capuchin Church is Count Raimondo Montecuccoli's, Prince and Duke in his older days, who was hailed as a military genius. And genius this hero of the Thirty Years' War must have been, if for no other reason than having written in his great work that to carry on war one needed three things, above all: money, money, and again money. The Trinity Column, erected by Emperor Charles VI, also deserves notice, because it shows what we miss by not living in the good old times. It commemorates the deliverance of the city from war, fire and pestilence.

Here the Danube expands and makes the impression of a river of opulence, but the famous whirlpools of Grein stop these ambitions short. Castle Persenbeug, standing over the angry river, was a Habsburg palace. The last ruling Habsburg, Emperor Karl, was born here into a life of sorrow. He lost his throne, although he deserved it more than most of his predecessors. He tried to regain it with bold strokes which had driving force but lacked plan. He died of shame. There are few greater tragedies than his in all the Habsburg annals.

The Wachau, which begins about fifty miles west of Vienna, does not suggest tragedy. This part of the Danube river is the embodiment of gaiety and that type of beauty which surprises even travel specialists. The monastery of Melk, perched on a lofty promontory, marks the entrance to this land of fascinations. The river flows between steep banks, covered with vineyards and orchards, dotted with picturesque ruins. A master builder could

49

not have created a more pleasing proportion of the width of the Danube and the hills, which perfume it with a blend of odors, such as only Southern France produces in early Spring. Stream-lined canoes streak the water, and the backwash of the Vienna boat gives them the impression of an ocean ride.

The fortified church castle of St. Michael rises out of a sea of roses that bow to the breeze. Dark and aloof, it leans against the mountainside, thrusting its tower to the attention of the ghostly river pirates who haunt these parts. Angel Cell Monastery, *Stift Engelszell,* displays the Danubian church architecture, which lacks the elaborate art of Western religious buildings. Austria's church triumphant could afford to be simple; it did not need to fight for recognition. Castle Aggstein rises out of rocks piled on the river bank by a prodigiously esthetic natural force. It looks as bold as its occupants must have been when they plied their trade of war and plunder. In the castle of Duernstein Richard the Lion-hearted was jailed on his return from the Holy Land by pious competitors for sacred honors. Here he was discovered by his own people, according to legend, when his alien-tongued servant sang a song of woe.

Now we are on the outskirts of the enchanted land which has inspired the immortals of music. The Vienna Woods stretch southward, waves of green hills, crisscrossed by sunlit paths, which in normal times echoed Vienna's tolerance. All creeds and nations of the Danube valley worshiped nature with spon-taneous song. The bold outlines of the church of Klosterneuburg announce the approach of Vienna. Here the Danube curves sharply to the southeast. (A separate chapter is devoted to the former capital of ex-Austria.)

The Vienna Woods have receded to the south, but the Little

Carpathians have picked up the Danubian trail to the north. Former Czechoslovakia is a jump from here, and Hungary is not much farther. There is greater difference between the western and eastern approaches of Vienna than between Bavaria and Austria. The breath of the East strikes us fully as we leave the Austrian capital. The houses are smaller and longer; their windows have shrunk. Agricultural machinery is rare and the cultivation of the soil less advanced. Here, too, the climate begins to change. Up to this point the Danube valley is under the influence of the Gulf Stream, which brings life to Europe. The climate is mild, rainfall abundant, the meadows green. The wall of mountains which closes in upon the Danube near Vienna keeps much of the temperate weather from penetrating the valley farther east. After the Austrian capital, the green is less luscious in the Summer heat, and gradually the continental climate begins its reign.

Has climate anything to do with cultural advance in Europe? It can surely be no accident that the warm Mediterranean saw the rise of man. It can be no accident that subsequently the Atlantic seaboard became the outpost of civilized man. The Central Danube valley radiated culture in the distant past, when its climate was warmer. Today it is temperate too, but as we reach the Hungarian Gate the warmer rains of the Gulf fall behind. Until this point there was little difference in the cultural level of the German and Austrian Danube. Now we are beginning our journey into the past. Numerous trips down the Danube have convinced me that one descends a rung of the cultural level at nearly every fifty miles. The Gulf Stream may be one of the factors to be considered.

The Danube influences the life of all Austria. But in order to avoid the danger of obtaining a distorted view, let us see for a moment another part of the "Ostmark," the one strategically most important for many centuries: the country around the Brenner Pass. It is the shortest and most convenient route between Northern Europe and Italy. It was through the Brenner that the ancient Romans extended their sway to the Danube. It was through it that the barbarians of the North invaded the plains of Italy. Through the Brenner endless streams of pilgrims marched on their way to Rome. Various Emperors crossed it sixty-six times in the Middle Ages, penitent and militant, bent on war and peace. Here Napoleon met an unexpected defeat at the hands of liberty-loving mountain folk.

The Brenner is the widest gap on the two-hundred-mile frontier between Italy and Germany. Barriers, fifty yards apart, separate the two countries. At both boundaries all persons desiring to cross from one country into the other are carefully scrutinized. On the German—former Austrian—side of the Brenner the mountain slopes are dotted with whitewashed houses adorned with wooden carved balconies on which much native workmanship has been expended. Glacial moraines, deposited by the slowly moving ice rivers, furnish the stones with which the roofs of the houses are weighted in the fight against sudden squalls. The façades of many houses are ornamented with inlaid shrines of the Virgin, or decorated with water-colors of flowers and folklife. An abundance of taverns bears the traditional sign: *Weisses Roessl*. Here Alpine vegetation is luxuriant. Special laws protect the highly coveted edelweiss, keeping haughty company with the columbine, wormwood, sowbread, starwort, sea-holly and hellebore. Pine and larch are in evidence everywhere. The green of the meadows is almost unreal in the crystalline air. These are the *Almen,* on which the native brown cattle graze all summer.

Almond and Mulberry Trees

Villages are widely scattered and look like hamlets anywhere in Southern Germany. Large storehouses are, however, a special feature, reminding the tourist of the merchandise which North and South exchanged along the route. The churches are high-steepled, Gothic, many of them with rich altars and valuable frescoes. Thirty houses of worship may be seen from one observation point.

This is also the land of many castles, now mostly in ruin, almost theatrical in settings of boulder-strewn slopes, unbelievably inaccessible. On the main north-and-south route of Central Europe, the robber barons of past ages carried on their predatory pursuits. The competition was keen, evidently, and unwelcome guests could be eluded through underground passages into trailless mountains.

On the Italian side, which was Austrian before the war, the mountains recede gradually into the plains of Venetia and Lombardy, beyond the horizon. Although the names of the villages are Italian, they do not look any different from those on the northern slope. Italy's dictator gave orders years ago that the German names in the cemeteries must be Italianized. Some twenty-five miles south of the Pass, old Bozen, now Bolzano, affords the first glimpse of the South. Cypresses give the mountainside a Mediterranean look. Chestnuts, almond, fig and mulberry trees attract the eyes. The palms of the public gardens weather the Winter winds. In the early Spring the town is an unforgettable sight of colors running wild in its perfectly tended orchards.

On both sides of the Pass people speak a Tyrolean dialect, closely akin to Bavarian. They are a thick-boned mountain folk, the kind of Teutonic type that quickens race-conscious pulses.

53

In some sections the mixture of Southern blood may be seen. On holidays the village natives in the valleys of Tyrol still wear picturesque costumes. The men wear broad-brimmed hats, cocked at a rakish angle. They have wide belts, and their dark vests, jackets and knee breeches are gaily ornamented. Their woolen stockings are white. The women's dresses are studies in black and white. Their strange hats are peaked and made of the wool of native sheep. In the side valleys there is a rich variety of costumes.

The occupations of the inhabitants of this district are mostly pastoral and agricultural. The men are famous as hunters and fishermen, and as foresters they have little competition. Since the country once was a great attraction to foreign tourists, there was a large field for guides and innkeepers. Small industries also employ a few people.

Nature gave all to pre-war Austria: minerals, water-power, soil, coal, healing waters, the Danube, sea, natural highways, an industrious population. Man deprived her of these blessings at the end of the World War and left the Danube without its hinterland. Post-War Austria had a surplus of beauty: her Alps, Vienna, the green pastures of Tyrol. She had iron ore, some lignite, lumber and water-power; the rest was taken away. The Danube wharves lost much of their precious cargo. But the ships and other means of transportation continued to export Austria's genius in the form of goods: luxury articles, textiles. Those attractive young men seen from the Danube boats probably have little to do in their woodwork, furniture and paper factories— leading industries in Austria. A small country is at a disadvantage in carving a market for itself and particularly so if its people have lost heart. The quick descent from the peak to the bottom of a mountain is apt to take many breaths away. About one-third of post-War Austria's people were engaged in agriculture, which showed great improvement after the War. Before it, there was little need to turn over the soil, since other parts of the Empire specialized in this type of work, and it was more profitable for Austria to stick to her lathe. She also began to make better use of her abundant supplies of water-power which she did not need before the War, because parts of the Empire were rich in coal.

There were times when the history of the Austrian part of the Danube valley was only that of the Habsburg dynasty, an amazing family of nonentities with a genius for organization. Nearly the entire valley was theirs or under their influence at one time.

"Whoever is master of Vienna is master of the Danube valley," Prince Metternich, the shrewdest and most successful statesman of the river basin, publicly proclaimed. "If there were no Austria, she would have to be created," Prince Bismarck of Prussia and Germany said a half century later, after he had beaten Austria in the decisive battle of Koeniggraetz. The Danube made Austria great, and the Habsburg dynasty made her even greater. She is the hub of a compass whose needle points to Rome in the south, Constantinople in the east, Berlin in the north, and Paris in the west. The House of Austria did not conquer all these cities, some of which had their own forces of attraction. But, as pointed out before, it ruled the best part of Italy, was nominal head of Germany, and was master of the strategic Netherlands and of Spain.

The Habsburgs built their world power upon the Danube valley. There they were the strongest among a host of weak dynasties. The Danube attracted tribes and nations, as flame attracts the moths. They came from all over the East, urged onward by hunger, as the steppes of Asia began to dry up. They

55

were also attracted by the fame of the Danube pasture and the rich soil of the lower valley, which is the best in Europe even today. Dumped into the Danube basin, these fragments of peoples fought one another with all the bitterness of thwarted ambition. In assembling these fragments, the Habsburgs became the most powerful rulers of two worlds.

They fell, as we shall see, when each of the component parts became nation-conscious. It took several centuries for this concept to travel the seven hundred miles between the Seine and the Middle Danube. The medley of nations in Central Europe was not particularly anxious at first to become nation-minded. The Habsburgs were not bad rulers, although their brain capacities were not large. Occasionally they were downright stupid. More important still, the Danube represented a natural link, broken only when the national idea became a universal obsession. Prince Metternich and Prince Bismarck knew whereof they were talking.

Austria was one of the hundreds of tiny countries dotting the Central European landscape when her recorded history began in the early ninth century. A lance and a stout heart were then sufficient for a knight to get himself a country. The "eastern realm," Oesterreich, was set up by the Frankish Emperors as a bulwark against the Slavs. The entire realm of the *Ostarrichi* was some sixty miles from west to east. Emperor Otto II gave the frontier province to the House of Babenberg, whose members he raised to the rank of Margraves, frontier Counts. The Danube would have forced this family to become great, against its better judgment, if it had not become extinct in the middle of the thirteenth century. Meanwhile, Frederick Barbarossa, the legendary Emperor with the long beard, who is still asleep in his subterranean cave, raised Austria to the rank of a Duchy.

56

The usual feudal wars ensued, several families laying claim to a piece of land of great potentialities. Finally, it was Ottakar, son of Wenceslaus I, King of Bohemia, who obtained the Austrian provinces. Thus Slavdom made its bid for the possession of the strategic Danube valley. "If" histories are nearly always misleading, but it is tempting to think of what might have happened if in a decisive battle Ottakar had been able to hold his own. Would the Slavs have won Austria and the rest of the Danube valley? Would they have become Holy Roman Emperors? Would the perennial battle between Slav and German have been decided in Ottakar's favor?

It was then that a Count of little distinction was elected German King, not because he was strong, but because he was weak. The German rulers wanted a nominal head they could dominate, and their selection fell upon Rudolph, Count of Habsburg, whose ancestral castle, Hawk's Burg, was in what is today Northern Switzerland. Was it intuition or genius that told the first ruler in the House of Habsburg that he should try to win the country around Vienna from the Bohemian sovereign? He knew, of course, that as a German king he was merely a figurehead unless he had a hereditary domain to supply him with soldiers and money. The decisive battle took place in 1276, and from then until 1918 the Habsburgs ruled over Austria. Thus the war between German and Slav was decided. It was because of this battle that, less than four centuries later, Bohemia was conquered by Austria, with which she was forced to remain until the Habsburgs' fall. It may have been because of this battle, too, that twenty years after the end of the House of Austria, the Chancellor of the German Reich re-annexed Bohemia to a Greater Germany.

The story of Austria and the Danube now became the story of the House of Habsburg, a remarkable family, which was in power when knights marched to battle with spears and much later when airplanes cleared the skies of eagles, the symbols of family might. No other dynasty anywhere had such a vast collection of crowns as they possessed in their long history. The "small title" of the head of the House of Austria reads as follows: "Emperor of Austria, Apostolic King of Hungary, King of Bohemia, Dalmatia, Croatia, Slavonia, Galicia, Lodomeria and Illyria, King of Jerusalem, etc., Archduke of Austria, Grand Duke of Tuscany and Cracow, Duke of Lorraine, of Salzburg, Styria, Carinthia, Carniola and Bukovina, Grand Duke of Transylvania, Margrave of Moravia, Duke of Upper Silesia, Lower Silesia, Modena, Parma, Plaisance and Guastalla, of Auschwitz and Zator, Teschen, Friaul, Ragusa and Zara, Princely Count of Habsburg and Tyrol, Kyburg, Goritz and Gradisca, Prince of Trente and Brixen, Margrave of Upper and Lower Lausitz and in Istria, Count of Hohenembs, Feldkirch, Brigance, Sonnenberg, etc., Sovereign of Trieste Cattaro and the Wendish Marches, Grand-Voyvoda of the Serbian Voyvodina, etc., etc."

Their contemporaries gave nicknames to many Habsburgs, indicative of their characters and accomplishments. There were, for instance, among the first, Werner the Pious and Albert the Rich. The handsome features of Frederick the Fair were perpetuated on many canvases. Leopold the Habsburg was known as the Flower of Knighthood, and a Heinrich was known as the Lame and the Wise. History speaks of Otto the Gay; John the Parricide, whom legend made to play a part in the drama of Wilhelm Tell; and Frederick with the Empty Pocket. But history has given to no member of the Habsburg house the name of

58

Genghis Khan (*after a painting*)

Divide et Impera

"Great." Yet if individual genius did not help the Habsburgs to reach the highways of fame and power, they did possess a collective genius that made the family survive countless trials and vicissitudes. They were, in fact, adept at playing one nation off against another, and cornering the marriage market for the benefit of their house.

The Habsburgs never belonged to any specific nation. Thus, and thus only, were they able to set up their own first League of Nations of Europe, which consisted of a large number of nationalities. Their allegiance was to no race or country, but solely to their dynasty. The Danube made them great, and it may be said, perhaps, that theirs was a Danubian nationality. If a member of the house had been asked to name his nation, he would have been put to it to reply. He could not have said he was an Austrian without forever alienating Hungary's sympathies. Nor could he have said that he was a Hungarian without disqualifying himself for the Austrian throne. And he would also have had to think of the sensibilities of other nations over which the Habsburgs once ruled—perhaps may rule again.

From the ancient Romans the Habsburgs acquired the policy of *divide et impera,* which was admirably adapted to the Danube medley. To it they adhered until the very end, when the river's tide of nationalism became too strong for them. On the eve of the collapse, in the Autumn of 1918, the streets of Hungary's capital were patroled by Bosnian soldiers, while Hungarian soldiers performed police duty in the mountainous villages of Bosnia. Austria's German soldiers kept order among the Czech inhabitants, while Czech inhabitants did military service in the part of land where the Roumanians were at home.

Because the Habsburgs could claim no nationality, their court

was at times a Babel. When the first Habsburg entered the scene
he probably spoke a Swiss dialect at home and bad "kitchen
Latin" to noble companions. As the dynasty branched off into
Spain, its members adopted both the court etiquette and language
of the Spanish peninsula. When the Habsburgs conquered many
Italian cities they were conquered in turn by Italy's language,
which they took back to the Danube. Some time later the Austrian
court fell under the spell of Versailles and thrilled to the music
of French. It was only during Maria Theresa's reign, less than
two centuries ago, that the Vienna court began to speak German.
Later, members of the house spoke not only German, but some
Hungarian and Slavic.

Another instrument of the Habsburgs' success was their marriage policy. Most of their large territories were acquired at the
altar. Take, for instance, the case of the founder of Habsburg
greatness, Count Rudolph I. He was born into the ownership of
a castle and several small patches of land, but he married Anne
of Hohenberg, and this fortunate step meant additional land and
influential kinsmen, who helped him become the German King.
When he was impelled to extend his rule into the Danube valley
he offered the hand of one of his daughters to the heir of the
Bohemian King; then he changed his mind, met the King in
battle, defeated him and broke the engagement. When Rudolph
died, the Habsburg pennant was flowing on Vienna's ramparts,
and his dynasty was well on the way.

Habsburg's most spectacular son, Emperor and King Charles
V, was engaged ten times (for political reasons) before he was
twenty. One of his successors more than two centuries later,
Francis II, Emperor of Austria, tried to defeat Napoleon at arms.
Failing, he gave his daughter, the Archduchess Marie Louise, in

marriage to the little Corsican, and thereby accomplished his purpose. While Napoleon was on his way to Elba, his wife was on her way back to the court on the Danube; and the Habsburgs, after their appalling losses at Austerlitz and Wagram, were once more the victors.

Perhaps it was not mere coincidence that the decline of the House of Habsburg began when it was no longer customary for sovereigns to give whole countries as dowry. In any event, before the twilight of the marriage market, it was with envy that less successful sovereigns remarked: "Other countries may carry on war, but thou, happy Austria, shalt marry"— " . . . TU, FELIX AUSTRIA, NUBE."

Although history has not recognized any of the Habsburgs as great, it has acknowledged that some of them had caliber. Stature was achieved by Charles V, Holy Roman Emperor and King of Spain; by Maria Theresa, Queen of Hungary, and her son, Emperor Joseph II; also by Franz Joseph I. There were few byways of the world, old or new, that Charles V did not seek to conquer. He pursued the Turks down the Danube and penetrated their haunts in Northern Africa. His armies descended upon the North and South of France and came within sight of Paris. His lieutenants conquered Mexico and Peru. His protégé, Fernando Magellan, planted Charles' flag on the newly discovered soil of the Archipelago of San Lazarus, which in later years came to be known as the Philippine Islands. The Emperor was among the first rulers to insist that natives of America be treated with consideration. As a soldier he had few equals, and it was said that with his passing the world's best light cavalryman was buried.

The Danube valley has produced few rulers more picturesque than Maria Theresa, mother of the Queen of France, Marie

Antoinette, who fell a victim of the fury of the Revolution. It has been said of Queen Maria Theresa that she saved her dynasty. In this book of the Danube she is entitled to more extensive treatment, particularly since I am able to draw upon secrets long dormant in the Austrian Secret Archives. While most other Habsburgs were mere machines geared to signing their names, the personality of Maria Theresa emerges clearly. In an age when it was natural to act unnatural, she dared to be natural and act without pose of any sort, even that of simplicity. Her atrocious spelling mistakes did not prejudice posterity against the view of her bitterest enemy, Frederick the Great, King of Prussia, that she was a "great man." Klopstock, one of the leading poets of the age, called her the greatest of all the Habsburgs. Forced into a fight against almost the whole world, she saved her dynasty and the unity of the Danube valley.

Her historical rôle began in the late Autumn of 1740. Throughout the night the cobblestones of Vienna resounded with the heavy footsteps of the town guard. The capital of the Habsburg realm slept uneasily under a gloomy sky. Burghers in nightcaps, fright written on their cheeks, peered into the darkness. A few nights before, a luminous red meteor had shot across the sky, frightening the imperial city on the Danube, and only last night the guard of the suburb of Wieden, just outside the gates, had found a man writhing in the street, shouting in agony that the world was approaching its end; and tomorrow a young girl was to ascend the ancient throne of Habsburg.

Emperor Charles VI, father of Archduchess Maria Theresa, had hoped in vain for a male heir. Then he had taken his cap in his hand and made the rounds of the courts of Europe, begging them to permit his daughter to rule. As a bribe for their accept-

ance of her as his heir, the Emperor had turned over a large slice
of fertile Lombardy to the King of Sardinia, had promised the
Grand Duchy of Lorraine to the French King, and had been
forced to cede much of Serbia and most of Walachia to the
Turkish Sultan. Yet, on his deathbed, Emperor Charles VI had
feared that his passing would be a signal for the rulers of Europe
to rise and snatch away his daughter's crown.

In the early morning hours of coronation day the Danubian
metropolis had ample reason to be fearful. From the villages of
Floridsdorf and Aspern, across the Danube, peasants armed with
scythes and hoes were clamoring at the Roter Turm gate. They
had come to attend the coronation, their spokesman said, but
Vienna knew better. Rumors had reached the capital that the
peasants were armed to keep the young girl from ascending the
throne, and the town provost was able to send them about their
business only on the pretext that the coronation had been post-
poned.

As the hour of the ceremony drew near, Vienna's depressed
mood deepened. The envoys of Bohemia and Silesia, two Habsburg Crown lands, had received disquieting news. Young Frederick II, King of Prussia, who was to be known to posterity as the
"Great" and at that time was known to Vienna as the "Mean,"
threatened to overrun Silesia. His father had received no bribe
from the late Emperor. Frederick's neighbor, the elector of
Bavaria, had designs not only on one crown possession, but on the
entire Danube valley, hereditary land of the Habsburgs. Even the
King of Sardinia complained that he had been dealt with unfairly
and demanded a larger share of the spoils. And the Magyars—
what would they do? On them, more than any other nation under
the Habsburg rule, depended the future of the dynasty.

The coronation ceremony was short and depressing. Maria Theresa took possession of the Habsburg heritage, which included the Danube basin—Austria, Hungary, Bohemia, Silesia, Styria, Tyrol—and the Austrian Netherlands as well as a part of Lombardy. "A comely wench," the Hungarian noblemen admitted, twirling their waxed mustaches. Tall, slender, blue-eyed and blonde, Maria Theresa at the age of twenty-three appeared to them very much like the angels they had admired so long above the high altar of the Capuchin Church. Yet, they reflected, in a world kept in order by hard blows, angelic looks were of little use.

With the coronation over, the burghers scurried back to their homes. Frederick's army might appear on the Danube at any moment. Never before had locksmiths been so busy. The luminous red meteor could not be wrong. As night again descended, only the steps of the guard resounded on the cobblestones.

The red meteor did not lie. Maria Theresa's accession was a signal to the crowned heads of Europe to deprive her of the Danube lands. In the trail of wars which now ensued came pestilence and death. Four months after her coronation, the armies of Frederick II had invaded Silesia. Shortly after the outbreak of the hostilities, the Prussian King wrote the following letter to the Hungarian Queen:

"Madame, My Sister: Nothing could grieve me more than the knowledge that you have misunderstood the motives which have actuated the occupation of the Silesian provinces by my armies. The danger to which the menacing attitude of two of your neighbors exposed your crown lands impelled me to occupy a strategic position from which their movements can be controlled and their offensive purposes frustrated. My heart is for you, even though

64

my arms must be against you, but believe me, Madame, my sister, that the stability and future of your successful reign could be best vouchsafed by the move which I had to undertake and which, history will show, was solely motivated by my desire to be of service to you and of the illustrious house of which you are a member. Madame, my sister's affectionate brother

"FREDERICUS REX"

("Sister" and "brother" are metaphorical terms, used in the correspondence of sovereign rulers.)

Frederick the Great thus took Austrian Silesia under his protection, and it has been Germany's ever since. "He is a bad man," Maria Theresa wrote to a confidant. "He has stolen Silesia from me and I shall never forgive him. He took unfair advantage of me when I was hopelessly forsaken and when I had to fight the entire world. Nothing will ever make me see him in any rôle except that of a wicked man. His motives are far from being those by which he pretends to be actuated. In his diplomatic dealings he is unscrupulous and stoops to any practices, no matter how objectionable."

To her, as well as to almost everyone else of that time, it seemed inconceivable that the Prussian King, short, rotund, very young and very inexperienced, would develop into one of the supermen of the eighteenth century.

All Europe responded to the Silesian campaign with a cry of disgust. Sir Thomas Robinson, the English Ambassador to Vienna, protested against what he termed an outrage and a flagrant violation of international law. Even Berlin, unaccustomed as yet to the antics of the philosopher-king, sided with the Habsburg Queen. Little did Berlin suspect at that time that this was not merely a predatory expedition but that the King of Prussia was

65

taking the first steps toward procuring for Germany that place in the Danubian sun which a dictator contrived to obtain two hundred years later.

The second Silesian war followed closely upon the first campaign and confirmed Frederick's position of the occupied provinces. The Seven Years' War, which was the greatest effort of Maria Theresa, brought to a head the struggle between the Habsburgs and Hohenzollerns for supremacy. In a bold attempt to down the invincible Prussian, Maria Theresa headed a league of royal women. Their front was held in the East by the Czarina Elizabeth, autocrat of all the Russias, the most beautiful member of the league. In many respects she was as brilliant as her legendary father, Peter the Great, but she was even more unreliable. Madame de Pompadour, *maîtresse en titre* of King Louis XV of France and the real power behind the bedroom curtain, was the representative of the royal Amazons in the West. France had been Austria's traditional enemy, and through many generations Europe's history had been little more than the struggle of the Habsburgs and the Bourbons. With a stroke of genius which gave Austria's foreign policy an entirely new direction, Maria Theresa concluded an alliance with the French. She was assisted in her negotiations by Prince von Kaunitz, the Chancellor. It was he who drew Mme. Pompadour into the plot which resulted in the dynasties on the Danube and on the Seine fighting as allies. When the war came to an end seven years later, when the dead, the maimed and the widows were counted, Europe found that between Austria and Prussia not one village had changed hands. It also found a new world power—Prussia.

Maria Theresa regulated and liberalized the government machine. Before she issued her decrees, specifying the amount of

66

tithe serfs owed to their masters and the nature of public works they had to perform, the peasant population was a prey to the whims of arbitrary landlords. A rudimentary form of feudalism survived her father's rule, with the magnates in power and the occupant of the throne the executor of their will. Maria Theresa made the will of the State supreme, and thereby paved the way for the enlightened autocracy of her son, Joseph II.

She discarded export and import restrictions, opened new markets for the products of the Danubian lands. She gave the keynote of Austria-Hungary's later policy to cultivate better trade relations with the Balkans. She forestalled some of the worst flood menaces of the Danube by regulating its lower reaches and extending its navigable area. She took the first steps toward making Trieste Austria's outlet to the sea and improving the highways leading to its harbor. She cut down the number of holidays which, up to her time, took up nearly one-fifth of the calendar. The Queen did more for higher education in the Danube valley than any of her predecessors. She built universities, military and scientific academies and introduced important reforms to spread literacy among the rural population. She built theaters and concert halls and imparted to Vienna that air of dignity and beauty for which it is famous throughout the world.

"In the secrecy of her cabinet," her enemy, Frederick the Great, wrote, "she prepared the great schemes, which later she carried into execution. She introduced order and system into State finances, entirely unknown to her ancestors. Her revenues far exceeded those of her father, even when he was master of Naples, Parma, Silesia and Serbia."

But she performed her greatest work in the reorganization of the army. From her father she inherited a rabble of some 15,000 unruly rascals who had to be flogged into obedience. When she died, she left behind an army of about 170,000 soldiers, well cared for and disciplined. The morale of the army underwent a remarkable change during her reign, partly because she treated common soldiers as respectable human beings.

In the midst of so many preoccupations, Maria Theresa lost nothing of her native charm, which found many imitators in Austria. This is illustrated by a postscript to a letter to the President of the Supreme War Council, which, in the Habsburg archives, is unique in its unaffected simplicity. To explain the stains upon the paper, she apologized in her disarmingly naive way: "I am frightfully ashamed for pouring a cup of coffee over this letter."

As the years passed, the suspicion and distrust of the peasant for the woman sovereign gave way to unqualified confidence and affection. They now thought that she could cure children by merely taking them into her arms. Maria Theresa thus succeeded to an unusual degree in combining feminine tenderness with masculine fortitude. The Magyars described her best in their enraptured enthusiasm by calling her *"Domina Rex,"* our Lady King, instead of *"Regina,"* Queen, which would have been more grammatical.

Of the sixteen children of Maria Theresa and Francis I, the ninth child, Marie Antoinette, is best known to history. The young Archduchess spent many happy days on the banks of the Danube. It must have been one of the most charming incidents of court life when Herr Leopold Mozart, official violinist of the Archbishop of Salzburg, took his son, Wolfgang Amadeus, a six-year-old prodigy, to the Hofburg on the Danube, to play his own compositions on the harpsichord. Little Archduchess Marie

68

Marie Antoinette at Fourteen

Antoinette, one year his senior, was in the audience, and she made a great impression on him. "Tony" took "Wolfel" by the hand and showed him around the palace. On the polished floor he slipped and the Archduchess helped him to his feet. "You're very kind," Wolfel whispered into her ear. "When I grow up I'll marry you." Fate was not so kind to Marie Antoinette as to make her Mozart's wife. She was a mere child when she left the banks of the Danube for those of the Seine and was married to the Dauphin of France, the future King Louis XVI. She was hardly more than fourteen when, in her bridal dress, she took the imperial coach for Versailles. She squeezed the prayer-book her mother had given her in her childish hands. Into the book Maria Theresa had slipped a *règlement,* which was to serve her as a guide through life. After Marie Antoinette's execution the *règlement* got back to Vienna in some tortuous way.

Maria Theresa was not to blame if her daughter's tempestuous life contributed in later years toward provoking the population of Paris to the excesses which culminated in the Reign of Terror. The Austrian Queen always kept an eye on her daughter. Her most interesting letters were so confidential that, in accordance with her wishes, they had to be destroyed. Although they no longer exist, we do know that she urged her daughter to improve her relations with Mme. DuBarry, the new mistress of Louis XV, Marie Antoinette's grandfather-in-law. The Queen of the Danube lands was long dead when her daughter mounted the guillotine amid the angry shouts of a tumultuous populace thirsting for her blood. Had Maria Theresa any premonition of the impending danger? Did she suspect what tragic fate her Tony would meet?

The end found Maria Theresa at her desk, writing letters in her own hand. She wrote the following, preserved in the Habsburg Archives, presumably on the day of her death: "I am not so courageous today. Coughing bothers me. There is a trifling change for the better, but it makes little difference. As I am not accustomed to sickness, it appears to me more serious than it actually is. I hope I will have a good night."

Her night was restful; she was dead. Ever active, she had been about to move from her couch to a chair, when death overtook her. "Are you comfortable, Mother?" her son, Joseph, asked. "Comfortable enough to die." These were her last words. She ruled the Danubian lands for forty years and when she died her nations were plunged into deep sorrow.

Her son, Emperor Joseph II, had vague ideas about a united Danubian world under Habsburg's benevolent despotism. "The revolutionary Emperor" was a contemporary of old Frederick the Great of Prussia, Catherine the Great of Russia, and Voltaire the Great of Europe. It was the Emperor's ambition to be remembered by posterity as Joseph the Great. For his rôle he had a first-class mind, heroic intolerance, immense ambition and the desire to save the world. But he was a hundred years ahead of his time, and he failed heroically.

Joseph was an autocrat in the best sense of the word, who sacrificed his health, happiness and life for a cause. Playing the rôle of a Haroun Al Rashid blended into a Diderot he turned the Danubian lands upside down in search of a monarch's stone of wisdom. He also made a foredoomed attempt to turn the feudal lands of his realm into a modern empire, and he died broken and execrated. Among the enlightened monarchs of the eighteenth century, Joseph II was the only one for whom enlightenment was neither a caprice nor a fad, but a matter of the heart and mind. He must be considered one of the heroes of human enlightenment, the great friend of the underprivileged, and that meant the vast majority of his people. "Emotionally he was driven to improve the lot of the common people," his biographer, S. K. Padover, writes. "In reality, absolute monarchy, for which he stood, automatically spelled misery for the masses." He was desperately anxious to be just and good and forgot that the masses in his days forgave a good heart only in combination with an iron fist.

The tragic clash in his life began in his early youth. There could hardly have been two human beings more different than were he and Maria Theresa, his mother. She was well-meaning, but, compared with him, bigoted and intolerant. She was unable to understand her son, who wanted to be something infinitely more than a mere Emperor. "You are an intellectual coquet," she wrote to him. "You are only a thoughtless imitator where you think to be an original thinker." She warned him that there could be nothing more ruinous than his persistence in religious toleration. Joseph, on the other hand, wrote: "The distinctions between nations and religions must disappear, and all citizens must consider each other as brothers." For similar views, his nephew, the future Emperor Francis, sent scores to the scaffold. To Joseph the State was to be a community providing the greatest good for the greatest number.

He had many shortcomings, inherited from his Habsburg ancestors. As a born bureaucrat, he thought that paper decrees could save the world and bring about Utopia. During the ten years of his rule he issued some 6,000 decrees and 1,100 new laws. Nothing was left to chance or initiative.

In short, Joseph was too much an intellectual to be a success in a world in which banditry was legitimate diplomacy. Although he tried to be as unscrupulous as Frederick the Great, he failed in his major diplomatic ventures, and with that relentless perspicacity of his which struck terror into his heart he knew that he was a failure. He realized too late that his contemporaries wanted to be ruled, and not to be saved. His Hungarian subjects celebrated the news of his death with public festivals, and his coffin was the center of hostile demonstrations.

Napoleon came and went, leaving behind a dazzled mankind which was not to recover its breath for generations. Foreign troops were stationed on the banks of the Rhine and once again the Danube began to make world history. At Vienna seventy Kings and Princes bowed to Chancellor Metternich, the same Kings and Princes who, not long before, had paid homage to Napoleon at Erfurt. The world was safe from democracy, legitimacy was vindicated, and the reforms of the French Revolution had been thrown overboard. Metternich was the host of Europe at the Congress of Vienna, where the Danubian lands were to rewrite the history of the world. The Kings and Princes did not do much writing, however. They had brought their wives and daughters, and there were gay celebrations in the imperial palace. The real work was left for Metternich. He dazzled society with his wit and promoted a score of royal matches. Between parties he retired to his study and hatched his plans for autocracy to rule the world. He was autocracy's chief instrument, and its victory was his triumph. His enemy was the idea of Bonapartism, which covered all sins, an elusive enemy, synonymous with free opportunity for all. Bonapartism had to be stamped out.

The Prince had three potentates to win over, and had to play the rôles of courtier and lion-tamer at the same time. His master,

An Unholy Alliance

Emperor Francis, began to insist on settling the world's troubles according to his own lights. The King of Prussia, Frederick William III, balked at almost every project which he could not claim credit for originating. The most dangerous of the three was Alexander, Czar of all the Russias. He was a revolutionist—at least, Metternich called him so—and tried to realize dreams that could occur, the Chancellor confided to the Emperor in a memorandum, only to a madman. One of his favorite plans was for establishing a League of Nations. He was also mad enough to think Napoleon a great man. Metternich determined to exploit his "insanity" and encourage him to bring about the unity of the countries of continental Europe. When the new League should be formed, Metternich hoped to be its master. The Czar's admiration for Napoleon, however, had first to be changed.

Just then a fanatical woman was wandering about Europe preaching hatred against Napoleon. She was Baroness de Kruedner, a member of the Russian high aristocracy, a mystic and "seer." She would go to live in a forest with a few disciples and invite the peasants of the locality to come and hear the gospel of hatred. Metternich selected this woman to convert the Czar, a mystic himself. An interview took place between them, in which the Czar was sufficiently converted to satisfy the highest expectations of the Austrian Chancellor. The Holy Alliance became a reality. Alexander meant it as a sort of League of Despots directed against Bonapartism and all it connoted: a measure of freedom and enlightenment. It brought the leadership of the continent to the banks of the Danube, and bound Prussia and Russia to Austria. This "agency of peace, conforming to the words of the Holy Scriptures," was used by Metternich to stage the worst reaction Europe had known in centuries. He did not

73

like the unctuous phrasing of the instrument, but he did like its aim.

But Napoleon was not yet dead. One night, while the capital on the Danube celebrated the victory over the man whom Herr von Stein called "the enemy of the human race," a bomb fell among the Kings and Princes of the Vienna Congress—a dispatch saying that Napoleon had escaped from Elba. So great was the terror of his name that they forgot their chivalry and fled from the ball-room, upsetting the ladies as they ran. Napoleon might be already at the gates of Vienna!

The horror of the Princes was soon allayed. The Battle of Waterloo ended the Hundred Days' Rule and sent Napoleon fleeing for his life. His first thought was to seek refuge in the United States, but a lady of his entourage prevailed upon him to throw himself on the mercy of the English. He surrendered to the Captain of the *Bellerophon,* and three months later found himself on the rocks of St. Helena.

When news of Waterloo reached the Vienna Hofburg the band struck up a Hungarian *csárdás* and the ladies, having recovered from the effects of the stampede, graciously accepted the renewed homage of the cavaliers. When the dance was over, Metternich retired to his writing chamber and penned these lines: "The powers declare that Napoleon Bonaparte has placed himself outside the bounds of civil and social relationships, and that as an enemy and disturber of the peace of the world he is consigned to public prosecution." Next day he submitted the document for the approval of Emperor Francis, who signed it. Francis occupied the seat of honor at the Congress of Vienna. Was it not he who had brought the outlaw to his downfall by marrying him to his daughter?

L'Aiglon

L'Aiglon and His Golden Cage

Out of the Vienna Congress grew a great human tragedy, which had its epilogue on the banks of the Danube. Napoleon's son, formerly the King of Rome and now the Duke of Reichstadt, was ten years old when his father died on St. Helena with his name on his lips. "I recommend my son," Napoleon wrote in his testament, "never to forget that he is a French Prince and never to consent to be used as an instrument in the hands of the triumvirate who are oppressing Europe." He made the curious provision that his stomach should be given to his son. Napoleon died of cancer of the stomach and feared that his son might fall victim to the disease. He thought that by means of a thorough autopsy the physicians might be able to protect the boy. Marie Louise, his second wife, was to receive his heart, which she never claimed and never received. She did, however, claim through Metternich the largest part of Napoleon's estate.

In his golden cage on the Danube, L'Aiglon was dreaming about the Seine. Dreaming about him were the oppressed, as year after year the Holy Alliance crushed timid thoughts and sent Europe back to sleep in its intellectual dungeon. Millions of eyes were turned toward the Danube where the son of the eagle was trying his wings—so at least he thought. He was hailed as "The Son of Man," and "The New Messiah." Most of the political disorders of 1820-1830 were connected, directly or indirectly, with the Duke of Reichstadt, L'Aiglon. Revolutionary plots sprang up in France, where dissatisfaction with the Bourbons threatened to disrupt the government. Colonel Fabvrier was collecting Bonapartist sympathizers in the South. In Lyons the Duke of Reichstadt was proclaimed Emperor. In Saumur and Colmar the mob grew hysterical during a celebration of Bonapartists. Two French officers were dispatched to spirit the Duke

75

away from Austria. A French interior decorator followed them. The eyes of Belgium turned toward the imperial château on the Danube.

In the Balkans, where a newly awakened nationalism was full of promise, the name of Napoleon II had a magic power. In Poland, newly dismembered and still bleeding, there grew up an underground movement with the aim of enthroning the Duke of Reichstadt. In Hungary, too, the new idea began to germinate. But the Holy Alliance was still vigorous.

All this agitation made the keepers of the golden cage on the Danube watch the Duke more closely at the same time they were hunting down his sympathizers. Instructions were sent to the secret-service men of the Holy Alliance to spare no efforts in uncovering Bonapartist propaganda. Czar Alexander's idea for international co-operation of peace lovers degenerated into an international co-operation of spies. It was deadly espionage with a tendency to detect not only real conspiracies but also non-existent plots. Metternich permitted the rumor to spread that Napoleon's son was a very disappointing young man. Efforts to transform him into an Austrian Prince were redoubled. Metternich was sure that the rebels would not wish to place an Austrian ruler on the throne of their countries. The boy tried to battle against the Habsburg influence, but the environment was too strong for him. He who once said that he would never speak German had difficulty in expressing himself in French.

Metternich won against the boy by stirring his ambition for a military career. At fifteen, the male members of the dynasty were usually made officers of the army. He felt disgraced in his sergeant's uniform. One of his exercises in composition was an imaginary army order of Hannibal, full of eloquent phrases

76

about "heroic determination" and "sweeping victories." He would do anything to earn his share of glory. The Church-State and the Duchy of Modena were harassed by revolutionary outbreaks, and the Duke of Reichstadt, scarcely more than a child, acted in the spirit of the Holy Alliance by offering his help to crush them. The domain of his mother, the Duchy of Parma, experienced similar disorders, engineered mostly by Bonapartist sympathizers, and the young Eaglet expressed his desire to put them down. When the rule of his father's old enemies was menaced, he was ready to help them in an anti-revolutionary crusade. He wrote an essay on Prince Schwarzenberg, the Austrian General, who beat Napoleon in his last struggles for the domination of Europe. It refers to the author's father as "Bonaparte," showers praises on the Austrian General and gives scant recognition to the Emperor of the French. "It was an unforgettable sight," wrote the boy, now seventeen, and a captain of the Austrian cavalry, "to behold the closed ranks of the Austrian army so gallant in battle." If Metternich aimed to save the boy from the sin of inordinate ambition, he failed completely. Ambition was not killed; it merely took an unforeseen turn. A casual visit to the catacombs of St. Stephen's Cathedral gave his ambition a definite object. His attention was called to the tomb of Prince Eugene of Savoy, leader of the Austrian army that pushed the Turks out of the Danubian domains of the Habsburgs. Prince Eugene was a Frenchman. The resemblance struck the imagination of the Duke of Reichstadt and he devoured all information about his great prototype.

Now at last he was an Austrian because he did not know how to be otherwise. He tried to reconcile the opposing tendencies that confused him. He had heard in some illicit way that his father was popular with the people and he, too, decided to seek popularity. His tutor complained to Marie Louise, the Duke's mother, that the young man persisted in shaking hands with subordinate officers. This unheard-of practice might easily give offense to the Emperor. Another cause for complaint was the Duke's fondness for returning the greetings of the crowd when he drove out. "He has an irrepressible disposition," the tutor complained, "to make friends with everybody." His teachers now endeavored, and to an extent succeeded, in correcting his democratic tendency. With his military career at stake, he displayed a certain timidity in following his own inclinations.

In this alien environment, on the banks of the Danube, Napoleon's son lived under a pressure sufficient to have bowed the neck of the greatest. He was supposed to uphold a great heritage, of which he was reminded by his own conscience and the curious gaze of the world. On the other hand, his attempts at greatness were thwarted; he was denied scope for his talents, if he had any. The great tragedy of his life was that he did not know whether he had any talent. He had the consuming ambition of Napoleon the Great, the man who had used the French Revolution to make himself the tyrant of Europe. He yearned to get into the limelight of history from the obscurity in which he was kept by Metternich.

He was now an Austrian Duke, an Austrian colonel, and a French Napoleon no longer. The drama of L'Aiglon was nearing its last curtain; he was stricken with a mortal illness. The upholders of the old order in Europe must have breathed easier. In spite of his poor health, his life in Vienna became gayer. Contemporary accounts overreach themselves in their enthusiastic description of the debut of the young Duke of Reichstadt at the ball of the English Ambassador. As soon as it was announced there was a rush for invitations. The boy had often been seen riding in the Prater, the favorite amusement place of the Viennese, and innumerable girls had fallen in love with him. His dramatic story had prepared the guests for a dramatic entrance.

A hush fell on the ballroom, when the court filed in after the Emperor. Eyes were fastened not on the richly dressed Archduchesses, but on the slender lad in white uniform. Even the French Ambassador, whose government had proscribed the youth, had to admit in his report: "His first appearance in public was an overwhelming success." The Duke hoped to please the assembled diplomats rather than the ladies. The diplomats might be useful to him.

The conflict between his ambitions and his opportunities was burning him alive. He would shout himself hoarse commanding his battalion. He insisted on trying to tame fractious horses, galloping one till it broke down, then jumping on another. He would leap wide ditches where his aides were afraid to follow. On the banks of the Danube this was the only possible outlet for his furious energy. His physician may have guessed better than he knew when he said: "It looks as if he performed these feats to commit suicide." Officially he now diagnosed pulmonary tuberculosis. He counseled moderation, but he might as well have advised the fire not to burn.

The Duke was ordered to take a rest. The Emperor went out to the parade ground with the doctor and unintentionally humiliated his grandson by ordering him to the château. The boy turned to go, but could not resist saying in an aside to the court physician: "Thank you, Doctor, for having me arrested." At times, when his fever abated, the youth would get up and take long rides to Baden and Helenenthal, his favorite haunts, or spend hours in the Hietzing suburb, just outside the castle or in the Prater. One day, coming from the Prater, in an open carriage, he was caught in a cloudburst. He reached home pale and exhausted, and next day came down with pneumonia. He could not sleep at night, and by day he often fell into a coma. The Duke hovered between extreme optimism and pessimism. He was to have a new carriage and then go to Italy to recover his health. The thought of the new carriage that would take him out of his prison made him happier than anything else since his childhood. The sacrament for the dying was administered to L'Aiglon through the tact of a sister-in-law of his mother. She was expecting a child and asked him to make the birth a doubly blessed one by joining her in the holy communion. The Duke received the mass for the dying without realizing it.

On the night of July 21, 1832, a storm broke over Schoenbrunn, according to belief handed down to us. The son of the eagle was about to follow his father into the sun, while Nature shouted a thunderous godspeed. At 3:30 in the morning the Prince felt intense pains in his chest. A gust of wind swept a stone eagle from the cornice. A gurgling sound came from the Duke's throat. At five began the final agony. He rose in his bed. "Get the horses ready!" he screamed. "I am going to visit my father!" He fell back. Presently he moaned: "Mother, mother, save me!" These were his last words. He was twenty-one years of age.

His mother was asleep when he died. The court chronicler says that she was in the castle and, when she was informed, ran to his room. She left the city before he was buried. Marie Louise had forgotten Napoleon, and, as the gay Duchess of Parma, soon she was to forget her son.

Burial in the Church of the Capuchins

Different parts of the bodies of the Habsburgs were buried in different places. The heart was deposited in the Loretto Chapel of the Augustine Fathers in a sealed silver cup, the entrails in the underground churchyard of St. Stephen's Cathedral and the embalmed body in the mausoleum of the House in the Church of the Capuchins. On the day of the Eaglet's funeral the streets were black with a silent crowd from the Chapel of the Hofburg to the Church. The Viennese never forgave Napoleon for bombarding their city, the city of Mozart and Beethoven. But *"der huebsche junge Napoleon,"* as they called the Duke of Reichstadt, had won their hearts. Marengo, Austerlitz and Wagram were forgotten on the day of his burial. Surrounded by members of the Austrian court and the ducal household, the body of Napoleon's son was taken to the resting place of the Habsburgs. At the closed gate of the Church of the Capuchins the Court Marshal tapped three times.

"Who is it?" came the challenge.

"We have brought the dead body of Franz Joseph Karl, the Duke of Reichstadt."

"Who is he?"

"He is the son of Napoleon, Emperor of the French, and of Marie Louise, Archduchess of Austria."

The gate was opened and the body was carried down the steps into the vault where the Habsburgs lie. The crowd in front of the church dispersed slowly and with real tears.

"My cradle and my coffin will be my history," the Duke had prophesied shortly before his death.

No Habsburg has been more violently discussed than Franz Joseph I, "the last of the Caesars," who ascended the throne in the revolutionary year of 1848 and was forced by death to leave it during the World War. His rule of nearly three score and ten was symbolic. He became Emperor of Austria in the stagecoach era and joined the other Habsburgs in the Capuchin Church in the airplane age. Although he was wide awake to his work and duties, his was the fate of a modern Rip Van Winkle, transported into an age that was alien to him. Some observers say he was a genius of persistence, credited with holding together a realm that was creaking in all its joints. Others say that his clinging to the old was responsible for the great collapse that followed his death. They believe he might have staved off the final hour by yielding to new ideas, especially to the forces of nationalism stirring in the Danube valley. There is no denying that Franz Joseph had a certain genius, if close attention to detail may be called genius. Even at the age of eighty he was at his desk, long before the morning star had paled from the Danubian sky. His finger was always on the pulse of his country, yet he could never diagnose its illness.

For seventy years, Franz Joseph was the fate of the Danube. In his mind every problem was reduced to a common denominator: How will it affect the interests of my dynasty? For him things were either good or bad—good if they were favorable for his House and bad if they were unfavorable. In his system there was very little conscious compromise, since good cannot be made better by mixing it with bad. An inevitable progress, which broke upon his monarchy during his reign, emanated from forces over which not even the Emperor had control. He saw the world as an immutable mass which always remained the same, provided agitators were kept away from it. This was closely linked with the belief in a special divine Providence, operating in the manner of the Austrian military system, where things had to go *im Dienstwege,* through the proper channels, and the Emperor was the intermediary between heaven and the common people. "Franz Joseph ruled in opposition to the tendencies of the times," wrote the late Karl Tschuppik. "Against the external forces threatening his empire he pitted the traditions of his House."

Yet the Emperor favored the extension of suffrage during the latter part of his rule, an attitude which was at variance with his extreme views. This seeming contradiction may be assigned to the paradoxical nature of the Emperor, who could be easily stampeded by sudden fits of fear into the exact opposite of what he really wanted. After the defeats his country suffered at the hands of the Prussians and Italians he had to adopt reform measures if he wanted to prevent his hereditary lands from being detached from the Habsburgs' realm.

The result was another paradoxical situation in which the House of Austria appeared as the champion of human rights. The aristocracy of Hungary, of which Franz Joseph was the King, was fearful for its privileges. Thus, the Emperor, an arch-reactionary, was advocating reforms which appeared radical to the Magyar ruling classes, while they were staging a spectacular fight against Comrade Franz Joseph, as he was nicknamed at that time. As a matter of fact, the Emperor and King was in favor of an extension of suffrage and opposed the class rule of the Magyar barons not because of any liberal sympathies, but because he wanted to deprive the Hungarian noblemen of sovereign rights which he claimed for the Royal House.

It was under the rule of Franz Joseph that the reconciliation was effected between Austria and Hungary, which led to the constitution of the Austro-Hungarian Monarchy, about which more will be said in a later chapter. The reader is merely reminded here that the Danube played its nature-made part in the sixteenth century, when the House of Habsburg extended its rule over a large part of Hungary. For three successive centuries the Hungarians quarreled with the Habsburgs for concessions and sometimes even for full independence. It was not until 1867 that this question was solved, when Franz Joseph became Emperor of Austria and King of Hungary. The two countries, united in the Monarchy, collapsed at the end of the World War.

The golden age of both countries came during the rule of Franz Joseph. Never was Austria gayer and more prosperous—Hungary advancing faster. This was not the result of the Emperor's statesmanlike qualities. Prosperity would have come even if the throne had been occupied by a man of less industry. It was the result of the new machine civilization, which raised the general standard of life, and stimulated consumption to a degree undreamt of before. Situated at the threshold of the agricultural States—having agrarian Hungary as part of the Monarchy—Austria could not help exploiting her large supply of natural resources and human ingenuity, and becoming the purveyor of industrial products to her eastern neighbors. Thanks to her geographical position and charm, Vienna had become a clearing house of goods between the Orient and Occident. Franz Joseph took great interest in developing the beauties of the capital of his House, an interest which proved to be one of his most human traits. His court was the most glamorous in all Europe, inheriting the glory of Versailles. It attracted distinction and wealth from all over the Danube valley and far beyond. It set the social tone. To be introduced at the court of Vienna was an event never to be forgotten. Let us, then, cast a glance at the glory that was Habsburg at the turn of the century.

The grand ballroom was aglitter with a forest of bulbs disguised as candles whose light was reflected in trembling cutglass ornaments. From the galleries hung immense tapestries, the handiwork of Dutch and Spanish masters, depicting the lives of antique gods. The estrade for ruling sovereigns faced the main entrance gates, through which filed an endless crowd of guests. His Majesty's favorite *Kapellmeister,* Joseph Strauss, youngest brother of the sovereign of music, was standing on a podium to the left. The soft carpets, which felt like deep grass, were hemmed by living statues— lackeys whose immobile features would have earned them applause on the vaudeville stage. Oriental potentates were dazzled and foreign princes of European courts were taken aback by the spectacle of all this splendor. Here they were made to realize that they were guests of an imperial family that had led crusades, raised Turkish and Tatar sieges, fought religious wars, crushed revolutions. When the gates had closed with elaborate solemnity, and the chief master of ceremonies knocked on the floor three times with his golden staff, the band struck up the *Gott Erhalte* and Their Majesties appeared, followed by their proud retinue. A smile from Franz Joseph was a triumph, a word from him was the crowning of a career, and his handshake lifted a man into the company of immortals. The ball began.

How did an Emperor live in his private life? Franz Joseph was part of the Danubian scene and a few words from the recollections of his valet, Eugene Ketterl, are not amiss. Every morning at 3:30 the valet stepped to the Emperor's bed and woke him up with these words: "I throw myself at Your Majesty's feet and wish him good morning." His Majesty answered with a cordial "good morning" and got up. He had a masseur with whom he had no end of trouble. This man who had been selected to be a support of the Crown saw no reason why the Crown should not support him. It was no pleasure to get up at three o'clock in the morning, especially in the dead of Winter, and this good man must have thought: "There is only one thing that can mitigate the horror of getting up so early and that is not to go to bed at all." He acted upon this idea and became the most diligent guest of the Vieroeckl Cellar in the immediate neighborhood of the Vienna Hofburg, not far from the Danube Canal. In order not to fall asleep, he drank copiously and thus succeeded in keeping awake. For this he had to pay with the loss of not only his mental but also physical balance.

At first the Emperor was amused by the antics of his masseur, who not only did not help him with his bathing but even needed the Emperor's aid. The masseur would have been forgiven if one day he had not lost his balance and clung to His Majesty's neck with both hands, thereby upsetting the tiny rubber tub in which the Emperor was bathing.

At five o'clock the head valet gave Franz Joseph his breakfast: coffee, butter, roll and ham, except on fast days. In the last years of his life, the Emperor took tea instead of coffee, but it had the potency of three ordinary cups. From five until twelve he ate nothing—never asked for anything to eat and was evidently under the impression that the kitchen could not meet such an unexpected request. When the Emperor opened the Millennial Exposition in Budapest he remarked to his head valet that it would be difficult for him not to eat or drink anything from five in the morning till four in the afternoon. Ketterl advised him to take a second breakfast at ten, whereupon Franz Joseph asked hopefully: "Could I really get something to eat at ten?"

Franz Joseph was horrified at the thought of using the telephone, and his entourage succeeded only in persuading him to make one call. This was when Crown Princess Stephanie, the widow of his son, Crown Prince Rudolph, married Count Elmer Lonyay in 1900. After several days, he congratulated the couple over the telephone. Shortly after its installation, an amusing incident occurred with this telephone. The Emperor was in his small rubber bathtub, when the bell began to ring. "Wait a minute," the Emperor shouted. The ringing continued. "You should wait," the Emperor shouted again at the top of his voice, as if the man at the other end of the wire could hear him.

The Emperor had a dear friend, Mme. Catherine Schratt, friend of his wife, Empress Elizabeth, who, realizing that she was no spiritual mate for her husband, threw him into the company of the celebrated actress of the Vienna Burgtheater. When the Emperor was in Schoenbrunn, on the outskirts of Vienna, he would lay down his pen at three o'clock in the afternoon and walk between a hedge of trees along the broad alley. In her villa, Mme. Schratt would be waiting for the Emperor and he would help her make tea. Then he would sit at her feet, telling her his worries and asking for her opinion. When the Emperor was in Ischl, the summer resort near Salzburg, she would join him with a coach full of aristocrats and statesmen. Since she had no fortune and had to be thrifty, she traveled in third-class carriages. Naturally, the high officials and peers of the realm who knew that one good word from her was worth more than a volume of memoranda preferred to sit on the uncomfortable wooden benches. The Emperor would await her at the railway station and display

87

no surprise to see how humbly his friend was traveling. Franz Joseph was seldom surprised. He simply thought things had to be the way they were.

He was so thrifty that he never noticed when others were spending money for him. Mme. Schratt had to go to great expense to keep a household worthy of her imperial friend, yet it did not occur to him to help her. He did not want her to be his friend for financial reasons. Only when it was brought to his attention in a roundabout way that she was in financial straits did he instruct his private treasury to pay her debts. But the head valet will tell us more intimate details of how careful the Emperor was with his money:

"If you think that the Emperor had a large supply of underwear and shoes, you are mistaken. His underwear was of the cheapest linen. My own underwear was incomparably better in quality than his own. His civilian wardrobe was especially inadequate. Besides a few hunting uniforms, an antiquated full dress and an old evening dress suit, he had only one or two costumes. For a long time I wondered why the number of the Emperor's civilian suits was so small and the number of tailors 'By Appointment to the Emperor of Austria and King of Hungary' so large.

"Franz Joseph had not the faintest idea how to dress. He would, for instance, pick out a bright blue tie to wear with a green suit. He was never angry when I called his attention to these mistakes; he would merely repeat them. He would wear high boots or heavily nailed military shoes with full dress. I was considered something of a revolutionary when for the first time in many years I had the Emperor's trousers pressed. They were wrinkled, baggy at the knees and showed distinctly the lines of the high boots. When I entered his service, the Emperor had only one overcoat. It had been given to him by his best friend, Czar Alexander II. When I humbly protested that after twenty years that coat deserved a rest the Emperor was shocked. 'A new coat costs an immense lot of money.'

"At first I could hardly believe my eyes when I found that in none of the imperial castles of Vienna, Schoenbrunn and Ischl was there a bathroom. The Emperor's wash bowl in Schoenbrunn was incredibly primitive. It was a wooden contraption, extremely small, with sharp corners, against which the Emperor was always bruising his body. Inasmuch as, for reasons of economy, the Emperor would not permit me to buy a new bowl, I had to resort to a trick. I told him that in an unused room of the castle I had found a very good china bowl which would fit into His Majesty's bedroom wonderfully."

If nominations were in order for the most mismated royal couple in recent history, again we should have to turn to the Danube valley. Emperor Franz Joseph was unimaginative, hard-working, punctilious. His wife, Empress Elizabeth, was fanciful, poetic, fantastic. He was a conservative; she was a revolutionary, revolting against her own dynasty and the world it created. "We are sitting on a powder barrel," she wrote in her diary. "Why should the people . . . love us who live in luxury and abundance, while they, even if laboring hard, can scarcely earn enough to keep themselves alive? Our children are dressed in silks and laces, while theirs go about in rags, barefooted."

Elizabeth selected as her "guiding spirit" a man who had been excommunicated by his own country, whom opposition to its dynasty made an exile—the arch-revolutionist and enemy of the traditional: Heinrich Heine. Because she was the Empress of an almost absolute monarchy, she understood Heine's meaning when he assailed royalty. The very iconoclasm which appalled European courts, appealed to her. "Heine's hope and desire was," she wrote, "to see the day when the peoples would refuse to serve their rulers as abject puppies do, when the rulers would cast off their glittering rags, their royal purple, looking for all the world like the red cloak of the executioner; the golden coronet, drawn down over their ears to make inaudible the voice of the people; the golden scepter placed in their hands as the symbol of their power, their despotism. Heine yearned for the time when monarchs would be free—as free as their peoples to dispense charity and good-will and to bring happiness to all. . . . This Heine called the Emancipation of the Kings."

Degeneracy in the House of Habsburg and in other ruling houses did not escape Elizabeth's attention. She was descended from the Wittelsbachs, in which insanity was not infrequent. She herself often feared lest she become mentally deranged and feared for her children. How she hated the loafers who, although they must have seen her frailties, burned incense to her and her imperial consort! "There they are," she wrote about the courtiers, "on their knees, gazing with stupid eyes at their masters 'by the Grace of God' and they never realize that there is among the admired ones many a ruler 'by the Grace of the Devil.' "

"Why cannot we be what God has made us?" the Empress exclaimed. "Why must this life be one continuous comedy in which we all play a part and which, in our dying hour, is sure to fill us with repulsion?"

She had no home in the imperial palace, next to the man who understood only documents, not human hearts. She ordered a castle built on the island of Corfu—the one the German Kaiser later acquired—but it was too gorgeous. She craved simplicity.

Emperor Franz Joseph I

The nearest approach toward a normal life was traveling incognito in foreign lands. "All around the world my journey shall take me. I will sail the seven seas like a female Flying Dutchman. I would take on my journey only men who have nothing to lose. The best thing would be to take a crew of men that had been sentenced to death. I should have then no scruples in exposing them to dangers."

Elizabeth might have been impelled to follow those of her relatives who had renounced their titles and embarked upon careers free of the pompous slavery of the Vienna court. For there was hardly anything on which she could agree with her husband. He feared the inroads of modernity into the hallowed precincts of the court. He distrusted parliamentarism, which he considered the work of the Evil Spirit. She, on the contrary, carried by her impetuous nature to extremes, advocated the immediate and radical democratization of the Habsburg Empire. Her insurgent spirit found Hungary congenial, the country which in the Emperor's mind was connected with the obnoxious adjective "rebellious." In search of dreams she went to Switzerland, where the glaciers and exotic clouds attracted her. She listened to the echoes of thunders in isolated valleys, and she kept on weaving dreams. It was becoming increasingly difficult for her to be alone with herself. She had to be going about, seeing new countries, new peoples, yet keeping herself aloof from them, keeping herself aloof from her own real self as well. It was a wild chase of the unknown, always on the trail of chimeras, living outside of this world in all but her body. The end had to come as it did. She was returning to a boat on Lake Geneva when a man suddenly struck her in the breast. She fell, but, somewhat dazed, rose and walked to the boat. "What happened?" she asked, surprised.

On board she fainted, and when her bodice was opened a small blood stain appeared—an assassin's awl had pierced a heart which was as revolutionary as his own. Anarchist or madman, no one knows, nor is it important. The awl changed nothing in the fate of Empress Elizabeth. It was a fulfillment of a wish: her will to die.

The Danube in Austria is the setting of the tragedy of Crown Prince Rudolph, son of Franz Joseph and Elizabeth. Few royal dramas have exercised the imagination of the world more than the one enacted in the Mayerling shooting lodge.

Around 9 o'clock in the morning of January 30, 1889, a man of distinguished presence rushed up to the stationmaster of Baden, a few miles south of the Austrian capital, introduced himself as Count Josef Hoyos and asked that the Vienna Express, scheduled to pass at 9:18 should be stopped. The stationmaster was sorry to inform the Count that stopping a train exceeded his authority. Impatiently, Hoyos exclaimed: "His Highness the Crown Prince has had a hunting accident. I must report to His Majesty." The train was stopped.

Quickly news of the accident spread in Vienna. Immediately legend began to take shape. A few undisputed facts also became known. The Crown Prince's dead body had been found in the early morning hours; next to him lay the lifeless Baroness Marie Vetsera. The skull of the heir to the throne was shattered. "On the side of the Crown Prince's bed," wrote the semi-official *Wiener Zeitung,* after an earlier ineffectual attempt to attribute death to a paralytic stroke, "close to his right hand, lay a discharged revolver. Its position left no room for doubt that the deceased had discharged it with his own hand."

Rudolph's body was taken to Vienna, where it lay in state. In storm and rain Marie's body was hastily buried in the churchyard of the nearby Heiligenkreuz Cistercian Abbey. Strict censorship was applied to the Austrian press, but Vienna was athrob with rumors.

The main character in this Danubian drama—Crown Prince Rudolph Francis Charles Joseph, Archduke of Austria, 31 years of age, attractive, genial, gifted—was a Prince Charming if ever there was one. As next in line to the throne of a realm of more than 50,000,000, he was to have become the head of the oldest dynasty in Europe. His tragedy was that the rôle of a passive Crown Prince did not fit him. His ferocious energy sought outlet in endless discussions, the writing of books and newspaper articles, the drawing up of tradition-defying plans to save his dynasty and his father's crown, as if the House of Habsburg would not endure forever! Shackled to the past and unable to break through the inexorable splendor of his prison, he took refuge in evanescent pleasures, became addicted to drink and, perhaps, also to drugs.

His companion in death, the Baroness Vetsera, was an attractive Vienna débutante of eighteen; she was of Armenian origin. Her mother, Baroness Helena, was an ambitious woman who sought to replenish the family's depleted treasury by marrying her off to a wealthy husband. But Marie's Oriental blood played havoc with her mother's plans and she plunged headlong into an adventure from which there was no escape.

The Mayerling tragedy occurred about twenty miles southwest of the Austrian capital, on the outskirts of the Vienna Woods. At the foot of timbered hills, the slender chimneys of the hunting lodge of the Crown Prince peeped out beyond the clumps of fir and oak. It is now a Carmelite nunnery, and the room in which the dead young man was found is a chapel. The royal drama has given rise to several theories. Although the court said it was suicide, the world became suspicious. Why should Rudolph have taken his life? Was he not idolized by his people, and did not the world lie at his feet? Reports in the respected daily, *Neue Freie Presse,* attributed death to a stray bullet. There were also rumors of murder. "The Prince with the Velvet Mask," was the title of a pamphlet secretly circulated. Its authors asserted that gashes on his cheeks, inflicted with murderous intent, were covered with a velvet mask.

And the murderer? It was the head forester of the imperial reserves, said one group. He was supposed to have found his daughter with the Crown Prince, whose face he shattered with his rifle. No, said the other group, it was the drinking companion of the heir to the throne, Herr Alexander von Baltazzi, a dissolute youth, who was himself wounded in the brawl and taken to Baden, where he died. When ex-Grand Duke Ferdinand IV of Tuscany was escorted into the room where the dead Crown Prince lay, he saw the Habsburg family physician extracting pieces of glass from the head of the dead man. They were bits of a champagne glass hurled at him in Mayerling the night before by a suitor of Baroness Vetsera whom he had taunted with jibes, one version goes. Finding her Crown Prince lover slain, Marie committed suicide.

The story would not be complete if diplomatic intrigue in the Danube valley did not enter into it. It was the Black Hand Mafia of one country, said one faction. This is the hand of Herr Bismarck, others asserted. Wilhelm II, the new German Kaiser, was the Archduke's pet aversion. Rudolph did not favor the idea of linking up the fate of Austria, which he meant to make into a peace-loving nation, with that of a militant Reich. A third group hinted darkly that St. Petersburg had a hand in the death. Russian aristocracy was apprehensive about a suspected radical's becoming a neighbor sovereign. The extreme reactionary ultramontane party was also seen in the background, fearful of an "atheist" Emperor.

If theories of murder were numerous, those of suicide were even more so. Leaving out inconsequential details, all of the motives may be reduced to two: love and politics. The story is often told how desperately the Crown Prince wanted to get a divorce from his wife, Stephanie, so as to marry Marie, but the Emperor offered implacable resistance. It was politics, say others. A cousin of the Prince, Countess Larisch, shows him just about to kill himself because of political intrigues when the Baroness entered his room, upbraided him and he, driven by drink and an irrepressible temper, killed her and then himself. The Countess believed that behind it all was a plot to make Rudolph King of Hungary. The suggestion has often been made that he was engaged in a conspiracy to have himself proclaimed both Emperor of Austria and King of Hungary, and thus "save" the monarchy. Still others quote a mysterious Dossier No. 25, said to have been sunk into oblivion by the ruler's orders, showing the Emperor's son plotting with Hungarian patriots in an effort to set up a Magyar army to take the place of one branch of the Austro-Hungarian armed forces.

Analyzed critically, what does the evidence show? The autopsy was performed by five internationally known professors of Vienna University and the family physician, who reported that it was a case of suicide; death was caused by a shot from a medium-caliber revolver fired at close range. A gash above the left ear was the exit of the projectile. Before his death the Crown Prince wrote farewell letters to his wife, his mother and sister. His letter to the Crown Princess is reproduced in his own handwriting in her recollections, and reads as follows: "Dear Stephanie, you are now untrammeled by the bane of my presence. Live happily in your own way. Remember me to . . . . (names). I go calmly to my death, which is the only way of saving my name. Love and kisses, Rudolph."

Next to the deathbed were three letters by Baroness Vetsera. "We are wondering what the Great Beyond looks like," she wrote to her mother.

When turning over the files of the Imperial Chancellery to the Secret Archives in 1918, Count Polzer-Hoditz, head of the Chancellery of the late Emperor Karl, found a sealed satchel belonging to the tragic Crown Prince. It contained, in addition to indifferent objects, an onyx ash tray with the following words in violet ink: "Revolver is better. Not poison. Revolver is surer." It was Baroness Vetsera's handwriting.

The Crown Prince seems to have suffered from a suicide obsession. "I am tired of the unchecked life urge," he wrote to his friend, Moricz Szeps, a left-wing newspaper editor. "I am looking for opportunities to see moribund persons take their last breath."

It is the view of the ex-Crown Princess, of her daughter, Elizabeth, of Countess Larisch, and of Count Polzer-Hoditz that the Crown Prince died by his own hand. It is also the view of Baron O. von Mitis, who devoted years of study to this case. This opinion is shared by nearly all the competent historians. But if

A Question of Insanity

there is near-unanimity about the suicide, what does first-hand information reveal about the cause of this Danubian tragedy? Was it love or politics?

Princess Stephanie states categorically: "He did not love her; she was in love with him. Marie was only one of the girls." Yet the ex-Crown Princess may be biased. She had been deeply humiliated. We also learn that his telegrams to Marie were cold, while hers were ardent. Gently he was trying to make her understand that their day was over. If it was not love, which evidence seems to rule out, was it politics? The Crown Princess knew vaguely of her husband's political work but was never initiated into details. Among the several motives mentioned, which one bespeaks the truth? It is here that we come upon an impenetrable barrier. The documents which may have shed some light on this point seem to have been lost or destroyed. The published writings of the late Crown Prince, while critical of the Emperor and his government, are merely those of a young radical chafing under the restrictions of court life. If ever there was some treasonous material, no one in authority has ever disclosed its real nature.

It has also been suggested that Rudolph was of unsound mind. At the end of their report the physicians express the view that the deed may have been done in a state of mental aberration. This was a conventional formula, enabling the church authorities to grant religious rites to suspected suicides. The Crown Princess, who ought to know, says that Rudolph was inconstant but normal.

The evidence thus indicates that death was due to suicide, unmotivated by overwhelming love, and probably owing to political entanglements. Rudolph wanted to accomplish heroic deeds but was defeated by his environment. The hero of this Danubian

97

tragedy appears to have been a split personality, owing partly to heritage and partly to his surroundings. Modern Prometheus was doomed. Whatever else posterity may say about him, he was the most tragic Prince in modern times.

His successor as heir to the throne was also a tragic Prince. There can be no doubt about the causes of his death. Nor can there be any doubt today that the murder of Archduke Franz Ferdinand was not the real cause of the World War. But it was a convenient pretext, and the proverbial spark that ignites the powder box. That his death should be violent was written in the stars. His life was violent, too, a succession of explosions which shattered his nerves and his position in the world. He hated and loved violently. He hated Emperor Franz Joseph, whom he was to succeed, and the sovereign hated him. He hated the Italians, English, Magyars, Poles, Serbians, and was hated by them. He was egocentric, bigoted and autocratic, an Oriental potentate on a rampage in a semi-constitutional monarchy. Franz Ferdinand's capacity for affection was just as violent. He stormed past all obstacles and swept away all dynastic objections when this greatest hater in the House of Habsburg finally found a woman on whom he could lavish the pent-up love energy of a futile life. He who hurled defiance at the gods of his day found only tender words for the woman who was to share his tragic fate.

History has treated him with something akin to scorn. He was the man with the Iron Mask who never showed his face. He was called a sphinx, because people did not take the trouble to understand him. His immense capacity to repel frightened away even those who like to investigate the motives of violent emotions. His rudeness discouraged attempts to understand him. The world has forgotten that he had been brought up under abnormal con-

ditions and that he displayed admirable qualities when he over-
rode the objections of the Court and married a girl of inferior
social rank. Given the temperament of Franz Ferdinand and the
conditions under which he lived at the court on the Danube, he
had to become a high-strung instrument of violent extremes.
His ambition was overpowering, elemental. He faced the new
Sun King, Franz Joseph, a ruler awed by his own might. Franz
Ferdinand had the torrential energy of the man of action, while
the Emperor depended upon the mystic power of his crown. The
struggle was uneven, and for Franz Ferdinand the only way out
was to fall like the defeated hero of a Shakespearean tragedy. It
was a strange destiny that his death was the prelude to the world
catastrophe that broke on man.

Both the Emperor and the Archduke were autocrats, but the
latter was in the opposition and that made all the difference in
the world. Franz Joseph saw himself as an apotheosis, the center
of the universe. Franz Ferdinand battered the walls of the Hofburg to save the dynasty. He went about this work in such a tact-
less way as to antagonize those whom he needed most.

The Archduke's hatred of the world originated at the time he
was suffering from tuberculosis of the lungs and had been given
up as hopeless. "Friends" and parasites turned away from him
and prostrated themselves before the new god, Archduke Otto,
the heir presumptive. "You and my valet are my only friends,"
the Archduke complained to his physician in his characteristic
vein. Recovering from his illness, he saw himself being sent
around as an imperial messenger boy "placed at the disposal of
the All Highest orders of His Majesty." He wanted to do heroic
things and it did not take him long to see that under Franz Joseph
heroism was as great a handicap as brains. Through the mist of

99

incense he beheld the carved image of a bronze Buddha, inscrutable and torturingly impersonal, his uncle, the Emperor. At each step he was confronted with obstruction, the smiling images of small Buddhas, old Admirals, decrepit Generals, antiquated Hofrats, the survivors of a dead age.

Franz Ferdinand was not in the crowd of incense burners. While he had not a towering intellect, he had the good sense to see that the monarchy was headed toward Nirvana. In order to forestall the worst, he decided to overhaul the foundations of his future realm. He wanted to transform the dual monarchy of the Austrians and Hungarians into a triune Kingdom of Austrians, Hungarians and South Slavs. If the Archduke's ideas had been followed, the World War might have taken a different turn or, as some say, may even have been averted. He wanted to revive the three Emperors' alliance of Austria-Hungary, Germany and Russia. The Italian alliance, in his emphatic opinion, was not worth the paper on which it had been covenanted. It was an irony of fate that the man who wanted to co-operate with the South Slavs should have been considered their worst enemy. It was a South Slav young man who killed him on June 28, 1914. Franz Ferdinand had seen the light when he maintained that the monarchy should be overhauled and placed on a broader basis.

Tragedy dogged the Habsburgs' footsteps. Soon they were to fall and with them the Danubian dynasty. Someone had to pay for their past successes, and for their lack of planning. One of them had to pay for their many mistakes, also for the repressed forces in the Danube valley. For a long time, the House of Austria had lived not on its merits but because of the force of traditions. It had become a force supposedly as fixed as the sun and stars. People took it for granted, and did not inquire into the reason of its existence. It was one of the political myths, which live on and on, and then collapse suddenly, while the world wonders how it could have lived so long.

It was young Emperor Karl I of Austria (and the Fourth Károly Király of Hungary) who had to pay the price, and in all Habsburg history it would be difficult to find a monarch more unjustly punished. The Viennese called him a *"guter Bursch,"* a nice fellow, shrugged their shoulders and smiled indulgently. He ascended the throne in the middle of the World War. Few Viennese realized that the "nice fellow" was much more than an amiable handshaker, and that he risked all to save them from the worst. The Emperor had a clearer view of the War than the incomparably more gifted statesmen of Central Europe. While most of them were disposed to call America's intervention a "bluff," he knew better and warned his Allies against provoking the United States. He was emphatically opposed to the stringent U-boat regulations of Germany on the ground that they would infringe the neutrals' rights. "Germany always under-estimates its enemies and the United States, and over-estimates her own strength. Berlin is stricken with blindness and is headed for ruin," the Emperor told the head of his Chancellery.

No sooner had Karl ascended the throne than he began to work for peace. He invited his brothers-in-law, Princes Sixtus and Xavier, officers in the Belgian Army, to visit him near Vienna. He and his wife, Empress Zita, drew up a memorandum on the war aims of the Central Powers, which the Princes were to transmit to the President of the French Republic, Raymond Poincaré. The Emperor was ready to conclude a peace with the Allies behind the German Kaiser's back. He conceded the justice of the principal Allied claims. It required real heroism to sign such a document. From the Central Powers' point of view it was high treason, the punishment for which was death. The Allies were so wrapped up in the conduct of war that they had no time to think of peace. Besides, peace in those days meant defeatism, and that was treason. Not one of them realized the full import of the Emperor's move.

In his own country, too, Karl was misunderstood, and whisperers called him weak because he had the courage to be good. The following incident, told by Count Polzer-Hoditz, the chief of his Cabinet, sheds much light upon his real nature: "Emperor Franz Joseph was dead. There was a woman in Vienna for whom his death meant more than for his closest relation. Catherine Schratt, the actress, now an old woman, was the sole companion and best friend of Franz Joseph. While he was alive, the Court treated her with the utmost reverence; now that he was dead they refused her admission to his bier. The Spanish etiquette did not provide for such emergencies. Emperor Karl noticed Mme. Schratt standing helplessly at the door of the funeral chapel, took her by the arm and led her to the dead sovereign."

The World War was over, and so was the Habsburg dream. The Danube was the same, but its rôle had changed. The Austro-Hungarian monarchy was no more; there was an Austria and a Hungary. There was also a Czechoslovak Republic, comprising the northern parts of Austria and Hungary. A new Roumania was added to the old, containing Austria's Bukovina and Hungary's rich Transylvania. A new Poland rose, including Austria's Galicia, famed for the beauty of its coronation city, Cracow, and for its oil wells. Little Serbia, of pre-War days, became the Yugoslavia of post-War times, having absorbed Croatia and Slavonia, autonomous parts of old Hungary, and the Slovenia of Austria,

102

not to speak of Bosnia-Herzegovina, where the heir to the throne was shot. Italy got her share, too—from Austria the beautiful southern Tyrol, where the South meets the North, and Hungary's only seaport, Fiume.

The Habsburgs were on their way into exile, dispersed throughout the world, outlaws in their own countries. Karl and Zita were yet to try to change history, and their attempt will be recorded in the chapter on Hungary. Austria was now a small country of some 6,000,000 inhabitants, including 2,000,000 in poverty-stricken Vienna. The little Republic had the mountainous beauty of Tyrol and Salzburg, but had no coal and food. They will be able to get on, foreign well-wishers asserted. "Look at Switzerland." Yes, but it took Switzerland centuries to make a success, and Vienna was growing hungrier every day. The Austrians had no desire to live alone, and the names of prospective adoptive countries were passed in review: Italy, Switzerland, Germany. The last country seemed to be a logical choice. The majority of the Austrians did not change their opinion about the Prussians, and they would have preferred to live alone. But the Allies had taken good care to mutilate them to such an extent that they should not be able to stand on their feet. Then the peacemakers forbade Austria to join Germany. "The independence of Austria is inalienable," says Article 88 of the Treaty of St. Germain, "otherwise than with the consent of the League of Nations."

Did the Allies know what they were doing? They saw only part of the way, fascinated by the Danube. They remembered Metternich's words: "Whoever is master of Vienna. . . ." The Romans and the Habsburgs had shown that the Danube valley tended to become a natural unit. The Germans should not be rewarded for having lost the War. Austria would have opened to them the way to the Balkans, and the Berlin-Bagdad dream would have become a reality. But the Allies did not see Austria's side of the problem, and they would have had to be more than mere statesmen if they did. The three old men sitting around the peace-conference table felt tremendously strong. Their countries had won the greatest war in history and thought it was won forever. Their power was uncontested; they were firmly anchored in a myth. They supposed that the world would never change and that the vanquished would always be obedient. Without their help, Hitler could never have taken Austria. But let us not anticipate history. For twenty years the union of Germany and Austria, *Anschluss,* was the great issue.

The Austrians wanted to join the Reich because they were hungry, and the Germans wanted to take Austria because their pride needed a salve. Republican Berlin could not have had the sinister motives some of the French statesmen attributed to her. Again it was the former Allies who helped Hitler reach the peak by their refusal to listen to Austria's tearful voice. If only the *Anschluss* had been accomplished, Hitler would have been deprived of his strongest argument. A closer co-operation of the Danubian countries could have prevented German hegemony. The new Reich of the early post-War era was Socialist and pacifist.

The life of republican Austria at the beginning was an endless search for food. The name of the food was sometimes coal and other times it was a League of Nations loan. Her spokesmen stood at the gate of Geneva, hope of mankind, and coins were dropped into his hat. Much of the hat-holding was done by Ignaz Seipel, Chancellor and prelate, whom a friendly press had built up as a superman. He sought to weaken the Socialists, Austria's strongest party, and thereby played into the hands of the Nazis, who entered the stage after he had departed. But he knew that the only durable solution for Europe's troubles was a loose United States, and he also knew that a start would have to be made in the Danube valley.

Then came Hitler. Austria's tragic tale took another turn. The Nazi Fuehrer was an Austrian himself, and his position at the head of a supernationalistic Reich was abnormal. The prohibition of the *Anschluss* was a real grievance, and he would have been a poor politician had he not taken advantage of it in his war against the treaties. He saw the opportunity the Allies gave him by letting Austria float in mid-air. His movement was dynamic, warlike. He saw that Austria's strategical position in a future war would be invaluable.

The Italian dictator, Benito Mussolini, could have stopped him, and Il Duce did, in fact, keep him in check for years. His Fascism is no less dynamic than Hitler's Nazism, and it, too, needs its own *Lebensraum,* space to expand. The Danube valley is not merely Germany's, but Italy's, lifeline of Empire. It leads into the Balkans, with its unexploited raw materials and potential markets, an ideal jumping-off point to the East. Besides, Italy had a quarter of a million Austrian Germans in South Tyrol, spiritual descendants of Andreas Hofer, the mountain-innkeeper, who fought Napoleon. A dynamic Reich on the Brenner Pass, Il Duce knew, would be a stronger attraction for his Tyroleans than decrepit Austria. He marched his troops to the Brenner Pass in 1934 when Hitler seemed to be ready to jump on his prey. Mussolini proclaimed many times Italy's vital interest in an independent Austria.

The little Republic had meanwhile changed its mind about *Anschluss.* Its largest party, the Socialists, loathed Nazism, arch-enemy of trade unionism in the Reich and leader in world reaction. The Catholics formed more than ninety per cent of the population. The followers of the House of Habsburg saw that Hitler was the greatest danger to their cause, and the wealthy Vienna Jews had little cause to love the Fuehrer, even though he appeared as the savior of capitalism. For years the Austrians tried to hold back the Nazi steam-roller.

The country's forces were organized under tiny Engelbert Dollfuss, nicknamed *Millimetternich*. So small was he that, according to popular belief, one night when worries kept sleep from him, he was walking up and down under his bed. Yet, he was Austria's Chancellor and dictator, because there was fire in him. His blue eyes flashed a winning smile and the petitioner left happier when he said "no," than when others said "yes." He radiated energy and good-will, and his eloquence, combined with will power, swayed the masses. In this age of average-man dictators, he also had the proper antecedents: peasant parents. The village priest urged his father to send the little chap to school. No taller than an overgrown midget, he distinguished himself in the highly regarded Corps of Imperial Chasseurs during the War.

Although a Doctor of Laws, his interests were rural. He founded the Provincial Chamber of Agriculture of Lower Austria, flinging his energies into helping the farmer. He occupied a high position in the peasants' association, *Bauernbund*. As a member of the Christian Social Party, he rose to a cabinet position. One day, in 1932, the President of the Republic asked him to form the government, and Dollfuss promised his reply in the morning. Wandering off by himself into a nearby church, he spent the night in prayer, asking for God's guidance. Next morning he became

Prince Ernst Ruediger von Starhemberg
and Chancellor Engelbert Dollfuss

Austria's Chancellor—David facing the German Goliath. He needed popular support to fight the Nazis, and the Austrian Socialists would have followed him through thick and thin. But he rejected and then fought them, and thereby prepared his undoing and the end of Austria. Surrounded by Fascism in the North and South, he considered it his best policy to fight fire with fire. He adopted Mussolini as his guardian angel, thinking that self-interest would keep Il Duce on the narrow path. He did not know that Fascism embraced chaos as its ally and that Mussolini was subject to self-destructive fits of temper. Since there was no Fascism in Austria, it had to be created, and the *Heimwehr,* Home Defense Corps, turned out to be a bundle of broken reeds. Instigated by Il Duce, a renegade Socialist, nauseated by his own past, Dollfuss rejected the help Liberals offered him. So far did he veer toward reaction that before Nazi bullets ended his career, he ordered the magnificent Socialist apartment houses of Vienna shelled. Hundreds of his countrymen were slaughtered.

The waters of the Danube reflected the Austrian Nazis' bonfires celebrating the deathly blow which their weak enemy dealt their stronger foe. A midget dictator could not cope with the German Juggernaut. Explosions disturbed the serenity of the Wachau, and tear gas bombs brought Vienna theater audiences to their feet. The Nazis' political opponents were killed and maimed. The world was to see that the Dollfuss government could not maintain law and order, even though it took all the ammunition of Germany to prove this point. The Nazis set up an Austrian Legion whose avowed enemy was their own country. Anyone found guilty of loyalty to Austria was convicted of high treason by the Nazis. Incendiary leaflets were smuggled into Austria from the Reich and distributed by the millions. The Nazi songs of Munich out-thundered the Vienna waltz. High pressure agitators swarmed over the Austrian mountains, and swastika-wearing bullies terrorized the countryside. The army, State services, the police were honeycombed with Nazis in disguise.

Dollfuss countered the Nazi campaign by advertising Austrian patriotism. He reintroduced the military uniforms of the imperial régime, popularized the old national heroes, encouraged the return of members of the former dynasty, and revived the cult of the past. His job was well done, but its echo was thin because the real friends of the Republic had been driven underground. In July, 1934, the Nazis decided to put Dollfuss out of the way. The police got wind of the plot, but became entangled in its own red tape. A group of Nazis were smuggled into the Chancellery in the uniforms of the Austrian Army.

The plotters had agreed on a code. "Old samples of cutlery arrived" meant that Dollfuss was dead, "old samples of cutlery on the way"—Dollfuss captured. The Austrian Legion had been drawn up on the frontier, ready to invade the country. The government broadcasting station in the heart of Vienna announced that a new government with Nazi participation had been formed. In the Chancellery, several members of the government were in conference. The plotters met no resistance. The building was old even in Napoleon's time, full of labyrinthine passages. Dollfuss heard the scuffle and wanted to get out of danger's way. As he sought escape, he ran into one of the plotters, Sergeant Otto Planetta. Two bullets from Planetta's gun struck him down. The little Chancellor was laid on the sofa. He begged for a physician, then for a priest. Both were refused to him. The Nazis let him bleed to death.

That night there were no bonfires on the Danube, and the advertised Nazi uprising did not materialize. The Austrian Legion remained beyond the frontier and Italian troops began to climb toward the Brenner Pass. "The independence of Austria for which Dollfuss fell is a principle," Mussolini telegraphed to the Austrian Vice-Chancellor, "that has been defended and will be defended by Italy even more strenuously in these exceptionally difficult times."

On whose shoulders would fall Caesar's mantle; who would save the Danube valley from Nazi rule? All eyes turned to Prince Ernst Ruediger von Starhemberg, leader of the Fascist Home Guards of Austria. For a day he played an important rôle. Opinions about him have always differed. The irreverent Vienna café said of him: "The Prince was a child prodigy. As intelligent at the age of four as he is now." Others have maintained that he did not lack the small dose of intelligence expected of a successful statesman.

It was in the castle of Efferding on the Danube, a few miles out of Linz, that Starhemberg was born at the turn of the century. In his childhood and youth he was surrounded by memories of the Middle Ages. In the principal room of the castle the place of honor was occupied by the likeness of an ancestor, the "Turk-beater," who in 1683 defied the Grand Vizier Kara Mustapha Pasha. In the family, tradition had a strong hold, yet Ernst Ruediger's parents despaired of their son's chances to re-dedicate the Toledo-made sword of the ancient house to new victories. In the reign of Franz Joseph the world seemed to have gone to slumber, and there was no market for heroism. The Starhembergs had a score of castles, on which hundreds of servants lived, wearing the princely colors. The Princes were kind and treated their servants with as much solicitude as if they had been their serfs. With the outbreak of the World War, hope would have beckoned to the Starhembergs to increase their collection of laurels if Ernst Ruediger had been just a little older. He became only of military age when the War was nearly over, and then, too, he was sent into the hinterland. He was tall and slender, his face a joy to look upon. He tried to appear very masculine, and in order to emphasize his manly virtues he liked to use *Kraftwoerter,* strong words.

When the debacle came, sadness settled on the Starhemberg castles. Vienna was in the hands of enemies worse than the Turk. They were the Social Democrats, who appeared to him as the wreckers of the civilization his ancestors had saved. What was a young Prince to do in a Republic run by the common herd? He set out on a trip of adventure, offering his sword to the champions of noble causes. Germany was not far from his village, and in 1921 the Prince was a member of the irregular bands trying to save Upper Silesia from the Poles. Two years later he was in the Mecca of the reactionaries of all countries, drinking in Hitler's incendiary words. We are told that the young Prince took part in the Beer Hall Putsch, which was to result in a march on Berlin.

After Hitler's failure, Starhemberg returned to Austria, disappointed but not dismayed. Now he began to drill his hundreds of servants. Such private armies were in vogue then along the Danube. A few years before, Tyrol had formed the *Heimwehr* in protest against the transfer of South Tyrol to Italy. At about the same time Carinthia, which was to decide between Austria and Yugoslavia at a plebiscite, formed a home defense corps for the protection of her interests. Starhemberg was inspired by these examples. But now that Mussolini was Italy's master and

Carinthia had gone Austrian, the corps had to dedicate itself to some other cause. Vienna was run by the Social Democrats and the Prince decided that they were an international danger. Since he had money and spent it lavishly, the *Heimwehr* came under his influence.

The world was getting ready to forget Starhemberg when, in July, 1927, Vienna had a fit of nerves, after a mob had set fire to the law courts in revenge for what its leaders called a "reactionary miscarriage of justice." The Socialists were blamed for this riot and the newspapers of the Right demanded the extermination of *Austrobolshevism,* their name for Socialism. Starhemberg now devoted all his time to organizing the reactionary forces throughout the Republic. So great was his zeal and so lavish his expenditures that he went bankrupt. What was more natural than to try to find a way to the heart of Mussolini, also a Socialist-hater? Soon large shipments of arms were rolling into Austria, consigned for the *Heimwehr.* These shipments, which originated in Italy, were disguised as "scrap iron" and "machine parts." As Mussolini's *homme de confiance,* Starhemberg's reputation grew, and so did his self-confidence. Now he thundered against the "red rascals of Vienna" in country papers. He had to be taken seriously, because he took himself in such deadly earnest. When Karl Vaugoin, known as the *Sozifresser* (Socialist eater), became Chancellor in the Autumn of 1930, he took the young Prince into the government as his Minister of Interior. Inspired by the example of Prince Metternich, whose reign of terror was the delight of his early youth, he tried to transform Austria into a "police-State." The political department of the police was strengthened, the Socialist press harassed, the radical leaders shadowed. The

III

Socialists resisted and the Prince decided to change his tactics. He was now to plot against the régime of which he was expected to be the pillar.

On an Autumn day, ten trainloads of *Heimwehr* troops were awaiting their transfer from Graz to Vienna, where they were to occupy the City Hall, the national telephone and telegraph buildings and government departments. It was at this juncture that a strange event took place. The Acting Police Commissioner, Herr Pamer, took matters into his own hands, thereby violating official rules. He called out the entire police force, occupied the railway stations and other strategical points, and defied his own Minister. The Prince was so greatly incensed at his subordinate's conscientious performance of his duty that he had him removed from office. Austria now saw what an anomaly it was to have a man in the government of which he was an enemy. The electorate passed an unfavorable judgment on the Prince by returning a larger body of Socialists to parliament. The *Heimwehr* got only five per cent of all the votes cast.

The Prince now decided to achieve his aim unconstitutionally. The coup which his *Heimwehr* attempted next year was meant to succeed even at the cost of bloodshed. The revolt started in Styria and was a great success, so far as the vaudeville stages were concerned. The army surrounded the *Heimwehr* forces, which submitted without as much as a show of resistance. There was a comic-opera trial—very *gemuetlich*—at which the princely "master mind" behind the putsch was acquitted *in absentia*. Austria laughed, but Mussolini's brows were contracted.

The Prince would have been swept into oblivion by a tidal wave of ridicule if he had not been saved at the last moment by the Third Reich. Adolf Hitler's shadow now fell over Austria. The Nazi chieftain grew more menacing every day. The persecution of the Catholics in the Reich antagonized the Austrian common people. The aim of the Hitlerites to annex Austria and fill the principal offices with Prussians antagonized the politicians. Mussolini intervened. He financed Starhemberg against the Nazis, and his money enabled the Prince to build up his *Heimwehr* to a strength of 100,000 men—four times greater than the regular army. Chancellor Dollfuss joined forces with the Prince. Since the Chancellor was not a reactionary—and the Prince was—the question has been asked: "What was the explanation of this unnatural alliance?" Mussolini's policy had the merit of simplicity; he merely wanted to weaken the Austrian dictatorship by splitting it between two dictators. Starhemberg admitted that he was the one who started the civil war in Austria. The combination of Mussolini and Starhemberg was too much for the Little Dictator.

After the death of Dollfuss, Starhemberg was the Vice Chancellor and, supposedly, the power behind the throne. But he had a way of being on vacation when vital events broke in Vienna. At first these absences were attributed to superior statesmanship. Then it was found that the motive was love. The object of his admiration was a beautiful actress, whom he later married. His meteoric career came to an abrupt end on a beautiful May night, two years after the death of Dollfuss. The Prince was dismissed from the government while having a hilarious time at his favorite Kobenzl Bar. From there he could see sleeping Vienna and the light-flanked ribbon of the Danube. His Home Defense forces were absorbed in the Fatherland Front, led by Chancellor Kurt

113

von Schuschnigg, the last head of the government of independent Austria. When he fell, the "beautiful blue" Danube became brown indeed.

For a moment, Chancellor Schuschnigg rose to heights where he kept company with immortals. In that moment he was an instrument of Danubian fate. His prime concern was Austria, but, indirectly, he sought to save the lifeline of mankind. In a history of the Danube, his name must be mentioned with reverence, even though he, too, was heir to many human frailties.

Nothing in his early life suggested that one day he would be called upon to face such a tragic fate. Nothing suggested that the lifeline of the Habsburg Empire, the Danube, would become the lifeline of the Nazi Empire under his dictatorship. Star-gazers would have probably foretold for him a brilliant career as a lawyer. He was one of those who seemed predestined for a life of quiet ease. Franz Joseph was the symbol of a seemingly indestructible imperial power when Kurt was born in Southern Tyrol, later detached from Austria and attached to Italy. His father was a high army officer and his grandfather was also a general, known and feared as the "Thunderer." His was an Austrian military family which worshiped *Dienst,* service, for the All Highest Imperial and Royal family. Kurt did not spend much time at home. His parents were mostly on the go, today in the garrison of subtropical Meran and tomorrow in Northwest Austria, near the Russian steppes.

He was sent to the school of aristocratic boys—the Jesuit gymnasium, Stella Matutina, the morning star, at Feldkirch, familiar to foreign tourists as the first Austrian station on the way from Switzerland. Kurt was very popular with his teachers, who praised his gifts, but less popular with his schoolmates, who thought him too reserved. He made a name for himself as the star of the school stage, where he excelled in classical rôles. His school career was abruptly interrupted by the War when he was seventeen. The following year he joined the army and was assigned to the 4th Regiment of Mountain Artillery, called by the Austrians a "life-insurance company." Young Schuschnigg was within sight of his lieutenancy when the War ended for most of his countrymen, but not for him. The Austro-Hungarian forces were in retreat and the Armistice was to be signed the following day, when he and his father were caught by a British group doing auxiliary service on the Italian front. This meant eight months of captivity in Italy.

After his return to Innsbruck, Kurt took up law, graduated in no time, and settled down as a country lawyer. But his eloquence was wasted in the Innsbruck courts. Prelate Seipel discovered that young Schuschnigg was of first-class legislative timber, and also that his family was good. To be picked out by the statesman-priest as a promising young man meant an assured career, and at the age of twenty-nine Kurt became a member of the Vienna Parliament. His ability and background qualified him for a leading part in important judicial and budgetary committees. Since he possessed more than common political sense he knew that mere ability was not enough in those troublous days. He must have his own semi-military cohorts, if he wanted to make an impression, and he set about organizing his storm troops. The Danube valley had learned from the Rhine, where Hitler in a brown uniform was reaching for the stars.

Schuschnigg was thirty-four years old when he became Minister of Justice, and the following year he also received the portfolio of the Ministry of Education. Upon him fell the task of rewriting

the Austrian Constitution in order to conform to the less liberal
spirit now prevailing in Austria and of giving education a religious basis. In this work he earned the respect of his party
friends and the hostility of the Socialists. He had a remarkable
aptitude for making people believe that his rise in the political
world was against his will. It was a common saying among his
colleagues that "Kurt is harmless," which meant that he was
not a serious rival. Jealousy thus disarmed, he forged on to victory—prelude to tragedy.

Meanwhile, Prince Starhemberg made his bid for power with
the aid of his Fascist army. The Vienna cafés, which sometimes
had remarkable intuitions, were buzzing with stories about the
Prince's impending step. He wanted to become the Regent Governor of Austria—almost a King. It was then that Schuschnigg
stepped in and clipped the Prince's wings in his disarming way,
and became the strong man of his country. To be.Austria's dictator was not a safe occupation in those days. The Chancellor
was constantly being threatened with violence and warned to be
prepared to meet his Lord. His wife was killed in an automobile
accident, when their car ran into a large block of stone lying at
a bend in the road. Although a Nazi plot could not be proved,
it was freely mentioned in Vienna.

Schuschnigg was now the dictator of Austria; at least the
world thought so. He commanded the Fatherland Front, which
was to unite the entire country in the pursuit of common ideals.
Did the majority of the Austrians follow him? The Austrian
Nazis maintained that he was merely the leader of a one-man
movement, himself, and that the entire nation was in their camp.
The vision of a dominant Third Reich was, undoubtedly, tremendously attractive to many Austrians, used to the imperial

glory of the Habsburgs. Since the Monarchy could not be restored, the union with a Germany feared and respected appeared to them the best solution. The overpowering success of Nazi propaganda blinded many Austrians—Germans at heart, heirs to the dreams of the Holy Roman Empire. The music, hysteria, the goose-step, the uniforms, stirring speeches, and the identification of the drab little man with his country's greatness, exerted an overwhelming influence.

The Austrian Chancellor knew the value of symbols in stirring up the mass-man, and he gave Austria her own symbols. There is some magic in the number "three": Third International, Third French Republic, Third Reich. It denotes completeness in the Hegelian sense: thesis, antithesis, synthesis. Schuschnigg sought to popularize the idea of the Third Austria. The Habsburg dynasty ruled over the First Austria, which collapsed at the end of the World War; the Second Austria grew up under the aegis of parliamentary democracy; its place was taken by the Third Austria, an authoritarian country, seeking to weaken the impact of Nazi onslaught by insisting on the country's Catholic heritage. Schuschnigg wrote a book, *My Austria,* which was to become a political testament in the manner of Hitler's *My Battle.* "Doubters have been in this country," Schuschnigg wrote, "as long as its name has endured. But it has survived the Thirty Years' War, the disorders of the eighteenth century and the Napoleonic period, the destructive decades before the World War, lastly, and despite all, wounded to death yet still alive, it survived even that."

Opposition to the Nazis was crystallizing along the Austrian Danube: the Socialists, Catholics, legitimists and Vienna's wealthy Jews. Could a *mystique* be created, a religious fervor, as strong as the Nazis, to save the Danube's pride? Mussolini still considered the Danube the lifeline of the Italian Empire, and Austria a necessity. So he wrote in the February 13, 1935, issue of *Popolo d'Italia:* "I believe that with the end of the year, with the renewed strengthening of the State and the recovery of the economic situation, everybody will be convinced that Austria can live; and thus that a second German State can exist in Europe, German, but master of its own destiny."

Bonfires continued to burn on the banks of the Danube and in the mountains. There was a lull while the Nazis strengthened their reserves. Then activity was renewed. The government was trying to guess where the next blow would fall. Chaos was systematized, as the climax was approaching. Germany exerted economic pressure on Austria. Tyrol was stripped of tourists from across the boundary. When Mussolini went to war in Ethiopia, the props fell from under Austria. He could not afford to fight on two fronts and had to secure his country's rear.

Then Hitler set to work. First he laid down a smoke-screen to cloak his preparations for the final offensive. "The German government recognizes the full sovereignty of Austria," read the treaty he concluded with Schuschnigg on July 11, 1936. The world sighed with relief. Hitler had agreed to keep his hands off Austria. "He is a fanatic, but he is honest," was the consensus. For years he had elaborately built himself up as a crusader of honesty, an angel of light against the powers of darkness. The world gave him the credit he demanded, taking his statements at their face value. In coming events his reputation helped him more than his army. Without this belief in his integrity he could not have taken Austria. Chancellor Schuschnigg himself was hypnotized by Hitler's campaign of self-praise and began to concentrate on Austria's economic reconstruction.

Hitler now made his final preparations for the coup, still protected by the smoke-screen. But unexpectedly he encountered opposition among the leaders of his own army who were convinced that the Great Powers would not tolerate Austria's absorption and that, if the Fuehrer moved, a major conflict would ensue. The march of Il Duce's divisions to the Brenner was not forgotten, and Czechoslovakia had an excellent army, backed by the former Allies. The Fuehrer struck at his own military. Austrian frontier posts reported the nocturnal arrival of German generals. The former German Crown Prince himself had crossed the frontier without a passport, without even a toothbrush. In the early Spring of 1938, Hitler purged his army of the belief in the Allies' readiness to fight him. The time had come to strike. Hitler now needed a Nazi spokesman in the Austrian government, and to get him there, he had to use his hypnotic power of persuasion on Schuschnigg. The German Ambassador to Vienna, Franz von Papen, prevailed upon the Austrian Chancellor to visit the Fuehrer in his mountain chalet in the Bavarian Alps, where he was spinning his web for the capture of Austria.

Schuschnigg let himself be persuaded that he could induce Hitler to conclude a truce. Nazi agitation in Austria had flared up anew. On the day he left for Berchtesgaden he gave instructions to the Salzburg garrison to declare a state of alarm if no word came from him by four in the afternoon. He left the Austrian frontier posts behind and was lost to the world for hours. Noon came, then early afternoon, three o'clock, and the hand of the clock was approaching four. No sign of life came from the Austrian Chancellor. At four o'clock sharp the telephone rang. Had he not sent this message to Salzburg Danubian history might have

119

taken a different turn. The garrison would have been alarmed and so would the world. We know the rest of the story from Schuschnigg himself, who told it to Guido Zernatto, the General Secretary of the Fatherland Front and member of the Cabinet, probably the most important Minister in Austria next to him.

Hitler greeted Schuschnigg coolly, then showered him with reproaches. He told him that he considered the Austrian government a tyrannical régime, and that the Austrian Chancellor had no right to persecute an entire nation with a handful of his followers. He called the assassins of Chancellor Dollfuss martyrs to the German cause. He accused the Austrian government of leaning on the bayonets of a foreign power—Italy. The time was over, Hitler said, when the German Reich would stand such treatment. It had been his intention to march into Austria on February 26, but he was willing to consider another plan. Meanwhile, the heads of the German army and air force were waiting in the antechamber. The main points of the plan were the appointment of an Austrian Nazi spokesman, Dr. Arthur Seyss-Inquart, in the Vienna government and the technical co-ordination of the armies of Austria and Germany, beginning with the exchange of two hundred officers in the first year. Schuschnigg defended his point of view with vigor, rejecting Hitler's charges. He was either to accept or to reject the German plan, and in the latter case the Reich's army would march. The Austrian Chancellor pleaded lack of authority in such a vital question; he must first consult the President of his country.

Then they sat down to luncheon, where Hitler was again formal but polite. He told his guest that in Hamburg they had the alternative of building a tunnel or a bridge. The bridge would be more expensive. Nevertheless, he chose the latter, so

120

that Germany should have a longer span than the Americans. He also planned to have several skyscrapers built in Hamburg "so that the Americans can see when they visit Europe that the German people can do as well as they." They also talked about international relations. Hitler said that Mussolini must depend upon his friendship, because the wars in Ethiopia and Spain had weakened him to such an extent that he could not do without Germany's help. "He thought very little of the fighting value of the Italian army, and, in conflict, he said, 100,000 German soldiers would suffice to rout the Italian army." Hitler declared that the Dominions would not follow England in a war that did not directly affect their interests. He thought the downfall of the British Empire possible and, in case of war, even probable.

Schuschnigg returned to Vienna. Events were now moving rapidly. Under duress, the Austrians accepted the German ultimatum and Seyss-Inquart became a member of the Cabinet. He was admirably fitted to play the part of a Trojan horse. The studious, intelligent type, his very looks aroused confidence. He deprecated violence and professed to be a good Catholic. In short, he was the ideal person to lull Austria into a false sense of security at the last moment. The foreign Powers, headed by Italy, which had Austria's cause at heart, could not fear such a harmless-looking young statesman. While Austria complied with her part of the treaty, Hitler broke his by appointing a new leader for the Austrian Nazis, in violation of their agreement. Hitler knew that he must act quickly before the Great Powers shook off their lethargy. Although he did not overestimate their striking power, he could never be quite sure.

Responding to the signal of an invisible conductor, the Austrian Nazis began to riot, first in Graz, the hotbed of Nazism, and then closer to the Danube. They displayed the swastika flag, sang the "Horst Wessel," defied the authorities. Schuschnigg now saw through the plot: to create chaos and then march the German army into Austria to restore order. He had to act quickly, and he did. He called a plebiscite of all Austrians to decide: "Are you in favor of the independence of Austria or not?" It was to take place on March 13th. In the last moment it was called off, as all the world knows, except in a village lost in the Tyrol mountains, which heard nothing about the changed plans. Ninety-five per cent of the population of the village voted "yes." Ninety-five per cent of them would have probably voted "no" out of fear if Hitler had asked the same question. Schuschnigg knew it and he made a dash to get in ahead of the Fuehrer. Incidentally, he wanted to call international attention to Austria's plight.

It was then that he rose to heroic heights, afire with his mission. When he spoke in Parliament for the last time, it was the spontaneous recognition of greatness that greeted his proclamation of Austria's devotion to her historic ideals. This greatness sustained him in the performance of what was probably the most tragic task in modern Europe: his farewell to Austrian independence. Schuschnigg had only a noble cause, but Hitler had a strong army. The final part of the plan was completed. At the invisible sign of the political orchestra leader, the Austrian Nazis broke into a crescendo. Riots were staged throughout the land. The innocent-looking Dr. Seyss-Inquart took over the Chancellery and invited Hitler to "restore order." Hitler, knowing that this invitation was to come, had several divisions assembled secretly on the Austrian border two days earlier. During the night of March 14, his divisions began to move. When Signor

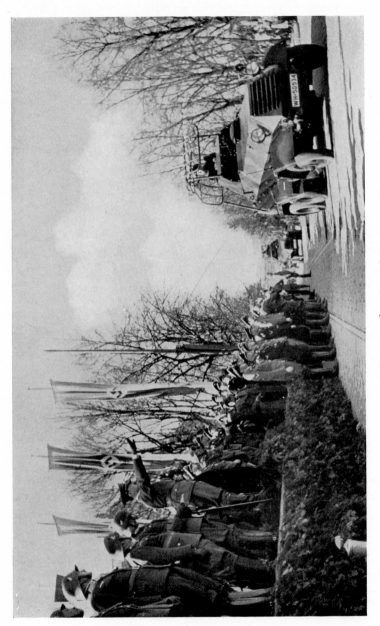

Hitler invades Austria

The End of Austria

Mussolini of Italy, M. Benes of Czechoslovakia, M. Daladier of France and Mr. Chamberlain of England woke up, they could comfort themselves with the thought that nothing could be done for Austria. The Czechs were solemnly assured by the Fuehrer that he had no intention to occupy an inch of their land. If the Great Powers had decided to prevent the rape of Austria by commissioning Prague to take over Rome's previous rôle, we are assured that the German army could have been blasted out of the Vienna road. Mr. G. E. R. Gedye, a brilliant observer, saw the wrecked Reich tanks from the former German border to Vienna, when Hitler's army invaded Austria. His informants told him how the Fuehrer raved at what he called an international scandal.

This was the end of Austria. With one stroke Germany became master of the Danube valley, and the War which the Allies thought they won in 1918 was lost in 1938. The Reich now had a larger territory than before the War. The millions of lives lost and millions of dollars spent for victory only benefited the vanquished. No country lost as much as Italy, bottled up as she was in her tight little peninsula, deprived of the lifeline of the Fascist Empire, the Danube, the countries of which Il Duce had rallied under his flag. When the first German troops marched up to the Brenner Pass and hoisted the swastika banner alongside the tricolor of Italy, Mussolini lost the World War for his country. He was too weak to fight, and the next best thing for him to do was to jump on the victor's band-wagon. Thus at least he could make the masses of his people believe that Germany's victory was also theirs. Having no illusions about the political education of his countrymen and about the efficacy of truth against the power of concentrated propaganda, he had no doubt that Italy would accept the *fait accompli.* "Mussolini, I shall never forget you for this," Hitler wired to Rome, and he had good reason for this spontaneous outburst of joy. At one stroke he conquered both Austria and Italy.

Moviegoers may recall the hysterical joy of the crowd greeting Hitler the Conqueror upon his arrival in Vienna, the Vienna he had left as a poor young man with bitterness in his heart. They did not see the eighty per cent of the city's population that stayed behind, shutting themselves up in their homes. They may have overlooked the thirteen police cars that protected the Fuehrer, and the keen-eyed special troops of the police, with the sinister skull and crossbones on their caps, scanning the crowds, and the triple row of Berlin police, in pale-green uniforms, facing the packed masses. Nor did they see the tragedy in the wake of the occupation. "You will shrug your comfortable shoulders," writes Gedye, "and say 'bogey tales' when I tell you of women whose husbands had been arrested a week before without any charge, receiving a small parcel from the Viennese postman with the curt intimation—'To pay 150 marks for the cremation of your husband—ashes enclosed from Dachau.' . . . Hurrying down the stairs of my flat to hear Hitler make his first speech in Vienna, I was delayed by men carrying out the bodies of a young Jewish doctor and his mother, who had lived quiet, decent and hard-working lives two floors below. The man had been dismissed from his hospital overnight, without a hope of even being allowed to earn another penny. Nazis had forced their way into his flat and thrust a great swastika banner out of his window. Being a doctor, escape was easier for him and his mother than for most; they had found it through a hypodermic syringe."

Silence Falls on Vienna

Thus Austria again became "Ostmark," as she was at the time of Charlemagne, a spearhead in the Danube valley of a conquering nation. A recent visit revealed the new character of the land, and I wrote the following upon my return:

The silence falling on Vienna impels the fear that she may become a modern Bruges, a dead city. According to a popular story, a Viennese deputation called upon Hitler, asking him to retain Vienna as an express station for through trains. Although I found many of the cafés open, their old clientele was gone. They are no longer a social center, where conversation was an art. Who would dare to talk under the eyes of the political police? The blinding light no longer attracts light-hearted pleasure-seekers. *Judenverbot*—Jews forbidden—is written on many doors. The Opera on the Ring has seen its star cast decimated by Aryan laws. Gone are the days when youth began at dawn to form a line for standing room. The concert halls have lost the bulk of their devotees. Even Vienna's famed operettas have suffered. The performers sometimes outnumber the audience. The theatres have banned the top-notchers, such as Max Reinhardt, and light comedy's place has been taken by heavy drama, where heroism is murder. The chic shops of the Kaerntnerstrasse are now displaying the last remnants of the city's genius in dressmaking, but there are few customers. Folksy dirndls dominate the street scene. The men flaunt their Nazism with bared knees in Tyrolean breeches. The brown uniforms of the storm troopers, the black tunics of the special troops and the army gray lend the street a military air. No longer is it chic to be well dressed in Vienna.

"Vienna is to become greater than ever," Nazis insist. Now that Germany has acquired a commanding position on the Danube valley, they argue, trade with the Balkans and the Near East will increase; and Vienna will become the great transit station between the Third Reich of 80,000,000 inhabitants and some 100,000,000 of the countries to the east. A prominent Nazi assured me that the city's fairs will surpass those of Leipzig, her banks will resume their

125

former positions, and Danubian shipping will be revived. In a decade, predict the Nazis, the former capital will gain an additional million inhabitants. The Nazis have also announced an ambitious housing program. A garden city is to be built to the south, on the way to Italy, and will house a quarter of a million tenement inhabitants.

Public programs have already been begun. The armament industries, the building of strategical roads and uniformed organizations have absorbed the unemployed. But one hears complaints that emergency wages are near the starvation level. Confidential reports and official statements indicate that Vienna's general standard of living has deteriorated rather than improved until the time of writing. Wage levels, expressed in mark currency, are lower than they were when Hitler took the reins. Working hours, on the other hand, are on the increase. The ten- and twelve-hour day may soon be back, as it is already back in the old Reich. Food is more plentiful than in Berlin, but Austrian cities also know the "one-dish" day. Is there much dissatisfaction with Hitler's rule in Ostmark? Now anti-Nazi slogans are scribbled on the walls of workers' houses—and are erased by special squads. In these sections Hitler's unsmiling picture must be protected by wire netting. The authorities have not dared to remove the names of Socialist city officials who built the municipal homes. And to win over the former Socialists, the Nazis have even released from jail those of them who rose against the previous régime under Dollfuss.

One sees harmless-looking leaflets, advertising everything from cradles to coffins, distributed by mysterious hands. The first few sentences of these leaflets speak of whatever products they are supposed to advertise; then they slide into a thundering indictment of the Hitler régime for its destruction of labor's few remaining rights and its policy of war. "Song to be Whispered" is the underground anthem, written by an Austrian scribe. Many know it by heart; a defiant voice may shout its militant lines into the night. The illegal radio station, *Freiheitssender,* broadcasting from behind some frontier, has popularized it among Vienna's workers.

126

Disappointed Old Fighters

Nevertheless, the former Socialists did not strike me as particularly active. Many are weary of a fight that cost many lives in 1934. Others see no sense in fighting one brand of Fascism for the sake of another which might take its place. The opposition to Hitler's rule from his original followers seems somewhat more serious. They are the "Old Fighters," who publish an illegal sheet of the same title, *Der Alte Kaempfer*. They are the ones who terrorized the countryside with shootings, bomb-throwing and nocturnal burnings of weird swastikas in forest clearings. They are the ones who formed the Austrian Legion, which was outlawed in Austria, and sought refuge in the Reich for years. The Old Fighters envisaged an Austria of which they would be the masters. They did not dream that others would be given the key positions in their country—that Austria would lose her army—that she would be completely suppressed. They had in mind a federal system under which their country's native ways would be respected. Many of them are bitter and give vent to their feelings in explosive words. Some of them are in the dreaded Dachau concentration camp; others were sent to East Prussia and still others were drafted into service under Generalissimo Franco, when the insurrection in Spain was fought.

Outwardly there is little change in the serene Austrian countryside. Some villages flaunt the swastika, while others are more wary. What has Hitler done for the rural part of the country of his birth? In one year of his rule, Ostmark's production of pig iron increased some 140 per cent. The lumber industry was also thriving; hydroelectric power production increased. Hitler also started the first auto-express highways, such as his engineers have been building in the Reich for years. They, too, are of strategical importance for his penetration of the Danube valley. And what about the tourist industry that loomed so large in the nation's life? At the height of the Salzburg festival, I was told that in that city of music there was plenty of room for all. How different it was in previous years, when the late-comer had to put up with improvised beds, if he could find one at all! Official statistics published at the end of the first year boasted of an increase in tourist traffic. This may have been true,

127

but many of the visitors were "knapsack tourists" from the older Reich, while the "valuta guests" from America, England and France were largely absent.

Several monasteries and church schools had been closed on the ground that they overlapped. The Nazis in Austria, however, are less vehemently anti-Catholic at present than in the rest of the Reich, probably realizing the strength of Catholic opinion. But pro-Habsburg sentiment is hardly in evidence. The Emperors' names have disappeared from street signs, being replaced by those of Nazi leaders.

Sullen opposition is more noticeable in Tyrol and Vorarlberg, Ostmark's west. This is all the more remarkable because some of the Tyroleans were the most ardent supporters of Nazism before it took their country. Anti-Nazi Austria was defied then by a huge swastika on the bald rocks of majestic Hafelekar Peak near Innsbruck. Austrian Tyrol was convinced a strong Reich—instead of an anemic Austria—would be able to liberate the Germans of the southern slopes. When Hitler's troops marched up the Brenner Pass, the valleys echoed the rumor that South Tyrol would be returned to the Fatherland. Instead of that, Hitler pledged his word that the frontier between the two Fascist countries stood for all time, and resentment took the place of hope in mountain huts.

Hitler is heir to the Habsburgs' most precious heritage—Austria. When that famous family took Vienna in the thirteenth century, they could be sure of the rich Danube region. From there they extended their rule to the farthermost Occident. Hitler employs this endless power to conjure up intolerant nationalism and the threat of war. Austria's traditions of song and music have been disavowed. Is there no limit to the dictator's might? Although Austria is too tired to move, the world wonders: "Can she forget her past?"

3. Vienna—Dream and Reality

$\mathscr{T}$HE picture of Vienna one paints before seeing it consists of magnificent palaces, inhabited by women of unearthly beauty, who sing rather than speak, dance rather than walk. When I first saw Vienna, it disappointed me. I arrived at the Eastern Railway Station, *Ostbahnhof*, probably Vienna's poorest terminus—although none of them shines with beauty—and directly went to a hotel in a business section. On my way, I saw houses with peeling walls, peddlers with pushcarts, and girls bound for work, looking anything but dream-ladies. I found out later that beautiful Viennese women would rather die than be seen in the city during the Summer.

The next time I saw Vienna I went to live there for two years, not long after the World War. It was then a run-down and suspicious city, hungry, too. It took a full day to find a hotel that was willing to admit a young foreigner. Early next morning I wanted to present a letter of introduction to a Viennese, ready for a joyous welcome. Instead of that, a pair of suspicious eyes peered at me from behind the casement, a cautious hand opened the door as far as the chain-bolt would permit, and an unfriendly voice wanted to know who I was, what I wanted and why.

Nor was the headwaiter in our hotel joyous and jovial when he withheld the slice of bread which was coming to me on my ration-card. He forgot to give it to me, probably in the belief that shy young men did not like to ask for pieces of bread. Tired of fighting for my slice, I advertised for a furnished room, and a lady answered. Although I looked not more dangerous than an average person in my station, she asked for my passport and references. After investigation, she informed me several days later that the room was at my disposal, but that I was not to use electricity and must buy my own fuel if I wanted heat. One evening I had to break the commandment about the light. She caught me in the act. Hastily I drew my conclusions about Viennese charm.

In the two years of my stay, I came to know Vienna from a different side. I found it possessed of a mellowness which has a touch of the Southern and the Oriental. It takes time before the beauty of the city gets into your pores. The Viennese at their best were an unforgettable sight. You had to see them on Summer Sundays in the Vienna Woods, radiant with joy and song, fully justifying their fame. You had to see them in enchanting *Stadtpark,* when the dynamic orchestra leader conducted a Strauss waltz. The very statues of the park seemed to be athrob with joyous expectation.

The real Vienna, of which poets sang, could never recover its

130

spirits after the World War. Before the *dies irae,* it was the spiritual capital of the entire Danube valley and Eastern Europe, not merely the capital of the Habsburg monarchy. It attracted seekers of fame and elegance, devotees of pleasure, geniuses and adventurers from half the continent. It was the home not merely of the aristocracy of the Habsburg nationalities, but also of Russians, Poles, Turks and all the Balkan nations. It was the musical center of the world, a center of elegance, and the trading and banking capital of many countries. It was the last outpost of sophisticated culture. Its university was world-famous, so were its concert halls and theaters.

Vienna was a gift of Nature. Geologists tell us that the so-called "Gate of Vienna" is a mountain gap where the Alps are pushed back to give way to the Danube. To the east, the Northern Alps reappear in the continuous chain of the Carpathians. On an airplane trip down the Danube, this gap may be clearly seen. The chain of mountains is broken by this depression, filled out by Vienna's ripples of houses. Here the two great historical routes intersect: The Amber Road, connecting the Baltic Sea (largest source of amber) with the Adriatic and the Danube. The Amber Road was one of the main gates of nomadic invaders. Later, when the Habsburgs took Vienna, they reversed the trend and extended their rule north and south, along this historic highway. It is bisected by the Danube, Europe's transcontinental highway, created by Nature to link up East and West. Here first the Orient sent the Occident its treasures. Then the Occident returned the favor by sending the East the crusaders' spears and the heavy guns which shelled the Dardanelles.

At Vienna's railway stations the geographical significance

of the "gap" may be clearly seen. The signs on the trains read: "Paris-Budapest-Bucharest-Istanbul" (Orient Express), "Vienna-Trieste-Roma," "Vienna-Warsaw."

Vienna saw the approach of Europe's principal races: Germanic, Latin, Slavic, and for hundreds of years the fight was on for the possession of this crucial stronghold. Rome could not feel safe from the hungry nomads until it filled the gap. The Germanic tribes were admonished by their instincts that theirs was a precarious life unless the site of Vienna was in their hands. It was here that the expansive Slavic East sought to obtain a firmer footing in the heart of Europe. From this key point of the Danube it could have controlled all vital approaches to its own "living space." But the Asiatic Magyars kept the Slavs from this part of the river and thereby injected a new problem into Europe's life.

Again we are reminded of Prince Metternich's famous saying: "Whoever is master of Vienna. . . ." When the Romans were masters of this gap, they were drawn into a campaign of conquest which took them as far as the delta of the Danube and the Black Sea. When the Germanic Habsburgs asserted themselves in Vienna they were bound to draw their Slavic, Latin and Magyar neighbors into their orbit. Theirs were the most fertile parts of Italy: golden Lombardy and Venetia, the gifts of God. Theirs were Hungary and Bohemia, filled with Nature's treasures, inhabited by self-willed nations, which were powerless to counteract the magnetic force of the Danubian Gate. Now that Germany is the master of the metropolis, she, too, is bound to pursue a dynamic policy.

Let us now look at Vienna, its people and how they live. Strangely enough, this "Queen of the Danube," which inspired

The Vienna Woods

the Blue Danube Waltz, has only its outlying suburbs on the river. But the center of the city is built on the Danube Canal, so-called, although it is not a canal, but a wayward arm of the river, some sixteen miles long.

The hilly Vienna Woods stand guard at the western entrance of the city, perfuming its nights and cooling its air. Bold Kahlenberg rises over the Danube, as if wanting to see what such a metropolitan monster looks like. Is there a more enchanting sight than Vienna in the evening from this vantage point? There it lies half-buried by green leaves, if you can penetrate the mysteries of darkness. You can see that half of Vienna consists of farmland; yet it is one of the largest cities in Europe, three times as large as Berlin, with only half of the German capital's population. From Kahlenberg you can also see the semi-circular row of lights marking the world-famous "Ring," which is one of the most beautiful streets—if not the most beautiful—to be found anywhere. Its two miles are concentrated delight, filled with buildings, parks and monuments. Less than a century ago it was the site of the fortification that surrounded the Interior Town. Along the Ring we can trace the symbols of Vienna's greatness and why she played such a vital rôle in the Danube valley. The massive masonry of the one-time War Ministry—now headquarters of the Fifth German Army Corps—speaks of a proud Empire, now defunct. The contrast with the *Stadtpark*, next to it, could not be greater. It was one of the most popular show places of Viennese *Gemuetlichkeit*, joviality. There everyone used to sip his favorite raspberry drink, *Himbeersaft*, at hundreds of small tables, sprouting in the shade of multicolored parasols, while the orchestra struck up the latest operetta hit, *Schlager*, setting blond and brown heads swaying. There guests

133

sat for hours under the benevolent eyes of the headwaiter, accustomed to see tables occupied all afternoon for the equivalent of a quarter, which bought not only the drink and music, but also the right to peruse countless newspapers and flirt with friendly girls.

The Opera of Vienna is not merely a building, but a hallowed institution. At one time it was "the" Opera of the world, with the best orchestra and singers. Its performances were recorded not merely in the press, but also in conversation. To attend them was not only a custom, but a passion. Next to the Opera is the *Burggarten,* continuing in the *Volksgarten,* and between the two parks is the *Burg,* the imperial palace, where the Habsburgs had their residence for centuries. It is haunted by long traditions, now discarded. Its Swiss wing was built in the thirteenth century, while the new wing is only a half century old. It was here that Emperor Franz Joseph saw the world change from the stagecoach to the airplane in the sixty-eight years of his reign. Pre-War Viennese were passionately fond of watching the changing of the guards. In multi-colored uniforms and bobbing feathers, the troops wheeled into the cobblestoned court of the *Burg.* Behind the drawn curtains, their Imperial Master may have been watching, and every soldier did his best.

The Imperial Library forms part of the palace, and when all its secrets—as well as those of the Imperial Secret Archives—are unearthed, mankind will know more about its own history.

Facing the *Burg* is the former Chancellery—known to the world as the palace on *Ballhausplatz*—the Foreign Office under the Habsburgs. It was there that Metternich wove the threads that ensnared Napoleon and gave his imperial masters their victory over the spectacular Corsican. It was there that the

Vienna Congress wrote a historic document while dancing, and gave Europe the Holy Alliance which employed religion once more to veil the hatred of the strong for the weak, of the oppressor for the oppressed. It was in this building that the ultimatum was issued which gave the signal for the outbreak of the World War. A memorial tablet on the wall commemorates the deed of murderers. The Nazis put it up in honor of the men who killed Chancellor Dollfuss.

Those marble philosophers you see are not meditating why they are there, although they would have every reason to do so. They are sitting in front of the marble Parliament, which, even when built, was more impressive than important. The Habsburgs never believed sincerely that the masses could or should take care of their own destiny. In this part of the Danube valley, parliamentary democracy lacks old traditions.

There is deeper significance to the fact that the City Hall, *Rathaus,* out-towers the Legislature. Even in her heyday, Austria would have been merely one of a dozen countries without her incomparable Vienna. She was unique, the capital for the genius of a dozen countries, soaring far above the cultural level of the rest of Austria. Vienna's recognition meant fame, career. It beckoned to the young Serbian as much as to the young Hungarian, neither of whom would think of wasting his energies in his own country. The City Hall of Vienna symbolized its international importance.

To the Viennese it is famous also as the battleground of their most picturesque Mayor, Dr. Karl Lueger, now more a legend than a historic figure. To readers of Hitler's *Mein Kampf* he is known as leader of the anti-Socialist Christian Social Party, which inspired the future Fuehrer with anti-Semitism. But Lue-

135

ger himself had many Jewish friends, and when accused of inconsistency, he answered in his thick Vienna dialect: *"Wer ein Jud' ist bestimm' ich."* (I decide who is a Jew.) His name is written in marble wherever you go in Vienna, for he laid out parks, built bridges and public buildings—at least he took credit for them.

St. Stephen's Cathedral is to Vienna what Notre Dame is to Paris. Its 450-foot tower can be seen from afar, and for centuries its sentinels saw danger threatening the Danube valley. The lacelike lightness of its stone masonry does not betray its strength, which has defied age and two Turkish sieges. That venerable dirt on some of its stone began to accumulate in the twelfth century, but the master builders' hands were stayed by war and Black Death. Its catacombs contain the remains of a long row of Holy Roman Emperors, all members of the House of Habsburg, products of the Danube valley. The entrails of the later members of the House of Austria were until recently deposited in its urns. The *Stock im Eisen* (tree in iron), diagonally across the street from the Cathedral, is a place of pilgrimage today, as it was in those dim times when the Celts venerated their deities in the sacred grove, of which this is said to have been a part. It was customary for traveling craftsmen to drive nails into the stump.

A few steps away lie the dead bodies of the later Habsburgs in the basement of the unimpressive Capuchin Church. Fresh white flowers, deposited for years, attracted attention to the bronze coffin of the young man who was born a King and died a Duke, Napoleon's son, L'Aiglon, lying between his mother, who loved herself with passionate devotion, and his grandfather, the Emperor, who loved the young man, yet killed him by keeping

136

him in a golden cage. The Habsburgs who are not here had tragic ends. The brother of Emperor Franz Joseph, Archduke Maximilian, became Emperor of Mexico and died before the firing squad of Juarez. Death relieved him of the martyrdom of a mistaken life, packed with good intentions and irretrievable errors. The body of Archduke Johann is absent. He is better known to the world as John Orth, merchant, who exchanged his golden prison for the humdrum of everyday uncertainties. He was shipwrecked off the coast of Patagonia, if popular belief may be trusted, although many saw him years after the supposed tragedy, sharing the fate of romantic Princes whom their contemporaries do not even allow to die. The body of Archduke Franz Ferdinand is not here either. He had married a lady of less exalted rank, and the two of them were banished from the exclusive burial ground of the Habsburgs.

"Downtown" Vienna was aristocracy's residential section. Its somnolent streets are flanked by the palaces of the former great, now dead, in exile, retirement or concentration camp. These palaces bear not only German, but also Slavic, Latin and Hungarian names, because exclusive Vienna attracted the nobility of the entire Danube valley, basking itself in the sun of the imperial court. In those days the Hotel Sacher was a landmark for the rural aristocracy that came to town for riotous times. What it lacked in comfort, the hotel made up in expensiveness. The visitors paid for its patina.

Vienna's Kaerntnerstrasse bisects the Inner Town. It was the rue de la Paix of the imperial capital, the meeting place of elegance in the Danube valley. It exported fashion and imported feminine beauty. You could do no better than stroll along this famous street in search of long-missed friends. The intimate

137

revues and cabarets of its tributary streets were places of rendez-
vous for pleasure-seekers from a vast hinterland, extending all
the way to Asia and the Pacific Ocean. For thousands of miles
behind Kaerntnerstrasse there was no street comparable with it
in magnificence.

Although foreign visitors were often inclined to believe so,
aristocratic sections and fashionable quarters did not monopolize
all Vienna. Some of the worst slums of Europe were in this
glittering capital. They were filled with dreary rows of houses,
which popular language called *Zinspalaeste,* rent palaces. Their
crowded rooms were breeding places of disease, and bathrooms
were unknown.

Vienna changed her looks after the World War, when the
Socialist city government began to build municipal apartment
houses on a larger scale than the world had ever seen. A shy ex-
bank clerk, Hugo Breitner, was the mastermind of this scheme.
He could be found at his desk in City Hall at eight in the morning and nine at night, because he had a dream which had to be
realized. Vienna was desperately poor, living on short rations,
but the hope of a new day was in the air, and *Stadtrat* Breitner
was the instrument of destiny. Socialism wanted to show that
poverty was no handicap. In spite of its meager resources, the
Austrian capital set an example to rich countries in wiping out
slums and building apartment houses, models of beauty and
efficiency, for the poor. The Karl Marx Hof, as it was originally
named, contains nearly 1,400 apartments—the largest in the
world. Breitner had 64,000 municipal apartment house dwellings
built for about a quarter of a million. They had gardens, libraries,
playgrounds, swimming pools, community kitchens and laundries.
Rent was based only on the cost of maintenance. It was these

houses which the Home Guards of Prince Starhemberg and Chancellor Dollfuss had shelled in February, 1934.

The Danube Canal, which forms the base of the Inner Town, separates it from the *Prater,* Vienna's Coney Island and the Leopoldstadt, its ghetto. "The Royal and Imperial Prater" of pre-War days was the popular amusement area of the Danube valley. Its unique giant wheel, Hansel and Gretel shows, and merry-go-rounds are still there, often streamlined, but the old spirit is gone. The green canopy of linden trees shaded countless wooden tables covered with checkered chintz. The flicker of the candle, protected by glass, shed sufficient light on steins and mugs, but did not betray moist eyes and craving lips. This was the paradise of Dragoons, Huszárs and Uhlans, not to speak of cavalry and plain infantry, who proved to be a tremendous attraction for romance-famished servant girls of all countries in the Danube valley. *Der fesche Gefreiter,* smart lance corporal of the Imperial Army, could not have been more admired if he had been the Crown Prince himself. The green canopy looked down upon a mass of ecstatic dancers when the band struck up the quick polka. Smiles came spontaneously, and a Sunday in the *Prater* was something to live for all week.

Leopoldstadt, the ghetto of Vienna, has entered world history as the starting point of the anti-Semitism which Hitler adopted as his basic policy. On a Sunday afternoon, a few years before the War, bricklayer Hitler, dreaming of an artist's career, crossed the Danube Canal. There and then he discovered the Jew. In the old Leopoldstadt he still wore a kaftan and ear-curls, the first Hitler ever saw. The Jew looked different and he was the traditional scapegoat. He had money, popular belief held, and Hitler had none. The young bricklayer's hatred cried out for a

139

target. The idea bred conviction, and conviction led to a mania. His enemy was not of flesh and blood, but a phantom. The Leopoldstadt was the Oriental Jew's entrance gate to Western Europe. As soon as he crossed the Danube Canal, he was transformed and became a Western Jew.

The Viennese developed certain traits as a result of his peculiar environment. He is almost as much a mixture as the New Yorker, and no amount of Nazism can make him "racially" German. The reading of the Vienna telephone book should be compulsory for Nazis, to teach them how cosmopolitan is the former Austrian capital. The lure of Vienna attracted a rich racial medley. The city was a miniature League of Nations under the Habsburg reign.

The melting pot produced a pleasing type. German thoroughness was improved by Latin vivacity and Hungarian vitality. The Slav's brooding spirituality was combined with the Teuton's passion for precision. Intermarriage has produced Viennese women famous for their beauty. One of the two headquarters of elegance was in Vienna before the War.

The mixture of blood alone does not account for these traits. The characteristics of the Viennese were modified by the unique position of the city. For centuries the Habsburgs beautified it, and ransacked two continents to lay their treasures at the feet of the Queen of the Danube. In those days unemployment was no problem and food was not lacking even for the slum dwellers. The aristocrats attracted to the Court sounded the keynote for the higher classes. Since Vienna was the amusement capital of half Europe, it also specialized in entertainment, and its people were infected with the joyous spirit of all merry-makers. The tone of the town was gaiety. The middle classes reflected Vienna's pride in being rich and the center of a powerful empire.

140

The Musical Capital of the World

Vienna was long the acknowledged musical capital of the world. Marble memorial tablets haunt you in the Alsergrund, Hietzing, Doebling districts—wherever you go. This was the house where "Papa" Haydn composed the *Emperor March,* adopted by the Habsburgs as their own. In that house young Mozart lived before Maria Theresa first heard the child prodigy. That was the house in which Schubert's dreams took shape. These quiet streets inspired Beethoven's *Ode to Joy.* There Brahms captured the moods which sum up the mystery of life. It was in that house that Wagner read the derisive criticism which inspired him with the idea of the *Meistersinger.* The marble angels soaring skyward around Johann Strauss embody the ecstasy of music.

The Austrian capital made you love music; it was its very air. When I first went to Vienna, I pretended to love Beethoven and Wagner, while wondering how people could bear such noise. I told my friends about my reactions in an unguarded moment. The next time they took me to a concert, they said little in explanation of the music, but what they did say carried meaning. They made me hear fate knocking at the door of life in the opening of the *Fifth Symphony.* They made me hear the sexual ecstasy in the climactic scenes of *Tristan.* I heard the struggle of light and darkness in tonal poems, listened to emotions which neither words nor color could explain, the deepest stirrings of the human soul, expressible only in sound, man's most primitive way of self-expression, elevated into a world of transcendent beauty. Because of the spirit of Vienna I cannot hear Beethoven or Wagner without being moved to momentary flashes of understanding everything that is baffled by logic.

Vienna became the musical capital of the world partly because the Danube and the Amber Road brought to her the fertilizing genius of many races. The Danube was, in truth, the lifeline of the world's musical Empire. The Slavs and Magyars took to Vienna the nostalgic folk tunes of the peasants, so clearly heard in Brahms. The misty North sent it the doubts of self-seeking souls trying to force the inexpressible to yield its secrets. The South infused Viennese music with that sunny charm which enthralls the world in Mozart's compositions. Vienna, the amusement center of the Danube valley, inspired Strauss to classical masterpieces of popular music.

The Austrian capital was a magnet for musical genius because of its liberal court and generous aristocracy. It was a social obligation for a rich man to have his own musical protégé. It was not always merit that received the best treatment, and often titans of music knew hunger and need.

Before the debacle, the arbiters of Viennese society were those connected with the Court. It was not part of life, but far above it, high in the social stratosphere. The Court was regulated by the Imperial and Royal House Laws, made for demigods. Every step of members of the Court was prescribed by the rigid Spanish etiquette. Members of the ruling family committed a crime against the law by following the dictates of their hearts. Archduke Franz Ferdinand's sons lost the right to succeed their father on the throne because he had married for love. Even the lowly, living in the shadow of the Court, were raised high. Viennese youths envied the position of His Majesty's coachman and of the imperial forester.

The army, too, was "imperial and royal," and its officers held a privileged position. They far outranked public officials and enjoyed a social distinction which was the envy of civilians.

Their resplendent uniforms enhanced their value in the love and marriage markets. The Hungarian Huszár officer's gold braid would have put to shame the operetta uniforms of glittering French comedies. Visiting army officers were often invited to the Imperial Ball, which provided them with a subject of conversation for life.

Next in line came the *Staatsbeamter*, the public official of a vast and intricate bureaucracy. His social position was much higher, even though his income was much lower, than that of an industrialist. The magic prefixes of "K.K."—imperial-royal —to which he was entitled, made him a member of a privileged class. He, too, reflected the glory of an august Court. Most of his compensation was not in money, but in the respect of his neighbors for a man who was part of the government.

These privileged classes comprised, of course, only a small part of Vienna's population. It may seem unjust to dismiss the rank and file with a few words, but the hard-working technicians behind the scenes do not get even a small share of the recognition which the public showers on the featured player. The bulk of the Viennese lived and loved, struggled and fell, as the rank and file does always the world over. Some of them tried to climb higher; few of them succeeded, since life was constricted into the mold of a strict caste system. Privilege was jealous to retain its position by monopolizing the good things of life. The average Viennese usually had as much as he needed to live, sometimes a little more, sometimes a little less. He was the mass-man, *Massenmensch,* and sometimes he was saved from despair by apathy.

The World War changed the social stratifications of Viennese life. The Court was gone, its members voluntary exiles except for those who renounced their titles. A young ex-Archduke became an auto-mechanic and another one found a job as a clerk. Some of them were involved in money scandals, but none of them distinguished himself. They may have been unable to adjust themselves to a new mode of life so speedily, or they lacked ability. If they had become rulers, some of them might have given good accounts of themselves and might have been hailed as noble and wise.

Disgusted with the new age, the aristocracy retired into its palaces, its revenue greatly diminished. It is slowly dying out. Some of its members took refuge in the more congenial atmosphere of England and the South of France. The Austrian army was reduced by Allied command to a force of 30,000, about one-twentieth of its former number, and it could have no use for most of the former officers. Many of them had a hunted look as they watched the busy life of the city hungrily. Most of the former public officials shared their fate, as the tiny Republic of 6,000,000 inhabitants could accommodate only a small part of the civil service of an Empire which once boasted a 53,000,000 population. The rank and file Viennese were divided into two classes after the War, depending upon their political allegiance. The majority of them were Socialists, and theirs was the city government until the Fascists came. "Red Vienna" had many enemies, more friends. It gave an honest and efficient administration and was moderate. Not all were of the same view, however, and the latter called Vienna "Bolshevist," which certainly was far from the truth. But in such matters it is not truth that people seek, and the result was satisfactory to them, because the Austrian countryside could be aroused against the "Reds."

Members of the Christian Social Party belonged in the other

group. With them the accent was on the Church, which had a strong hold on Austria. They were willing to permit the rich man to keep all he had, while trying to induce him to be kind to the poor. The two parties had a fairly good time attacking each other, while, at the same time, injecting the proper dose of *Gemuetlichkeit* into their quarrels.

The life of the Viennese in the heyday of the capital had more leisure and probably less work than in other cities of its size. The *Heuriger* and the café were two institutions that gave the Queen City of the Danube its stamp. When leaves were beginning to pale under the Autumn sun, bundles of hay on poles were displayed on the street front of the taverns. Most of them were—and many of them still are—on the outskirts, at the foot of the Vienna Woods, in a setting for the gods. The pole with the hay was an invitation for lovers of new wine to enjoy it in the taverns. *Heuriger* was Vienna's vernacular for new wine. In the mellow air of tavern gardens Viennese joviality had a field day. Even if that man in the hunting costume was the Crown Prince himself he would have been a killjoy had he refused to join in the merry-making. Social divisions were discarded and all became high priests of Bacchus. The more guests there were the higher soared their joy.

The cafés of Vienna have a long tradition. According to popular belief, the retreating armies of the Sultan left behind them a bag of coffee beans in the seventeenth century. Vienna took up the coffee-drinking habit not merely for the sake of the beverage, but also because it meant, since the earliest days, a feeling of camaraderie for its devotees. The cafés on the Danube Canal became social and political centers. It was here that the Viennese hatched the plots which overthrew Metternich.

Today cafés are nearly as numerous in Vienna as drug stores in New York. Their terraces help the curious to while away time by watching street scenes. Under Hitler's rule, however, cafés are going into eclipse. "Life must be heroic," says the militant Nazi. Before this change, a man was merely expected to be happy. Every type of day-dreamer, every purse had its café. Everyone was expected to have a *Stammtisch,* favorite table, to which one was expected to be as loyal as to one's Fatherland. Horse-dealers and, later, auto salesmen had their cafés, and so had journalists —the renowned *Herrenhof.* Political plotters from all over the Danube area met in the Café Imperial. The Hungarians had their favorite meeting places, and so had the Croats, Poles, Serbians, Roumanians, Albanians and other nations. The Socialists had theirs and so had the Fascists.

Guests transacted business, made love, wrote books. Mothers cast nets for daughters' prospective husbands; young men looked for mates, permanent and temporary, for social contacts, jobs, or for a rich American to help them save the world. Coffee was also drunk in the cafés. It had a variety of names, depending upon its strength and the proportion of milk: *Schale Gold,* a cup of gold; "black and white"; *"mélange"; "Natur."* Timid talkers could have music for their background. *Herr Ober,* the headwaiter, saw to it that glasses of fresh water would always be on the guests' table. He knew whether you were a member of the reading sect, and what papers you liked. In short, Vienna's cafés were clubs, reading rooms, forums, lecture halls, plotters' havens, and public drawing rooms.

Since it was Nature that made Vienna and not a despot's whim, it was natural that it should have been a Roman fort. Its present and its Roman names, *Vindobona,* have given rise to speculation, and on this question many doctor's dissertations have been written. To complicate matters even more, the Hungarians call the city *Bécs,* which seems to indicate Slavic origin. Serious students seem to agree, more or less (unless they are Nazis) that Vienna (Wien) is a Slavic word, derived from old Czech or Slovak and that it means "by the water," a reference to the Danube. Nazis do not like this explanation, which would give the Slavs a prior claim to the gate in the Danube valley.

The Roman era, when Vienna garrisoned a cohort of archers, showed already that the masters of this gap in the hills were masters of the Danube valley. The fertile plains of the North invited Roman greed, and the gold and ore of the lower reaches of the Danube were standing temptations. However, the early history of the town need not detain us long. Many of its pages are left blank; Vienna must have been in a No Man's Land, between the end of the Western and beginning of the Eastern world.

It re-entered history when Rudolph of Habsburg made it the capital of his dynasty and thereby gave evidence of political perspicacity. Vienna was to become the Rome on the Danube, the most important capital of Europe. The Habsburg capital grew, keeping step with the importance of the Empire. "The city is friendly and attractive," wrote a visiting Spaniard of the early sixteenth century. "There is no lack of society, for people stream in from everywhere, from Bohemia and her dependencies, from Silesia, from Hungary and from neighboring Italy."

Hans Sachs, hero of the *Meistersinger,* sang:

> *"Vienna, the great, broad, crowded town,*
> *Girded by stone walls all around. . . ."*

A schoolmaster with more ambition than ability exulted:

"When first the Town dawned on my eyes
Methought I was in Paradise."

That was not the view of the Viennese when the Grand Vizier Kara Mustapha led his army of a quarter of a million up to the very walls of their city in 1683. A previous attack of the Turk had failed a quarter of a century earlier, but this time Islam seemed determined to storm this bastion of the West. The Christian powers were divided, and French and Italian experts assisted the Turk in the siege. If the Sultan should be able to obtain a foothold, he could push onward into Germany. The eternal craving of the East for the conquest of the West might then have been satisfied.

The forces of defense were led by Count Ernst Ruediger von Starhemberg, ancestor of Dollfuss' rival. The crowded city offered an admirable target to the enemy. Dysentery wrought havoc with the population. So furious was the Turks' onslaught and so panicky was Vienna that sentiment counseled surrender. The Count urged the people of the capital on to a crusade, and where exhortation failed the headman's ax carried conviction.

The Janizaries were a frightful sight, and their battle-cry sent cold shivers down the burghers' spines: "Be merciful to the infidel dog and burn in Gehenna!" Evidently they did not want to take any such chances. But this time the conscience of the West was aroused. John III (Sobieski), King of Poland, was an ally of the Austrian ruler and it was for political rather than religious reasons that he threw his support to Vienna's defenders. There is a tendency now to romanticize about him as a seventeenth-century crusader, defender of the Western world.

148

It must not be forgotten, however, that for forty years previously he did nothing to keep back the advancing Turks. Rather, he helped them by his constant plottings against the Polish crown, until he succeeded in taking it himself.

The relieving army of the Polish King came from the direction of the Vienna Woods, and it was a question whether it could reach the plains in time to save the defenders from the final offensive. In the last minute, the generalship of the over-confident Grand Vizier failed. There seemed to be no doubt that his would be the victory when the Turkish forces inadvertently swept the hesitating John III into battle. In endless streams the forests disgorged the allied soldiers. The Turks began to stampede, and Vienna was saved. The Islamic myth was broken, and soon Hungary was relieved. The entire middle reaches of the Danube were purged of the Turks.

Never again was Vienna in such danger. Now an era of growth began. She was improving in looks, too, according to the standards of the age. The houses of the well-to-do were five or six stories high, an English diplomat's wife wrote, shared by as many families; their apartments were magnificent, composed of eight or ten large rooms, all inlaid with mosaics, the doors and windows richly carved, and furnished, such as was seldom seen even in kings' palaces. The apartments were adorned with hangings of the finest Brussels tapestry, prodigious mirrors framed in silver, Japanese tables, rich Genoa damask window curtains. The whole was made gay by pictures, vast porcelain jars and large lusters of rock crystal. The meals were Gargantuan, sometimes fifty dishes of meat, served on silver, and as many as eighteen kinds of wines. The English Lady found the women ugly, carrying a prodigious burden of false hair, and a

149

fabric of gauze, a yard high, consisting of three or four layers, and countless yards of heavy ribbon.

An English aristocrat of the eighteenth century, Lady Vernon Lee, found Vienna a mixture of French elegance and levity, Spanish solemnity and vacuity, Hungarian pride and love of display, Oriental splendor and misery, and Italian love of art. The common folk amused themselves by seeing robbers and murderers broken on the wheel. Dogs tore bulls to pieces in the grand circus and horses were eviscerated. Vienna was described as a perfectly balanced specimen of an unbalanced eighteenth-century German court—a mixture of refinement and bigotry, vice and pomp. Questions of etiquette were of deadly importance. Two coaches met in a narrow street at night, her Ladyship recorded, but their occupants were unable to decide which should go back. They were determined to die on the spot rather than yield. They sat there till two in the morning, and the street would not have been cleared until their deaths if the Emperor had not sent his guard to part them. "And even then they refused to stir, till the expedient could be found out of taking them both in chairs, exactly in the same moment. After the ladies were agreed, it was with some difficulty that the *pas* was decided between the two coachmen, no less tenacious of their rank than their ladies."

In his *Biography of a Bygone City,* Henry Dwight Sedgwick gives credit to Emperor Leopold for having helped Vienna become the musical center of the world. "He made all his dependents learn music," he quotes Lady Vernon Lee. "He sent his little Archduchess, Maria Theresa, onto a miniature stage, when she was still an infant. . . . He accompanied Farinelli on the harpsichord, and well nigh gave singing lessons to the greatest of the living singers." The very same little Archduchess became a great Queen in due time. The statues of Gluck, Haydn and Mozart are in the niches of her monument, facing the Burg.

The golden age of Viennese music was approaching. Gluck was so successful that he never had to go hungry. That was not Mozart's good fortune; he gave lessons and wrote immortal music. He was perhaps the most gifted human being that ever was born. Yet he had to write on his death-bed: "I have come to an end before having had the enjoyment of my talent." The royalties of American broadcasting companies on his compositions performed in one year would have given him luxury and ease.

Coming between the two, Joseph Haydn had his ups and downs, playing in the gutter and composing in a garret, where his jug of water froze in Winter. Luckily, he found an aristocratic patron who made him sign the following provisions, among others: "He must be temperate, and not show himself overbearing toward his musicians, but mild and lenient, straightforward and self-controlled." He and members of his orchestra were to appear at performances in white stockings, white linen, powdered and either with a pig-tail or a tie-wig. He was also to abstain from vulgarity in eating, drinking and conversation. . . . "The said Joseph Heyden [the name was misspelled] shall appear in the Prince's antechamber daily, before and after mid-day, and inquire whether His Highness is pleased to order a performance of the orchestra."

Haydn stayed with His Highness for thirty years. He was mild, wore his uniform, abstained from vulgarity and had plenty to eat. He also composed music, including the oratorio and the Austrian national anthem, not to mention many other immortal pieces, in all of which he displayed a spirit entirely "free from vulgarity."

A cross-eyed young man, ugly, brooding, dark and short, was to make his name in Vienna and also to help the capital make its name resound throughout the world. He was Ludwig van Beethoven, an inscrutable creature, about whom a society lady wrote: "When he visited us, he generally put his head in at the door before entering, to see if there were anyone present whom he did not like. . . . His face was red, covered with pockmarks, his hair quite dark. His dress was very common. . . . He spoke with a strong provincial accent; his manner of expression was slightly vulgar; his general bearing showed no signs of culture, and his behavior was unmannerly."

By this time music was Vienna's great passion. The most celebrated Austrian general of his time, Archduke Charles who fought Napoleon, carried a spinet in his luggage and listened to Haydn's music the night before the battle. "The Emperor at the end of his business day took part with his chamberlains and aide-de-camp in a violin concert." A distinguished piano virtuoso admitted to a friend that in Vienna there were a hundred ladies —all amateurs—who played better than he did.

Twice the armies of Napoleon advanced upon Vienna. The second time the Austrian Emperor gave orders to resist the French. A rain of fire descended upon the moats and walls, and a cry went up from the population that the treasures of many centuries would be ruined. Bombs fell close to Haydn's house, Schubert was in the choir school, and Beethoven in the cellar. The guns were moved into Haydn's little garden, and from there hundreds of shots were fired into Vienna. The old composer's servants were frightened out of their wits, but Haydn got out of his invalid's chair and admonished them: "Why this terror? Know that no disaster can come where Haydn is." But the excitement was too much for him. He was carried to bed and three weeks later he was dead.

It was from Vienna that little Marie Louise, daughter of the Austrian Emperor, left for Paris to marry the Corsican "ogre." It was to Vienna that she returned with Napoleon's son into a world dominated by Prince Metternich. "He is a very amiable man," Napoleon had said of the Prince, "and he talks well, but he lies always; one can lie once, twice, three times, but one cannot lie always." Because Metternich did that, he earned his reputation as a great statesman. People admired him because he was as wicked as they would have liked to be.

After his fall, the swing to the Left was short-lived, as it always is. But while it lasted, the spirit of 1848 stirred hopes of a better social order. Youth was swept away by its own noise and the vernal urge. Bonfires were burned, street lamps smashed, torches carried in parades. Vienna was ready to welcome Utopia; the imperial court got its coaches ready and departed for the north. But noise and ardor win batles less easily than cannons. The revolutionaries of 1848 lacked the latter. The imperial army swept back the revolters; reaction returned, and, after having punished the little man for his big dreams, gave him most of what he had wanted. It could afford to do so, since this was only a fraction of what was due him. When the smoke of the cannon had lifted, a novelist overheard a man of the street talking to his wife: "Wife, do you know what I should like above all things? I long like a child to hear a little good music again."

Meanwhile Franz Joseph had been given the throne of his uncle, Emperor Ferdinand, a high-grade moron. This had been the wish of the House of Austria no less than that of the ex-monarch, who was as much afraid of cannon as of men. Franz Joseph spent most of his eighty-six years in Vienna. When he took the throne, a Roman Senator, come to life, would have found scant cause to marvel at what he saw. But what would he have said three score years later when the Capuchin Church received the remains of the "last Caesar"?

During his reign Vienna was growing rapidly and became the beautiful city it is today. But it was growing less rapidly than Berlin and Budapest, and that was a portent. On the battlefield of Koeniggraetz Austria was beaten by Prussia in a war which lasted only a few weeks. To us it is only one of the many wars that seem a casual part of the European scene. But to people living in 1866 it must have appeared an event of tremendous importance. Was it really possible that the upstart Hohenzollerns of Prussia should have beaten the most powerful dynasty of the world, and with such ease? This beating was against all rules—an infraction of the divine order that the strong should always be strong and never the weak shall rise. This meant too that Prussia was taking the lead in the unification of Germany, while the Habsburgs were to look after their Danube valley. Vienna had to make her peace with the Hungarians, who now became nominal partners in the Austro-Hungarian monarchy. That is why Berlin and Budapest eclipsed the Austrian capital.

The Viennese aristocracy was moving into the country. It considered itself partly responsible for the defeat, was shamed and humiliated. Lost wars must have their scapegoats. The aristoc-

154

racy had received much of the credit for Austrian success and had to bear the blame.

In the face of adversity, the natural characteristics of the Viennese were accentuated. In the rôle of Wotan they had failed, while that of Hans Sachs, the mastersinger, fitted them to perfection. Now they could afford to indulge in their love of music, to take things easy. *"Kann man nichts machen"*—nothing doing—became Vienna's watchword. Smiling cities are apt to lose the vigor of their muscles. Vienna did not know that she was on the down grade. Could life be mellower and laughter more spontaneous than Vienna's was at the turn of the century? It was the golden age of the Danube valley. All had work, and music was being played everywhere. Vienna whirled to the tunes of Johann Strauss and entertained tourists from all parts of the globe. They came to see the habitat of music and gaiety. The future cast no shadows on the path of man. For a long time there had been no war, and with the interconnection of financial interests and the growth of civilization this menace was thought to have been banished. It was with the abandon of the carefree that young couples were dancing around in the *Heuriger* taverns of the Vienna Woods. Time was moving on. The first horseless carriage aroused some hilarity on the Ring, especially since it made a tremendous racket but little headway. Then the people of the capital resigned themselves to these buzzing contraptions. The French Channel flyer, Louis Blériot, paid a visit to Vienna with his airplane and was cheered. But the guard was changed in the courtyard of the *Burg,* as it had been changed for longer than man remembered.

The newspapers printed ominous dispatches about troubles in the Balkans, but one was far more interested in football than in this dry stuff. Besides, all the world was familiar with the bad name of the Balkans. Then the newspapers reported the murder of the Serbian King and Queen, and even the most ardent sport fans had to take notice. Yet Vienna was a cozy place, growing more beautiful every year, and it was a pleasure to live. Emperor Franz Joseph was in the *Hofburg,* although he spent much of his time in the Schoenbrunn castle, but that, too, was in the capital. The Habsburgs were there, as they have always been and as they always would be. A world without them could not be even conceived.

Gradually, newspaper stories from the Balkans forced themselves upon the attention even of the most indifferent. War broke out between the Turks and their former subjects south of the Danube. At café tables in Vienna people were beginning to take sides. Some of them suggested that it was time their country made some order in that junk closet of the world. Others were more interested in football, and all were interested in the waltz. Few people noticed that lights were burning late in the Foreign Office.

Then the Archduke and his wife were murdered in Sarajevo. Vienna was precipitated into the center of world events. She issued the first ultimatum and the first declaration of war. Her statesmen head the list of war criminals. They went blindly into the disaster from which there was no return for man. The city of music became the city of death. War came and with it long lines in front of the bakers' shops. Vienna was on the verge of starvation, and the conscience of the world was aroused. For the sake of Schubert and Mozart, Beethoven and Strauss, for the sake of Vienna's charm, the sins of Count Berchthold, the man who sent the ultimatum and the declaration of war, were forgotten. But Vienna never recovered from this blow. Never was she to become her former self. She still attracted admirers from all parts of the world, but Vienna's smile was sad and when visitors praised the famous *Gemuetlichkeit* they merely quoted text-books. This is how Vienna lived until the German army took possession of the *Burg* in the Fuehrer's name. Cities do not die overnight; they decline. No matter what will be done for Vienna, she can never be what she was. Her streets resound with the tramping of Nazi boots. Once the capital of the world, today she is a German provincial town.

4. The Danube Greets the Slav

$\mathscr{P}$AST Vienna the Danube flows and past the Hungarian Gate. The Little Carpathians close in upon it from the north. The Vienna-Budapest steamer approaches a spur, crowned by the ruins of the former royal palace. We are approaching Bratislava, capital of Slovakia, at present a satellite State of Germany. For two hundred and fifty years it was the capital of the Hungarian Kingdom. Then its name was Pozsony. More than a third of her population is German, and they call it Pressburg. The three names reflect the confusion at this point in the Danube valley, where Germans, Hungarians and Slavs meet.

Now the Germans are left behind, although they reappear in language "islands" over much of the middle basin. The North Slavs, too, disappear, as if afraid of the open plains, and are concentrated in the mountains lost in the northern haze. Here we are in the heart of the Little Hungarian Plain, inhabited by the Magyars. This was the frontier of Czechoslovakia for twenty years, all this and all the way to Esztergom, where the Danube turns south. The river was a strategical frontier and not, as social scientists say, an ethnographical one. The Czechs asked for it at the Peace Conference for the protection of their newly born country. They got it because three supermen were in a generous mood and gave away freely the ex-enemy's land.

Czechoslovakia was a Danubian country only because the river was her southern boundary. She was broken up into Bohemia and Moravia, which German troops occupied in March, 1939, and Slovakia, which was temporarily allowed a semblance of independence. The two former are not on the Danube and the latter has merely a window on the river at Bratislava. The rivers of Bohemia and Moravia are mostly tributaries of the Elbe and Oder, which flow into the North Sea and the Baltic. The rivers of Slovakia, on the other hand, are tributaries of the Danube. Yet Bohemia and Moravia could not be left out of a book about Central Europe's principal river. For three hundred years they were part of the Habsburg Empire, and for a longer time they were in the orbit of Vienna.

"Whoever is master of Bohemia is master of Europe," Prince Bismarck said long ago. Bohemia cuts across the vital arteries leading into the Danube valley. "The Bohemian basin," writes Colonel Emanuel Moravec, a Czech military authority, "represented from ancient times an extensive fortress which defended the Danubian area against pressure from the northeast, and at the same time protected the northwest of Central Europe from pressure issuing from the south and the southeast." Through her Moravian Gate the Oder opens the eastern German plains to the Czech highlands. Through the historic Uzhok Pass, farther east, the Avars, Huns, Magyars and Tatars thrust into the Danube valley. Bohemia lies athwart the highways leading into the Slavic world. "Bohemia is a salient into the heart of Germany," Nazis said. "In a few minutes swift Czech planes could bomb our annual Party Congress at Nuremberg, where all our leaders are assembled on a platform." Bohemia's fate was decided.

Czechoslovakia as she existed until the Autumn of 1938 was about the size of the State of Arkansas, and had about 15,000,000 people. Nature lavishly stocked her hills and plains with wealth. Her black soil was of the best, her industries large, her armament and shoe factories had few equals. Her chemicals, metallurgy, sugar and textiles ranked high. She had the largest coal mines in Central Europe, and her mineral wealth was the envy of "have-not" nations. She possessed about 75 per cent of the late Austro-Hungarian Empire's key industries. The shape of the country should be remembered—an elongated sausage. In the north she was protected by the Sudeten mountains, a name made famous in history because of the great betrayal. This chain of hills gave its name to the 3,500,000 German inhabitants of the country, occupying, for the most part, the heights overlooking the central plains. Bohemians, Moravians and Slovaks are all Slavs, and in an hour or two you can travel from the one to the other. Yet the Slovaks live in another age; between the Bohemians and Moravians the difference is small. The Bohemians, including the Moravians, engage our attention briefly, and the Slovaks even more so. They may help us to understand the problems of the Danube region.

Take, for instance, the village of Zhor, a Bohemian-Moravian "Middletown" (Czech, if you prefer, since both are the same).

160

A Simple Village

It lies on the boundary of Bohemia and Moravia, in a country neither very hilly nor very plain, neither too rich nor too poor, but uniformly beautiful. It is near the town of Ceska Trebova, about three hours by train from Prague, west from there. The village can be reached by bus; it has no railway connection. It hugs a winding road and its bypaths shoot off into waving fields of wheat and rye. Under its bower of oak and beech, Zhor, in normal times, is a picture of peace. In the reflection of the rich foliage, the white and light-blue houses provide a color symphony. Their tiles and slate look shyly through the tremulous green. Small mansard windows wink drowsily in the transparent blue of the air. The wooden ties connecting the pillars of the older houses with their roofs have seen at least a century roll by. The protruding roofs seek to give protection against sudden squalls. The windows of the houses are wreathed with flowers. The barbed iron fences are reminders of the days when the Czech village was under Habsburg rule.

The scene is dominated by the school, which would not be out of place in a rural district of the English-speaking world. The whirr of the threshing machine is heard in a nearby field. An ox-team treads the path to the loft, piled high with hay. Swallows scuttle back and forth from their mud-nest. The lark shoots into the air. In lisping Czech, the farmer exhorts the horse Jancu to go along. About thirty per cent of the Czechs are farmers, and the number of those engaged in forestry and agricultural industries is large. Indeed the typical Czech is represented as a farmer, and as such he has been immortalized in song and story.

He is the westernmost representative of the race which spreads for nearly 7,000 miles to the east, as far as the Pacific. His hair is light and he is a little above medium height. If it were not for

161

the strong Slavic nose it would not be easy to tell the Czech and Bavarian apart. Their women began not long ago to cultivate the modish line through sports and diet. Hundreds of thousands of them were members of the vast gymnastic association, the Sokols. The Czech farmer is literate and articulate. He is not a peasant, in the sense the word is used in Central Europe, but a *sedlak*, settler, who would not feel out of place in a farming community of the United States. His hands are skillful, and if machinery is not more widely seen it is because the farmer's holdings are small.

Until 1919 more than forty per cent of the land in old Bohemia belonged to large estate owners. In that year the Czechs began to break up these holdings and give them to the landless. When Czechoslovakia lost her independence, the average size of farms was fifteen acres. The soil is of the best in this part of Europe and it is cultivated nearly as intensely as Denmark's. In addition to the more usual crops, the Czech farmer cultivated and exported sugar beet, flax, hemp, poppies, caraway, currants.

The village craftsman is in a class by himself. The old Austro-Hungarian monarchy knew him as a jack-of-all-trades. Even today large numbers of Czech tailors and shoemakers, whose background is the village green, may be found in such over-critical foreign cities as Vienna and Dresden. "The national genius reveals itself in painstaking work," a native student of Czech character says, "rather than in flights of fancy." The country's greatest men were organizers, such as Thomas Garrigue Masaryk, nation-builder and first President, although Smetana's music stirs deep emotions and Capek's fantasies are profound. You associate the Slav with individual brilliance and collective dullness. That Russian of the Tolstoy novels knew all the answers to all the questions, except to the one as to how to make a living. He probably had brilliant theories about the universe and garbage collection, but did not know how to fill the job of a bank clerk. In conversation he must have been a most delightful person, but the most deadly person to work with.

The Czech is unlike this typical Slav. He has lived in such close proximity with the German that he has acquired his thoroughness and efficiency. Often he lacks a sense of humor. Compare him this time not with a Slav, but with the Hungarian, in the Middle-Danube regions, who works less well, but laughs better. Outsiders prefer the latter's company and find him delightful. The average Czech is more human, as shown by his superior social institutions, hospitals and orphan asylums. The Hungarian takes with condescension, as if he were giving, when the Czech often appears to be taking when he is giving. He had to take orders so long that he lost boldness and self-confidence. In order to compensate for his lack of these qualities he is often over-assertive.

It was during the last Summer of Czechoslovakia that a world-famous English author told me on the terrace of the Café Ambassador of Prague, while tens of thousands of young Sokols were marching in front of it: "I have never known the Czechs were so nationalistic." This was no compliment on the lips of this Left-wing democrat, lover of the Czechs and hater of the Nazis. Let me give you another illustration about the way this spirit worked, not throwing stones at a nation's tomb, but in order better to understand the greatest disaster of the Danube valley.

Take the case of the General Post Office in Prague, with which every visiting tourist is familiar. It had no inscription in any foreign language, although Prague attracted many visitors, and a Frenchman or Englishman could hardly be expected to understand the language of such a small country. The Czechs did not want to be impolite, but if they had employed English inscriptions, for instance, they would also have had to use German signs. This would have been fully justified in the capital of a country with so large a German minority, but the Czechs were afraid it might be taken as a sign of weakness.

The Czechs treated their minorities—Germans, Hungarians, Jews, Roumanians, Ukrainians—better than any other nation in the Danube valley. They gave them better schools, parliamentary representation and the right to use their languages. The minorities had their own nationals in the government. The Czech leaders were open-minded, conscious of their obligations. But the results show that the minorities did not appreciate this liberality. The Czechs' neighbors, the Poles, employed opposite methods. They suppressed the minorities and deprived them of their rights, and yet, so far at least, there is an independent Poland. Minorities are touchy and they can more easily forgive persecution than inconvenience. The persecutor's argument is the whip, which all the world understands, but a democratic government employs persuasion, which presupposes full equality. The fact that some postmasters in the German section spoke bad German counted more against the Czechs than if they had purged the Sudeten agitators. The lower officials' policy of pin-pricks enraged the minorities, which took Czech concessions for signs of weakness.

Let us now continue our visit to the typical Czech village before it lost its independence. It had only a couple of public officials. The elder, *starosta,* had been selected by his neighbors because of his seasoned views. He knew the world, having spent several years in old Austria, and his opinions were listened to with respect. He solved contentious problems with matter-of-fact simplicity. The local policeman, like the elder, was a half-time farmer. It would have been difficult to give details about his constabulary duties. There was no need for a lockup in the village; the nearest one was in town. The Czech language does not lend itself to effective shouting, and brawls were rare. Chance vagrants were not frequent, and the self-discipline of the rural folk took care of the local ordinances.

"The peasant's life is a round of griefs," the folk tune says, "but he bears his burdens lightly." His life all the Summer day is in the fields which extend to his very windows. At night he returns to his supper, the traditional *knoedel,* dumpling, served with kraut. He eats meat, too, perhaps even roast goose, a favorite dish. A tall glass of Pilsen beer, brewed in this very country, helps him appreciate his food.

Social life is for the most confined to the family. Czech village life has its roots in the *zadruga,* the family community. Kinsmen form a round table. Common interests and traditions hold them together as they talk over their problems in the light of an electric lamp, a recent acquisition. For more ambitious occasions the Inn of the Crown provides the proper setting. There the villagers used to indulge in their favorite pastime: political discussion. The majority of the local farmers belonged to the Agrarian Party, a minority were Socialists. One or two of those present liked to call themselves Communists. The twoscore of parliamentary parties which dotted the political landscape might have differed on all minor points; they strongly agreed on the need of national defense. In that respect the Communists held particularly vehement opinions. It was not because of them that Czechoslovakia was lost.

Leisure plays a rôle in the village, as life goes on and sorrow is numbed. Since the place is too small for a movie house of its own, the young ones take the bus to town, where they treat themselves to Hollywood super-colossals of two years ago. Else they must wait until the ambulant cinema calls on its fortnightly rounds. On such nights the setting of the movie tent evokes memories of circus days. Rural festivals belong largely to the past, except for church feasts in certain parts of the country and a few remnants of traditional merry-making. Choral music is the farmer's great favorite, but the radio has all but displaced home-made music. "By its tunes thou shalt judge a nation," Karl Capek used to say. In normal times the Czech countryside and town were enchanted by a blend of Vienna waltz, with a hint of German march, and Slavic nostalgia for the unknown.

In the thoughts of the Czech village the totalitarian State was associated with oppression. The introduction of the totalitarian system has not changed this opinion, except that it has driven it underground. Rural philosophy rejected the idea of the Fuehrer and deemed the totalitarian State a denial of human rights. "The Czech farmer is an inveterate individualist," the late President Masaryk said. "His respect for human life is too profound to make him yield to tyranny. He is eager to form a part of a State that makes him free, and not one that enslaves him." His patriotic excesses were explained by the ex-President: "The unused energies of hundreds of years accumulated in our nationalists and sought an outlet. This may explain the excesses of some of our friends after the great change came."

For the Czech farmer nationalism sprang from an instinctive devotion to the soil. An atavistic memory kept him informed about the long struggle for self-realization under the Habsburg rule. This new country of his enabled him to work his own land.

The Struggle of German and Slav

He knew that it was coveted by Germany. "We shall not surrender!" was written as a permanent slogan on the blackboard of the village school. "*Nedame se!*" They were surrendered with no chance to fight for themselves. Their supposed friends delivered them to the Germans.

The Czechs have two histories, depending upon the nationality of the historian. Their history, written by Germans, seeks to show that the aborigines of the Bohemian plains were Teutons and that the Slavs were later comers, pushed into this promised land of wheat and coal by the westward pressure of Asiatic tribes. Czech history, on the other hand, says that the original inhabitants of the plains were Slavs and that the Germans began to come, first, as missionaries and, later, as merchants.

No matter what version of history we accept, this part of the Danube valley has for centuries witnessed the struggle of German and Slav. When Ottakar the Bohemian fought Rudolph the Habsburg, he probably did not realize that he was fighting the cause of the Slavs. He was interested in power for himself and for his dynasty, rather than in the vast Slavic race. When the Czechs were preparing to get rid of the Habsburg rule some seven centuries later, they consciously embraced the Pan-Slav cause. Many of their leaders wanted to march with Russia, in spite of ideological differences, because the "big cousin" seemed to be in a position to support the Slavic race on the Danube. If the Czechs could have depended upon an extended Slavic hinterland, they might have ousted the Germans from both Bohemia and the Vienna Gate. They lost the battle at the end of the tenth century when the legendary Árpád of the Magyars beat the legendary Svatopluk of the Slavs in the Middle-Danube valley and

167

paved the way for Hungary. The Magyars thus introduced a wedge between the North and South Slavs, and the Czechs were delivered to the Germans' tender mercies.

Recent events can be best understood if we keep the basic facts in mind. In this millennial struggle the Slavs have been pressing westward and the Germans eastward. The former had some of the best soil of Europe, but were landlocked, while the latter had access to the sea, but lacked soil. The Ice-Age glaciers, which corroded the Nordic land, deposited rich debris on Slavic land. The struggle was not decided overnight. The Slavs were victorious first, their history tells us, although the Germans deny their claim. But there is the eloquent evidence of the names of such towns as Buckow, Lankwitz, Rudow, Spandau, Teltow—Berlin's suburbs. Then there are the Slavic Wends a few miles southeast of the German capital, vestigial remains of the eastern tide.

The Slavs might have triumphed if they had not lacked a fundamental quality. They might have been able to prevent the Magyars from pushing into the Middle Danube area and, later, prevented them from taking root, had they not lacked the capacity for organization and self-government. The Russian steppes were first organized by the Norsemen of Rurik. For three hundred years they were under the rule of the Tatar Golden Horde. Peter the Great went to the West for his ideas of statecraft. Catherine the Great was a German. The Baltic Germans played a leading rôle in the government of pre-War Russia. The Russians made an effort, which was not always conscious, to set up a Pan-Slavic State. They subjugated the Poles, Ukrainians, Lithuanians, White Russians, but they spent themselves in the tremendous struggle to push to the Pacific Ocean and to reach the warm waters of the Mediterranean via the Straits. They built up a country comprising

one-sixth of the earth's land surface not because of their organizing ability, but because the Far East was exhausted and they were
the only ones to take the land.

Besides, the Russians developed a dynastic-religious-national
autocracy of the most exclusive kind. Their Czar was first in
command on earth, second in command in heaven. He yielded
first place to God merely because He had no army and, therefore,
could not be a serious rival. But he was stronger than He, because
the Czar needed no thunderstorm to strike blasphemy dead.

All the time the Germans were pushing eastward. Their Teutonic Knights took the Baltic coast, fighting the pagan Prussians
for the greater glory of God. They were missionaries before God,
but empire-builders before history. They probably did not know
that they were fighting not for Christ but for the German race.
Any such admission would have been sacrilege.

When Frederick the Great took a large part of Poland he
merely pursued the policy of the Teutonic Knights. His Prussia
was the successor of the fighting Order—a Prussia which no
longer wore the mask of religion. When William II forced
Communist Russia to sign the treaty of Brest-Litovsk in the last
year of the World War he, too, followed in the victorious footsteps of the Teutonic Order. The richest lands of the Ukraine,
most of Poland and the Baltic coast were to fall under German
control. The German was triumphant and his eastward march
continued.

A few months later the situation changed and Germany was
beaten. Now it was the turn of the Slav to forge onward and when
newly born Poland carved her access to the sea out of Germany's
living body, she merely followed historical precedent. Czechoslovakia was set up—a salient into the Reich. When Hitler took

the Czech's country in the Autumn of 1938 and the Spring of 1939, he followed the Teutonic Order, as Frederick the Great and William II had done. For the first time he discarded the religious pretexts of the Order and the nationalist ideas of the two monarchs. His Third Reich was set up as a race and not as a nation. It was to comprise all Germans, whether they belonged to Bohemia, Poland, Hungary, Russia and several other countries. It was to be super-national, even anti-national, which was more than the Communists could say of their country.

In the course of this struggle, the Germans acquired a militaristic spirit, but not so the Czechs. For the average German the "goose-step" is a philosophy of life, *Weltanschauung,* and not merely a parade-ground step. To him it represents unity, discipline, precision. He thrills to the rhythm of uniform movement. It makes him part of a machine, gives him the confidence of being in a herd. While the Czech has learned much from the German, he has not become militaristic. He would have betrayed his Slavic origin by surrendering his real nature. Nowhere did this difference strike me so forcefully as in Nuremberg, at the time of the Nazi Party Congress, and in Prague, at the time of the great Sokol festivals. In that year the Czechoslovak Republic died.

The spectacle in Nuremberg was indescribable, frightening. Imagine a hundred thousand men marching as if they were one. At a word of command, which sounded like the cracking of a whip, all these tens of thousands moved with the precision of the machine. Not one of them made a saving mistake. The most frightful part of it was that they seemed to enjoy it, if machines may be said to enjoy anything. This miracle of uniform movement was inspired, not human, but super- or even sub-human.

In the Masaryk Stadium of Prague a hundred thousand youths

participated in the Sokol gymnastic festivals. They were boys and girls, men and women, wearing blue trousers and red skirts, which ran into vast lines of color. Music gave them the cue and they began to move onward. They reacted to the tunes, as the flowers of a fairyland garden react to a gentle breeze. It was beautiful—the beauty of rhythm, of motion for a higher aim, of peace. . . . An invisible orchestra struck up a waltz and the vast field turned into a ball-room, two hundred thousand feet gently tapping the ground. This was Utopia, compared with Germany, and many eyes were moist with tears.

This was the doomed Czech Republic, the only successful democracy in the Danube valley. The Nazis could not tolerate its success. It would have been a reflection upon autocracy. Good is abhorrent to the vicious: it invites comparison, sets up higher standards. The German Fuehrer destroyed Bohemia, but permitted the formation of a State of the Slovaks, at least a hundred years behind the Czechs. The ape-man hates the superman. Bohemia could ask no higher compliment.

Bohemia's name is probably derived from the *Boii,* a Celtic race, said to have inhabited part of the land three thousand years ago. Historians are fond of the Celts. They can always be cited to explain what historians are otherwise at a loss to explain. We might as well leave them, because they are enwrapped in a mystery which ignorance has made more charming. We are more interested in the struggle between German and Slav, which began in the early years of the Christian era, when the Teutonic Marcomanni took the land. Several centuries elapsed before "forefather" Czech arrived with his Slavic tribesmen. One of his successors was Prince Samo, originally a merchant, who beat the enemies East and West, liberated slaves, punished the mean and rewarded the good. He was such an exemplary Prince, indeed, that his existence could be doubted if the Czechs did not insist that he had really lived. Libussa's name must not be omitted. She was a mythological Princess who ruled the country and founded "golden Prague," *Zlata Praha,* in which she displayed a shrewd taste, since the pleasing combination of river and hill makes it an unusual sight. One day she came across the beautiful peasant, Premysl, plowing his field. She married him. He became the founder of the Premyslid dynasty, which ruled over Bohemia for five hundred years, until the beginning of the fourteenth century. When the dynasty became extinct, power passed to the Luxembourg and later to the Habsburg family through the female line.

The struggle between Germans and Slavs took a decisive turn under Ottakar II, called the "Man of Gold" because of his wealth, and "Man of Iron," because of his might. From the Giant Mountains in Bohemia to Istria on the Adriatic he ruled with a strong hand. In the battle which he and Rudolph the Habsburg fought, history was made. What would have happened if some of the Bohemian nobles had not deserted their sovereign? Would the Czechs have become masters of the Danube valley? In spite of this setback, Bohemia remained a key country, her ruler an Elector of the Holy Roman Empire. "Nothing can be done in the world," was a contemporary saying, "without the help of God and the King of Bohemia."

It was in the thirteenth century, Czech historians tell us, that the Germans began to move in to Bohemia in large numbers, attracted by her increasing prosperity and the need to carry on export and import trade. Four centuries later more of them were

John Huss

to come, refugees from their native Germany. They settled in the mountains around Bohemia. There the enemy's march was impeded and the salubrious air was an ally of man against the plague. After the Habsburgs had taken the land, they settled on the soil deserted by the native aristocracy. This is why the Sudeten Germans occupy the heights overlooking the Bohemian plains and the "language islands," scattered throughout the land.

Let us return now for a moment to the martyrdom of John Huss, Rector of the University of Prague, and national hero of the Czechs. A century before Luther he wanted the Church purged of politics and corruption. His ideal was the religion of the early Christian, a creed of broad humanity, which recognized all men as equal before the throne of God. He wanted to return to the teachings of the Bible. Huss was not a reformer of doctrine and dogma, but an orthodox Catholic. His aim was to help the poor, impoverished by the exactions of an un-Christian clergy. Theirs was the law of God, and opposition to it was rank heresy. Huss preached that the sinful should not be obeyed, even though they were invested with authority. How could such men command the respect of their neighbors and be acceptable to God? "He who follows his lustful passions is an animal, but he who lives according to his reason is a reasonable man." The Archbishop of Prague alone owned some 400 towns and villages; the Church in Bohemia possessed one-third of the land.

The preachings of Huss were declared heretical. "The regularly appointed authorities must be obeyed, not because they are good but because they govern in virtue of the powers conferred upon them as representatives of the law." Authority is divine, this opposing camp held. Institutionalized virtue was set up against individual goodness. The holy offices are above man's weak-

173

nesses. If all were to judge if the Church was just, where would authority be?

The Emperor summoned Huss to the Council of Constance. He gave him a safe conduct, to have full freedom to defend his teachings, and be allowed safe return home. Huss had a foreboding and took leave of his disciples: "Should my death be to His glory and your welfare, may He accord it to me to face it without fear." Immediately upon his arrival in Constance, he was arrested by the Church authorities. The Emperor protested mildly against this violation of his promise, but the Council declared that heretics were beyond the pale of human law, and this argument could not be gainsaid. Huss' crime was heinous; he had dared to utter an obvious truth. " 'Tis better to be vanquished speaking the truth," he admonished his judges, "than vanquished lying." In his jail he wrote: "Many dogs have surrounded me, many spoke angrily against me without any reason. Instead of taking care of me, they robbed me and repaid with evil my kind deeds and with hate my love of them."

It was on a July morning in 1415 that he was burned at the stake. "His truthful voice had to be burned out of this world," Thomas Carlyle said.

Huss had no idea when he preached that he was a Czech national hero. His tragic fate aroused his countrymen and the Hussite wars followed. John Huss became the father of Czech nationalism. "Truth wins," *Pravda vitezi*, became the battlecry of the Czechs.

History also remembers the name of John Zizka of the Chalice, leader of the Hussites, because his religion meant more to him than the recital of prayers and the acceptance of dogmas. The

174

war was on against the "Romanists." It was not merely a religious war, but a national and social conflict, one of the first of its kind. Zizka signed himself "Chief of the Taborites, in the hope of God," and his soldiers were "God's Warriors," whom he addressed as "Dearest Brethren." This was another phase of the struggle between German and Slav. His enemies were the Germanic Princes. He fought them with his peasants, even women. Theirs was to be a religious democracy, patterned after the early Christians. His enemies carried church banners to battle. On both sides the Hussite wars were cruel, conforming to the pattern of religious wars. The enemy was the devil, and it was a good deed to rid the world of him. Out of this war grew the creed of the Bohemian Brethren, who reject all war, because Christ conquered by love and not by violence.

The Danube valley was to see the reshaping of a world. The most cruel conflict, probably, of many centuries was to start in Prague. The Reformation had swept Germany, but the Habsburgs in the Danube valley sought to stem the tide. The Church of Rome still exerted its magic and its influence penetrated the Danube basin across the Brenner Pass. Bohemia saw the danger signals and sought to draw closer to Hungarian and Pole. They were to form a united front against the Habsburgs, then extend their rule to most of the Danube valley. Little did the Czechs realize that geography is one of the most formidable forces of history. In the secular struggle of German and Slav, the former was bound to win.

The Thirty Years' War was precipitated by Bohemia's troubles. Another World War, three hundred years later, was precipitated by troubles in South Slav regions. In both cases the enemy was the

House of Habsburg, who represented the Germanic idea against the Slavs. The World War of the seventeenth century began with a comic-opera prelude. Several Bohemian spokesmen called at the royal palace of Hradčany at Prague to protest against the violation of an undertaking by King Matthias to respect the Protestants' rights. In the heat of the argument the Protestant Bohemians tossed the Catholic imperial advisers out of the window. The councilors fell on soft straw in the moat below and only their dignity was ruffled. The "defenestration of Prague," as historians like to call this incident, caused a world conflagration lasting for thirty years. When it was over, half of Germany's population was dead and civilization was killed, too. Entire sections were inhabited by vultures and cannibals feeding on their neighbors.

On a November day in 1620 Bohemia expired in the battle of the White Mountain, which lasted only a few hours. This was a war of the Bohemian nobility, of divided counsel, uncertain whether their interests would not be best safeguarded by the Habsburgs. The days were gone when women and children rose in defense of their human rights. Bohemia's population of 2,000,-000 had decreased to 900,000. Leading nobles were executed, others fled the hangmen, and their possessions fell into Habsburg hands. "Murder them all, without exception," the Emperor was advised. "The unholy nation should be extirpated," the Spanish court admonished Vienna. Bohemia lost her higher classes; peasants fled, too. That is why Poland shelters descendants of Czech refugees and Pennsylvania has her Moravian Brethren. Bohemia could not recover the loss of blood for three centuries. Their story now became the Habsburgs'. The Czech language was all but forgotten except by the peasants. There was too much Germany all around Bohemia, and the Danubian battle of the Slav against German seemed to be lost.

Bohemian nationalism was revived only in the middle of the last century. This was a reaction against the Holy Alliance and the system of Metternich. The Czechs began to study their language and history. The gymnastic organization of the Sokols began to focus national ambitions on a common objective. If the Habsburgs had fully realized the importance of this movement, their dynasty might have been saved. Even so, they had to reckon with the Czechs, who occupied some of the most responsible positions in the Danube monarchy. More than one Austrian Cabinet in the last quarter of the nineteenth century was dominated by the Czechs. This was particularly true of the government of Count Hohenwart. A new era seemed to dawn in the Danube valley when Minister-President Count Badeni introduced his famous ordinances which legalized the Czech language in the government offices throughout the whole Kingdom of Bohemia. But the German nationalists rose and prevented the execution of the ordinances. The Habsburgs had acted too late.

The World War gave the signal for the peoples of the Danube valley to rise. The Czechs were in the van, testing their strength, not being quite sure how far they could go. If the Central European Powers had won, the Czechs would have lost. The fight of the Czechs began against the country of which they were nominally citizens. What would happen if the two Kaisers lost? Would Bohemia become an independent part of the monarchy under Habsburg rule? This was a beautiful dream. Few, if any, dared to think that she might become an independent republic, having no connection with the Habsburgs, and containing not merely Bohemia but also Slovakia. This became the great epic of the Danube valley. The story of Eduard Benes, second President of the Czechoslovak Republic, last President, too, at the time of writing, exemplifies the struggles of the Czech nation.

As a child he hoed his father's land near the village of Kozlany, a few miles west of Prague. For three centuries the Austrian had been sitting in *Zlata Praha,* golden Prague, the pride of all Czechs, and a living symbol of past greatness. But three centuries had not dampened the patriotic ardor of the Benes family; they were still good Czechs. Eduard's parents were dirt farmers, having little time to pamper their ten children, of whom he was the youngest. Although the Benjamin of the family, he was not its pet. He was too dreamy-eyed for that, and the way he handled the hoe was ludicrous. He had unexpected outbursts of temper and was particularly cross with the children of the neighboring village, whose native language was German. He could give no satisfactory explanations of these flashes of anger, beyond saying that the German children were arrogant and haughty.

Some of the Benes children did not want to spend all their lives on the farm. Two of them had gone to Prague and become teachers. While still in school, Eduard followed them, and it was his hope that one day he would also obtain a teaching position. At school he did not excel, except in football. In a reckless moment he made a bold jump and broke a leg, after which there was little hope of his ever being able to join the team. He was in despair. He did not know then—and no one else did—that by breaking his leg he had qualified as one of the saviors of his country. After a few years in Prague, young Benes scaled his ambitions higher. He no longer desired to be a teacher of some primary school; he now wanted to be a high-school teacher or possibly a lecturer at the Czech University. Interested in languages, he learned long chapters of the Bible in French and broken English. He began to have a great compassion for the poor. The unhappiness he often felt for the woes of humanity and especially of his native Bohemia filled his heart with the augury of a world in which he would be an important figure. But these were childish dreams. In those days he was entirely unconscious of his future vocation. The thought of entering the foreign service never even occurred to him, and he would have been mad to think that Bohemia could become an independent republic in less than a score of years. The old order seemed to have taken permanent quarters.

Benes turned to France for further light. He had sixty crowns in his pocket when he arrived at the Gare de l'Est, hardly enough to live on for a fortnight. Paris was not unknown to him. He was familiar with the glories of the Quartier St. Germain and the slums of the Ménilmontant through the writings of his favorite authors. In a dingy room of the Left Bank he made his new home. How he liked the creaking stairs, which led to his *gîte*, his sleeping quarters. He was in love with the Sorbonne, where he studied sociology and philosophy. Murger's Latin Quarter had a special charm for him. He made friends with young anarchists and terrorists who fainted at the sight of a finger cut by glass. Over a cup of *café au lait* he settled the affairs of the world. He would sit for hours in the Chamber of Deputies, dreaming and scheming, the hero of imaginary battles in parliament. "I became attached to France," he wrote later, "because of the traditions of her great revolution, the broad perspectives of her national history. . . . I returned home a convinced radical and revolutionary."

Before returning home, however, he matriculated at the Uni-

179

versity of Dijon, which was a meeting place for Czech students, and there took his doctor's degree. He selected his subject: "The Austrian Problem and the Czech Question," and suggested autonomy for the Czechs in the existing framework of Austria, under the continued rule of the Habsburgs. In those days before the War no young Czech revolutionary extremist dared even to dream of an independent Czechoslovakia. Back to his native country young Benes went and at Prague he had an invitation from Professor Thomas Garrigue Masaryk to call on him. The professor was the hope of the Czech patriots; but what could he do to give expression to national will? With Masaryk's help, Benes was appointed teacher at the Prague Commercial Academy. He was then twenty-five years old. Three years later he was lecturer of sociology at the Czech University of Prague. His career was now clearly outlined; he would become a professor in due time.

If it had not been for the World War, Eduard Benes would have been writing history instead of making it. It would have landed him either in a university or a jail. The World War swept Dr. Benes from his academic surroundings into the European whirlpool. Masaryk and he grasped the importance to their country of the world conflagration. They saw the weakness of the Habsburg Empire and hoped it would be unable to stand up against the terrific pounding it would receive at the Allies' hands. A handful of Czechs were ready to take the ultimate consequences. It was decided to send Masaryk abroad; he was to put his country on the map. Benes and his friends stayed behind to supply him with news and to organize discontent. They formed an underground organization, the *Mafia*. His broken leg saved Benes from the army. He collected money and information, made the Czechs concentrate on their enemy: Austria. Twice he visited

An Old Typewriter and a Stenographer

Professor Masaryk in Switzerland, once to warn him against returning and the second time to supply him with fresh news. Benes was very ingenious in sidetracking the police. He would go for a walk with the other members of the *Mafia* in a Prague public garden and discuss their plans under the policemen's eyes. The authorities could not be fooled indefinitely, however, and Benes had good reason to believe that he was on the list of suspects. It was decided that he would have to join Masaryk in Switzerland. But how was he to leave Austria? His passport was forged and he did not dare to face the frontier officials with it. He sneaked out of Austria by night, and if a dog had barked at that spot, an observer says, arousing the guards' interest, Czech history might have taken another turn. But he got safely beyond the boundary, and joined Masaryk in Geneva.

A marble tablet on a rickety old house not far from the Seine marks the spot where Masaryk and Benes labored. With an old typewriter and an ill-tempered stenographer they set out to build a country. Technically, they were enemy aliens, citizens of Austria. How could the French know that they were not spies? They had to convince the Allies that although they were Habsburg subjects, and therefore enemies, they were, in reality, friends. At a time when the spy scare was at its height, such a task was far from easy. They had to make the Allied statesmen learn where Czechoslovakia was. They had to sell their fanatical belief in the Czech cause to Paris, London, Washington and Rome. They had to get their program accepted as an Allied war aim.

But a good cause and fanaticism carried less weight than help with arms. Masaryk and Benes then did the dramatic and unexpected which arrested the attention of the world. They built up a Czech army fighting for the enemies of the country of

181

which they were citizens. The Austrians kept on sending the Czech soldiers to the front. There they surrendered to the Russians and Italians. Soon the Czechs had their own divisions fighting against the Austrians and Germans on the Eastern, Western and Italian fronts. Now the Allies were finally convinced of the good-will of the Czechs. At home the friends of Masaryk and Benes were arrested and put in jail. Some of them were sentenced to hang, but the Habsburgs knew well that the execution of the sentence would have further aroused the Czechs' ire and furnished them with martyrs. In their shabby flat of two rooms the two Czech leaders and their friends set up the first Czech government. It still had the old typewriter, but no country. Dr. Benes became the Foreign Minister of this shadow Cabinet. If the Allies had lost, the two men's attempts would have been drowned in ridicule. But the Allies won.

Masaryk, helped by Benes, set out to build their country. The Allies recognized them as a provisional government. The Russian Revolution broke out and the Czech legionaires were marooned, exposed to the crossfire of Whites and Reds. Masaryk took command and the Czechs smashed their way to the Pacific, there to embark for the West. Not since Xenophon led his ten thousand across the plateau of Anatolia to the Black Sea had mankind seen such a feat.

Masaryk was now in the United States. President Wilson was the Jupiter of the warring world, hurling his thunders, proclaiming the word. His power was immense because back of him stood the untapped resources of the richest nation, also because he was surrounded by mystery. He had to be won over to the Czech plan. Besides, the United States had a large number of Czechs and Slovaks, to whom their former countrymen overseas looked up as leaders. They had money and a will to help their native land. At Pittsburgh, Pennsylvania, the Czechs and Slovaks agreed to set up a common household. This was a fact of great historic significance. The Czechs and Slovaks had lived apart for a thousand years; the former were under the rule of Austria and the latter under Hungary, although both of them had to obey the Habsburgs. In Washington Professor Masaryk issued the new country's Declaration of Independence. In the United States he drew up its Constitution, with the help of an American college professor, Herbert Miller of Bryn Mawr. Masaryk was still in the United States when he became the first President of Czechoslovakia. He left New York to get a hero's welcome at home.

Czechoslovakia was the creation of Masaryk, the master, and Benes, the disciple. They were the two and only Presidents of the Republic, and both of them were philosophers. All of their country's neighbors turned to army leaders and strong men. Germany went Fascist, and the Austrians followed her example. Poland turned to a Marshal, Hungary to a Rear Admiral and Roumania to a military-minded King. Czechoslovakia seemed to many the realization of Plato's *Republic,* modernized and improved. In all fields of social legislation she was in the front rank. She had no aristocracy of blood or money, neither did she have slums and widespread misery. The peasant was given land, the factory worker decent wages. All could worship the political gods of their choice.

Do not draw the hasty conclusion that, because Czechoslovakia is no more, the government of Masaryk was a failure. There are times when it is a distinction to fail. I had the privilege of calling upon the President a year before he retired from office. He spent an average of two days a week in his official residence, the Hradčany palace, although he was eighty-five years old. From all over the capital you could see the Presidential banner of white-red-blue on the tallest tower of the palace. As I mounted the hill, I read the motto on the banner: "Truth triumphs." The car passed through ancient fortifications, then a vast gate at which Czech soldiers stood guard. Taken in hand by a courteous aide-de-camp I was shown into a lift, the center of which was occupied by a throne-like chair. In the palace everyone talked in whispers, as if fearful to disturb the memories of the past.

While waiting for the audience I looked at the paintings of Correggio and Palma Vecchio on the walls. In a few more minutes I walked endless corridors, landing finally in the antechamber of the President, which contained the overflow of his library. The door opened and I was in the study of the President, which one would have been inclined to describe as a scholar's lair. Books were heaped high on several tables, keeping company to sheets of yellow and pink paper. On the former the President made notes of his research and on the latter he marked his own thoughts. Masaryk stood up and rubbed his eyes for a second, as people do who have been reading long. He spoke flawless English. His French was as good as a Sorbonne professor's, his German had no accent and he spoke Russian with ease. His voice was hollow—the sign of old age—except when he touched upon subjects closest to his heart. Then it became metallic, although slightly muffled. When he spoke, you could hear not only the statesman, but also the professor. Where other men of politics saw only the present, he also assayed the past and visualized the future. He was proud of his work, the Republic of Czechoslovakia, but never overlooked its weakness. "Monarchism and Caesarism have left something of aristocracy and absolutism in many of us." He liked to repeat what he considered the first principle of statesmanship: "We are part of the world as a whole."

Mr. Lloyd George once said of Masaryk's patriotism that it was not imprisoned within the front lines of the State, "for it has been ennobled and enriched by his love of mankind." Emil Ludwig, the German biographer, called Masaryk the "greatest European." He was a wise and good man. "Everywhere there are heaps of patriots," he told Ludwig, "who make profitable business out of their patriotism." "I am not a ruler, but I know that the masses must be led. My method of leadership is not despotic, but more by the way of suggestion." "The meaning of life cannot be merely to soak in knowledge as if one were a sponge. This is only a luxury, just pleasure-seeking." "What I have often called 'world-humanity' is but another name for the inborn desire and striving of men for general friendship and union." "Chauvinism, that is to say, political, religious, racial or class intolerance, is nowhere justified, least of all in our country."

The problem of the peace-makers was to deal with the nearly 3,500,000 Germans in historic Bohemia. Under the Habsburg rulers they considered themselves superior to their Czech neighbors, although intermarriage was common among the peasants and the industrial proletariat. The middle class of these *Deutsch-Boehmen,* German-Bohemians, was violently nationalistic and more extreme than the Habsburgs. They were a frontier people in constant struggle with the Slavs, and they developed the usual frontier symptoms of the Danube basin. They were suspicious of their neighbors, jealous of their progress and fearful of becoming an oppressed minority. Hitler got most of his racial ideas from them. His National Socialist German Labor Party originated among the Germans of Bohemia.

Lloyd George says in his recollections that the problem of the Sudeten Germans was considered from all angles at the Peace Conference. Before the War they belonged to Austria, which was no more. But there was a Czechoslovak Republic, which the Sudetens hated with all their heart. The heights, on which they lived mostly, and the plains, inhabited by the Czechs, were never separated in historical times. They were complementary: the one furnishing the raw materials of industry, the other the raw materials of agriculture. The plains could not have been defended against the heights. The question of Austria was ruled out. The Sudeten-Germans shared Hitler's hatred for his native country and its dynasty. Both of them appeared too effeminate to them. Should they become independent or should they be attached to Germany? But if they had become independent they would have had the empty shell of nothing. For centuries they lived together with the peoples of the plains. Their entire economic system was geared to this union. They could not have lived independently for any length of time and would have fallen into German hands. Technically, the easiest solution would have been to attach the Sudeten land to the Reich, because they are contiguous. The most articulate of them were in favor of this Great-German solution. More Prussian than the Prussians, they would have felt at home in a warlike Reich. But it was not the object of the Allies at the Peace Conference to strengthen the Germans. They remembered the words of Bismarck: "Whoever is master of Bohemia . . ." The plains would have been at the mercy of the Reich on the heights and the Germans would have been rewarded for having lost the war.

The Allies attached the Sudeten lands to the Czechoslovak Republic. Several Sudeten leaders thereupon proclaimed the independence of their country and set up a cantonal government. The Allies forthwith ordered the dissolution of this country. Austria, too, announced her claim to the *Deutsch-Boehmen.* The inhabitants of several mountain villages removed the frontier stones between themselves and the Reich. Many new countries were made and lost in those days, and the general uncertainty furthered political ambitions.

Gradually, the Danube valley was returning to a more normal mode of life. Love of an ideal was elevating, but food was more important. The destruction of four suicidal years had to be repaired. The Allies were backed by the myth of an invincible power and even the Sudetens grew tired of trying to shatter a stone wall with bare arms. Austria fell into a lethargy, having strength only to beg at the four corners of the earth. In Germany the Left was fighting the Right and vice versa. All were trying to fight famine, and the French Right government was fighting them all. The German mark took a plunge and the Reich experienced an endless number of Black Fridays.

The economic hurricane was halted at the Sudeten mountains, as if by magic. Need was rampant on the German side of the hill, while the Czech side was well off. Czechoslovakia was heir to an ideal country, in which agriculture and industry were well balanced. It was the most self-sufficient nation east of France. Its government was led by inspired statesmen, the world agreed. The Czech miracle was accomplished: food and work, social reforms. The country was in a fever of construc-

tion. Modern Utopia was being built in the Danube valley. The
lesson of the two mountain slopes was not lost on the rank-
and-file Sudeten-Germans. The majority of them were now willing to co-operate with the Czechs. They called themselves the
"Activists," and polled 65 per cent of all the German votes at
a national election. But the minority still held out, refusing to
have any truck with the *Saisonstaat* (season State), as they
called the Czech Republic. These were the die-hard "Negativists."

What would have happened if the depression had not struck
the world full force? Hitler probably would have remained a
hysterical politician, and Austria would have retained as much
independence as she had. The Sudeten "Activists" would have
continued to roll up large majorities at the polls. But let us not
write "If history." The depression struck the Danube valley
before it did the rest of Europe. The crash of the *Creditanstalt*
of Vienna was the signal for the economic disaster. The depression swept Hitler into power, because if the average German
has not enough bread he turns to *Weltanschauung* and that is
not always a good thing for the world. His political creed had
an unusual fascination for the Sudetens, long won over to the
idea of racial superiority. In many cases one-half of a village
in the mountains belonged to the Czechs and the other half to
the Germans. The German half resounded with the stamping
of uniformed legs. Big streamers proclaimed to the German
side: "One State, One People, One Leader." When work is
scarce any change seems to be attractive. The part of the two
mountainsides was reversed. On the German side factories were
working overtime. One State—one armed camp. The New
Reich set the tempo for the armament race, and production

was speeded up, until the race took the breath of the world away. German workers no longer formed a line of 6,000,000 in front of the unemployment bureaus, where pittances were doled out. Glad to have work, they were not greatly interested in how this terrific race to arms was paid for. Nor did they care to know how they were going to finance it in the future.

On the Czech side, however, factories began to slow down, and then to cease work. The Czechs now began to realize that a showdown between German and Slav was inevitable. Most of their industries were in the Sudeten area, which the advancing enemy would try to take in his stride in the first days of hostilities. The mammoth Skoda arms works at Pilsen could be reached in less than five minutes from the German border. The airplane as an important new weapon in war necessitated ← the relocation of the arms industries. Russia had done it on a large scale; Germany and France were doing it on a smaller scale. The Czechs began to close down factories in the frontier districts and transferred them to the Moravian Quadrangle, behind the Bohemian-Moravian range, in the center of the country, which they sought to make impregnable. They also transferred them to mountainous Slovakia, out of sight. The Sudetens found the jobs moving away from them, and they were bitter. The number of the "Activists" began to dwindle and the number of the "Negativists" to grow.

The Nazi Party began to make inroads. The Czech government dissolved their movement, which thereupon re-appeared as a sports organization. It was then that Konrad Henlein appeared on the stage, and his Sudeten German Party began to spread its wings. Henlein's great asset was that he looked honest. He was not a great organizer, political manipulator, or an eloquent speaker. He looked so honest that when he said: "I am a good Czech and my Sudeten Germans are good Czechs," nobody told him: "You are a liar." Looking honest was his principal occupation, and it was important in Hitler's fight against the Czechs.

Henlein was born in that very town of Asch which was a salient of Bohemia into Germany and which became Austrian in the distant past merely because of the vagaries of treaty-making. He joined the Austrian army as a volunteer because he, too, like his master, Hitler, was irked by the unheroic life of a drab townsman. He was wounded, then taken prisoner by the Italians. After his release he became a bank clerk and, later, an instructor of gymnastics, trying all the time to find a more heroic occupation. He found that heroism could not be accomplished in the penumbra of a *Turnhalle*. It required the support of masses, who would repay the investment of effort a thousandfold. How he got in touch with the Nazis of the Reich is a story which will probably be told one day. That genius of political management who pulls the strings saw the tremendous advantage of having a man with innocent blue eyes and disarming glasses. He would have discarded Henlein promptly if he had looked like a bully.

Time and again Henlein asserted that he was a loyal son of the Republic and that his Sudeten Germans wanted no more than their rights. They were annoyed, he said, by postmasters in the German area who could not speak German, railway guards who spoke only Czech. They wanted more schools and more say in the local government. The Czech Cabinet was ready to consider the Sudetens' grievances. Every time such a step was made, Henlein added to the list of German demands. The economic interests of the Sudetens should be better safeguarded, he said. The government should not discriminate against them. They should have the right of self-government in the districts where they formed a majority.

On March 14, 1938, Hitler's army marched into Austria. The Fuehrer assured Prague that Czechoslovakia's territory would be respected. The world did not heed the warning given to it in a book published as far back as 1932. "If success be achieved in uniting Austria with Germany," wrote the author of *Der Kommende Krieg*, Professor Ewald Banse, "the collapse of Czechoslovakia will follow; Germany will have common frontiers with Italy and Yugoslavia and Italy will be strengthened against France." The world did not believe the professor because Konrad Henlein had innocent blue eyes and because he had said that he was a loyal citizen of the Czech Republic. The master mind who picked the blue eyes knew that they would be helpful in gaining a country of 15,000,000 inhabitants, with all its treasures. The Allies still did not know what the game was about. Although they had forbidden the union of Austria with Germany, they seemed to admit to themselves that the situation was untenable, and as long as Austria did not resist by force, the *Anschluss* could not be prevented.

The Czechs themselves had not realized the gravity of the situation. They had concentrated on the "Hungarian menace" and had neglected to build any large-scale fortifications against Germany. The Little Entente, consisting of Roumania and Yugoslavia, in addition to their country, had been formed to keep the Magyars at bay. The Czechs had also thought the Habsburg family a more serious danger than the Reich. For years they had repeated their veto to the restoration of the youthful Otto to the Vienna throne. If the young man had taken the crown, Hitler's task would have been more difficult.

It was only after Hitler had marched into Vienna that the Czechs launched their defensive program. They studded the mountain frontiers with pill-boxes. Heavy fortifications protected the Moravian Gate, where the river Oder opened a gap to German invasion. In the west, they built line after line of trenches, beginning at the language frontier, all the way down to Prague. Their diplomatic line of fortifications was already built up. If they were attacked, France would hurry military aid to them, and Russia would follow the French example. The Czechs were convinced that they were so essential to the defense of England and France that the British would side with them as a matter of course.

The scene was set for the rape of Czechoslovakia. Hitler never says: "I want to commit a crime." He says: "He is a Bolshevist," and packs the word with such frightful meaning that all respectable people begin to shudder. Although these respectable ones are a minority, they are the ones that count. Hitler gave the signal for the propaganda campaign: "Czechoslovakia is an outpost of Bolshevism." It was perfectly orchestrated in the Ministry of Dr. Joseph Goebbels. His press gave detailed descriptions of Russian airports through the length and breadth of the Czech Republic. They were imaginary descriptions, but people did not know it. In vain the Prague government tried to answer: "We invite German government representatives to see for themselves that we have no such airports."

Hitler knew that his fate was in the hands of the English ruling class. If they believed him and his baby-blue-eyed messenger, Henlein, all would be well. He could not afford to go to war yet against a combination of major powers. He had been arming for only three years, while France had been arming since the War. The Fuehrer knew the language of the English higher classes, led by Prime Minister Neville Chamberlain. He and they were spiritual brothers, pursuing identical policies. He confronted them with a problem: "I don't want these Czechs even if you wanted to give them to me. Our Germany must remain racially pure. But I do want self-determination for the Sudeten-Germans. They are entitled to it, and it is a right in which you profess to believe. If you want to go to war on this issue, you will have the Bolshevists with you, perhaps. Do you want them, who want all that you have, or do you want me, who wants nothing from you?"

It was then that Henlein stood up and his innocent lips formulated the "Karlsbad Program." It demanded full autonomy for the Sudeten area, but it said nothing about independence or union with the Reich.

Hitler knew that he was behind the enemy's diplomatic line of fortifications. The *Daily Mail* could not have been more affectionately pro-Fuehrer if it had been published by the Berlin Propaganda Ministry. The London *Times* published an editorial in which it went as far as Henlein. A well-known professor of the Sorbonne wrote a featured article in *Le Temps* of Paris, in which he sought to show that the Franco-Czech pact was invalid. Public opinion in both countries was being prepared for the great betrayal.

Meanwhile, Czechoslovakia was planning a solution of the Sudeten problem. In the Summer of 1938 I spent much time in Prague, and one evening a man close to the Foreign Office called me to see him. Without any further ado, he began to

193

outline a government program, designed to give a measure of autonomy to the Sudeten Germans. Without my asking for it, he gave me authority to publish the plan. Obviously, this was a trial-balloon of the Czech Foreign Office, eager to know whether it would satisfy the German government.

The Czechs were also getting prepared on the military front. In the third week of May, 1938, word was received in Prague about German divisions on the march up the mountains. The French and English intelligence services confirmed this information. On May 21st, a quiet, partial mobilization was effected in Czechoslovakia. In a few hours all men were at their appointed posts. Tanks, guns, anti-aircraft forces were on the move. A few hours later the entire Sudeten area was manned. Nothing like this had been seen before. It was not merely the clock-like precision of the mobilization that took the breath of the world away. The partial mobilization would not have been such a signal success without the whole-hearted support of all Czechs. In their quiet, undemonstrative way, they accomplished a military miracle.

This was a setback for Hitler, which made matters worse for the Danube valley. A man of his type is infuriated by any opposition. How did Czech worms dare to show Him their puny force? In his Alpine chalet he consulted his hunches. He knew that his victory in Czechoslovakia would finally seal the defeat of the Allies. He also knew that the Czechs were determined to fight for their independence as a man. A rifle shot might be enough to set off endless rows of powder boxes. He was not yet ready for a major war, but he was ready for a war with the Czechs. It would be better to save ammunition for the great day of reckoning.

"The Hangman with His Little Bag"

Czechoslovakia was also making preparations. Half a million went to Prague for the Tenth Sokol Congress. They were to take home the sacred fire with which this incomparable sight inflamed them. They were ready to lay down their lives to save their human dignity. That Summer in Prague surpassed all others in beauty probably because of the unconscious realization of the fact that it was a season of leave-taking. The *Mala Strana* exuded that sweet odor of wet soil and flowers, which imparts to that part of Prague its particular perfume. The thirteenth-century synagogue, with its oversize gable, served to remind the visitor that the city had a long tradition of tolerance. The Hradčany palace overlooked this scene of grandeur in all its magnificence. The Presidential banner was up all Summer, indicating that this was not a year to take vacation. The big hotels of the *Vaclavske Namesti* were crowded with the international crowd of sensation-seekers, attracted by impending death. A high government official told me: "We may yet witness a Mongolian invasion, but it will be from the West."

The world should have had its eyes opened when London announced that Viscount Runciman would go to Prague. The Henleinists received him with salvos of applause as he alighted from the train, and their newspaper greeted him as the friend of justice. He came as "the friend of all and the enemy of none," Lord Runciman said. But that acute observer of Danubian tragedies, G. E. R. Gedye, knew better. "The hangman with his little bag came creeping through the gloom," he quoted Oscar Wilde. The London of Neville Chamberlain was preparing its alibi. If the Czechs could not accept Lord Runciman's suggestions, the English Fuehrer could wash his hands of the last and only democracy in the Danube Valley.

195

This was a signal for Hitler to go ahead, and he did. From the conductor's desk, Minister Dr. Goebbels gave the sign, and a full blast replied. "Czechia [a word of contempt] is Europe's Danger Center," "The Czechs are Bloodthirsty Bolshevists," "The Season State Must Be Swept Away!" Then the Minister of Propaganda gave the signal, and a part of the Paris press responded promptly. The sonorous sound of cash-registers was clearly heard. France was to be split up into pro- and anti-Czech camps, the latter predominating. The scene shifted again to Berlin. The conductor's baton brought in the brass. Even the heroic inmates of the Teutonic Valhalla would have been frightened by the shrieking of trumpets! "The Czech *Untermensch* [ape-man] Tortures Germans." Czech frontier guards shot two Sudeten Germans who had refused to halt. Berlin gave the signal for the crescendo: "Mass Murder in Czechia." "Bloody Murderer Benes Killing Thousands of Germans," "Martial Law Declared in Murderland," "How long?" The Fuehrer's patience was on the wane.

The climax approached when Hitler gave his first speech in Nuremberg. "I speak of the 'Czechei,' " he screeched. The Nazis always used the word with a sneer. "The Czechs beat up bloodily three and a half million members of a race of nearly eighty million people if they sing a song, wear white stockings, or use a greeting which does not please them." The world was holding its breath. What was to be his last word? Was he going to demand the Sudetenland for the Reich? That would mean war. The Czechs would not stand for that. No, Hitler was laying down a thick smoke-screen. He demanded merely self-determination for the Sudeten Germans. "It is not my will that in the heart of Central Europe, through the talents of other statesmen, a second Palestine should be created. The poor Arabs are defenseless and deserted; the Germans in Czechoslovakia are neither defenseless nor deserted."

Then Hitler took a long breath for his last attack. The walls of Jericho fell at the sound of trumpets, the Roman capital was saved by the cackling of geese. "Other countries carry on war, thou, happy Hitler, maketh speeches." If on September 26th, when Hitler made his speech in the *Sportpalast,* he had been suffering from a sore throat, history might have taken another turn. He had the world hypnotized, listening to every word he uttered, as the sick man analyzes his physician's words. Has one man ever had an audience so large? On that speech might depend the future of mankind. On that speech, too, depended Hitler's fate. He would have to back down or go to war—for which he was then unprepared—if he failed to score. This speech was not going to be so easy as the march into Austria. Now his words would have to be heard in a country entrenched behind a line of fortifications which cost nearly half a billion dollars— a fabulous sum in the Danube valley. His words would be heard, too, by the Czech army, one of the best equipped in the world. England and France were also listening in and so were the Russians. Prague's people were scanning the eastern sky for the Russian air armada.

Those who saw Hitler on that day will never forget the scene. The *Sportpalast* was packed, and well-tried methods whipped the crowd into a frenzy. There was music, the martial kind, and there were flags, brown shirts, black uniforms, gray uniforms, and music again, splitting the ear-drums. It all contrived to pour assurance into the herd, which was afraid of some unknown danger. Terroristic Fuehrers have a place only in the

midst of cowards. But cowards are more dangerous than the
brave, because they are swayed by animal impulses. Thus the
Roman scum of the Colosseum gloated over the mangled bodies
of Christian martyrs.

All eyes were focused upon the Leader. He did not speak
to the brown shirts and black uniforms. He spoke to Mr. Chamberlain and England: "Do you want the English to die for
Czechia?" He whipped himself into a frenzy. He screamed
about hundreds of thousands of Germans driven out of Czechia,
tens of thousands put in prison and thousands mowed down.
And the villain was *"der Verbrecher Benes,"* Benes, the criminal.
"The tyrant Benes wants to shoot, arrest and imprison everyone
who displeases him." "The existence of Czechoslovakia is based
on a lie and the father of that lie is Benes." "Benes has never
kept his word in his life. Now he is going to be made to keep
it. I have made Benes an offer. It is nothing more than the
realization of what he has promised already. Let Benes
choose. . . ."

Hysteria reached its climax, but it was scientifically worked
out, and every drop of the Fuehrer's venom had been weighed
on a precision scale. Why this tirade of hatred against Benes,
whom the League of Nations had come to admire as the ablest
young "elder statesman"? Why Benes, who has settled more
disputes, devised more new instruments of peace than anyone
else? From Hitler's point of view Benes was the logical choice
to be built up as the enemy of peace and mankind. The average
person cannot hate a nation; it is too abstract, too diffuse. The
leaders of Allied propaganda during the World War knew it
when they concentrated their barrage on the Kaiser, whom they

198

represented as Evil Incarnate. It would have been difficult to make them hate a hundred and fifty million people of several nationalities, including women and children, paupers and orphans. The same was true of the average German in the Autumn of 1938. His hatred had to be given a focus in the form of a man stripped of all humanity.

Hitler issued his ultimatum: the Sudeten areas must be ceded to him in four days, else he would march and take them. There was no longer any question of self-determination of the territory. Blue-eyed Henlein had fled to the Reich. He no longer said: "I am a loyal Czech citizen." The smoke-screen had lifted, and behind it were the muzzles of the most beautiful cannon man ever devised for his own destruction. The world had been lulled into a sense of security. The British Prime Minister declared he had no cause to doubt the sincerity of the Fuehrer. The French were not ready, physically or psychologically.

Prague was preparing for the war. Food prices began to rise, gasoline was unobtainable, lines formed in front of shops selling gas-masks, telephone and telegraphic communication was curtailed, trains were reserved for the military. The city was plunged into darkness when dusk came. Pedestrians walked with pocket-lights, and motor-car headlights were dimmed. Most people walked the streets with gray gas-mask canisters; policemen joined the army and their places were taken by elderly men and boys wearing Sokol caps. Air raid shelters were designated by broad arrows on the pavement and large posters gave the addresses of first-aid stations.

Meanwhile Lord Runciman was preparing his report. He has been left with the impression that the Czech rule, "though not actively oppressive and certainly not 'terroristic,' has been marked by tactlessness, lack of understanding, petty intolerance and discrimination." He admitted, at the same time, that the Henleinist leaders had from the start been wasting his time by pretending to seek a remedy for minority grievances, when in fact they were openly preparing for a rebellion, after the failure of which they fled the country.

Riots broke out in the Sudeten areas. Czech gendarmes were attacked and killed; Czech police opened fire in self-defense. The Nazis' policy was to create chaos, and then march into the Sudeten area to restore the rule of "law and order." The pattern was familiar; it had worked in Austria and it was going to work in "Czechia." But was it really? The Czechs were not Austrians, weakened by years of misery, suffering from a sense of insufficiency, hesitant about the merits of two conflicting views. The Czechs were united and they would fight. And if they did fight, the French would be drawn in and the English, too, not because the Czechs were close to their hearts but because they could not let the French sink. And the Russians would come in, too. It would be another World War, for which the Germans were unprepared. One can end a war on short rations, but the Reich would have had to begin it with that handicap. The words of Montecuccoli were remembered: "Three things are needed for war: money, money, and money." The Germans had none of these three things, and they lacked the wherewithals of mechanized warfare—oil and rubber. The first line would follow the Leader into the fire in any type of war, but the older generations had not yet forgotten the banks of slimy blood at Ypres and on the Somme. If Hitler suffered a reverse early in the war, what would the 65 per cent of German electors do who at the last free elections, in November 1932, voted against him? How many of them would employ their arms against him instead of the enemy? And what was the potential value of Italy as an ally? She had spent billions in Ethiopia and Spain. A dictator with a powerful jaw can do many things, but miracles of carrying on three wars in as many years may be beyond him. And the third war would be nothing like the previous ones.

Hitler knew that England and France wanted a war even less than he. They had all and could gain nothing more in a new conflict. They were rich and fat. The issue of "Czecho" would have been most unfortunate for both countries. Why should a young Australian lay down his life for a country whose name he could not even pronounce? Hitler knew that Chamberlain was willing to meet him more than half way, especially if another country would pay the bill. Let me sum up chronologically the principal events leading to the destruction of Czechoslovakia:

On September 15th Chamberlain visited Hitler in his Berchtesgaden retreat. After his return to London the following day, his government asked the League to make optional the military and economic sanctions against aggressors. On September 17th all Czechoslovakia was placed in a state of emergency. On September 18th, Premier Daladier of France conferred with Chamberlain in London. Dictator Mussolini said in Trieste: "The solution has only one name—plebiscites for all nationalities who demand them." Premier Milan Hodza said in Prague that a plebiscite was unacceptable. On September 19th, the British and French Cabinets voted to support Hitler in demanding the right of self-determination for the Sudeten Germans. The following day they proposed to the Czechs to cede the Sudeten areas. Prague suggested arbitration, but on the 21st London and Paris informed her that there must be an immediate agreement to cede the area if armed invasion by Germany was to be avoided. In a last-minute conference the Czech government yielded to pressure.

"As the news of the surrender came to be known," Gedye writes, "a nation broke into tears." As the day wore on, curses began to mingle with tears; a new phrase was born: "Surrender Government." Toward the evening the whole city seemed to be pressed into the *Vaclavske Namesti,* processions formed, shouting: "Away with the government!" "Long live the army!" "Military dictatorship!" "We want Syrovy!" The one-eyed Commander-in-chief had fought his way across Siberia. "Dismiss the capitulators and put the army in charge!" a quarter of a million people demanded of President Benes on Hradčany Hill. On September 22nd the Hodza government was replaced by a Cabinet of Jan Syrovy. On the 23rd, Chamberlain again called on Hitler, this time in the lovely Rhine resort of Godesberg. The Fuehrer stiffened his terms of surrender, and Chamberlain returned. He placed the Nazi terms before the Czechs, who rejected it. "The proposals go far beyond what we agreed to in the so-called Anglo-French plan." On the 26th, President Roosevelt wired Hitler an appeal not to break off negotiations. On the same day Hitler spoke in the *Sportpalast.* On the 27th Hitler wired to Roosevelt declining all responsibility if hostilities should break out. The English were digging trenches and fitting gas-masks. Chamberlain and Roosevelt appealed to Mussolini to intervene with Hitler. On the 28th, the Fuehrer invited the heads of the English, French and Italian governments to meet at Munich the following day. The Czech delegates were denied admittance to the confer-

202

ence of the Big Four at Munich. It was only late at night that they were ushered into the presence of the supreme judges.

"The atmosphere was oppressive," reported Dr. Hubert Masařik of the Prague Foreign Office. "Sentence was about to be passed. . . . Mr. Chamberlain was yawning continuously without making any attempt to conceal his yawns." A map had been prepared, detailing what parts of the Sudeten area were to be occupied outright and what parts were to decide of their own fate through a plebiscite. The Czechs were not even asked to give their approval. "Chamberlain had just played a clever hand against us, with the unfriendliness toward our nation," a Czech diplomat said, "and the affection for Herr Hitler that in our hearts we had always expected."

The Germans marched in and took what they wanted; the Czechs did not even ask for a plebiscite. Now that their fortifications were gone, they were at the enemy's mercy. The Poles marched in and they, too, took what they wanted. The Hungarians were on the move and got a chunk of Czechoslovakia. The Slovak autonomists raised new demands and the Czechoslovak Republic became Czecho-Slovakia, with the accent on the hyphen. Less than six months later, Hitler took Bohemia and Moravia. Now he showed his true colors. The two provinces were alien land and not German. The most successful democratic experiment in the Danube valley was over. For three centuries it had been England's basic policy to prevent any continental power from acquiring hegemony. In defense of this principle she fought the Spanish Armada during the reign of Elizabeth, fought the Dutch at the time of Cromwell, went to war with Napoleon early in the nineteenth century and sought to crush the Kaiser in the World War.

Neville Chamberlain threw this basic policy overboard. He acted as a good Fascist, but a bad Englishman, and perhaps repents the day when he surrendered England's bastion on the Danube.

Slovakia was set up as an "independent" country, but the Germans retained the right to occupy her River Vag, the largest tributary of the Danube in these parts. The country thus constituted was made up almost exclusively of mountains; most of her three million inhabitants lived on the slopes of the Carpathians. Whatever may be her nominal form of government, Slovakia is a part of Germany.

When the train emerges from the Jablonka Pass on its eastward way, Bohemia-Moravia are behind the traveler and Slovakia is in front of him. The contrast between the two slopes is dramatic. The houses on the western side would not be out of place in France, but on the Slovak side they exude an Oriental air. Here life is geared to a slower rhythm and the twentieth century is remote. The Slovak mountains produce an unlimited quantity of beauty but not much food, and Slovaks are poor. The older ones are slow to discard ancient habits. You can recognize them by their long hair, broad-brimmed hats and white baize trousers. The braided hair of the young women tells which of them are unmarried. Most of the inhabitants are peasants and shepherds. In the Spring the shepherd-in-chief drives the sheep to the meadows, where he and his younger assistants lead a primitive life. With the first snow the sheep are on their way to the village. Before the War, food shortage drove many of them to foreign lands. Hundreds of thousands of them sought a living in America, and as a result ex-Americans have played leading rôles in Slovakia. They worked in the mines of West Virginia, saving their dollars for the day of their return to the native hills. Back home again, they built their homes in the shadow of the Tatra and Fatra mountains. The older folk still understand English in these American villages. A Hungarian aristocrat, running for office before the War, was unable to make himself understood in Slovak, while his would-be constituents understood no Hungarian. He spoke to them in English and was elected by a large majority.

For a thousand years the Slovaks lived under Hungarian rule, hence they have hardly any history of their own. Because of centuries of oppression the Slovaks at first lacked the self-confidence for nation-building, when the Czechoslovak Republic was formed after the War. It was soon discovered that the Czechs and Slovaks were mismated. The Czechs hushed up the secret, but the Slovaks began to divulge it. They wanted equal rights with the Czechs to run their own part of the country as they saw fit. The Czechs replied that the Slovaks had equal rights, as attested by the fact that the names of both of them were on the signboard of their joint enterprise. Slovakia protested that she did not want to partake of all the happiness which came by the way of Prague. They pointed to the Pittsburgh Agreement, which provided for full equality between Czechs and Slovaks. They wanted to set up a Czech *and* Slovak Republic, not a Czechoslovak one.

The Slovaks decided to fight for their rights. It was largely a youth movement, headed by a very old man, Father Andreas Hlinka, a country priest, whose name is now enshrined. Nearly a half century before, he fought Slovakia's Hungarian masters; he was sent to prison for years and fell so dangerously ill that doctors gave up all hope. Some thirty years later he resumed the fight, this time against the Czechs. Two warrants for his arrest were framed

205

in the waiting room of his office, one issued in Budapest and the other in Prague. Hlinka's battlecry was "Slovakia for the Slovaks." His Populist Party opposed the Czech government at elections, and while he fell far short of achieving a majority, his party was important. He died at the age of eighty-four just before the Munich agreement.

The Slovak grievances were numerous. Hlinka arraigned the Czech government on the ground that it treated the Slovaks as an inferior race, pushing them into the background, while Prague manned the important posts. He pointed out that the Slovaks had no legislature of their own and that the educational system which the Slovaks introduced was alien to the soil. The Czechs, he insisted, tried to stamp out the Slovak language, sought to supplant it with their own tongue and culture.

It is true, the Czechs argued in rebuttal, that numerous Czech officials held office in Slovakia, but centuries of oppression had rooted out administrative capacity among the Slovaks, so that there was a shortage of higher officials. At the same time, some of the highest offices were filled by Slovaks. President Masaryk himself was half Slovak, and Premier Hodza, who headed the government for years, was a full Slovak.

"As soon as the new generation grew to manhood, most of the outsiders were withdrawn. And as to the language, Czech and Slovak are dialects of the same tongue. In a new country it would have been advantageous to standardize the speech."

The facts behind the twenty-year-old controversy reach back a thousand years. During those centuries numerous differences arose that could not be removed in two decades. The Czechs belonged to the West. For hundreds of years they formed an independent country, and even after the loss of their freedom in

206

the seventeenth century, their Habsburg masters treated them
with consideration. It was the Czechs who created the largest
shoe factory in the Old World and their Skoda arms plants vied
with the largest in all countries. The Czechs' fingers are skillful
and illiteracy is unknown among them.

Slovakia is closer to the East. Her villages have all the picturesque inconveniences of the pre-machine culture. Although
much was accomplished in the Republic, native conservatism
sticks to narrow roads, which are inexhaustible in producing dust
in fair weather and mud after a rain. Many of the inhabitants
still cling to the tallow candle and the wooden plow. Their
ramshackle houses are often overcrowded and their unsanitary
condition may be responsible for the ravages of tuberculosis.
Under the thousand years of Hungarian rule, the most elementary
human rights were withheld from the Slovaks. Under the Magyar
régime it was a common saying: *"A tót nem ember,"* the Slovak
is not human. As a gesture of protest, many young men attended
the Czech University at Prague.

Differences of attitude toward the Church accentuated the
conflicts. The Slovaks are devoted to the Roman Catholic Church,
and the village priest is often their political oracle. The Czechs,
on the other hand, came to identify the Church with the House of
Austria, which proudly bore the title of "defenders of the faith."
The Czechs sought to emancipate themselves from the religious
allegiance which, they maintained, had been forced upon them
by the Vienna Court. The Czech National Church, which derived
its inspiration from Jan Huss, came into being shortly after the
War.

Conflicts were inevitable with such differences in backgrounds.
The Czechs wanted to go ahead full speed, to make a success of

their country. Inspired with a missionary zeal, they set about the task of raising their backward brothers to a higher level. But the Slovaks misunderstood their intentions.

What will the historian of tomorrow say about Slovakia? Will he say that her independence was of short duration? For a thousand years quiet reigned in her valleys, but recently she was thrust into the center of Europe's stage. Her mountains cast long shadows in the path of her conqueror.

The Green
Danube

4. Hungary — Rural Landscape and a Conflict

*M*AJESTICALLY the Danube sweeps onward; deep calm broods on its waters. It swirls out of the Brown Empire, past Slovak Bratislava, into the country of the nation which claims it as its own. Farther up the Danube the hammer-strokes of Hitler's diplomacy forged a new pattern of empire along the river. But it had been the lifeline of the Hungarian Kingdom for a thousand years. Without the Danube, Hungary could not have existed. It was the natural source from which a wayward tribe of warriors derived its strength and maintained itself against a world of enemies. It was the might which enabled the Hungarians to extend their rule to the mountain frontiers provided by Nature. It was the dynamic energy which attracted scores of busy little rivers, continental commerce and a sweeping ambition. There are two Hungaries, and the Danube tells their tale. The pre-War Hungary of a thousand years comprised the entire middle basin of the

Danube. The Hungary of the post-War years had only one-third
of her former river basin. Recently she has recovered more of the
Danube. Will she ever recover all she has lost? The second Hungary was stripped of more than two-thirds of the territory of the
first Hungary and nearly three-fifths of her population.

The Danube is a river of whimsical moods. One would hardly
recognize the hilarious youngster of Germany in the mature
river parading its frothy waves of silver sheen in Hungary. It
is flanked by jealous reeds, looking like the river god's bayonets.
Here the perfume of trees, mingling with the odor of flowers,
produces that ingratiating scent which is the pride of Hungary.
Armlets of the Danube, chattering pleasantly, console the weep-
ing willow, tug at the branches of more sociable trees with irrepressible buoyancy, and perpetrate all sorts of childish pranks.
Here the long-legged heron resents the deep-throated greeting of
the steamer to the village around the bend. Here deep silences
are rent by the uninhibited concert of the bullfrogs.

The Vienna-Budapest steamer plows the Danube's ripples in
the midst of a rural landscape dominated by church towers. The
hayricks overtop the whitewashed houses, blinking in the strong
sunshine with their short-sighted windows. They are smaller than
the ones we left behind in the west. Agricultural machinery is
rarer; the peasant women's kerchiefs are more colorful; the scythe
and sickle flash stray glints back to the sky. Towns float into view,
as quiet as the countryside, their peace rarely disturbed by the
roar of motor-cars. Their houses are small, too, and the gait of
the townsmen leisurely. Dreamily the burghers look at the boat
from the terrace of the open-air café at the landing place. Dreamily the gypsy band plays burning Hungarian music. Life here is
in slow motion.

A Ruined Castle

The Danube of castles and ruins is behind us; the protection of hills is left behind. We are passing through a country of plains, parts of which are among the best lands in the Old World. Castles thrive on hilltops; not here. Even if there were hills in this region, they could not have survived the massed attack of the East. This beautiful land, ravaged by Tatar and Turk, still wears the scars of their visit. At the town of Esztergom the Danube forsakes its eastward course and turns southward boldly. Here there is a hill, topped by a vast Cathedral, resembling St. Peter's of Rome. In its shadow rests the residence of Hungary's primate. Excavations now in progress have brought to light the thousand-year-old church in which St. Stephen, Hungary's first King, worshiped. Our steamer makes its first call on historic Hungary.

It calls again farther down the river, where Hungary's only Danubian ruined castle greets us, recalling the times when history was royal murder. A primitive ferry, carrying a horse-team, may cross our way. The joyous crew of the rowboat from the near-by Summer resort waves us a friendly greeting. A small freighter pants upstream, carrying a string of barges. It flies the swastika flag of Nazi Germany, or the flag of Yugoslavia or Roumania, farther down the river. We overtake a chain of rafts, which Spring waters floated in the Carpathians on their way down-stream. The turning of propellers, the tooting of craft fail to dis-turb the slumber of the Danube. This quiet is in contrast with the lively Rhine, a smaller river. Here we are in the agricultural belt of Europe. The small factory chimney we see belongs merely to a flour mill or distillery.

Now we approach Budapest. If we look closely we may see the outlines of Aquincum, a Roman outpost. On the outskirts of the capital we are greeted by a forest of chimneys, because here Hungarian industry is concentrated. The Danube has no greater surprise for the visitor than the Hungarian capital, Budapest, which demands a chapter of its own. Now we are concerned with the rest of the country.

You arrive on the Vienna boat just before dusk falls, at a moment when the scenery is at its best.

"Isn't this a magnificent view?" a native asks as he points to the pageant of hills across the river. "Was it not a crime to dismember our country?"

Had you mentioned the weather or the price of sugar, he would have brought up Hungary's dismemberment just the same. It is Hungary's perennial subject, the local substitute of football and baseball, motor-cars and crops. What they mean, of course, is the breaking up of Hungary after the War. It is a vital problem of the Danube valley, and its importance bears no relation to the size of the country. Some of the smallest countries are larger than Hungary, with her fifty thousand square miles and her present population of slightly more than ten million.

A glance at the map shows us why Hungarians always talk about the first Hungary. It was as near perfection as a geographical unit could be. The Danube occupied the center, inviting hundreds of little rivers to accept its hospitality. That big river, running parallel with the Danube, slightly to the east, is the "Magyar stream," the Tisza, so called because it was born and died in pre-War Hungary. Other rivers drained the Northern Carpathians for Hungary, where the High Tatra, tallest of the range, stood guard over the lesser peaks. In the east, the rivers cascade down the Transylvanian mountains, bidding hail and farewell to picture-book towns whose architecture has felt the hands of German settlers. For those who remember that Transyl-

214

vania was the eastern outpost of the Reformation at the time of the religious wars, the rivers furnish an explanation. They open this country of woods and hills to the west, while the Eastern Carpathians close it to the nearby Orient. The tourist is puzzled to find such a highly developed Western culture so far in the East.

A relief map tells the story of the mountains. The Carpathian range curves northeastward at Vienna, then embraces the Danube in an ellipsis, three-quarters of a circle. Then there is a gap, out of which grows the chain of the Dinarides, all the way to the Adriatic Sea. There it becomes part of the Alps, sweeping northward, as far as the Vienna Woods. Pre-War Hungary's frontiers were the crest of these mountains. Nature made Hungary a natural unit, and man followed Nature. All railways and trunk highways converged upon Budapest. Hungary was as highly centralized as France.

The variety of her soil helped former Hungary become an entity. In its center is one of the largest plains of Europe, the *Alföld,* on the left bank of the Danube all the way to the hills of Transylvania. It comprises the entire Middle Danube region and its sand, black clay and loess produce wheat and corn. West of the river is the region known as Transdanubia, where the Alps end and the wine of Badacsony ripens. The vapor-laden clouds of the Gulf Stream come all the way here from the Atlantic. This region looks back upon an ancient culture, reflected in its garden-like fields that please the eye as much as Northern Italy's. Straddling the Danube, north of the country just described, are the green fields of the Little Plains, *Kis Alföld,* where sugar beet yields large returns. The Northern Highlands provided the first Hungary with precious timber, also coal and salt. In pre-War Hun-

215

gary's East are the ore mountains, which fascinated the Romans and Turks. The most luscious pastures of the Alps do not eclipse those of Transylvania, famed for its cattle and sheep. Hungary had flourishing iron-ore mines in the Southwest, close to the Adriatic Sea.

The second Hungary of post-War days contained only the core of this rich land. She lost her access to the sea and mountains, her timber, ore and salt, the natural gas of Transylvania, its minerals and metals. She also lost the jewel-box towns of the East, some of her main arteries of travel. After Munich, Hungary recovered Ruthenia, a country of woods and tinkling brooks in the far Northeast. She also recovered much of the left bank of the Danube, before it turns south.

The Hungarian Danube only yields its secret when you stop at one of the villages bunched on its banks. The houses turn their side to the street, while the small windows open on garden or court. The street was the enemy for centuries, and the Turkish Pasha's henchmen were curious. "A bad neighbor is a Turkish curse," the Hungarian proverb says. "All neighbors are curses," village architecture seems to say. In Turkish times they were often spies as well, and village memories reach back hundreds of years.

The street twists and turns between rows of acacia trees. An ox cart ambles down the street, its drowsy driver scarcely able to keep himself erect. A gang of barefoot children watch their flock of geese. Women of all ages paddle their daily wash in the brook behind the village. Thus their ancestors in Asia did two thousand years ago. When the Autumn rains begin to fall, the street becomes an obstacle to traffic, and in the Winter each house is a world unto itself. Inside, the houses are impeccably clean. The Hungarian peasant woman is a fanatic for cleanliness. Her "clean room" is a shrine, opened only for weddings and burial feasts. The sun is not allowed to shine into the living room, which is cool even on the hottest day.

In the evening the social life of the village moves to the well. The scene could not have been different in Abraham's day. A tall pole stands over each well, and an immense beam swings across it like the yard of the mast. A weight at one end is so arranged as to balance the bucket at the bottom of the well. When the beam is swung upward the bucket is sucked into the well; and when the end with the weight is pulled, the bucket rises full of water. In this setting village gossip thrives, public opinion is created, and Mihály woos Piroska.

Away from the Danube, yet under its influence, is the *puszta,* the Hungarian prairie, the life of which has a different rhythm. Here the Magyar cowboy, *csikós,* bestrides his charge when rounding up his horses. He is the aristocrat of the plains, while the pigherd is its proletarian. They sit with their heavy *suba,* mantles, on their shoulders. In Winter they turn out the fleecy wool of the *suba,* in Summer its leather lining. The cowboy believes that the sun's rays glance off the leather, and in this belief he feels cool. On hot days, of which there are many, you see an endless flock of sheep floating on the crest of curling waves. Behind them strides a giant, his head piercing the clouds. Onward the sheep float into the endless horizon. Then the sun is extinguished by a cloud. The apparition vanishes. This is the *Délibáb,* the Hungarian mirage.

Life on the farms is on a lower level than in the village. The owner of the land provides the house to have his workers closer to the fields and farther from temptation. Scattered all over his estate they have no chance to organize. The farmhouse is nearly buried under its tousled thatch. The mud walls keep out the Winter cold, but the crevices let it in. Sometimes two or three families share a room with pigs and geese. In full view of the public, the family members live. The atmosphere is always over-charged because of the lack of privacy, and the children grow up under high tension. The damp walls help keep the mortality high. Paris is only nine hundred miles from the *puszta,* but it might be on another planet.

The Hungarian towns are small. Only one of them has a population of more than a hundred thousand, besides the capital. Industry and commerce invite large masses, and Hungary has little of either. If each town suggests a composer to the musical-minded, as has been asserted, Hungary's towns are haunted by Liszt's rhapsodies. The sleepy streets are pervaded by his tunes, ground out by romantic misses. Small-town Hungarian life recalls the French province. Its sleepy charm appeals to retired public officials. The local aristocracy, including the doctor, lawyer and druggist, meets on the terrace of the *cukrászda,* ice-cream parlor. They seem to be as proud of their social status as if theirs were the glory of Napoleon. Over a plate of ice-cream they discuss politics and solve the most difficult problem with remarkable ease and a superior smile. Sometimes it is only a glass of native beer which sustains their garrulity.

Some of the towns enjoy a rich community life. The town of Szeged stages some of the best open-air performances of the Danube valley. Shakespeare is a familiar author in the theaters of the Hungarian towns. Music is cultivated with gusto, and the literary circle may produce a rustic genius of local fame. Most

218

of the featured figures of Hungarian literary life had their start
in a small town.

Who are the Hungarians; to what "race" do they belong?
Some of them are tall, others are short, about half of them are
blond and the other half dark. Some look as Teutonic as the
Vikings of picture books, others as Southern as Neapolitans.
Obviously, the Hungarians are a mixed race. The Middle
Danube invited greed and devastation. Several times the land
was emptied of its human contents, and new settlers sought to
turn the tide of fate. In the population of Hungary you find
Germanic, Slavic, Latin, and all kinds of Asiatic strains. The
"synthetic" Hungarian is of medium height, neither blond nor
dark, broad faced with high cheek bones. On the whole, they
are better looking than the Danubian average, except where
extreme poverty has affected their health.

But the Hungarians are neither German, Slav, nor Latin.
Scientists long tried to find their ancestry. The prevalent view
today, and for the last fifty years, has been that the Hungarians
are of Finnish-Ugrian origin—an Asiatic race. Their nearest relatives in Europe are the Northern Finns. The older theory was that
the Hungarians were related to the Turks. "The most probable
truth is," says Count Paul Teleki, Hungarian Prime Minister and
noted geographer, "that Turkish warriors subjugated a greater
mass of Finnish fishermen and farmers. Turkish shepherds and
warriors had been driven by drought from their pasturelands in
Asia. They fell upon peasants acquainted with irrigation, the
Finns, destroyed their works and conquerors and conquered set
forth to seek a new home." The name "Hungarian" is derived

from the word "Magyar" through its German corruption, "Ungar." Magyar, in turn, is thought to be derived from the name of mythical "Magor," brother of "Hunor," legendary ancestor of the Huns.

The language of the Hungarians is related to Finnish, mostly in grammar and a little in the composition of words. Incidentally, Hungarian is one of the most difficult languages, more so than German and the Slavic tongues, with which it has nothing in common. Nor is it related to any other language in the Danube valley. The Hungarian speech has many strange traits, one of which is that a person's first name is his second name, just as in Chinese. John Smith in Hungarian becomes "Smith János." Some of the names of agricultural implements are of Turkish origin, and about two thousand words are Slavic, suggesting that Magyars and Slavs have been neighbors for long.

In pre-War Hungary the majority of the population were not Hungarians; they were Slavs, Roumanians, Germans, Italians. It is worthy of notice that as strong a race as the Magyars, who have maintained themselves in a hostile Danube valley for a thousand years, should not have been able to absorb these nationalities. The task was not easy because the minorities could fall back upon the help of their kin living beyond the borders of the Kingdom and outnumbering the Hungarians. For reasons which we shall see later, many races were attracted to this particular portion of the Danube valley, making more difficult the task of assimilation.

Long ago Europe dubbed the Hungarian "hospitable" and "chivalrous." Older Hungarians still remember the day when the master of the manor tied the wheels of his guests' coaches to the highest tree tops, so as to prevent the breaking up of the

220

party. To leave a feast before it was three days old was considered bad taste. Even the poor liked to entertain in a way that reminded one of Biblical times. The isolation of the Hungarian countryside in Winter encouraged long-term hospitality. Once the host received a guest he was well-advised to keep him, as no traveler might stray his way after the rains came. Meanwhile, what was he going to do with his nectarlike Tokaj wine? Besides, the Hungarians were pioneers, dependent upon one another's help and therefore sociable. Tradition dies hard in this part of the Danube valley, and bad times have not changed the Hungarian character. Visitors to Hungary find hospitality overwhelming even today. Many of them have to eat two lunches a day, unable to bear the silent reproach on the housewife's face.

Hungarian chivalry has a trace of the Middle Ages, when troubadours sang the praises of exalted womanhood. Women are paid extravagant homage, although words are not always translated into deeds. The cult of women is another trait of pioneer civilizations, where life is hard, and raw edges of the struggle for women must be dulled. Before the War, chivalry also took the shape of sympathy for lost causes.

Nowhere in the Danube valley and nowhere in all Europe are there more remnants of the caste system. In no other country do rank and title mean as much as in Hungary. The Magyars themselves are familiar with this affliction and diagnose it as *rangkórság,* title disease. A man with a small shop employing a bare dozen of employees expects to be called "director" and be treated as a superman. Even if you are merely in charge of the weather reports of the local gazette, you are addressed as "Mr. Editor" and not plain Smith János. Since many families

consider it a disgrace to live without a handle to their names,
they send their sons to the University from which they emerge
as "Herr Doktors." The headwaiter of a Hungarian railway
dining car was addressed as "Doctor" in my presence. If you
visit a Budapest café for the first time and your title is unknown
to the waiter you may be prepared to be called "Herr Director"
or "Herr Doktor." The number of excellencies is extremely
large, since not only all ex-cabinet members and former privy
councilors are entitled to its use, but all kinds of councilors
who have enough *pengoes* to contribute to the treasury of the
ruling party. In today's Hungary, as in pre-War Russia, Excellency is not the highest title. The Regent Governor, for instance,
is *Durchlaucht,* a compromise between Your Highness and Your
High Excellency. Not long ago I overheard this fragment of conversation in a telephone booth of the Danube embankment:
"His Excellency X advised me that His High Honor Y informed
His Excellency Z that His Honor X would pay his respects to
him."

Feudal influence is reflected in the tone of everyday lan-
guage. The city man still addresses the lowly peasant as the
Liege Lord spoke to the serf in the days of the Honorable Bede.
The other day a friend of mine, who is a businessman, received the following request from an unknown young girl in
Hungary, asking him to facilitate her coming to the United
States: "Your Excellency: An unworthy poor girl takes courage
with deep humility to write to such a powerful lord. In grief
I turn to Your Excellency imploring Him on bended knees to
listen to me. . . . I beseech Your Excellency to accept my peti-
tion. With eternal gratitude, praying for a favorable reply, I
am, a poverty-stricken girl, XY."

Aristocrats and Traitors

The Hungarian of the highest social classes occupies a unique place. He is an aristocrat, a Prince or Count. Often he bears the title because his ancestors once betrayed Hungary. These forebears received their titles and estates from the House of Austria which needed traitors in order to keep the Magyars quiet. The Károlyis, for example, received the second largest estate of the Kingdom early in the eighteenth century as a reward for their betrayal. Before the days of compulsory conscription the aristocrats were also repaid for placing their private armies at the disposal of the Habsburg rulers. As the head of a private army of his serfs, *banderium,* the aristocrat was then a General as well. In those days Marshals were born in castles and not made. For their services on the battlefield the highly born were exempt from taxes. Even after a standing army had been set up they insisted on such exemption. "The greatest Hungarian," Count Stephen Széchényi, was called a renegade because he wanted the nobility to pay tolls on a newly opened bridge. The aristocrat was expected to decorate the country with his presence, and he considered work degrading. Anyone caught in the act of working promptly lost caste.

Since every aristocratic child inherits the father's title, their number is large. They still live behind social moats, although not entirely immune to change. Until the end of the War they tried to isolate themselves completely from the common man. The older aristocracy did not mingle with the younger aristocracy and the latter looked down upon the millionaire Jewish "sugar Barons" who monopolized Hungary's sugar industry. Strict laws of etiquette among members of the higher aristocracy approached the rigor of the Habsburgs' dynastic laws. Their life was surrounded with social taboos, violation of which entailed ostracism. Before aristocratic boy could meet aristocratic girl socially, their parents went into family history, producing genealogical tables and charters of nobility. Aristocrats led a life of cultural incest. The sphere of their interest was greatly limited. To mention money in company was taboo, although it was not taboo to make it by underpaying laborers. Farming was a gentleman's occupation, not actual work in the fields. Industry was frowned upon. Hunting was an occupation worthy of the highest rank. Horse-races were favored; many other sports were ruled out. Monte Carlo had its contingent of Magyar nobility. Gambling on a large scale was gentlemanlike, and losing money at baccarat was admired. Herr von Szemere gained great fame by losing a hundred thousand gold francs in one night without batting an eye. Had he won money, many eyebrows would have been raised. The army was the traditional home of the landless nobility—the cavalry, of course, not the infantry. Politics and government service stood high on the list of desirable work. Even when Hungary turned her back for a short time upon aristocratic tradition at the end of the War, the head of her progressive government was an aristocrat, Count Michael Károlyi. "Even the Communists must have their King," was the sardonic comment. Many aristocrats were younger sons without an assured living. Some of them found a ready market for their titles in the United States. The more unpronounceable their names, the greater their marital success.

The Hungarian aristocracy, together with the Church and banks, controlled a disproportionately large part of the land. Twenty per cent of Hungary's total income went to 52,130 persons, representing only .6 per cent of the population in 1930, when the census was taken. Of a total population of 8,688,000 in that year, some 1,800,000 were entirely landless rural laborers

224

and "servants." Nearly as many peasants had holdings from 1.5 to 15 acres—insufficient to support a family. Nearly 50 per cent of all the land was owned by .7 per cent of the population, while 67.3 per cent had no land or less than the minimum. Today Hungary is the classical land of large estates. Recently some of the aristocrats were forced into less exalted occupations. They sold their titles to banks and industries as members of their board of directors. Some of the younger men even went to work.

The aristocratic code of ethics is responsible for Hungary's reputation as the duelists' paradise. Members of the high nobility are apt to fight a duel at the drop of a hat. An unfriendly glance, an involuntary frown are resented. In no other country on the Danube or elsewhere is dueling in such great vogue. When Alexander Hamilton lost his life in a duel, Americans began to take a great dislike to this type of manslaughter. Today *une affaire d'honneur* in the Bois de Boulogne is news. In Hungary it is an everyday occurrence. Not long ago a Hungarian lawyer was fêted on the occasion of his hundredth duel, and another lawyer challenged two score opponents for an alleged slight to his wife. "Here you may kill for only five days in jail," may well be written on the portals of Budapest's fencing halls, since this is the penalty of a fatal outcome. However, no such duel has been reported in Hungary for years, and when the enemy is pinked, honor is saved, and the former antagonists adjourn to the nearest tavern.

Not all Hungarian aristocrats lead frivolous lives. On their estate of three hundred thousand acres, the richest Hungarian family, the Count Festetics, long maintained a sanctuary for genius. Situated on beautiful Lake Balaton, at Keszthely, their hall of living fame and literary festivals attracted talent from far and wide. Brahms' Hungarian dances might never have been composed without them.

The "gentry" class of Hungary shares many honors with the aristocracy. *Bessenyöházi és tarcsfalvai Berzenczey János*, meaning simply that the gentleman in question comes from the first-mentioned places and that he is a member of the nobility. The voice of the gentry is as cutting as the aristocrats' when talking to the peasant, but most mellifluous when addressing a member of the higher castes. Before the War, the gentry's principal occupation was politics. He was either a man of 1848 (year of the revolution), or of 1867 (year of the compromise with the Habsburgs). The members of the two parties talked endlessly about politics, but seldom achieved a practical aim. Adherents of the former wanted a Hungary entirely independent of Austria, while the latter were more content with the Austro-Hungarian monarchy. Then as now the gentry has specialized in "serving" the State. If you have anything to do with the Hungarian government you soon find out that the word should not be taken literally. It is really the State, you and millions of others, who serve the public servant. The government is all-powerful and without its "assistance" you can take no step. The country is small, the gentry is large and public offices are limited. But the nephew has a right to obtain the uncle's help in getting a government job, and the Ministries are crowded with sinecures obtained by nepotism. Since the official has an excess of time, he scrutinizes petitions with magnifying glasses. The public stands at attention before him, embodying the formidable State, and meekly mutters: "Yes, sir."

Here is a typical example, as told by a friend. He wanted to get married, had the bride and, just as important, all kinds of documents. They were properly stamped, signed and counter-signed. First he had to present the documents to the janitor of the office, who turned over every page and finally returned them as insufficient. When he reached the official of the lowest rank, my friend was obsessed with a sense of guilt. By the time he reached the highest official with whom he had to deal—an under-registrar —he was intimidated and fearful. His brows ominously knit, the official examined the documents with tantalizing slowness, his gloom deepening. Obviously, he could find no fault. Then, suddenly, his eyes brightened. The maiden name of my friend's mother was not clearly legible on the moldy document. The official turned the whole sheaf of papers back to him, and his calvary began again.

On our way down the Danube, in Hungary, we find the peasant everywhere. For centuries he was treated no better than the native cattle. In 1848 he was emancipated. He was no longer a serf; he was free—even to starve. America beckoned to him, but the gates of the United States have been closed since the War, and the problem of the peasant has grown more acute. The peace treaties deprived Hungary of her hinterland, leaving to her some of the best wheatland. Even in the midst of plenty, the peasant still could go hungry. There were no customers for his crop. Hungarian wheat could not stand the terrific competition in world markets. It cost more at Hamburg, a thousand miles away, than Winnipeg wheat, which had to travel five times as far.

The Hungarian peasant looked at the rest of the Danube valley, where the landless had been given land. Hungary's early post-War land reform was worse than a farce. It merely gave a handful of peasants the questionable privilege of buying the worst of the magnates' lands—often swamps. Too long had the peasants lived under the shadow of the manor to expect a real change in their lives. An English writer recorded the idyllic life of the Hungarian Danube country before the War:

"At meal times people sit round the big pan armed with long-handled spoons which they dip into the *gulyás,* according to age and rank. They eat seriously, without talking. The people are swift to passionate outbursts, as the storms burst without warning. The women work sixteen hours a day, and the younger ones still dance in the courtyards. Festivals are given free rein. The boys marry young, for they can enter into manhood councils when married, and the wedding day is celebrated with long processions and feastings, and many quaint doings, such as the farce of stealing the wife, the killing of the cockerel for the groom, the crowning of the best man with laurel wreaths, and the drinking to eternal friendship by the newly married couple while still at the altar. Then all night long dancing goes on at the house of the bride's parents, and in the morning the pair, led by the gypsy band and escorted by the inhabitants of the village, are conducted to their new home. To it the bride has brought fine linen beautifully embroidered, and rich dresses, perhaps some jugs and plates which hung in the kitchen of her parents' house, for these form part of her dowry."

Much of the early life has remained, more has changed. A group of young Hungarian authors descended upon the villages in the late thirties, their object to "discover Hungary." They presented their findings in a series of books, which shocked even the shock-proof people of the capital. "From the heart of Europe," one of them wrote, "you can reach the heart of Asia for the price of a street-car ticket." Another one echoed: "Budapest is an oasis in a wilderness."

228

Bread for Breakfast and Dinner

In a Hungarian Middletown, the village of Tard, one of the investigators had the eight-year pupils of the local school write down what they eat in a day. The child of a "wealthy" family, with thirty acres, wrote: "Monday morning I ate grapes, at noon I ate soup, and grapes again in the evening. Tuesday morning: sausage . . . noon: bacon . . . evening: milk. Wednesday morning: bread . . . noon: soup . . . evening: bread . . . Sunday morning: grapes . . . noon: soup . . . evening: bacon."

The eleven-year-old daughter of a peasant with eight acres wrote: "Bread for Wednesday morning, bread for noon, and noodles for supper. Bread for Thursday breakfast, soup for dinner and bread for supper. . . . I don't eat meat because we haven't got it." A little boy bragged: "Once I ate an egg and it was very good. I'd like to eat an egg again."

In the best-paid families of agricultural laborers, another investigator found, each member earned less than four cents a day. Wages as low as a cent a day for each family member were found on some rich estates. At harvest times wages went as high as twelve to fifteen cents a day. About seven per cent of the population was found to live on such a low level.

Despair has bred semi-religious sects in Hungary. Some of them are nihilistic, professing creeds which deny the right to life. Adherents of the sect of the "Seedless" are landless peasants who have turned to the systematic destruction of their kind. They practice complete birth control. They tolerate no vegetation around their houses, except the acacia tree, which is the symbol of poverty. The "Starvers'" revival meetings recall those of the deep American South. Closely packed in their houses of worship, the murmur of their chants rises and falls, broken by the shriek of

229

the faithful to whom the light is suddenly revealed. Silence falls on the audience as a "seer" takes the word, his eyes piercing unfathomable mysteries far beyond the thatched roof of the hut. In the gibberish he talks, frenzied emotion can be poured out more easily than in intelligible words. The faithful are the elect, and the candidates are those who have not yet been purged, awaiting salvation from their sins. They abjure drink, swearing and carnal love. They are attached to doomsday, the day of fulfillment for them. The "Tremblers," too, prepare themselves for the final Day of Atonement. Their nocturnal services often end in flagellations. "Devil Chasers," "Whitsunwaiters," "Sabbathians" are some of the other sects. They bring back historic memories of the inhabitants of entire towns rising from their thresholds and following the firm steps of Pied Pipers. Despair is the *leit-motif* running through many centuries.

There is some difference between the status of the Hungarian farm-hand and factory-hand, but not much. The peasant has plenty of common sense and native intelligence, but his soul-killing work makes him anybody's victim. The industrial laborer has a little more time to learn, even when not in school, but Hungary is not sufficiently industrialized to make his a powerful group. Hungary's aristocratic traditions keep the laboring man under a cloud, and he is distrusted because occasionally he tries to stand up for his rights.

In the Angels' Quarter of Budapest, probably so-called because it is the Devil's Quarter, you can still see some specimens of "shacktown." Here are shacks with cardboard roofs, replaced after each downpour. They are inhabited by the lowest-paid factory hands, unemployed and drifters from town and country. Here members of several families swarm in rooms of seven to ten feet, reproducing in real life Gorky's *Lower Depths*. Not many years ago I saw a poster of a Budapest trade-union appealing to the public's sympathy for the raising of wages by a fraction of a cent.

This is the country which occupies the most strategical position in the Danube valley, east of Vienna. It is a country with a tragic history. No ruling class professes to be as patriotic as the Magyar, and no ruling class has done more to damage the moral fiber of the nation. Their patriotism is merely an attachment to their own caste. The worst treason in their eyes is sympathy for the underdog. An experienced English journalist called Hungary the "black spot" on the map of Europe. She is today a feudal country, such as no longer exists anywhere in the world. Although her population is much better educated than that of her neighbors, Yugoslavia and Roumania, she is more backward in social relations than they. In no other country is the ruling class as contemptuous of the masses it exploits. It sneers at its weakness and prevents its rise. It keeps the rank and file from making their country a leader in the Danube valley. It forces its political immorality upon the masses and calls selfishness patriotism.

The Hungarian ruling class likes to repeat that Hungary has the oldest Constitution on the European continent, only seven years younger than England's Magna Charta. There is, however, a difference between the basic laws of the two countries. The Hungarian Golden Bull vested the nobility with the right to rise against the King if he broke his pledges. It created an aristocracy in which only members of the higher classes had a voice. Nothing was farther from its intention than protection of the common man.

Hungarian history makes much of the statement of the French

231

historian, Jules Michelet, that the Magyars, along with the Poles, kept the Turks from Western Europe's gates. It is a fact that the Turks did not pass beyond Hungary, apart from their short excursion to Vienna. But one wonders if they could have maintained themselves for a century and a half along the Middle Danube if it had not been for the squabbles of the Magyar nobility and their fratricidal warfares. The Turks were already exhausted when they reached Hungary, having lost their driving force battling their way across the murderous Balkans. A united nation could have repelled them, but not a country which worshiped half a dozen political gods.

The Hungarians came from the East, driven onward by a blue sky which denied rain to the pastures of deep Asia. When they set out, they did not know that the Danube was their destination. The blue sky had drawn the moisture out of the tired fields and the smell of death filled the universe. It was the death of cattle, dying of thirst, and then the death of men. A series of droughts had parched the life-giving green. They followed the crowd, and were followed by others. The East stampeded toward the West. They cherished the illusion that Rome still flourished, her greatness enhanced by distance. It took centuries before Rome's fame reached the Amur region and the Gobi. The tribes of the Pamir began to move; so did the medley of races on the Iranian high plateau. Irresistibly they were driven onward by the force of historic gravitation. They had been on their way for a hundred years when the news reached them that Rome had died centuries before. The Fata Morgana of the sun-parched plains made them see the glories of a new Rome—Constantinople. At the very end of the world there was the Kingdom of the Franks, its black soil carpeted with luscious grass. The tribesmen kept riding onward, fighting and killing their way closer to the miracle of the West. They jostled one another and had no mercy for the weak. This was an irresistible onward march of the strong. He who did not kill was killed.

Between the Caspian Sea and the Ural Mountains lay their natural highway. The warrior peoples swept the peasants of the steppe belt aside, picked them up and carried them on to Europe. They rolled continuously westward. Their names were Avars, Bulgars, Huns, Magyars, Scythians. Now myth elbows out fragmentary history and shows the heroic Árpád leading his supermen across Verecke Pass, where the Carpathians form a natural route between the North and the Danube valley. These are the Magyars whom patriotic history has endowed with the traits of Ohrmuzd, the force of light, fighting Ahriman, the force of darkness. The year was 895, and the impetus which catapulted the Magyars out of Asia was so strong that in less than ten years they occupied the entire Middle Danube region, from mountain to mountain, from the Carpathians in the north, to the Carpathians in the south, from the Carpathians in the west to the Carpathians in the east.

They conquered the shadowy "Empire of Moravia," which exists in legends, perhaps even in history. Much of the Danube valley was swampy and sheltered death. Malaria was the nomads' great enemy, and no amount of armor could give protection. Earlier waves of tribesmen had swept down the Danube, in search of the miracle of Rome. Now they formed a defensive wall against the Hungarian arrivals. The impetus which had brought them all the way to the Danube drove the Hungarians onward. "Heaven protect us from the murderous Magyars," the faithful prayed. The

233

Burgundians of the Far West saw the savage tribesmen, and so did the people of Constantinople and Otranto in the South. The invaders sacrificed white steeds on the altar of "Hadur," the War Lord. They were the Huns of the tenth century.

At the meeting place of East and West, Hungary was subjected to the pressure of the Eastern and Western Catholic faiths. "The great chief of Hungary," Duke Géza said, "is strong enough to have two religions at the same time."

The Danube opens Hungary to the West, closes her to the East because of the rocky Iron Gates. St. Stephen, Hungary's patron saint, and son of Duke Géza, accepted Christianity from the West. Thereby he imported the Roman religion and an inferiority complex. He gave an ideal to his countrymen: the West. They cherish it unto this day, but are not sure whether they are truly Western. King Stephen was not merely a saint, but also a shrewd politician. He thought Constantinople too strong to sponsor a new country and rejected the Eastern form of Christianity. In his day, Hungary was the America of Europe, to which races and religions of all climates were flocking. "Weak is the country which is dependent only on one race," the King said. Some of the greatest names of the country are of German, Slavic, Transylvanian, Roumanian and Italian origin.

A shadowy figure is St. Emery (Imre), King Stephen's son. He fascinated the faithful with his ascetic life, concentrated on the beauties of heaven. His Italianized name, Amerigo, was popular in the Latin world. With the pride characteristic of small nations, Hungarians claim America's name is a memorial to their beloved Prince.

Having been forced to settle, the Hungarians applied themselves to the arts of normal times. That meant that the weaker

234

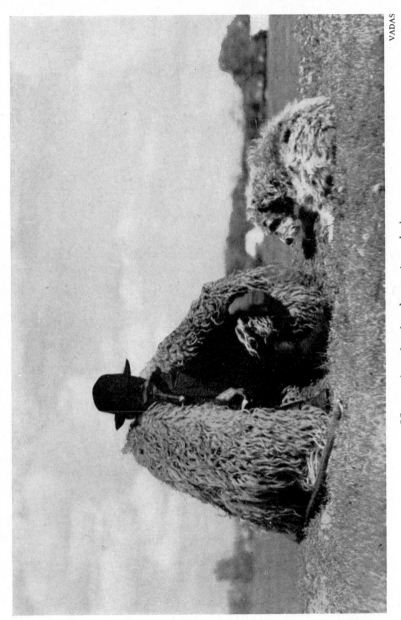

VADAS

Hungarian shepherd wearing *shuba*

had to work while the stronger heaped ignominy upon him. Christianity made little difference in the relations of man to man. "Thou shalt love thy neighbor . . ." applied only to his reward in heaven.

War was the occupation of the noble, and Hungary would have acquired a full-fledged medieval culture if it had not been for a catastrophe which is still a living memory, although it occurred some seven centuries ago. Its hero was Genghis Khan, the "Perfect Warrior," who ruled over an Empire larger than the Romans' or Napoleon's. It extended all the way from the China Sea to the banks of the Danube. The Mongol Emperor reared his throne on chaos, at an age and in a world which was in a flux. His Mongols anticipated the twentieth-century "totalitarian" warfare. As men of common sense they saw no reason why women should be allowed to live and bear soldiers and why children should become full-fledged killers. So they destroyed them. Thus they were preparing the way for the Mongol Peace, when all would belong to the ruling race. The inhabitants of the Black Sea city of Balti committed mass suicide, legend tells, to escape death at the hands of the sadistic enemy. One objective of the Mongols was the Middle Danube region, and Hungary felt the full impact of their lightninglike thrust. Entire villages were abandoned, their inhabitants seeking refuge only to be massacred "while trying to escape." King Béla IV of Hungary was just one jump ahead of the invaders, and he ran as far as the Adriatic coast. Genghis Khan died and carried an imperial dream to his grave. His Mongol hordes evacuated the Danube valley.

When he returned, King Béla saw the royal castle lined with long rows of vultures, unable to rise because of their weight. Pestilence completed the work of the enemy. The King encouraged the nobles to build fortified castles against future Mongol invasions. This weakened royal authority. When the last King of the House of Árpád died, Hungary was faced with ruin. For two centuries she was experimenting with alien Kings. Some of them were bad, others were worse, a few of them were great, others weak. The results of the Mongol invasion were not yet over. The warriors of Genghis Khan drove the Osmanli Turks from their original home in Northern Asia. Thus was set into motion the tremendous force that was finally to engulf half the Mediterranean, all the Balkans, and most of the Danube valley. Fifty years after the last Árpád King had died, the Turks crossed the Hellespont from Asia Minor to Europe. "They prayed like hyenas, fought like foxes and stunk like wolves," the contemptuous West maintained. Within thirty years they took the Balkans and were throwing their pontoons across the Danube.

János Hunyadi, whom four countries claim as their own, was the answer of the fifteenth-century Occident to the East. He was the Iron Duke of his age, the first general in the Danube valley who depended upon planning rather than unorganized pluck. He was a man of small stature, with long locks, smiling black eyes and rosy cheeks. He could neither read nor write, and he spoke no Latin, the language of the ruling class. That did not prevent him, however, from carrying the war into the Turks' own territory and beating them in every major battle. No greater figure was known to the Danube country until Napoleon shot across its sky. The name of the "Turk-Beater" was entwined in the lore of a half dozen nations. But for a fatal mistake to which he gave his help, the Turk might have been kept from the Danube for generations.

The mistake was made after Islam's best generals had been

slain in battle and Murad the Unconquerable had abased himself by suing for peace. King Ladislaus of Hungary agreed on the terms with the Turk and took an oath on the Gospel to observe the Pact. The fanatical Papal Legate Cesarini, used to the methods of the Borgias, saw the time ripe to kick the infidel out of Europe at the price of perjury. He prevailed upon the King to break his pledge with the argument that an oath to the infidel was invalid. The King thought this would be a walk-over campaign, although the Despot of Walachia, Vlad the Devil, warned him: "When the Sultan goes hunting he has a larger suite than thy army." The King marched all the way to the Black Sea, and there his small forces saw "Turks rushing upon them from marsh and sea." He himself was slain, and his former ally, Vlad the Devil, had Hunyadi kidnaped and thrown into a dungeon to pacify the Turks for his own perfidy. So great was the fame of the Turk-Beater that Murad ordered Vlad to set him free. The battle of Varna was the Waterloo of Christendom. Constantinople held out only for a few years, and when she was lost, the Turkish flood engulfed the East of Europe.

Night was to fall soon, but for a historic moment Hungary saw a glorious reign. The nobles were to elect a King, and they were captivated with the immortal name of Matthias Hunyadi, sixteen-year-old son of the Turk-Beater. Danger threatened on all sides: the Turks from the east, the Bohemians from the north, and Austrians from the west. The boy King set up a professional army to meet this challenge. The Hungarians like to boast that their ruler anticipated the great Western countries with his standing army. Again Magyar soldiers drove terror into German hearts. King Matthias took Vienna, the Habsburgs' capital. Never again was Hungary to see her armies score so gloriously. His soldiers came to be known as the Black Brigade of Matthias the Just because of their black armor. He created the cavalry of Huszárs, who made their name famous far beyond the Hungarian frontier. He had a river fleet of several hundred vessels, more than Hungary was ever to have again. He had artillery of the latest ballistic devices and the "Big Bertha" of the fifteenth century, which sixty horses could hardly move.

Under King Matthias' rule the robber barons kept quiet, and roads were safe. For the first time in the history of the Danube, piracy was banished. The nobility was compelled to contribute to the State household; they grumbled and talked of their rights, but the King appeared among them and they bowed to him. He raised the lowly to high official positions. A miller's son was one of his greatest generals. He codified the law, purged justice of venal judges. He was an eloquent salesman of Hungary's Tokaj wine. King Louis XI of France adopted Matthias' metallurgical reforms and Ivan the Terrible borrowed his master-miners.

The court of Matthias was the meeting place of great Renaissance artists. Italian tourists at Buda described his castle as more beautiful than the best in their native land. The elaborately bound books in his library, known as Corvinae, still are treasures of many museums. He provided a sanctuary for scientists and closed his eyes when their findings were not in harmony with the dogmas of the Church. He even made an attempt to equalize wealth, but he did not succeed.

His word counted in foreign affairs. He kept the Turks and Germans at a distance, and made history as far as Egypt and Persia. He helped the fighting monks, Teutonic Knights, as well as the Czars of Muscovy, who were trying to keep the Kings of Poland quiet. One is struck with the similarity of his rule and

238

Napoleon's. His reign, too, was founded on his individual genius. He carried on wars for personal prestige, burned his candle at both ends, fascinated his contemporaries, and was obsessed with the idea of building up a dynasty. His realm, too, collapsed as soon as he was gone. "King Matthias is dead and with him justice," peasants wailed at his grave.

His illegitimate son, János Corvinus, a lad of seventeen, was to have been his heir, Hungary's L'Aiglon. His father had bribed the nobles with princely presents and royal estates. But they wanted to have a King whose beard they could twist and elected the weakest pretender to the throne. They saved their privileges for a few more years, but paved the way for the Turks, who must have applauded their decision to elect *"Dobje László,"* the Yes King, Wladislaus II of Bohemia. *"Dobje, dobje,"* all right, all right, was all the King could say to his nobles' proposals. The Black Brigade was dissolved, the just laws of Matthias were repealed, the equitable system of taxation abolished, the scholars thrown out, and the Austrian possessions turned back to the German Emperor.

The Turks took their time in coming. Hungary reverted to the darkest Middle Ages. From their castles the nobles carried on their feuds against one another, also against the prosperous towns. One of the towns hired a mercenary army to protect it against the nobility. Each aristocrat had his own foreign policy, ignoring the King, who repeated: *"Dobje, dobje."* The peasants paid the bill.

In 1514 they could not bear it any longer and rebelled. They had no leader at first, and followed no plan. A group of famine-stricken peasants ran amuck and their neighbors were seized with shrieking madness. Raising their scythes, they marched upon the

239

nearest castle, forgetful of the consequences. The lord and his retinue were in a drunken stupor, and the peasants encountered no resistance. Word of their success got around. The countryside rose and found a leader in Dezsö Dózsa, not a peasant himself, but a member of the nobility. The little we know about him is colored by historians of the aristocracy, who describe him as a fifteenth-century "Red." His crime was all the more heinous because he had nothing to gain by the peasants' success.

The nobles, forgetting their own quarrels, formed a united front against the peasants. They had the soldiers and castles, the churches and the clergy. The peasants had only their raw strength and hysterical exultation. It was not so much superior military strength that defeated the serfs as the myth of the nobility's power. They crawled back into their caves, realizing the enormity of their crime; they had been fighting for human rights. It is said that Dózsa was seeking death at the head of his shrunken army, when all was lost. The nobles wanted to set an example. They caught him alive, put him on a "throne" of red-hot iron, placed a burning crown on his head, then, exhibiting him as "King of the Peasants," made his followers tear out his burning flesh and eat it.

The "Savage Diet" turned all its attention to the peasants' plight, but, instead of improving it, made it worse. If their condition was intolerable before the rising, now it became inhuman. The serfs were now completely at their masters' mercy, and so they remained for three hundred years.

Again the lure of the West fascinated the East. The Turks' religious fanaticism was blended with their craving for plunder. The palace of Matthias in Buda, and the Burg of the Habsburg Holy Roman Emperors in Vienna stirred the Oriental imagina-

A Barefoot King

tion. The Mohammedans were not interested in pasture for their cattle, black soil for their plows. They were a master race, and work was beyond contempt. Their eyes were riveted on the treasures of the Kings of France and Dukes of Burgundy, of the Doges of Venice and the burghers of Florence. They were familiar with the Venetian galleys which plied the Mediterranean.

On their way to glory, the Turks needed allies, which they found in the weakness of their enemies. They could have been kept away from the Middle Danube if János Hunyadi's spirit had survived. The Crescent would never have been raised on Buda's church towers if the Magyar noblemen had really been noble. "There is not a man here willing to pay three florins to save this realm," the Papal Envoy in Hungary wrote, and the Ambassador of Venice echoed: "Things cannot go on like this much longer." Hungary's boy King Louis II was sick with pellagra because of poor food, and he went barefoot. The wealthy aristocracy was busy with oppressing the weak and carrying on their feuds. Foreseeing the danger of Turkish invasion, a few patriotic Bishops built fortifications at their own expense. Sultan Suleiman could not believe that the Danube valley was in as bad shape as it seemed. He waited years before he let himself be convinced that the Hungarian aristocracy was rotten to the core.

In a tremendous hurry the Hungarian Diet proclaimed twenty-year-old King Louis the father of the country and dictator, *pater patriae*. It appropriated a large sum for the national defense, which it never paid, and ordered general mobilization, which it ignored. "The sky was black with the Turkish hosts when the Sultan rode to battle," a contemporary versifier wrote. Ill-nourished King Louis' stature grew for a moment. He issued calls to all Hungarians, describing the plight of their land. There were

241

only some 25,000 in the whole country who found it and their religion worth fighting for. August 29, 1526, was the day of the greatest disaster in Hungary's history. Symbolically, the Battle of Mohács was fought on the Danube. The King was drowned while trying to escape, and nearly all his soldiers were killed. It required only two hours for Hungary to lose her independence. The entire Christian world was plunged into grave danger. For a hundred and fifty years the best part of Hungary remained under Turkish rule. Even today the extent of the Turkish occupation in the Danube valley may be traced, just as one can trace the extent of Roman occupation. The Romans were constructive; the Turks were destructive. The only trace left by them is in the eyes of the Hungarian peasants. One could never do enough for the Turk. The more one labored, the greater were his exactions. Memories live long on the Danube. Although two centuries old, they are still fresh and vivid. The Turk is largely to blame—along with the Magyar aristocracy—for that resigned look in the peasant's eyes. The peasant is aloof and fearful, although the Turkish Pasha's ashes had been blown far away. He dislikes the government, which is his enemy, omnipresent, omnipotent, vicious, malicious. When the Turk finally was forced out of Hungary, he left behind a land inhabited by ghosts. From mountain to mountain, the entire country had a population of two and a half million. In a country with world-wide reputation for fertility, the density of the inhabitants was as small as in the sand deserts of Arabia, and in the Bánát, with the richest soil of the entire Danube valley, it equaled the density of Siberia. No towns remained in the occupied territory, none exists today, with the single exception of Szeged.

Before the Turks left, Hungary was swept by the Reformation.

The Habsburgs Come

The peasants turned away from Rome, and followed Wittenberg and Geneva. This was the only way they could shake off the hated present. This was their political revolt against both the Turk and their own Barons in the unoccupied areas. Some of the nobles, too, turned their backs on Rome, because their appetites were large, and so were the clergy's estates. The roads to Rome were no longer traveled by pilgrims.

Yet Hungary is a Catholic country today; only about one-quarter of her population is Protestant. The Counter-Reformation was directed from Vienna. "Whoever is master of Vienna is master of the religion of the Danube valley." This paraphrase could be made of Metternich's famous utterance. With the singleness of purpose and political genius characteristic of the Jesuits, Péter Pázmány conducted the campaign to restore Rome to her former glory in Hungary. A *Realpolitiker,* realistic politician, he concentrated his attention upon the powerful families, knowing full well that the conversion of one of them was worth more than the conversion of thousands of peasants. *"Cuius regio eius religio,"* religion belongs to the landowner. The Protestants fought back with religious frenzy. Hundreds of their clergy rotted on Neapolitan galleys, and some of the most touching religious poetry burst into life on the lips of these slaves of the oar. Again Rome was victorious in the Danube valley.

It was the Habsburgs who organized the struggle against the Turk and Protestantism. After the tragic death of King Louis II, the pathetic victim of the Battle of Mohács, Ferdinand, Duke of Austria, claimed the throne of dismembered Hungary by right of marriage. "Thou, happy Austria, marry!" His wife was Louis' sister. Some of the Hungarian nobles put up a fight, and a native ruler occupied a fiery throne. Later the Habsburg flood engulfed

243

the Middle Danube valley. Once the terror of the Danube, Hungary now was reduced to a pawn in a bigger game. She helped the Habsburgs bolster their strength; she was rich and strategically located. From time to time the memories of knightly virtues roused a romantic leader. None of these Habsburg-opponents is better known to Hungarian youth than Ferenc Rákóczi, who inspired Hector Berlioz' *Rákóczi March.* He pitted bare-handed valor against heavy artillery. He won the admiration of his people, but lost battles. Hungarian history is full of such romantic personalities and incidents.

Queen Maria Theresa made the Hungarians save the Habsburg throne with her romantic appeal. When beset by enemies, led by "that bad man," Frederick the Great, she made a dramatic appearance before the Hungarian nobles in the royal palace of Pressburg, holding her infant son, the future Emperor Joseph II, against her ample bosom. Tears flowing down comely cheeks, she appealed to the Magyars to save her throne against the enemies moving toward her capital. Swords flew from their scabbards and the assembled nobility cried: *"Vitam et sanguinem. . . ."* Our Life and Blood for Our Queen. Cynics observe that they said nothing about money. In a few days the first brigade of Huszárs was on its way to the Silesian front, where unromantic Frederick was plotting the downfall of innocence. Soon word spread in the Hungarian countryside that the occupant on the Prussian throne was the devil. The quick action of the Hungarians dramatized the Queen's plight and shamed the Austrian crown lands into action. Her dynasty was saved for two centuries, but Silesia was lost. Hungarian school children are willing to swear, on the strength of text-book testimony, that the entire House of

244

Habsburg would have been destroyed without the Magyars' help.

Her son and successor, Joseph II, made a name for himself as the most-hated King, and yet no one could be animated by better intentions. He emancipated the serfs, enabled them to buy and sell land, to marry, practice trade without their lords' sanction. He abolished torture and flogging to extract confession, and introduced equality of citizenship for all. The success of his policy would have redounded to the nobles' benefit, since serf labor was unprofitable and no amount of whipping improved its quality. The half-starved peasants, thwarted at every turn, were apathetic and stubborn. The nobles called Joseph a "Jacobin," which was to them synonymous with fratricide. They hated him because he was a renegade. At first he appeared to the peasants as a young god.

But his enemies were too powerful, backed by invincible aristocratic institutions. He could have won his aim, perhaps, to improve the lot of the common man if the common man had not turned out to be his own worst enemy. Again the Hungarian nobility proved that what it called patriotism was merely class privilege. Again their victims proved that they would side with the oppressor. The oppressor was strong, and therefore godlike and admirable. The slave found a deep affection for the whip, glorified as an instrument of divine order.

Thus those whom Emperor Joseph wanted to help turned against him. His subjects supported the aristocracy. His own courtiers called him a failure, and not even the luster of his crown could save him from pitying smiles. Defeated, he withdrew all his reforms on his deathbed, as impetuous in destruction as in creation. His death was celebrated in the Hungarian village he

245

had wanted to save from pestilential institutions, and villagers formed processions to thank the saints for having delivered them of a mortal danger.

The nobility, so courageous in defeating the reformer-ruler's plans, was less bold when it met Napoleon's generals in a battle which was over when it started. The noblemen would have thought it unworthy to plan a campaign. They wanted to fight as man against man, without organization, as the Crusaders had done. The French Emperor did not follow up his success in the Middle Danube valley. Why did he not march along the river on his way to India? Why did he march against the Russian Empire, made invincible by its vastness? Did he merely want to challenge fate by performing the superhuman? In Hungary he would have encountered little resistance and in the Danubian Principalities, farther down, he would have found assistance.

In no part of Europe did Waterloo have a stronger echo than in the Danube valley, where the man who beat Napoleon, Prince Metternich, was the uncrowned King. God was still worshiped in His churches, but real power was in his hands. Heretics were no longer burned at the stake, but dangerous political thoughts were mortal sin. Unto Caesar was given the share of God. Not that the Prince and his nominal chief, "Papa Franz," the Emperor, were vicious. They were as good at heart as Torquemada the Inquisitor had been, and they had the salvation of their millions of children at heart. Nationalism was the unforgivable sin; and its punishment was death. Yet the ideals of the French Revolution were not lost altogether; they were merely hibernating. Nationalism was in the air, and Metternich an anachronism. Hungary's social institutions were still those of the Middle Ages. The masses awaited a change; this was a messianic age.

246

Louis Kossuth's Revolution

It took sixty years for the ideals of the French Revolution to travel the distance of the few hundred miles between Paris and Budapest. The soul of the Hungarian revolution of 1848 was Louis Kossuth. He is what Cromwell was to England, Garibaldi and Mazzini to Italy. A member of the lower nobility, he made his name with his reports of the proceedings of the Diet. The Habsburg rulers kept it open as a talking-shop, where the deputies could let off steam in Latin, which the common people did not understand, but they forbade the publication of the speeches in Hungarian. Kossuth defied the authorities and was sentenced to five years in prison. There he imbibed a deep hatred against the Habsburg rule, which, incidentally, could have done him no better turn than make him a Hungarian martyr. In jail, too, he studied English with the aid of a dictionary, Shakespeare and the King James version of the Bible. Years later he astounded the Anglo-Saxon world as one of the greatest orators in the English language.

The February Revolution broke out in Paris; barricades were set up and the Bourgeois-King, Louis Philippe, was forced to flee. The air of the Danube valley was overcharged with hope. A new world was in the making, and magic words were bandied about: parliament, constitution. In an impassioned speech Kossuth demanded reforms. Two years before it might have been just an eloquent speech; two years later it would have been high treason. At that precise moment it was a statesmanly act.

Spring comes early to that part of the Danube valley, and it was the month of March. Not only Budapest's, but Vienna's youth listened to him breathlessly, and his speech was placarded in the imperial capital. Revolution broke out in Buda and Pest, the twin capitals, and was instantly victorious. A Hungarian cabinet was

247

appointed, and although Kossuth was only its Minister of Finance, he became the Hungarian government, a legendary person. His speeches were revelations from the Magyar Mount Sinai. Irresistibly he was carried into drastic opposition to the Habsburgs. He became *the* Hungarian Revolution. The liberal nobility which had supported him at first took fright at its own boldness, and Hungary had no strong middle class. Peasants in high positions would have been as anomalous as Negro women heading the Daughters of the American Revolution in Mississippi.

Kossuth became the virtual dictator. He set the serfs free, proclaimed popular representation, religious liberty, universal taxation, the right of public meeting and universal equality before the law. Carried away by their enthusiasm, young men began to preach freedom for the entire Danube valley. Soon a body of Hungarian fighters was marching to Vienna to help the Austrian revolution. Again the Magyars were moving upon the West, this time as torch-bearers of Occidental ideas. But they were beaten on the outskirts of the Austrian capital. Feeble-minded Emperor Ferdinand was deposed and Archduke Franz Joseph took the crown. The imperialists took heart, and in a short time reaction was shelling Pest from the top of Gellért Hill.

Meanwhile, too, the national minorities were moving down their mountain slopes, converging upon the plains, where the Hungarian Danube was the last stronghold of the new ideals. Kossuth was too much of a Hungarian to realize that the Kingdom sheltered a dozen other nations with ideals of their own. The cause of the revolution now seemed to be lost, but Kossuth did not think so. His romantic eloquence aroused the countryside. He appointed Artur Goergei to conduct the campaign against all enemies of Hungary. Goergei turned out to be a military leader of unusual gifts. The dictator and his commander-in-chief presented the greatest contrast. Kossuth was all soul, Goergei all brains. The former was a political poet, the latter a military mathematician. Kossuth trusted his impulses and distrusted "schemers," while Goergei distrusted spellbinders and trusted logic. Although they fought behind the scenes, the combination produced remarkable results. The "peasant rabble," as Vienna called it with contempt, routed the imperialists, whose defeat turned into disaster.

Then Emperor Franz Joseph turned to Nicholas I, Czar of all the Russias, urging him to keep revolution from the Danube, in the name of the Holy Alliance. The Czar's life was dedicated to sanctifying the name of God by imposing autocracy upon the world. In his soul, too, there burned the zeal of the Grand Inquisitor. With gladness in his heart, he responded to the imperial call, and soon his armies were streaming down the Carpathians, led by members of the Hungarian aristocracy. These latter were convinced that they could find favor before their God by seeing their country crushed. In this conviction they were guided by the thought that a country purged of their privileges was not theirs.

The armies of the Habsburgs were closing in from the west. The Hungarians were outnumbered two to one, and their arms were vastly inferior. On the plains of Világos the forces of Kossuth and Goergei were beaten. The Hungarian soldiers were decimated, and many of their leaders were hanged as traitors. Goergei lived to a very old age, shunned by the Hungarians for this last act of disgrace, for which he was not responsible. Kossuth fled the country, and the Turkish government gave him asylum. The Habsburgs demanded his extradition for alleged common crimes and placed a price on the head of his wife who, however, managed to escape with the aid of loyal peasants.

To the fifties he appeared as *the* champion of liberty. The government of the United States despatched a man-of-war to bring him to this country. He was received by the Congress and hailed by all on a triumphal tour of America. Kossuth was the great romantic Hungarian statesman, impulsive and eloquent, moving from spotlight to spotlight, giving the Magyars the reckless hero they adored.

Reaction followed revolution, and was followed by reconciliation. The revolution had failed, but its ideals triumphed: the serfs were free, equality before the law was covenanted. Thus the historical cycle was closed. The Habsburgs were forced to make their peace with the Hungarians because they saw the growing menace of the Hohenzollerns. On the battlefield of Koeniggraetz the final decision was made. The Austro-Prussian War of 1866 lasted only seven weeks, long enough for the Hohenzollerns to defeat the Habsburgs. Next year the latter concluded the *Ausgleich,* Compromise with the Hungarians, and the Austro-Hungarian monarchy was born. Both nations had sovereign parliaments. The Emperor of Austria was the King of Hungary. Each country had its own government. Hungary's official language was Hungarian. Foreign relations, national defense and finances relating to them were matters of common concern. The language of the bulk of the army was German.

The interval between the Compromise and the World War—nearly half a century—was Hungary's Golden Age. Agriculture prospered, although the unjust distribution of land worked great hardships on many. Commerce made marked headway. The products of Hungary's agricultural-machinery industry found a good

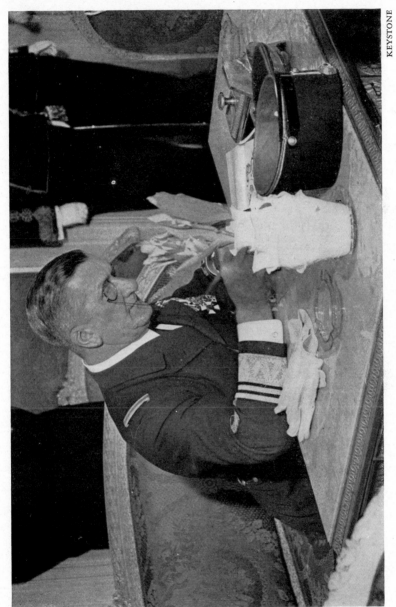

Regent Nicholas Horthy

market in the Balkans. Budapest, the capital, was Europe's fastest growing city, after Berlin.

In spite of the economic progress, Hungary's political stability was not assured. The legislature was afflicted with a mortal disease. It was elected by a small group of qualified voters, and the governmental candidates nearly always won at the polls. Electoral corruption was rampant, and intimidation often weighed more than arguments. As soon as the opposition party was in power, which occurred most infrequently, it adopted its predecessor's method. Although the Hungarian was passionately fond of talking politics, he only produced ideas detached from action. The movement to wrest power from the feudal clique had no popular backing. A large section of Hungarian opinion was in favor of an independent army and a bank of issue, but nothing was done about it.

The Hungarian ruling classes took no notice of the national minorities—Slavs, Roumanians, Italians, Germans—who formed a majority of the population. They were deaf to their requests to cultivate their languages in schools, in cultural and political life. The minorities were either unrepresented or insufficiently represented in parliament. Meanwhile, nationalism had struck the Danube valley. Slavs, Roumanians and Italians beyond the frontiers began to take an interest in their brothers in Hungary. After centuries of Turkish rule, the Balkans faced the emergence of a half dozen nations. The Magyar aristocracy saw none of the new problems, absorbed as it was in the contemplation of its greatness and in defending antiquated rights. It was they who pushed the bill through which raised barriers against the Serbian swine imports. Swine-raising was Serbia's staple industry and thus political animosity was intensified. The nervous tension in the Balkans grew. It spread to the adjoining Danube regions. Restless and dissatisfied, Europe fell a victim to the virus of war. Two shots rang out in Sarajevo. In the fateful Summer of 1914, the World War began.

Dominating Hungary in those days was Count Stephen Tisza, a man of courage, integrity and blindness. He was unable to see that the rule of the feudal aristocracy was outmoded. But he did see that a war would not help his country. He was fully aware that the military would seize power, and the influence of his class would be reduced. He felt, rather than saw, that the war would affect the fate of the Habsburg dynasty. His voice was strong when he objected to the ruthless ultimatum to Serbia, but the war party's was even stronger. They were blind, too, and plotted inadvertently the downfall of the House of Austria. Count Tisza's stand was then unknown to the world which called him a "war criminal." The secret was divulged only after the World War.

Hungary's heart was not in the War. She sensed probably the weakness of her cause. Popular enthusiasm at the time of the outbreak of the conflict was artificially stimulated. But as the War grew older, propaganda did its work, and where it failed, the threat of jail made patriotic ardor the better part of discretion. "Right or wrong, my war," provided an easy solution.

The Hungarian ruling class learned nothing and forgot nothing during the World War. It acted on the assumption that it could fool all the people all the time. It took for granted that the little man was craving a hero's death and a pauper's grave. The Western nations' trenches resounded with promises of a future country fit for heroes to live in. Not so in Hungary, where the aristocracy was sure of itself. Nonetheless, the Magyar soldier fought well during the War. Perhaps he would not have lost his head in the

252

last moment if he had known what he was fighting for. Hungary never suffered the agonies of near-starvation which turned Vienna into a city of ghosts toward the end of the War. Budapest was never bombarded from the air, and only a small section of hilly Northern Hungary was occupied by the enemy for a short time.

The Hungarian aristocracy had no sympathy for Emperor and King Karl's last-minute efforts to win over the national minorities of the monarchy. When Karl issued his manifesto in which his Empire was transformed into a federation, the Hungarian rulers outlawed such a solution for their part of the Danube valley. The end was drawing near. The Balkan front of the Central Powers had collapsed at Salonika and the "rear door" of the Austro-Hungarian monarchy was forced open. The Allied armies began their march from the southeast. Young Karl paid a hurried visit to the Hungarian countryside. He had heard ominous rumblings in Vienna. Could he depend upon the "chivalrous" Hungarians to save his dynasty as they had saved it under the rule of Queen Maria Theresa? If he only had the great Queen's sense of dramatic values! If he only could have seen his chance of a lifetime in a critical moment!

The visit took him to the "Calvinist Rome," as the Hungarians call their city of Debrecen. Its people are of the oldest stock, and, being Hungarians, they are romantic. Along with most other Hungarians they had a pet aversion: the imperial anthem *Gott Erhalte*. . . . It reminded them of long struggles against the Habsburgs and of their country's secondary position in the monarchy. The bands played this anthem every time the ruler appeared. The War was not yet over, but all knew that it was in its last throes. All knew, too, that in Debrecen the band would salute the Emperor and King with the imperial anthem, as prescribed by court etiquette. But somehow all hoped that by a miracle the band would play the Hungarian anthem. It would have been a revolutionary act and highly romantic, dear to Magyar hearts. It would have accomplished wonders. The city of Debrecen would have gone wild with joy and—who knows?—Hungary might have stayed the hand of fate. The imperial train came to a halt and the band struck up: *Gott Erhalte.* . . . The fate of the dynasty was sealed.

The Austro-Hungarian front collapsed, and millions of soldiers were streaming home, half-starved, tired, bitter. The old order collapsed, too, in the Danube valley. New governments were set up, new countries; the victors were ready to seize the prize. Something new was expected—a new world of peace and good-will, of plenty for all. "The Red Count," Michael Károlyi, second largest landowner of the country, was entrusted with the formation of the new government. He was a progressive, friend of the West, admirer of England and France. He was impulsive, full of good intentions, but had very little preparation for his task. His Minister of War declared: "I don't want to see any soldiers." His Minister of Finance frightened capital out of its wits: "I'll tax wealth out of existence." His Under-Secretary of State forgot important documents in his trousers pocket.

Peace and reconstruction were the keynotes of Count Károlyi's government. "The Danube basin is a unit," Oscar Jászi, the Minister of Nationalities, declared. He was an ardent champion of the Danubian Federation of States. In Prague and Bucharest, in Belgrade and Vienna he was known as a broad-minded scholar, who had been fighting the narrow and oppressive minorities policy of the Hungarian ruling classes for years. He was preparing a plan, according to which all nationalities could co-operate

254

with one another in the Danube valley. His plan had the merit of idealism, but the minorities were more practical. They also had the arms and armies. The Czechs seized Northern Hungary, rechristened Slovakia and Ruthenia; the Roumanians moved into Transylvania and the Bánát; the Serbians took Croatia, Slavonia and the Bácka. This was a bitter surprise for the Hungarians and, always incorrigible, they answered with a romantic gesture. Count Károlyi's rule had lasted five months. In reply to an Allied demand to evacuate additional territory, the Hungarian government turned the power over to a combination of Socialists and Communists, headed by a moderate Socialist, but actually dominated by extremists. Tens of thousands of Hungarian prisoners of war in Russia had brought back with them alluring tales of Bolshevism. It had the advantages of being new in the Danube valley and it may have had the advantage of frightening the Allies. At least it was dramatic and unexpected.

The compromise government soon developed into a purely Communist régime—Communist at least in purpose but not in accomplishments. Its leaders had excellent intentions, but execrable methods. Most of them were intellectuals and a few of them were Jews. The Tharaud brothers overdrew this era in their hysterical book, *When Israel Was King.* The most notable person in the government was its Foreign Commissar, Béla Kún. Like a true Hungarian, he was dynamic and over-eloquent. He loved the spectacular and melodramatic.

Some of the measures the Communists passed were long overdue. They expropriated the aristocrats' estates and were prepared to give land to the peasants. They introduced a large number of salutary social reforms, particularly affecting the factory workers, poor peasants, women and children. They organized folk festivals

255

which were to bring a little color into otherwise drab lives. They hated bureaucracy to such an extent that cabinet members wrote out important decrees long-hand. The Commissars moved dramatically and made long speeches. They were untrained in politics and believed they could change the feudal system at a stroke of the pen. They antagonized the "haves," and the Hungarian currency developed a sinking spell. Trade was paralyzed, and most of the industries stopped. Sabotage was rampant in the countryside. The former ruling classes began to organize themselves beyond the jurisdiction of "Red Hungary." They kept close touch with yesterday's enemy, trying to induce the Allies to invade their country. The credit of the Communist régime was approaching nadir as the patriotic élan of the population became exhausted. The Roumanians were moving closer to Budapest, and the Communist leaders engaged their forces in the hope that such a conflict would arouse the patriotic sentiments of the Hungarians.

The Communist government collapsed early in August, 1919. Béla Kún escaped to Vienna; other leaders committed suicide or were hanged. Reaction took the helm, and it was bloody. Police barracks and improvised jails were packed with suspects. An enemy's denunciation was sufficient to cause arrests, and night after night the shrieking of the doomed was heard. The political underworld rose to the surface, and mass murder became patriotism. The freebooters of Lieutenant Ivan Héjas rounded up scores of Liberals and Jews, made them dig their graves in the forest of Orgovány and buried them then and there. Concentration camps were opened for the politically suspect. The fury of the reaction vented itself with particular vehemence upon the Jews. Fourteen years before Hitler reached power in Germany, the Hungarian

256

white Terror anticipated his methods. Its victims are still un-counted.

A counter-revolutionary government was organized hastily, and the formation of the nucleus of a small army was entrusted to ex-Rear Admiral Nicholas Horthy de Nagybánya, who had an impressive appearance and an eloquently silent tongue. After the Communists had evacuated Budapest, the Roumanians marched in. They stripped the capital of the little that the World War had not devoured and then retired at the command of the Allies. Horthy's small army came on their heels. He was elected Regent Governor of Hungary, again invested with her former title of a kingdom, this time, however, without a king.

Before the War Horthy was an aide-de-camp of Emperor Franz Joseph. During the latter part of the struggle he com-manded the small Austro-Hungarian fleet and gave a good ac-count of himself at the Battle of Otranto, where he was con-fronted with a superior force. He did not succeed in running the enemy blockade but showed at least that there was an Austrian fleet. It is said that, although wounded in this battle, he kept his seat as well as head on the commander's bridge and retreated to his naval base with undiminished courage. Not much later he crushed a mutiny of the navy with much vehemence. When the end came it was he who had to turn over the ships to the enemy.

The government he appointed wore the label of "law and order." That meant that freedom of the press and assembly was restricted, and the proposed universal suffrage of the revolu-tionary era gave way to open voting in the rural districts, while secrecy was maintained only in the towns. The Communist Party was outlawed, and the Socialists had their wings clipped. The government's steam-roller was in perfect working order, although Parliament was kept open as an innocuous talking-shop, in deference to tradition. The land reform, long awaited by the peasants, failed to bring any relief.

Horthy's government signed the Treaty of Trianon, which covenanted Hungary's dismemberment. No fewer than seven States received territories formerly Hungarian: rump-Hungary, Austria, Czechoslovakia, Italy, Poland, Roumania and Yugoslavia. Roumania alone secured at Hungary's expense an area larger than the remnant left to Hungary. "These losses," says C. A. Macartney, in *Hungary and Her Successors,* "were proportionately far greater than those inflicted on Germany or Bulgaria." The Treaty limited Hungary's army to 30,000 officers and men. It deprived her of aircraft and a large number of arms, including the heavier types.

In the coming years Hungary's life passed under the shadow of Trianon. The whole nation went into demonstrative mourning. *"Toujours y penser, jamais en parler"*—Gambetta's warning after the cession of Alsace-Lorraine to Germany was not heeded in Hungary, where everyone not merely thought but talked of the national disaster.

More than three million Hungarians were turned over to their neighbors, Hungarians assert. More Magyar than the Magyars are the Székelys—in Turkish the word means "frontiersman"—a million of whom were transferred to the Roumanians by the treaty-makers. The purely Hungarian plains north of the Danube, including the former capital, Pozsony, were given to the Czechs on the ground that they needed them for strategical reasons. From the heights overlooking Budapest, the Czech frontier could be clearly seen, a mere ten minutes' airplane ride away. Half a million Magyars of the rich Bácka and Bánát were turned over

258

to Yugoslavia. Frontiers were often so drawn as to separate the town from its railway station, the village from its cemetery, the main building from its outhouse.

The whole country resounded with the defiant motto, *"Nem, nem, soha"*—No, No, Never. It was carved into bronze and marble, set on hilltop and the Danube banks. It became the political program of all parties, the creed of all Hungarians:

> *I believe in one God,*
> *I believe in one Fatherland,*
> *I believe in Hungary's resurrection.*

Since then children are being taught the pre-Treaty frontiers of Hungary, and the "occupied territories" are glossed over. Not one Hungarian in a thousand believes that the boundaries are fixed for long. They have torn out several pages of history and nothing can shake their belief that the "occupation" is temporary.

Tradition dies hard in Hungary, and a few decades do not eradicate the memory of a thousand years. The mirage of the *puszta* rides past the Danube, haunts the hills as well as the plains, lifts the spirit of all Hungarians, makes them see glory in the wake of defeat. Hitler was not the first to cut pages out of history. The Hungarians anticipated him, but lacked the strength, because of the smallness of their country, to revolt against the Peace Treaties.

Indirectly the Hungarians helped Hitler to attain power by diverting attention from the Rhine and concentrating it on the Danube. The defiant Hungarians were to be kept in place, and the beneficiaries of the Danubian debacle formed the Little Entente for that purpose. Fathered by the then Foreign Minister of the Czech Republic, Dr. Eduard Benes, it comprised Roumania, Yugoslavia, and his own country. The three had a population of some 45,000,000 and enjoyed the blessings of France, standing guard over them. While thus attention was focused on the Danube, Germany did what the Hungarians would have liked to do.

The disruption of the economic ties with the former hinterland wrought havoc with Hungary's everyday life. What was the peasant to do with the golden grain, what with the fruit of Kecskemét, the most luscious in the Danube basin? The countries which inherited Hungary's pre-War lands, the Succession States, did not want to feed the gods of war with their gold. The frontier railway stations lay deserted and wheat was rotting in Danubian granaries. At the same time, the Succession States built up their own industries on an ambitious scale, no longer willing to be dependent upon the products of Vienna and Budapest. The World War had taught them the lesson that industrial, no less than military, preparedness was vital to survival. What was the use of having the best soldiers in the world if they lacked arms to prove it? The Succession States concentrated upon their industries, and so did Hungary. Tariff walls began to rise in the Danube valley and behind them jealousy and fear peered into an uncertain future. The race of industrialization gathered momentum, and economic problems aggravated the underground political fight.

The post-War collapse of the Hungarian economic system was coming to a climax in 1921. The national currency began to fall. Jealousy kept the country's produce out of foreign markets. The demigods of the Left had failed, the gods of the Right provided no solution. Hungary was waiting for a national Messiah.

Conclaves in the Castle

In the castle of Prangins on Switzerland's Lake Geneva, visitors were frequent. They talked in whispers to a young man and a young woman, whom they addressed as "Their Majesties." They spoke of Hungary's misery, the messianic mood of her people, and the duty of the two young people to fulfill their divine mission. He was ex-Emperor Karl and she ex-Empress Zita, he a son of the House of Habsburg and she a Bourbon-Parma Princess. The ex-Emperor was kind and apologetic. He had wanted the best, was rewarded with the worst: exile and shame. He needed spiritual stimulants, which she provided. Her dainty chin was strong, and every morning she prayed in chapel for strength to carry out their mission. A ruler is true to his God, she maintained, only by performing his duty. During the World War, it was she who had induced him to approach the Allies behind the German Kaiser's back. It turned out to be an unsuccessful attempt to make peace, but it was a heroic failure.

In the castle conclaves a plan began to take shape. The young ex-monarch derived solace from the frequent letters of Regent Governor Rear Admiral Horthy, who now occupied the Budapest royal palace. In letters and through emissaries he assured Their Majesties that he was merely holding their place and would vacate it as soon as circumstances allowed. Not all aristocratic visitors were sure of the Regent's genuine sentiments. He was now the real power in Hungary, and life in the royal palace was sweet.

On Easter Sunday of 1921 a stranger gained admittance to the royal castle. So assured was he of himself that the guards dared not refuse admittance. An aide-de-camp of the Regent received him, and was thunderstruck to see that the uninvited guest was His Majesty the King. Horthy came on the run. With a self-assurance instilled into him by Zita, the King thanked the Regent for all he had done for him, announcing his royal will to assume the burden of government. In such moments history is made. Regent Horthy recovered his wits promptly, and without a moment's hesitation asked the young man to leave. He was holding the throne for him, of course, but his return would set the armies of the Little Entente on the march. Hungary's small army could not resist such an overwhelming force. Karl was not prepared for such an answer. If Zita had been near to prompt him, the history of the Danube valley might have taken another turn. But she was not near, and Karl was floored by the refusal. The precious moment which fate leaves for such answers was gone, and he knew that all he could have said now would have been uttered in vain.

Next day a car with drawn curtains was attached to the Vienna-Zurich express, and its occupant was a humiliated young man, who had gone to claim his throne and was thrown out of his own palace. News spread of the royal fiasco, and as the train stopped at the station of Linz on the Danube, laborers gathered around the curtained car, raising threatening fists.

It was a penitent Karl who was met by a sad Zita on the frontier railway station of Buchs in Switzerland. The Swiss government considered the imperial couple a danger to the security of Europe. The former Allies took steps, advising the Swiss to keep closer watch upon the exiles. The authorities thereupon informed Karl and Zita that their permit of sojourn would be extended only on the condition that they refrained from political activity and gave advance notice of future intention to leave the country.

Summer came and then Autumn. A bloodless war broke out between Austria and Hungary. Its cause was a frontier territory which the Allies had given to Austria at Hungary's expense. When Austria wanted to take possession of this strip of land, Hungarian "free troops" resisted. The opposing forces dug themselves in and some shots were exchanged. Colonel Lehár, on the Hungarian side, was an ardent legitimist, supporter of young Karl. His envoys and aristocrats conferred with the King in mountain retreats. They informed him that Horthy's betrayal had aroused public opinion and that more than ever this was the time to return. His Majesty could count upon Colonel Lehár's forces, if need be, to show the Regent his place. Zita was determined to fight. Her religious preoccupations crystallized the issue as a struggle between the usurper and the anointed King. This time the decision was for energetic action, well-planned and backed by force. Not even their children knew what they were doing when Zita and Karl motored out of their castle. Within an hour the occupants of a privately chartered airplane sighted the Danube on its eastward way in the October sun. A short time later the plane ran into a storm over the Vienna Woods. It outflew the gale and soon they landed on an improvised field of Western Hungary.

They spent their first night in the house of a loyal Hungarian aristocrat. In three hours they could have reached Budapest, but they did not take the train. The local populace learned of the sovereigns' dramatic arrival and improvised a torch-parade. Next day the royal procession got started, and picked up popular enthusiasm as it moved on. By the time they reached Budapest, they would have the entire country on their side. The procession took three days. From Budaörs they could see the royal palace overlooking the Danube. They could also see the trenches which their leisurely trip enabled the Regent's followers to dig. A few shots were exchanged. Zita was probably rehearsing the speech she would give the usurper. No doubt it was as strong a speech as her will to see Karl through to victory. But the country did not rise in support of the young King. Tired countries seldom rise in support of anything, and Hungary was tired, intimidated by an autocratic rule. The government provided the leadership and rallied inchoate public opinion, while the King looked romantic and forlorn. People felt pity for him, but it was of little help to the King who wanted to regain his throne. The Regent issued a proclamation: "Induced by traitors to their nation, His Majesty took a fateful step. . . ." The second attempt failed to recover the throne for the House of Habsburg, and the ex-King and Queen, ex-Emperor and Empress, were guests of the State; in other words, they were prisoners. In the monastery of Tihany, one of the most picturesque sites in Hungary, overlooking Lake Balaton, the former royal couple occupied two rooms hardly larger than cells. They could pray and look at the enchanting scene at their feet, where precipitous rocks rose out of the lake, but they could not leave the monastery.

What should happen to Karl and Zita? The Swiss government refused to re-admit them, insisting that they had broken their pledge. The Hungarian government turned to London to provide a minor St. Helena, and England complied. Soon the destroyer *Glowworm* was on its way, cleaving the waters of the Mediterranean, unearthly blue. Karl and Zita had tried and failed, were the laughing stock of the world, or, still worse, aroused deep sympathy. If they had not waited so long with their march on Budapest. . . . If . . . But why rehearse the past? Their St. Helena was to be Funchal on the Island of Madeira. No more beautiful place could be imagined than this jewel in the Atlantic.

Otto of Habsburg

Tourists find it an earthly paradise, but misfortune poisons the enjoyment of the sun and the welling of playful waters. On top of a mountain the family lived, forsaken by all but a faithful few, lacking the wherewithal of even a modest life. The ex-Empress had to perform common household duties. Karl fell ill with pneumonia, which he probably could have resisted if he had had the will to live. But he had the will to die, and was buried in Madeira.

His eldest son, Otto, became heir to the throne. The family moved to a small fishing village in the north of Spain—Lequeitio. The village reminded Otto of Habsburgs' former glory. In its vast church, centuries before, there had been divine services after a great Habsburg feat of arms. Spain had been a most precious jewel in the Crown of the House of Habsburg. A fishing village was no place for the education of a future Emperor and King. The Empress decided to move to Belgium. The Marquis Jean de Croix offered her the use of his Castle Ham in the village of Steenockerzeel, on the outskirts of Brussels. Otto was registered as a student of the famous University of Louvain. He wanted to become a physician, took up anatomy, biology and chemistry. He passed his first examination with *"grande distinction."* Then the big-wigs evidently discovered that the House of Austria had never had a physician-ruler. Next year he took up the history of diplomacy, canon law, international law and philosophy, and a few years later he graduated as a *"docteur en sciences politiques et sociales."* In the country of his exile he lived under the name of the Duc de Bar. In his long title, which covers about a printed page, he is described also as the sovereign master of the Duchy of Bar, which existed centuries ago and is now a part of France.

The Habsburgs did not abandon the hope of regaining one of

265

their thrones. But they were too fatalistic and old-fashioned to do anything about it. After her husband's death, Zita fell into a deeply religious mood. In past centuries prayers may have been effective in gaining thrones, but in our day planning and propaganda are more useful. Public sentiment could have been aroused, probably, both in Austria and in Hungary to favor Otto over Hitler. But the Habsburgs were too proud to win. They did not know that their petty intrigues are of little help in the twentieth century. They did not learn the art of shaping public opinion. Nor did they seem to realize that they could not go on living without national allegiance. Before the War, they could not afford to have it without antagonizing several nationalities under their rule. But nationalism had taken the Danube by storm, and the Habsburgs simply could not decide whether they wanted to be Austrians or Hungarians.

After Karl's second attempt, the Little Entente powers forced the Hungarian parliament to outlaw the Habsburgs. Regent Governor Horthy was now the real power. He appointed Prime Ministers and dominated the legislature. He lived in the aloofness of the royal palace, as far removed from the common man as if he were an ancient Caesar lording over the Danube valley. His unsmiling face reflected the awesome majesty of the State. The need that Western countries have to humanize their governments has not spread to this part of the Danube. Again Hungary anticipated the Nazi Third Reich. The State does not exist for the benefit of all, but all must live and die for the omnipotent State.

Then Hitler's shadow fell across the Danube. "Budapest next stop!" Nazi maps showed parts of Hungary as belonging to Greater Germany. Shortly after Hitler had marched into Austria, Germany announced the creation of a war fleet on the Danube.

266

German cannon could terrorize the Hungarian legislature in the magnificent Gothic parliament building. They could be trained on the former royal palace, the Prime Minister's mansion and key government buildings. When the Danube was the lifeline of the Habsburg Empire, Hungary was theirs. When the Danube became the lifeline of the German Reich, Hitler was heir to the realm of the House of Austria. It was feared that if Budapest were taken by a hostile force, the rest of this highly centralized country would go with it. However, the Nazi approach to the Hungarian problem might be quite different. Diplomatic conquest might be used instead of physical coercion. Magyar Nazis would prepare the way for the Fuehrer.

The Nazi forces began to operate under the command of the "Society of Germans Abroad" (V.D.A.), doing its work through the half million Germans of Magyarland. These Germans are more influential than their neighbors, because of their greater means and better organization. Their ancestors went to Hungary after the Mongol and Turk had left it, but retained their native language throughout the centuries. This is the strange influence of the Middle Danube, where the presence of many undigested nations has prevented the proper functioning of a Central European melting pot. At first the German Hungarians camouflaged their work with so-called *Kultur vereine,* cultural organizations, which later threw off the veil. Young Nazi students and older men of practical experience visited them, popularizing the idea of *Mitteleuropa,* a federation of German-controlled nations on the Danube. They told their hearers that Hungary was in the "trouble zone" of the world, exposed to "Communist danger." They also enlightened their audience that the Germans of Hungary belonged in the category of "frontier Germans,"

267

along with their kinsmen in Poland, Switzerland, Roumania and other countries.

The Hungarian Nazis themselves formed several Fascist organizations. The largest one turned out to be the Arrow Cross (*Nyilas*), which made great headway in all strata of society, including the national administration. Its program was largely Hitler's. It preached hatred for the Jews and Communists, demanded tearing up of the Peace Treaty. It offered land to the peasants. The villagers, starved for the black soil, listened eagerly. They had hoped many times and had been disappointed, but the Nazis spoke with trained conviction and their coffers were full. "Courage and tenacity," the Arrow Cross watchwords, were heard all over the Hungarian Danube valley. The semi-autocratic government could have stopped them but for the fact that they were Hitler's little pets and that its own policy of super-nationalism was in harmony with the Fascists'.

This movement identified wealth with Judaism, and combined anti-communism and anti-capitalism. Their leader was Major Ferenc Szálasi, a fanatic and a spell-binder. His father was a Slovak who, it is asserted, spoke a broken Hungarian. The curious parallel with Hitler, non-German dictator of Germany, is striking. His followers called him the *Vezér*, the Leader. Finally, the government found enough courage to send him to jail for three years.

Where else but Hungary could a movement such as the "Scythe-Cross" exist? When several members of this group were placed on trial, so tattered were their clothes that the judge withheld permission to have them photographed for fear that the pictures might tell the true story of Hungarian peasant misery. The movement attracted the least articulate social classes, which had lost faith in sane solutions. It was built up as a goose-stepping, uniform-wearing organization, inspired by Hitler, yet communistic in its aims. Its social-outcast followers tried to find compensation for humiliation in addressing one another as "general" and "colonel." "The Race-Protecting National Socialist Party" and other similar movements, the titles of which contain their programs, were born of despair.

All these groups overwhelmed the villages with startling ideas. Since some parts of the countryside are inaccessible in Winter even today, they broadcast German-made leaflets from airplanes. Thus the world-wide Fascist International penetrated the Danube valley. There it found uneasiness and a chaos of contradictory beliefs. To salesmen of world-saving ideas the afflictions of the Danube seemed to be curable with intensified nationalism. Did they know that Nature made the Danube a unit and that national boundaries were as many wounds on its aching body? Did they know that nationalism in the river valley defeated the very aim of the nation, which was to permit man to grow with his neighbor's help, and not to commit spiritual suicide?

$\mathcal{T}$HE capital of Hungary is a tapestry of hills and water, of an enchanted island, of music, leisure, elegance—and of slums and misery. "It's Europe's most seductive capital," enraptured visitors proclaim, swept off their feet by the discoverer's pride. But the shacks of Budapest's Angel's Field horrify the stranger. Budapest's soul is torn between memories of Eastern leisure and the Western urge to act. Her history is a struggle between the Orient and Occident. Although she lies in the heart of Hungary, she belongs to a different world—a world of rich culture on the threshold of Asia.

The right bank of the Danube, rising in hilly terraces, meets the sky. These are the last spurs of the Alps, geologists say. The chain curves away into the Bakony Mountains farther west, onetime hunting-ground of beloved bandits, Hungarian Robin Hoods. The right bank of the Danube is Buda, a town athrob with history. On the opposite bank is Pest, and she is athrob with youth. She stretches into the plains, *puszta,* land of the mirage, cosmic silence and infernal heat. A half dozen graceful bridges span the Danube, connecting the two.

A landmark tops each hill on the right bank. St. Johannes Mountain observation tower looks like a white-bodied nymph emerging from the moss-covered waters of a forest pond. Budapest takes immense pride in her setting, and the tower is the symbol of her pride. That entranced gaze of the natives surveying their enchanted capital from the hilltop is a declaration of love.

The Coronation Church crowns the northernmost Buda hill. Its seven centuries sit lightly on its native stones, which have witnessed some of the most turbulent chapters of the Danube drama. Here Hungary's Kings were crowned with a pageantry unknown to other parts of Europe. There are more monumental churches in Europe, but none has seen more pomp. Here the holy crown, a thousand years old, was placed on anointed heads. It is Hungary's most sacred relic. A special guard watches over it day and night in a building of its own. The crown has remained a symbol, even though the country is Kingdom only in name. The crown is the State, the government, a creed and even more.

Palace Hill supports the Renaissance vastness of the Royal Palace. Twice it was destroyed before the present castle was built at the end of the last century. This was the residence of the Habsburgs who seldom used it, except as visitors to enjoy Budapest's fragrant month of May. After their fall it was turned over to Regent Horthy, and it was here that he showed King Karl the door. In the chapel of the palace is the relic carried in a religious procession on the 20th day of each August. It attracts thousands to a ceremony which has never lost its magic. The relic is the mummified hand of St. Stephen, known as the Holy Right, miraculously preserved in the saint's tomb, according to legend, although the rest of his body turned to dust. When the Mongols took Buda, King Béla IV thought more of the relic than his own safety, again according to legend, and took it to the Adriatic coast, where it remained until the inhabitants of Ragusa returned it to Queen Maria Theresa, as a token of their affection.

Four stone lions guard the palace grounds. The two guarding the entrance look friendly, while the two standing at the exit seem to roar with indignation. The Late Emperor Franz Joseph is said to have asked the artist, John Fadrusz, for an explanation.

"They welcome Your Majesty's arrival," the sculptor is said to have answered, "and are indignant at Your leaving so soon."

The Prime Minister's residence, facing the Royal Palace, exudes an air of faded eighteenth-century baroque. Its tapestries speak of the joy the Danube valley has taken in war and hunting. The halberdiers scan the visitor's papers with care while swift-moving ushers appraise him with a critical eye. Although Hungary is a small country, her Chief Executive stands for an old tradition and embodies an aristocratic rule.

The square in front of the palace is the setting of a gruesome tale. Its hero was László Hunyadi, another son of the "Turk-Beater," a true Prince Charming in looks, chivalry and popular imagination. He was to pay for his father's greatness and the hypnotic power of his name. The high nobility accused him of having designs upon the crown. Young King Ladislaus V, weak and vain, lent himself to the horrid plot. He had himself invited to the young knight's Belgrade castle. He was to bring along his full retinue, and the plan was that they should kill the son of the Turk-Beater. But Hunyadi's friends saw through the

272

conspiracy and had the drawbridge raised before the mercenaries' mounts had arrived. Undeterred, one of the barons drew his sword at young László, but the latter's friends frustrated the attack. Fearing for his own life, the King pledged himself to spare the young Hunyadi and promised his mother protection for all the family. He appointed him Lord Treasurer and Captain General of the army, and returned with him to Buda. There, however, he had him arrested on charges of high treason and had his judges condemn him to death. In the long shroud of the dead, the young hero was taken to the execution block. Three times the executioner swung his ax, and three times the victim's long hair deflected the blow. After the third attempt, he struggled to his feet and demanded loudly that he be pardoned: "A common criminal should not be thus punished." As he moved closer, he stumbled on his shroud, was dragged back to the block, and a blow extinguished his life.

Silence is at home in the streets of Palace Hill. The clanging of the street-cars far below sounds like the echo of another world. The profound silence is accentuated by the strains of a Beethoven sonata pouring from an Old-World house. The cobbled streets along the edges of the hill are as dreamy as the music. Irreverent footsteps seem to frighten baroque ghosts out of their meditation. Some of the family escutcheons decorating the houses must have seen the raising of the Turkish siege. The gates of some of the old mansions are closed, the blinds drawn, the knockers left to rust.

The third hill along the water rises perpendicularly. This is St. Gellért's Mountain, a heap of dolomite rocks, topped by a low-walled citadel, which once served the Hungarians in their fight against the Turks. Strangely enough, the object of the present walls—built in the middle of the last century—was not to protect, but to intimidate the capital. The Austrian was its master, and he waged war against the Hungarian. On the precipitate slope of the rugged hill, a bronze St. Gellért grasps a defiant cross. A thousand years ago this sainted bishop of the town of Csanád defied the pagan rebels of Magyarland. He was about to cross the Danube on a tour of inspection. Just before taking the boat, he fell into the hands of the pagans of Vatha the Cruel, who began to stone him to death. The saint fell on his knees, imploring Heaven to forgive his attackers. They were so enraged by his appeal to a hostile god that they dragged him to the hilltop and hurled him into the river.

A picturesque grotto at the southern promontory of the hill reminds us that Hungary is a stronghold of Catholicism in the Danube valley. Yet a short distance away, a Turkish minaret not long ago pointed an accusing finger at an unfriendly sky. This district is known as *Tabán,* Turkish for "sole," and until recently the foot of the hill was covered with lopsided huts of ancient vintage, picturesque remnants of the East. In the Oriental baths on the Danube, Turkish tradition is perpetuated in a modern way. In Budapest a Turkish bath means what it says. In luxurious caverns, middle-class Budapest indulges itself in the manner of voluminous Pashas.

We cannot leave this bank of the Danube without a glimpse at a row of prosaic buildings, out of place in a setting so romantic. They are flour mills. Before the War Budapest was the milling center of Europe, the largest in all the world next to Minneapolis. At the wharves of the mills barges from all over the Danubian region, as far as the Ukraine, were tied up. Russia is no longer a Danubian country, and Hungary's neighbors are trying to become self-sufficient. The World War had taught these countries the danger of trusting a neighbor. Then Budapest was the only city well-supplied with bread, while the other capitals went hungry.

What Capri is to the Mediterranean, the Margareten Island is to the Danube. Its hundred and fifty acres, half way between Buda and Pest, are concentrated delight. The velvety beauty of its grass is the artist's despair. In the shade of that clump of giant oaks King Matthias the Just liked to listen to nightingales. The sulphur springs of the upper island attract a cosmopolitan crowd. The perfume of Budapest's largest flower garden is an aphrodisiac to the young. The *mondaine* elegance of this restaurant and that café, alive with music, makes the island a first-class social center.

The ruins of a convent recall the time when Princess Margaret, after whom the island is named, grieved here over the Mongol's wanton destruction under the rule of her father, Béla IV. Those ruins are now favored by lovers in search of a romantic setting. Here, too, we are reminded that this one-time Hares' Island, Lords' Island, Maidens' Island was a hunting ground, the meeting place of aristocrats and convent of high-born ladies.

Bridges are symbols of life with a unique structural charm. Those who planned Budapest visualized the importance of these spans. They blend into a country of plains and hills, enhance the beauty of the river. There are many bridges in the world that are larger than Budapest's, but proud citizens of the capital maintain there are few more beautiful. Their sweep is graceful, their decorations artistic. The Chain Bridge is the oldest of them all, and the first suspension span of this size in the entire world. It sways gently to the heavy truck, but is strong enough for any emergency. The late Thomas A. Edison described Elizabeth Bridge "as the most daring one-arched bridge in Europe." At the time it was constructed at the turn of the century, it represented the apex of the bridge-builder's art. An ornamental staircase leads to St. Gellért's monument and the Citadel. Franz Joseph Bridge perpetuates the name of the Habsburg ruler associated with the capital's phenomenal growth.

The "new" section of the city on the left bank, formerly officially and now popularly, known as Pest, is really older than Buda. Its exposed position laid it open to enemy onslaughts. Hence it was eclipsed by the rival on the right bank. The man-made beauty of the Danube Embankment compensates for the dramatic contrast of rock and green in Buda. This is the grand-tier from which the beauty of Buda can best be seen. Twilight hours at this vantage point should be lived and not described. The dying halo of the sun encircles Castle Hill. Floodlights throw the white Citadel, Fisher Bastion and Observation Tower into dramatic relief. The western breezes unload their burden of fragrance on the left bank.

Parliament Building arrests the eye on the left bank on our way downstream. Its four acres of limestone Gothic reflect a national will, recalling the monumental Westminster on the Thames. At the time it was built at the turn of the century, Hungary was anxious to show the world that she, with her population of twenty-two millions, was part of a Great Power, and that her Golden Bull, a basic law, was only seven years younger than England's Magna Charta. The World War reduced Hungary's population two-thirds, making Parliament Building disproportionately large. Nothing diminishes the patriotic Hungarian's

276

pride; and what Hungarian is not proud and patriotic? His answer has been given in four monuments of cement and not of marble—for a reason. These monuments on Liberty Square represent the four regions of which Magyarland was deprived at Trianon, and they are of cement because of the transitory nature of the peace. The North is depicted as a little Slovak boy, clinging to his mother's skirt, the South is a peasant woman, harvesting the wheat of the richest soil on the Danube, the East is a young man, upholding the shield of ancient Transylvania, and the West—given to Austria and now part of Germany—is an adolescent casting anxious eyes at Hungary's holy crown.

A few hundred delightful yards down the Danube Embankment brings us face to face with the National Academy, conceived by Count Széchenyi, "father of his country," who made it possible in the thirties by contributing his annual income of 60,000 florins for this structure. *Ex Occidente Lux* may be written on this symbol of Hungary's cultural aspirations. The Count was a typical enlightened Hungarian in his craving for the cultural treasures of the West and slightly apologetic because Hungary was so near the East.

Who could enumerate all the attractive buildings on the Danube Embankment, and who would have the patience to read a list that long? Between the Chain Bridge and Elizabeth Bridge, facing the royal castle and the sunset, the Corso is the chief attraction. It is the center of light and music, elegance and social arts. Flanked by hotels of dignity on one side and the Danube on the other, life pulses through the Corso to gypsy strains. In the shadow of potted jungles, open-air cafés and restaurants hem the Embankment, where beauty, wealth and talent are on display under multi-colored parasols. The strollers provide the chief attraction at lunch-time and twilight hours. A critical audience occupies rows of chairs, noting celebrities, appreciating gowns.

Here the actress of the moment absorbs her share of open-air admiration; the politician of the day is set upon by sycophants; the playwright of the week gets his homage; and the banker of the month puts his latest sweetheart on display. Budapest cannot afford to pay for the remarkable talents of all her children in full; she settles for the difference in admiration. The Corso on the Danube Embankment is a Vanity Fair, such as no longer exists in any other metropolis. But its smiling face occasionally conceals Disenchantment Fair. The Danube is only a few steps away, and subdued music, rainbow lights and elegance are an attractive setting for those who say good-bye. After a night of pleasure the wan dawn invites despair. The Danube has taken a great toll in life. Suicide police at one time sought to prevent mass self-destruction. It was in Budapest that the song of suicides, "Gloomy Sunday," was written; soon it swept the world. Its fascination was so great that the authorities had to forbid its public performance.

I spoke about the cafés of Vienna, described as an essential public institution before Hitler's time. The Budapest café is more than essential; it is indispensable. Paris could no more be imagined without her Champs-Elysées, London without her Piccadilly Circus, Berlin without Kurfuerstendamm than Budapest without her cafés. Wars and revolutions wrought havoc with old institutions, but not with this one. Some of them are magnificently ornate, others are distinguished, even attractive, recalling the best that France has produced. Yet it is in her cafés that the deep inner conflict between East and West is revealed. It is the blend-

Wit and Coffee

ing of a club, bar, concert hall, restaurant, library, with a touch of the American drug store and many other things. Guests pass the monumental portals with the grandiose flourish of sovereign lords. Promptly they fall heir to a pile of newspapers, also to dreams stimulated by popular opera. A heavy pall of smoke dances light pirouettes to frothy tunes. Short of an opium den, no better place could be found to put memories to sleep.

The traditions of at least two hundred years are behind the Budapest cafés. When Balázs Cafesieder opened his "coffee-drinking establishment" in 1715, little did he suspect that its progeny would provide the setting for an indispensable way of Continental life. It was in a small café of the Inner Town of Pest that the March Revolution of 1848 began. Revolution and counter-revolution of the twentieth century were thriving on the plush of the Budapest *kávéház*. It is the backdrop for high-pressure leisure as well as high- and medium-pressure activity. There are few places in which people can kill time more pleasantly than in a Budapest café. There the art of conversation has reached its summit in the Danube valley. In what other capital of Europe would people have the time to spend a night listening to a wit, contributing their own share to a feast of *causerie*? Ferenc Molnár, the playwright, was long known as a champion of wit festivals. Once he got started, his audience settled down to a glorious night. Theater-goers know him the world over as an author of charm and fantasy. His conversation was even better than his writing because he italicized its highlights with incomparable tone-inflections, expressive gestures and torrential improvisations.

Hungarian Abelards rallied their disciples at marble-topped tables. I remember one of these erudite young men enumerating the months of the French Revolutionary calendar without a flaw.

279

Another named all the Popes who reigned for two centuries of the Middle Ages, when the turnover in Rome was exceptionally large. Music and the arts, sciences and letters developed their experts. More than anything else, the patrons of Budapest cafés love to save the world. They do it with audacious finality, drugged with smoke and music. These stimulants also help to generate ideas of grandeur. The Budapest cafés were crowded with amateur generals during the World War, and they solved the most difficult strategical problems with alacrity and ease. The thorniest problems of diplomacy are trifles to these *kávéház* Metternichs.

The magnificence of the coffee palazzos induces a higher tone of life. There penniless Mme. Pompadours hold public levees and delight in their brief moment in the limelight. Heaven often delegates its authority to the café to help married bliss, sometimes without benefit of clergy. Here lawyers are in ambush for the first client. Businessmen without offices contract for deliveries which may never be made. Journalists, whose by-lines have only been printed on their visiting cards, look at the milling crowd with the scorn of unrecognized genius. Poets gaze into nowhere, praying for the inspiration that ignores them. Playwrights describe masterpieces which never reach the stage. Yet some of the best poetry and drama of Hungary have been written in the Budapest cafés. The Café New York on Elizabeth Ring was at one time known as Budapest's literary center. There the wild genius of the Magyar hills, Andreas Ady, brought forth his most savage indictments against life. He died shortly after the War. His fame has never traveled beyond Hungary's borders. His countrymen maintain that had he been born heir to the English language he would rank with the greatest of the great. Many of the front-rank playwrights of Hungary, who at one time had a near-monopoly on Broadway,

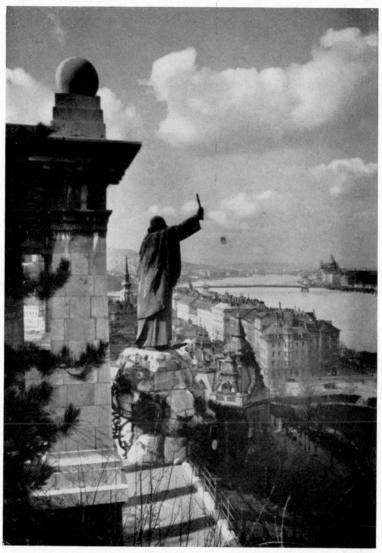

VADAS

Budapest from St. Gellért's

raised their brain-children in the smoke-charged atmosphere of the cafés.

Most of the little man's existence is spent in the shadow of tenements, not on the Corso and in the cafés. Visitors need not stray far from the Danube to encounter life as it is. Budapest has her own unadvertised misery, although the sights are somewhat less repellent than those farther east. One of the most populous districts of the Hungarian capital is called "Chicago," because of its rapid growth. It reminds us again that Budapest was the fastest-growing city in all Europe, next to Berlin. Her population increased more than 800 per cent, as compared with the increase of 343 per cent in Paris, from the beginning of the century until the World War.

Budapest's "Chicago" is as devoid of romance as the Main Street of a prairie town. Nor is the dreary spectacle mitigated by the physical comforts of America. Rows of small flats pulsate with resentment along open corridors. Children squawk piercingly, their nerves overstrained by sunless life. They are callous to unkind glances and loud oaths. The fabulous Corso might be a thousand miles away, so devoid are the streets of its glitter. A stroll in "Chicago" should be enough to convince the visitor that it is the headquarters of the grand army of despair. Yet life goes on, and the largest contingent of suicides is recruited from the better quarters. A sunless existence has its compensations. An excursion into the Buda Mountains, a stroll on sun-splotched paths of the Hüvösvülgy make up for the dreariness of an entire week. A trip up the Danube, with a couple of beer-filled glasses on checkered table-cloths, while music weaves its spell on cool waters, makes one forget the overcrowded tenements.

The Chicago of the Hungarian capital is not the worst. Dante's

inscription over the gate of Hell may justly be written over the
entrances of the shacks in Angel's Field in the capital's outskirts:
"Lasciate ogni speranza. . . ." Hope must, indeed, be abandoned. To be left by the wayside is heartrending everywhere, but
the West at least considers it a duty to redeem the body of the
unfortunate and unfit. Where there is no unemployment help—
only charity, and little of that—life shows a side which even the
author of the *Divine Comedy* would have shivered to portray.

Budapest, on the confines of the East and West, has a split personality. The Orient has infected its population with the love of
long siestas, while the West is pushing it to keep pace with the
Machine. Budapest looks up to the West, looks down upon the
East. Her geographical position has favored a half-submissive
and half-haughty way of life. An American or Englishman on the
Hungarian Danube finds all doors open, even the most exclusive
ones. The first condition of his success is an Anglo-Saxon name,
which no aristocrat of Boston loves more than does a citizen of
the Hungarian capital.

Budapest is attached to the aristocratic way of life. Hence her
inhabitants like to display what they have not. "How wonderful
it would be if we could afford to live as we do." It is said that
only a fraction of Budapest's more than a million and a quarter
people live within their means. This, too, may be partly explained
by the proximity of the extravagant East. The Balkan peninsula
is merely an hour and a half away by air. As in the case of the rest
of the country the aristocrats and bureaucrats were Budapest's
Tonangeber, social leaders, before the War. Loss of property and
the general demoralization of the stratospheric groups in the
Danube valley are opening the way to the bureaucrats. Hungary
is as highly centralized as France, and Budapest is the sun of the

282

Magyar universe. The caste of public officials is on the ascendant, and they have facilitated the advent of a Fascist-type régime. The Jews of Budapest occupy a unique position, and their problem deserves more than passing references. They like to boast that some of their ancestors lived on the site of Pest before the Magyar conquest, a thousand years ago. They fought the invading Turk side by side with the Gentiles. They lost more than ten thousand dead in the World War trenches.

The Budapest Jews are the most emancipated in the world. Not all of them, of course, as anyone can see who visits the neighborhood of King Street, *Király utca,* where ear curls are still on display. These are the remnants of the Orthodox Jews, whose fathers came from Austrian Galicia or Northern Hungary. But the majority of them provides the most convincing proof one can find anywhere that the Jew is not a "race." Most of the "Miss Hungarys" after the War were Hungarian Jewesses. They were not merely worthy of the honor because of their looks, but were typically Hungarian. Those beautiful blondes you see on the Danube Corso—real blondes—are probably Hungarians of Jewish creed. The high cheekbones which give their faces an exotic piquancy are probably the most characteristic traits of the Hungarian race. Those athletic young men, tall and muscular, are Jewish football players, members of rowing clubs.

Until recently, the Budapest Jews' percentage in professions of leadership and intellectual pursuits was disproportionately large. This was particularly true of physicians, lawyers and journalists. In the teaching profession, on the other hand, they have been discriminated against. They almost monopolized commerce and finance, and played an important part in industry. The plays that made the Magyar Danube famous on the stages of the world were written by Hungarian Jews. Those movie directors who revolutionized Hollywood and those producers whom you may consider the leaders of their art are also Jews of Hungary. That violin virtuoso, whose Hungarian name graces the billboards of concert halls from Tokyo to Cape Town, is a Jew. The Supreme Court of the Hungarian Kingdom, known as the Curia, had Jewish members before the War. Several Hungarian Jewish generals served in the Austro-Hungarian Army. Conversion opened the few doors still closed to them. One of Hungary's most prominent Ministers of National Defense was a Jew.

After the downfall of the Republican and Communist revolutions, the counter-revolution made an attempt to oust the Jew. The army was purged of them and so were high public offices. Government monopolies discriminated against the Jew. He forged ahead again, in spite of hostile governmental policy.

Some people believe that the Jew is doing himself harm by excelling. They evidently believe that the Jews should get together and decide to do nothing of exceptional merit, in spite of their gifts. The Hungarian aristocrat considered work defiling. He would have lost caste if he had gone into industry, commerce or banking. Agriculture was open to him without any such danger, but the financial operations connected with it were considered disgraceful. Hence he had to acquire a *Hausjude,* court-Jew, to manage his affairs.

Nature made Budapest one of the leading cities of the Danube. When peace came to her in the sixties, after the Hungarians and Habsburgs had concluded their pact, the capital began its dramatic spurt in the van of the great European cities. Very little would have been accomplished if the work had been left to the aristocrats. Not much more would have been achieved if the small gentry's co-operation had been called upon. They copied the aristocracy and found trade and industry degrading. These fields were left vacant; the Jews of Budapest had hardly any competition. The vast works of Manfred Weisz on Csepel Islands were a monument to his organizing genius. During the World War the Austro-Hungarian monarchy depended upon his arms and ammunition plants, as it depended upon the plants of other Jews. The banking palaces which began to rise on the Danube Embankment helped to get Hungary's share of international capital before the War. The lively newspapers, which, at one time, kept step with those of Paris, were built up by Hungarian Jews. The largest collector of arts was a Jew, and so were the theatrical producers. The audiences of concerts, opera and theater were predominantly Jews. On Jewish high holidays the vast majority of the capital's stores were closed.

Necessity drove the aristocrats to make their peace with money. Many of them married Jewish wealth. For several years they have consented to serve on the board of directors of corporations. A new generation of the gentry and the Gentile middle class has broken with aristocratic tradition. The auto and the airplane, electricity and machine have stirred their imagination. They have gone into industry; banking and trade are not wholly repellent. Down the Danube came the anti-Semitic wave from Germany. It appealed to many Hungarians, but not to the majority. The country people have lived amicably with their Jews for centuries. While the Jew is often better off than the peasant, he is part of the countryside, and the village would lose character without him.

In Budapest, too, the creed line was not strongly drawn. The Gentile Hungarian intelligentsia needed the Jew as audience and patron. It needed him also as a stimulant and a partner in intellectual adventures. Its own scope was so circumscribed that without such expeditions it would have been guilty of incest. But the War deprived Budapest of a hinterland, and competition became keener. Down the Danube swept new waves of Hitlerism. The Nazi tenet of anti-Semitism appealed to those not strong enough to stand on their own feet without a crutch. It enabled them to justify their lack of ambition by condemning merit as a crime against the blood. It enabled the inferior to see himself in a superior rôle. This resulted in laws reducing the participation of Hungarians of Jewish creed to a level they considered disastrous. Their contributions in making Budapest one of the most alluring cities on the earth were forgotten.

In Budapest, too, the majority consists of the drab average which lacks romantic appeal and therefore is often ignored. We now take it for granted that metropolises are identified with the industrial proletariat. Before the War about one-third of the total number of the employed were engaged in the milling, metallurgical, machine and ammunition industries. The aristocratic conception of life on the part of the employers made them look upon their factory-hands as serfs. They were ready to take care of them, so that they should not starve, should have shoes to go to work in and keep them in working condition. Most of them expended more care on their machines, because steel demanded its rights without a trade union. Property qualifications were so high that the factory workers had no voting rights.

Four and a half years of war brought about a change in the attitude toward labor in Budapest. Men who were good enough to die for their country must be good enough to have voting rights. The industrial proletariat was the strong-arm squad of the

Communist régime. When it fell, factory labor paid the price. Strikes were outlawed, the worker was shown his place, and employers completely dominated employment. "Slave markets" sprang up on the outskirts of Budapest, where desperate humanity was willing to exchange twelve hours' hard labor for food and shelter. Some found work, others did not, and were thrown upon public charity. Years of waiting took its toll; heads were bowed, shoulders sagging, eyes lusterless. Girls in their early twenties looked faded because of hard work and, worse still, loss of hope. Young men tried to extract a price from young women eager to marry. The marriage market became a racket, because young men could not set up a household with their own means. The Danube became a river for suicides.

The history of Budapest dramatizes the conflict of man and nature. Many times man destroyed it, and as many times nature has rebuilt the capital. For brevity's sake I shall speak only about Budapest, although Buda and Pest, two separate cities on the opposite banks of the Danube, were united only in 1872.

Much of the early history of Budapest is legendary, much of it is unexplored. Celts, Romans, nomads—the history of this part of the Danube is crowded with uncertainties. "The Scourge of God," as Attila was called, had his headquarters on the right bank of the Danube, if legend may be trusted. Why should we not believe it, since it accounts for the name of Buda? He led his Huns against the West, leaving his younger brother, Buda, in charge of his capital—Sicambria. Attila stayed away long and word of his death reached the Danube. The Regent thereupon changed the name of the capital to Buda. But Attila was not

287

dead; he returned to the Danube, slew his brother and changed the name of his camp to Etzelburg—his own German name. But Buda it has remained.

Visigoths, Vandals, Longobards, Avars, Slavs—the East poured its hosts into the Danube valley. The unity of the Holy Roman Empire appealed to Charlemagne. As there was only one heaven, there should be only one realm on earth, the realm of Christ. It is asserted that the great Frank liked the Buda hills and rested under its giant oaks. The Frankish army held its own against the Slav, but eventually was forced to retreat because of the great distance from its base. Under the Slavs, Pest was already a town—its name meant "kiln." Árpád the Conqueror came, but it seems that the Danube did not invite him. Then came St. Stephen, who made his home on the Danube. The pagans revolted when he introduced Christianity.

Generations rose and went to their graves. Again the East was in flames and the West in terror. Attila had been soft-hearted in comparison with the Apocalyptic Beast, Genghis Khan. The Mongols swept out of the East, then swept back—Buda and Pest were in ruins. The survivors built a wall around Buda; Pest was too much exposed. The Danube's turbulent waters swirled past the walls. In the fourteenth century Budapest fell under the spell of the Italian towns, where beauty made its home and murder stalked. Buda saw a regicide in the best Florentine manner. Queen Maria, lawful ruler of Hungary, was of Italian birth. So was her mother, Dowager Queen Elizabeth, and so were their ways of helping themselves. Charles of Durazzo was their major domo and an Italian himself. He was willing—insistent even—to carry the burden of the crown. Queen Marie demurred. He banged an armored fist and took the throne as Charles the Little, but not for long. A true daughter of the Renaissance, Elizabeth was familiar with the ways in which such disputes were settled in highly cultured Florence. She invited the King for a conference, which lacked none of the conventional courtesies. So absorbed was the King that he failed to notice a ripple of the curtain; and when he saw the Queen's vassal, Kálmán Forgács, it was too late: the steel of the assassin was deep in the royal chest. The King's residence of Buda did not see many such manifestations of Western culture.

The waters of the Danube froze to ice and thawed many times, but history paid little attention to the seasonal cycles. One year, in the middle of the fifteenth century, it was frozen so solid that it supported the private army of a powerful nobleman. If the ice had not been solid, the castle of Buda might never have seen King Matthias the Just. The throne of the castle was vacant, and candidates from all over Europe were in the field. The nobles were deliberating as to whom they should elect the country's king. Matthias Hunyadi, son of the Turk-Beater, was one of the candidates. It was the private army of his uncle, Mihály Szilágyi, which was drawn up on the Danube ice. At a signal, the army began to shout: "Long live Matthias, our King!" The shout was taken up by the populace on the bank of the river, spread across town and reached the conference hall of the nobles. The deadlock was broken; the voice of the people had spoken. Thus began the golden age of the royal castle on the Danube. The burghers of Buda liked their King's abrupt ways, of which the following order was an example: "From King Matthias, by the Grace of God. Good morning, burghers. If you fail to appear before your King, you'll lose your heads. In Buda. (Signed) The King."

The King liked to go among his people in disguise. His statue in the palace garden of Buda represents him as a hunter, in the company of a falconer and a country wench. Dressed for the chase, the King lost his way in the royal forest of Gödöllö. A sudden squall forced him to seek shelter in the house of the forester, whose beautiful daughter, Ilka, gave the young huntsman a jug of water and a blushing smile. He took a fancy to her, stayed on, and went for long walks with her. At last he had to leave, but before turning his face toward the Danube, he admonished the girl to look him up.

"Whom shall I ask for?"

"The royal huntsman."

The forester's daughter went to town a short time later and, seeing a group of reverent people at the palace gate, she saw her hunter in the gilded coach of the King.

"Long live Matthias, our King!" the populace cheered.

Ilka returned home without calling on the "hunter," and went to her grave shortly afterward. She asked to be buried alongside the path where the two of them had strolled.

Matthias was dead, and Hungary's dark ages began. The battle of Mohács was fought; the Turk took Buda. Boatloads of treasures were sent to Constantinople. Patrician houses were ransacked, allowed to fall into decay. The devastations of fire were unchecked, streets were overrun with weeds, and wild dogs fought for scraps of rotten food. "The streets were full of excrement and dung," a contemporary chronicler complains. "The windows were stuffed with mud and brick. . . . Painted spoons were the only merchandise offered for sale. . . . I asked a schoolmaster: 'Where is your school?' He pointed at five children: 'Here it is.' 'Are there no more of them?' 'No more in the whole town.' Dead bodies were lying everywhere."

The Turks and Black Death

Dead animals infected the water supply and the Black Death knocked at every door. Permission was withheld to bury the dead unless special burial tax was paid. The plague which swept the Danube forty-six times during the Turkish rule made Buda the hell-hole of the valley.

Islam lost its hold, and nationalism was beginning to grow in the river basin. The Turks had pitted their incipient consciousness of collective action against the moribund feudal system. That is why they had scored. But now they had settled down to a policy of plunder. Buda was liberated in 1686—a significant date in history. Islam's homeward journey began. It had lost its battle at Budapest. The two towns were in ruins, and it may have occurred to some to abandon them to fate. If the twin towns had not been natural products of their environment they would have been wiped out, but Buda and Pest were destined to live. The city fathers compelled transient merchants to fill their empty carts with waste for the homeward journey, to be unloaded beyond the gates. Thus the débris of devastated houses filled in the useless moat of Pest. The rest of the country looked at the twin towns with horror. *"Apage Satanas,"* the Biblical-minded mumbled, and the peasant paled. "The curse is on them." The new inhabitants came from afar. Shrewd "Razen" from Hungary's Southern plains settled at the foot of the hills. Adventurous French were lured by the promise of rich rewards; swashbuckling Spaniards came in hordes, attracted by lucre and glory. The Armenians took over the money market, the Greeks displayed their taffeta, the Jews settled in the Watertown section, and the Austrians followed the line of greatest profit. A miniature *Voelkerwanderung* set in.

The Kings of Hungary—now Holy Roman Emperors—granted

the twin towns much-needed privileges. Goods shipped via Budapest first had to be offered for sale to the local people, and the
resident merchants were entitled to commissions on such sales.
Still the Magyars were distrustful of their largest towns. Only
eight per cent of the inhabitants of Buda were Hungarians as late
as Maria Theresa's reign. The Kingdom's rural nabobs shunned
the towns, and took their money to Vienna. The Queen granted
the twin towns special privileges. Dead cats and dogs were disposed of by street cleaners, fire hazards were confined, government officials were ordered to lend a helping hand, social life was
encouraged, cafés were opened. But public safety was still a remote hope, though the hangman had a busy time. The sand and
dust of nearby Rákos Field plagued the housewives. Most of
the streets were unpaved, and the first street-lamps created a
sensation. Highest taxes were paid by those least able to afford
them; the burghers talked German, the noblemen murdered
Latin and only the *misera plebs* spoke Hungarian.

The remarkable development of Budapest toward the middle
of the last century is linked with the name of "the greatest Hungarian," Count Stephen Széchenyi. He knew that the Hungarian
Danube would be orphaned unless the aristocrats were induced
to help. They had to be kept at home, and not be allowed to spend
Hungary's wealth in alien lands. How were they to be weaned
from the use of Latin, French and German? He knew the value
of gambling in stimulating patriotism. He introduced horse
racing in the twin towns, and the result was remarkable. The
National Academy was the answer to the critics who maintained
that Hungarian was too crude a language for poetry. He was
instrumental in having the Danube regulated, where its flow was
impeded by titanic rocks farther down the river at the Iron

292

Gates. He opened river traffic all the way to the Black Sea, had the Chain Bridge built and introduced the first steamer on the Hungarian Danube.

The late Winter of 1838 had been severe, and when the thaw set in, ice floes were piled high above Margareten Island, and the Danube began to overflow its banks. The people were ordered to build dams, but the waters of the river crashed through the flimsy barricades, and the houses of Pest were in water up to their roofs. Many of the terror-stricken inhabitants were saved by Count Széchenyi, commanding a fleet of rescue boats. Slime covered Pest after the Danube had receded. Why was God's hand so heavy on the town? Flood, fire, plague and Turk appeared as heaven's punishment, but Count Széchenyi was more inclined to place the responsibility on man. "The flood was caused by lack of planning. The Danube must be regulated."

As so many times before, the will of the West prevailed against the apathy of the East. No longer is Budapest at the mercy of nature. After the agreement with the Habsburgs, the Hungarian capital entered upon a period of unprecedented growth. New houses were built, and the city began to spread toward the plains. New bridges spanned the Danube; new parks were laid out; a forest belt around Pest was to stay the march of *puszta* dust. Schools, libraries, scientific and literary societies began to flourish; Margareten Island enchanted the visitors; the Danube bank became the dreamland of today; the world's first underground railway was built in Budapest. The countryside began to move to town, its distrust overcome. The pioneer member of a peasant family explored the big city and fell under its spell. Work and adventure moved to the capital. A wave of Magyarization swept the city in the eighties as a reaction against centuries of alien influence. Magyar became the official language, and German was discarded.

During the World War, Budapest was the gayest spot of the Danube valley, frequented by soldiers on leave, who wanted to live to the full every moment of their absence from the trenches. The enemy never molested the hills of Buda and the plains of Pest. The armies of Austria-Hungary were on alien soil. Victories were celebrated—too many victories, probably, instead of just the one, and that was celebrated by the enemy.

The end of the World War found Budapest in a state of disrepair. It also found her the capital of a much smaller country—one-third of its former size. Yet Budapest grew, because many thousands left their homes in the territory taken by neighbors and moved to the Danube banks. She grew, too, as the State extended its influence into all walks of life and a new bureaucracy brought additional thousands to the Ministries on the hills. The city defied danger and dread, followed its own laws and improved its looks.

Budapest is more beautiful than ever, and much gayer than Vienna. At the gateway of East and West, she has remained a western outpost. Again her fate is in the balance; not only hers, but the fate of the entire Danube valley, just as it is of all Europe. "As Budapest goes, so goes the Danube valley," is still another variation on a now familiar theme.

The Red Danube

Rivers, unlike flags, do not change their colors as they flow from one country into another. The nations on their banks have emblems with different hues. When they are reflected in the water, all colors are lost, and only light and shadow remain. These nations also have armies and they kill one another. The soul of a river is not as complicated as man's.

The Danube is not red, since blood is washed away quickly, and its waters are in a hurry to meet the sea. This part of the river should be called the Red Danube because it flows through the site where blood has been shed for power and plunder. Wherever man reaches for the stars he bruises his neighbor. Here new cultures displaced the old. Roman ruins and medieval forts mark the highway of history along the river.

Rivers are born because of a great need. They are not the products of fancy or whim. They are driven onward by a dynamic

297

force; they live. Sometimes they start out and never reach the sea. Then they become lakes. The Danube meant no evil when it turned eastward at the southern corner of the Hungarian plains. It merely followed the line of least resistance.

Look at the pre-War map of Southeastern Europe, where the Danube turns east on its way to the sea, and you will find that the Danube was a frontier river throughout all its lower course. It separated Serbia from Hungary, and formed the frontier between Serbia and Roumania. Then it separated Bulgaria from Roumania. Just before disappearing in the sea, it became the frontier between Roumania and Russia. On the map of today Serbia is known as the Yugoslav Kingdom, and the Danube forms a section of the boundary between it and the Kingdom of Roumania. It continues to separate the latter from Bulgaria. Soviet Russia is not a Danubian power, and her share of the river was taken by Roumania.

Now more than ever before the Danube is a force which divides rather than links together. The Hungarian shore carried on war against the Serbian bank in the World War, and the Roumanians and Bulgarians were also at arms. Even today the villager on one side may have never set foot on the other bank. The simple fisherman must beware not to cross the halfway line. The color of the Danube does not warn him of trespassing, since it is the same under both flags. A shot, however, may warn him. He and his forefathers have seen the river run with blood.

The Danube separated the known from the unknown, the neighbor from the alien; it separated history, culture, races, traditions, religions and loyalties. It has been the scene of man's most savage cruelties against himself. This is the Red Danube, threshold of the Balkans, the bloody peninsula.

298

A Rural Scene

Small white-washed houses blink in the blinding sun with half-closed eyes. The acacia tree perfumes the Spring air, and barefooted children chase the ducks into the village pond. The scene is the same we saw higher up the river, and yet we are in the Kingdom of Yugoslavia. A few hundred feet of No Man's Land separates it from the Kingdom of Hungary.

We left behind Mohács, where the Danube valley lost its independence to dynamic Islam. Now peace reigns over the wheatfields, which shiver at the breath of the eastern breeze. The horizon is filled with a solid mass of golden stalks, rising and falling in response to a breath of air. This is the granary of the Danube, the fabulous Bácka of the black soil. A trawler swims into sight at the bend, dragging a string of boats, its chugging sound filling the universe yet deepening, and not breaking, silence. Its panting subsides; then a lark shoots into the air, and its chatter fills the sky. High-flying swallows perform prodigies of acrobatics, catching flies with lightninglike dips. Fledglings receive the stork with joy, as she gives them a choice worm. Then the sky is swept clear of sound and the eagle sweeps into sight at a great height, surveying its realm, ignoring the frantic lark. Nature is hushed; one can almost hear the sun's rays beating down upon the Danube. Bewildered herons squint at the boat and at the fleecy clouds. Fishermen spread their nets and fall asleep under the translucent sky.

The countryside is dotted with farmhouses looking like tousled birds. Slate roofs are getting fewer and houses smaller. The Danube is broad and it begins to take on the waters which swell its body to enormous proportions before reaching the sea. We approach the confluence of the Danube with the largest river we have seen so far on our journey, the Drau or Drava, which comes all the way from the Tyrol, suggesting the sights and scents of the Alps. It is at its confluence that the Danube changes its southern course to an eastern one, as if the strong river from the West had pushed it out of its way.

So far we have heard much Hungarian in the villages, although we are in Yugoslavia. Now we begin to hear more Slavic-Croatian and the dialects of Slavonia, Bácka and Bánát. South of the Danube a range of low mountains comes to meet us. Ancient trees cover its peaks; its slopes are covered with vineyards in which straggling villages are lost. Tanned youngsters wave a joyous welcome and gypsy strains strike our ears as we land in the shadow of the iron bridge. The Hungarian language which follows us reminds us that this town of Novi Sad was known as Ujvidék until the end of the War, when Hungary lost her. Today she is the capital of the Danubian provinces of Yugoslavia, and in all times she has been the center of the Bánát's grain trade. The range of Fruska Gora accompanies us on the right bank, crowned by convents, monasteries and forts. Small villages with big churches nestle in valleys which nature seems to have provided for their protection.

The Danube picks up speed as if driven toward a happy event by a mysterious force. As far as the eye can see the plains are covered with fields of wheat, except for a gap toward the north, where spearlike reeds stand guard over the largest of all Danubian tributaries, the Tisza, which the Germans call the Theiss. It was known as the "Hungarian river" before the War, because it came to life and gave itself to the Danube on Magyar soil. An unruly river, it often went on rampage in years gone by. At its confluence with the Danube stands the town of Titel, the great value of which was appreciated even by the ancient Romans, who had a settlement there. The powerful body of water seems to force the Danube to resume its southward course.

We want to hurry on because a remarkable sight beckons to us from the distance. Zemun was the frontier of Hungary and Serbia until the end of the War. The Romans built a fort there; the Huns destroyed it. Here the milky Sava, known to the Romans as Savus, rolls its waters into the Danube. The impetus it gives to the much larger river makes it change its course again.

We have reached the alluring sight on top of the hill; it is the Kalemegdan, a former Turkish stronghold in the capital of yesterday's Serbia, today's Yugoslavia. We shall return to Belgrade later on, but now we must complete our trip down the Danube as far as Roumania. The left bank is plain, the whitewashed houses, tall spires, acacia trees and flocks of geese are familiar sights. From there—Hungary—you could shout across into Serbia before the War, if your voice was powerful enough. It would have traveled from Central Europe into the Balkans.

This is the fateful Balkan peninsula. Unlike the left bank, the right bank of the Danube is rugged. The villages look different; often the houses are unpainted mud as if they wanted to make themselves invisible against the dark background. The churches are less numerous and their steeples less soaringly bold. The taverns look more rickety and the songs issuing from them are different. The men wear baggy trousers, hanging down in heavy folds, and are shod with sandals whose toes are upturned. For two centuries this part of the Danube formed the boundary between Turkey and Europe. The right bank is frontierland even today. The contrast of the carefree plains and the dark mountains reflects the difference between Central Europe and the Balkans. Here again we can read history in stones. The twenty-

301

four squat towers of Smederovo speak of the feat of the "God-fearing Despot Djordj" and his warriors who tried to save this part of the Danube from the Turks. Castles, Roman and medieval, follow the silhouette of the hills, until we reach the plain of Godomin, where the Balkans' largest river, the Morava, meets the Danube. We are not allowed to forget for a moment that we are on the Red Danube, colored by blood. The ruins of Golubac are memories of the day when the river still withstood the attacks of the East.

After Golubac the Danube undergoes a change. The plains of the left bank run up against foothills and these in turn lead to mountains, rich in ore and pines, watering places and beauty. The Transylvanian Alps rush forward and confront us with a solid wall of craggy rock. On the left bank of the river lies the Kingdom of Roumania.

The Danube is narrowed down to a fraction of its former size—now less than 300 feet wide. It has gained in depth what it has lost in width. For sixty miles the river flows between the Carpathian mountains and the Serbian highlands. Limestone walls are hollowed out by caverns; crystalline schist and granite form the rocky shoals. The air is so strong that it almost stabs lungs unaccustomed to such pine-perfumed purity. Not a sound reaches the ear from either bank, as if the entire world held its breath, concentrating on the stupendous fight between the river and the mountain. Gray hills narrow the water to a thin ribbon, and the Danube whips itself into a fury, its waters turning and churning, forming fantastic whirlpools.

At Drenkova the Greben Defiles begin, the rapid waters of the Danube smashing their way through rocks. On the right wall of the hills you can read the inscription of the legions of Emperor

302

Trajan, who built a road here along the Danube in the first century: *"Imp. Caesar Divi Nervae F. Nerva Trajanus . . ."* The mountains close in again, and now we are in a depression from which there seems to be no issue. Crags shoot out of the hard soil, some bare, others wooded. They recede before the furious river, only to close in again. We are now in the Kazan Narrows—Kazan means kettle in Serbian and Hungarian. And a kettle the Danube is, whistling and hissing, ready to explode in its mad fury. Its color is that of molten metal. The mountains are insistent, but the Danube is triumphant. The greatest struggle is yet to come. The two antagonists take a rest at Orsova, lying blissfully in the arm of a promontory, seemingly unconcerned by the gigantic strife.

Before the final curtain falls we reach Ada Kaleh Island in midstream. Here the river is broad and swift; the island is a half mile in length and width. If it were merely one of the Danubian islands, no more need be said about it, but it has a real distinction. One of Hungary's greatest novelists, Maurus Jókai, wrote a book about it under the title of *No Man's Island.* The village on the island consists of mud-plastered houses, such as one sees only in the Near East. At the appointed times the muezzin climbs the minaret of the mosque and his wailing voice summons the faithful to devotion as if this were the heart of the distant East. Old gates and neglected moats recall the time when this was a Turkish stronghold of the Danube. The population of about 500 wear turbans and veils, as if Mustapha Kemal had never lived, and they try to obey the Koran, except for the wine they press. This is a portion of old Turkey in the Danube.

The island belonged to Turkey, but the peacemakers forgot about it at the Berlin Congress in 1878, and when the river

banks went to Serbia, Roumania and Hungary, Ada Kaleh Island
remained with the Turks, an island floating in the air, as it were,
because there was no more Turkish land here. This was an ideal
arrangement for the inhabitants because the tax-collectors of the
river States lacked jurisdiction over them, and it did not pay the
High Porte of Turkey to send a tax-collector all the way. The
islanders brought in Turkish tobacco which they smuggled to
their neighbors. So skillfully did they conduct their operations
that for some time it was suspected that they had built a tunnel
under the river bed. After the War, Roumania annexed Ada
Kaleh.

The Danube steamer halts off the island, awaiting another boat
to clear the narrows, picturesquely known as the Iron Gates, toward which we are headed. So placid is the river, apart from its
swiftness, that we do not suspect what a hurdle it has to overcome. Again the mountains close in, again we see no issue for
the Danube. Fantastic crags shoot out of the water. "Grandmother's tooth" is one of them, and it looks decayed. The old
Romans built a canal and a road along the Danube to help their
ships. A railway engine helps upstream boats against the current.
Rocks and reefs protrude from the water, and the race begins
anew. It looks like shooting the rapids, except that a ten-foot
channel protects us. It was built toward the end of the last century, and the riparian countries would like to improve the Iron
Gates even more. The mountains recede to north and south; the
Danube broadens out, and at the next landing, in Turnu-Severin,
it is two miles wide. Through the mountains the Danube has
smashed its way from the Pannonian to the Roumanian plains. In
pre-historic times the mountains formed a continuous chain and
neither the Danube nor the narrows existed. The Hungarian

Alföld was then, some geologists believe, a great but shallow inland sea, drained by the water which broke its rocky bounds, forming the Iron Gates—the narrows. Near Negotin, the Danube leaves Yugoslavia and creates the boundary between Roumania and Bulgaria. From there it flows placidly toward the sea, accompanied by marshland, reeds, willows and tamarisk. Here we shall delay our journey and attempt to see the Yugoslav Danube in its proper perspective.

No city in Europe, it was said, saw more war than Belgrade, the capital of Yugoslavia. The Balkans have long been known as a political volcano. The World War started there two years earlier than in the rest of Europe and ended two years later. For centuries it was the battleground of the Turks, and, after their downfall, became the battleground of Western Europe. Today it lies along the lifeline of the German Empire. Three of its countries—Yugoslavia, Roumania, Bulgaria—flank the Danube, while the fourth—Greece—turns her face toward the south. Albania lives only in name; her ruler is the King of Italy. In the history of the Balkans, the Danube has played a vital rôle.

If you want to know why there is a curse on the Balkans, look at the map. You see the Danube and its tributaries flowing from the north and west. The Balkans lie to the south, and the Danube receives no important tributary from them. Ask which streams end in the Danube on their way north and no one seems to know their names, because they are unimportant, except for the Morava, which is not large either. The Maritza, Struma, Vardar fall into the Aegean Sea, and they, too, are only oversized brooks. Not one is a natural highway. Here you have the key to the "Balkan enigma." Nearly all of the peninsula is covered with craggy mountains which run into each other in a crazy zigzag. In fact, the very word "Balkans" is Turkish for "mountains." Crystalline schist rises against limestone; sedimentary rock is broken up by granite patches. Rocks of the Cretaceous beds intermingle with Tertiary crags. The traveler suddenly finds himself in a trap, from which the road leads backward. One mountain slope is barricaded against the next; each valley is a self-contained world. The Balkans lack the unity which only rivers can give; its streams are not arteries of travel. The Danube comes tantalizingly close, but it keeps itself aloof.

The mountains thwarted the Eastern and Western Roman world from gaining the Balkans' heart. Between Rome and Byzantium, it belonged to both at times and yet was a No Man's Land. Emperor Trajan tried and failed; so did the Eastern Emperors, who maintained nominal control. The peninsula was broken up into atomic units, as each valley worshiped its own strong man. Countless petty tyrants ruled over the valleys. Then came the Turks out of Asia. They were set into motion by the dynamic Mongols. As often happens in history, they triumphed because they were united. The Balkan atoms had exhausted themselves by smashing one another.

Along the Danube the Turkish conquerors penetrated Europe, and from it their power radiated in all directions. The Balkan people were brilliant fighters—too brilliant, indeed, to win. They were incorrigible individualists. Against the united front of the robbing, praying, fanatical Mohammedans, they were bound to fail. They held out as long as they could and were vanquished. They were a large majority in a rugged country, every nook and corner of which they knew. Their enemies formed a small minority in a land with which they were unfamiliar, and in

306

which they were interested only to the extent of plunder. Dynamic as long as they had to fight, the Turks became static as soon as the wars were over. They grew indolent, indifferent and apathetic —except to booty. Yet they ruled over most of the Balkans for more than four hundred years. Again the Danube and the curse of the Balkans were to blame.

Who were the inhabitants of the Balkans at the time of the Turkish invasion? They called themselves different names, and still do, but they were mostly Slavonic immigrants who engulfed the native Greeks, Illyrians, Latins, descendants of the tribes that sought to reach the West and failed, as well as tribes that sought to settle on the plains of the Danube and were pushed toward the barren mountains in the South. The modern Greek is predominantly Slav, and so are the Bulgarian, Serbian, Croat, Slovenian, and others too numerous to mention. "Racially," the inhabitants of the Balkans had as much unity as you can find anywhere, but they, too, are living illustrations of the fact that blood is sometimes thinner than water. Their high degree of "racial" unity did not prevent them from paving the way for Turkish victory.

How did the Turks overcome the great handicaps offered by the Balkan terrain? They made the best of the Danube's aloofness and of the fact that every valley was the enemy of the next valley. They applied the old Roman motto, *divide et impera,* divide and rule. If they had ruled over the Balkans themselves they would have had to work, which they did not like, and would have made themselves thoroughly hated. Instead, they gave Greeks authority over the Serbians, and invested Albanians with power over the Roumanians. The arrangement was ideal for all except the masses, and they did not count.

The Turks exhausted themselves in the course of the centuries. Who was weaker: they or their victims? Robbery as a principle of government is considered admirable by many and its practice is widespread even today. The Turks had depleted the visible resources of the peninsula, and their vigor was gone. The myth of greatness which sustained their vast Empire was fading. They took everything and gave nothing, destroyed everything and constructed nothing. They discouraged the natives from building on their folk basis, and offered no new culture. The influence of the East was on the wane in the Danube valley; the West was marching on. The Habsburg monarchy claimed the Danube as the lifeline of its Empire, and the Russians were forging onward in the Eastern Balkans. If the Turks had instilled loyalty among the people of the peninsula, they might have maintained their rule.

The Western powers saw a vast No Man's Land in the Balkans, with millions of prospective customers occupying vital sections along the Danube. What Genghis Khan the Mongol had done to the West, the West wanted to do to the East. It remembered that the Balkan people were Christian—Greek Orthodox—and that Western rapacity could be veiled with religion. The West began another crusade against the East, and this time, too, the Danube was its highway. Its objects were now the holy places of Mosul, where oil gushed from the ground, and not the holy places of Jerusalem. It also remembered that the Balkan people were oppressed, needed liberators who, in turn, needed markets. The Western Powers wanted the Turk to be beaten, but not too badly, since they feared the consequences of quarreling for the spoils. They were willing to let Christianity win, because it was merely an ideal. Christian nations, however, were competitors, and the Danube valley was precious. Thus, while helping the Balkan peoples, the Western Powers also kept them in check. The spread of nationalism in the peninsula partly solved their problems.

The Turk was ousted, but the curse was by no means lifted from the Balkans. The Danube could not change its course, and the Western Powers continued to be jealous of one another. The English were concerned with the road to India, and all roads, wherever situated, led to that magic land. The Russians insisted upon their policy of breaking through the ice blockade and gaining access to warm waters. Athwart the path of their ambitions lay the Turkish Empire. The Germans started to carve out a colonial empire in the Near East, a Promised Land of derricks. The Bagdad-Berlin railway was more a political than an engineering venture. The Austro-Hungarian Empire was fighting for its prestige, tottering on the brink of a disaster that, it felt, could be staved off merely by taking a slice of the Balkans. The peninsula was at its rear door, and to miss this opportunity would have meant to lose the entire Empire. Now that the infidel was out, the faithful began to quarrel among themselves. Each Great Power adopted a little Balkan pet, and the game began anew: "divide and rule." If Bulgaria was Russia's pet, then Bulgaria's neighbor, Serbia, became Austria's protégé. This was known as diplomacy.

The Balkans lack national unity because the rest of Europe kept them from fusing. As a consequence the peninsula is a museum of races and customs, religions and costumes, of languages and dialects. The typical town of Skoplje, in Southern Yugoslavia, reveals the split personality of the Balkans. A short bridge across the small river Vardar spans several centuries. The newer district, known as Seven Houses, lives in our age of electricity. Its streets are authentic imitations of French suburbia.

Their ladies diligently study Parisian fashion-plates. Electricity is generated by a municipally owned plant, and the council, not long ago, was headed by an ex-American mayor. This part of the town has a combination theater and opera, where Mozart alternates for honors with melodrama. It has a hotel without bed-bugs. Its terrace cafés are reminiscent of Old Vienna. Across the bridge is the old town. The *bit bazaar,* flea bazaar, displays a fantastic assortment of junk, from rusty nails to tattered trousers. The public porter, *hamar,* speeds down the street, a large sofa on his back. The begging gypsy was the hangman under the Turkish Sultans. In spite of the political disorder, these people are honest. The jeweler's store is left wide open, only a broom athwart the door to indicate that its owner is out. The police have little to do.

The old town has a varied collection of houses of worship. The mosque is near the flea bazaar and beggars display their exotic ailments with obvious relish. Its worshipers are Yugoslavs of the Mohammedan religion and a few Turks. The ancestors of the former embraced Islam centuries before, more out of neces-sity than conviction. Many of their descendants today are ready to die for the religion into which the Balkans had forced them. The Greek Orthodox church dominates the hill slope. It had to struggle for its life for centuries, because here the Cross and Crescent fought for supremacy. Pictures on its walls tell the lurid stories of martyrs. During Turkish rule this was the most graphic means of inspiring resistance to the challenge of the Crescent. The Roman Catholic church, subordinate in the Balkans, occu-pies a less conspicuous site. The synagogue is not far away, and is frequented by Sephardim Jews, whose ancestors were expelled from Spain at the time of King Ferdinand and Queen Isabella. They still remember the native *ladino* of their forefathers,

310

proving once again that traditions die hard in the Balkans.

At twilight the promenade is in full swing, and an audience takes its place at the tables of the open-air cafés. Some of the girls look like office workers from anywhere. The faces of some of the Mohammedan girls are veiled. The Koran forbids women to display their features, but says nothing about the length of their skirts. What these Islamic belles lose by keeping their faces covered, they make up by displaying their knees.

The architects of Babel would have delighted in the sight which the setting sun brings to life. Out of the ramshackle houses of the old town come the mixed Balkan people in steady streams. There are the baggy-trousered Serbians in their upturned sandals. The peasant woman wearing black is a Croat, mourning a national hero who died centuries before. Slovene salesmen from the Balkans' West take their seats at a café table. The undersized Albanians wear white caps; they come from across their dark mountains in search of a farthing a day. The Vlachs or Tzintzars of these parts call themselves "Romans," or Arumani and they like to be on the go. The Greek merchants from across the hills are on a business trip. One of the policemen at the Vardar bridge is a Hungarian. Those familiar with the many Balkan dialects can detect Bulgarians and Bosnians, Montenegrins and Herzegovinians in the crowd. Few of them look alike, as standardization has not yet swept the Balkans. The melting pot of Southeast Europe has never been in working order. The fez and fereddja, turban and veil, the national costumes are outward signs of the Balkans' real nature.

In the heart of the Balkans lies Yugoslavia, to which the Danube brings both the East and West. We have seen before that Hungary is devoted to the West, wants to be submerged in it, and feels aggrieved because of the distance from the Seine. Yugoslavia's problem is different. Her Danube is both Western and Eastern; one part of it feels attached to the West and the other part cannot break its ties with the Orient, and is not quite sure whether it wants to. Before the Sava and the Drava fall into the Danube they pass through Yugoslav lands, which were acquired only after the War as the reward of victory. They flow through Slovenia, which belonged to the Habsburgs for many centuries and was never under Turkish rule. Her people are proud of their Western heritage. Their language shows strong German influence and differs from the speech of other South Slav nations. The Slovenian part of the Kingdom does not belong to the Balkans, neither geographically nor intellectually.

The two rivers flow through Croatia-Slavonia (not to be confused with Slovenia, farther west), which for the better part of a thousand years enjoyed autonomy under Hungarian rule. Coming from the west, the rivers brought the Roman Catholic religion to the Croats. They also brought them fragments of Occidental culture and the desire to align themselves with the West. Croats do not like to be told that their country is in the Balkans.

The Danube merely skirts pre-War Serbia and does not even come near Dalmatia and Bosnia, Herzegovina and Montenegro. The religion of these parts came to them from the south and east. The Serbians are Greek Orthodox, and in the deep interior of the Balkans Islam thrives. No nation could have lived more than four centuries under the Turks without feeling its influence, and the Serbians would be superhuman if they had lived down the memories of the Sultan's rule. There is a world of difference between them and the Slovenes. Because of the proximity of the

West, the latter and the Croats occupy a higher level of culture than the Serbians. When the three of them, along with smaller fragments, were united in the Triune Kingdom of Serbians, Croats and Slovenes—Yugoslavia—after the downfall of the Habsburg realm, the struggle among them began. The Serbians had suffered most during the World War, had seen their country wiped out. They were the champions of the South Slav idea and, above all, were represented by a great politician, shrewd and dishonest Nicholas Pashich. They were allies of the victorious Powers, while Croatia and Slavonia had been forced to fight for the lost cause of Central Europe. The latter had planned a federal State, but the Serbians would hear nothing of it. Their historic memories did not suggest any such arrangement; they had grown accustomed, under the Turk, to pay homage to one supreme master. The Danube has brought the West to the front door of the Kingdom, but the dark mountains have kept it from entering its home.

It is a country of many contrasts, where the Parisian gown meets the veil, the Cross meets the Crescent, and East and West are mated, for better or worse. It is a country of old towns with long traditions and of haphazard mud villages, seeking protection behind primitive walls. It is a land of forbidding mountains peopled with the hobgoblins of superstition and of silent plains over which the deceptive Fata Morgana rolls. It is the country of Alpine snows and of sub-tropical climate under a dazzling sky. It is also a land of strong passions, where political opinions are accented with dagger and pistol. An airplane flight from west to east and thence south, across the length and breadth of the Kingdom, reveals its many faces and the strong contrasts of its culture. It is a flight from today into a lingering yesterday.

Ljubljana, the capital of Slovenia, was known before the War as Laibach, where the Habsburgs ruled as long as they did in old Austria. It was the center of the Slovenian movement. The fortress of Schlossberg, standing guard over turrets and chimneys, reminds us of centuries of Habsburg rule. The churches are Italian Renaissance and Baroque, combining Slav austerity with Italian serenity. The glacier-topped Slovenian Alps are only a step away. Here the Slav comes closest to the West; Italy is across the mountain range. The Slovenes' lips are sensuous and smiling. Who would not smile at the sight of the pines of Bled and the furious little streams racing down stone-strewn beds in a playful mood? They will swell the waters of the Danube, telling it about the winding mountain roads as merry as those of Lombardy and as clean as those of Bavaria. The air is crystal clear, but the forts on the hills cannot be seen because they are underground. For nearly twenty years this frontier-land between Yugoslavia and Italy was a front across which bombshells of strong words were hurled.

Situated at the river Laibach near its influx into the Sava, which rolls its milky waters into the Danube farther to the east, Ljubljana stands guard over a mountain gap into Italy—the historic Amber Road. Here Alaric fought his way across unyielding ranges on his way to Rome. Here the Huns justified their dreaded name by laying waste a thriving center on their ruthless march to the sea. The Magyars swept down the hills, following in the Huns' footsteps, destroying the fruits of an old culture. Then Ottakar the Bohemian chased the mirage of a union between the South and North Slav. For a brief moment he made them supreme in the Danube valley. Rudolph the Habsburg seven centuries ago blasted this dream and paved the way for Hitler.

Ada Kaleh Island

Nature made Ljubljana; man thwarted its will. It has a population of only 50,000, although it is 1,900 years old.

Now we can survey the Yugoslav Kingdom, with its 100,000 square miles—about the size of Oregon—and population of 14,000,000. We skirt the Julian Alps, the boundary between Yugoslavia and Italy. To take our minds off unpleasant thoughts of underground forts we turn our airplane toward the Adriatic Sea, a sheet of slothful blue, embracing green jewels. The South Sea Islands cannot surpass these gems of enchantment which a romantic spirit must have dropped into the water. The narrow coastline leaning against dark mountains is Dalmatia, another frontier. It is a land of palms and long siestas, of oranges and Southern dreams. It is a magic haven which has escaped the sad fate of commercialized beauty spots. Accessible only by sea and cut off by the mountains from its hinterland, this narrow Slavic Eden is a world unspoiled by tourists. "The Pearl of the Adriatic," Dubrovnik, once Ragusa, looks coquettishly at herself in the azure water under the bare limestone bulk of Monte Sergio. She sees a mass of aloe, palm, cypress, villas, Venetian balustrades, churches, flowering trees and shrubs. Once this dream city was great and its ships plied as far as America and India. Its name is remembered in the English language as "argosy," recalling the carracks of Ragusa, which Englishmen knew as Argusa or Aragosa.

No creaky brakes of motor-cars shatter the magic, and lazy sailboats ride the ripples raised by the *zeffiro*. It is sweet to dream under the fig trees, forgetting the troublesome world. The thunder of heavy cannon breaks the spell. Some Italian ships are engaged in target practice, out of their base at Zara, higher up the Dalmatian coast.

315

After this short detour to the Adriatic, we go back to the Danube, away from the West and into the past. Each minute of our flight brings us closer to the life of yesterday. The houses begin to shrink; red roofs turn black as tile becomes slate. We are now in the Croat part of the Kingdom over which the Habsburgs ruled for long as Kings of Hungary. The Karst Mountains loom up at the right as we leave the wooded slopes of Slovenia behind. The Karsts are barren, reminding us that we are on our way to the heart of the Balkans. The invading Venetians once entered fully into the spirit of the nearby peninsula when they stripped the mountains of their forests. Green patches proclaim the triumph of life in protected gullies, defying the cold *bora* wind of the North and the warm sirocco of the South. The frontier culture of these green spots draws strength from fighting the elements.

Beyond the mountains is the center of Croatia, long known as the Ireland of Yugoslavia. Now we are again in the orbit of the Danube. The plains are extensions of the Magyar *Alföld*. Along the Danube and the Drava they are remarkably fertile, yielding an abundance of grain, fruit and wine. Much of the plains, however, is fen-country, marshes and tedious steppes, where only isolated huts and artesian wells remind us of the presence of life. The capital of Croatia, Zagreb, looks snug between the Sava and the Sljeme peak. The Upper Town with its winding streets and the Lower Town with its shops are a study in contrasts. At every turn Zagreb accents her attachment to the West. Her university, academy of science, picture galleries, libraries, botanical gardens and monuments are signs and symbols of the Occident. Zagreb's life pulses on its café terraces to the rhythm of a South-German town. Time is not money; it is a medium of leisure. The large number of Roman Catholic churches remind us of the deep conflict between Croat and Serb. Catholicism means much to the Croat peasant because he bled for it for centuries. At every turn there is evidence of conflicts, past and present. The Croats' resentment at efforts to turn them into an Oriental nation is seen everywhere. Their Latin script is a challenge to the Cyrillic of the Serb. At every corner, too, we are made aware of the living presence of the murdered Stephen Radich, tribune of the peasants, who have adopted him as their martyred saint.

Eastward we fly again, drawn by the Danube which soon unveils itself as the river mist lifts. This part of the Kingdom is known as Slavonia—not to be confused with Slovenia farther west—that Slavonia which for centuries shared Croatia's fate. Here the Turk stayed longer, and you can still see his mark. In stumpy churches he hitched his horses to St. Christoph's image. "Where the Roman walks imperial roads sprout." "Where the Turk treads, no grass grows." The Romans too left their imprint on the countryside. This land of the three rivers was precious to them. The ruins of Roman culture are impressive, but the Turks have not left even ruins.

Now the Danube beats gently against the reeds and picks up the gossip of stolid herons. Here factory chimneys are extremely rare, and slate is yielding to thatched roofs. Farther east we float across the Danube, into the heart of the rich Voivodina, the granary of Hungary before the War and after it the granary of the Yugoslav Kingdom. The toylike peasants' houses are a blinding white; the streets are bordered with acacia trees. Here half a million Hungarians and hundreds of thousands of Germans add to the Danube's worries. When nimble fingers strip the maize at autumnal husking bees, the peasant girls weave stories about the

317

magic of the black soil, which is the best wheatland in all Europe.

Turning south, we approach old Serbia, the nucleus of the South Slav Kingdom before the War. This was the most troublesome part of the Balkans, and here the World War began. When we reach the capital, Belgrade, we must stop. *Beli Grad,* the "white town" of yesterday is the Beograd of today. Foreigners prefer to call it Belgrade. A French visitor has suggested that in view of the Balkans' reputation, "Red Town" would have been a more appropriate designation than "White Town." The Turks called it *Darol-i-Jehad,* the home of wars for faith. Sixteen times the town has been destroyed and has changed hands even more often. The gardens of the Kalemegdan, a former Turkish citadel, command the bluff above the Danube, where it receives the Sava. Looking down, one feels the slow rhythm of the Danube. Over it the silence of ages broods. It is the deep silence of the frontierland, where one world ends and another begins. The throbbing sound of the locomotive on the steel bridge to Zemun is an anachronism. The North Wind brings the warm breath of the overheated Hungarian plains, also the breath of the West. The South Wind from the Balkans is cool and mysterious. It carries the message of a land which is still trying to find its soul.

At every street corner of Belgrade East and West clash, merging for a moment, then going their way, only to meet again. Belgrade is a remarkable fusion of old and new, ambition and accomplishment. At the turn of the century she had fewer than 70,000 inhabitants (reduced to 47,000 in 1916, because of the War) and today her population is 300,000. On Terazye Square, in the heart of the capital, you can see the clash and fraternization of old and new. New buildings are going up, as modern as

318

any in New York or London. The vast parliament building was begun when democracy seemed to have won the War. The new ministries respond to an urgent need; post-War Yugoslavia is about three times the size of pre-War Serbia. Delightful mansions afford wealth the privileges it enjoys in the heart of the West. The white magnificence of the new royal palace attracts the eye. It was not often occupied by the late King Alexander whom an assassin's bullet felled in Marseilles. He preferred the simplicity of the Dedigne residence on a hill overlooking the Sava. The National Theatre occupies a prominent place as a symbol of Belgrade's efforts to get closer to Europe.

From Terazye Square you can also see the remnants of the Belgrade of yesterday. At a street intersection in the very hub center of the capital a ramshackle Albanian tavern stood not long ago, and may still be standing. Its petroleum lamps were not of much help in throwing light on its strange assortment of food. In many side-streets cobblestones still wreak havoc with rubber tires, and plaster houses, which look ageless and unsanitary, reel in all directions. In front of *cavarnas* sit sedate Serbs, sipping a mild spirit of plums, *shlivovitsa raki*. They may have come to town to transact some business with the government or to shop for their village co-operative. They look dignified, and do not scrape and bow, as do their Hungarian neighbors across the Danube. The peasant does not mince his words and calls the King "thou." I said before that the Turkish rule has left no trace on the countryside. But, evidently, it has left its mark upon the social institutions of the Balkans, as can clearly be seen when peasants talk to high officials about their problems. All citizens were equal before the Turks—all of them were dogs. Where all were persecuted, none could stand out, and the stratification of social classes was prevented. Hence the Serbian peasant is a born democrat, which cannot be said either of the Slovene or the Croat, who lived long under aristocratic rule. Some of the latter rose into the higher classes and became rulers themselves, but the majority were left behind in the race for social distinction.

Old Belgrade survived the War and yields to the new inch by inch. Many remember the picturesque filth of the Old Town. The name of Russian Town recalls memories of the Ekaterinburg merchants who tried to corner the wheat market of the Lower Danube. In their house, which became a center of Russian intrigue, the key-man of the Black Hand, the fateful "Apis" was often seen. Turkish Town, known also as Cross-Road, was shunned by the peasants because of the toll exacted from them.

"Whoever is master of Singidunum [Belgrade's Latin name] is master of the Balkans," may well have been the motto of Trajan's legions. This was also the view of the barbarians who took the natural citadel overlooking the Danube. Charlemagne's Franks penetrated as far as the confluence of the Sava and the Danube, chasing the mirage of a world-empire. The Bulgarians had the town for two centuries, then the Greeks took it, and the Hungarians. Sultan Suleiman seized it from the Magyars when the sixteenth century was young, and the Turks had it, save for short intervals, until 1866. But for a small mosque, which the Yugoslav government maintains as a relic, the signs of Turkish rule in Belgrade have been effaced.

Looking south from Belgrade on the Danube, we are facing the deep Balkans. Pyramidal Mount Avala is crowned by the ruins of a Roman fort, near the tomb of the Unknown Yugoslav Soldier. Flying over it one reflects that few small nations gave as good an account of themselves as the Serbians. Pushed out of

320

their country, they continued the fight in Greece and helped to turn the tide of war. Now we see the secret of the Balkan temper, as peaks rush at us threateningly, encroaching upon one another, thwarting man at every turn. Unruly ranges cut off stretches of fertile meadows, running into other ranges, gashed by streams that cascade down sharp inclines and disappear in the shadow of rocky masses. We follow the river Morava, which never seems to be able to make up its mind, darting in one direction, returning and rushing headlong, anxious to make up lost time. The roads in the west were like white ribbons streaking the landscape. Now they become rarer and bolder, climbing mountains and falling back into valleys. Farther to the north the mountains wore green, but here they are bleak and black, denuded of trees by former Turkish rulers. Far from the steel tracks that bring civilization, this part of the world is beginning only now to catch up with the twentieth century.

We make another short detour toward the sea and survey Montenegro for a moment, so named after the Black Mountain which shelters her from view. Before the War this was a Lilliputian Kingdom, ruled over by King Nicholas—informally known as Nikita—to whose quaint ways vaudeville writers were indebted for suggestions. If we fly low enough over the small town of Cetinje, the former capital, we may yet see the plane tree under which the late King administered justice and sometimes carried it out with his own hands. He had several beautiful daughters who found royal mates at the major courts of Europe. In this little country the printing press and prison were unknown until a century ago, when Prince Peter II, dictator and poet, introduced them. He needed the presses to print what he wrote, and the prison, it was suggested, for those who did not appreciate his

321

verses. When the War came, the printing press was transformed into bullets, but the prison remained.

Montenegro was so small before the War that any major power could have snuffed her out. In those days, the chivalry of the Great Powers placed such small countries under their protection. Since the World War, however, not even the smallest can find sympathy. For years the exiled Montenegrin royal family kept up a hopeless fight against the Yugoslav rule. Today she is as much part of the Kingdom as Serbia. When the mountaineers found that their bare-fisted valor was of no avail against machine-guns their savage patriotism subsided.

We cast a sidewise glance at Bosnia, made famous by Sarajevo, where in 1914 the shots rang out that announced the World War. Sarajevo today has all that the real Orient lacks. In smell and noise her bazaars are not inferior to those of Cairo. The copper-smiths' streets still echo the sounds that were familiar to Abraham's ears. The waterboy still carries a gourd which Lot's wife would greet with joy. Here veils and fezzes still predominate, and orthodox education is based upon the motto: "If it is already in the Koran it is superfluous, if not in the Koran it is a sacrilege." As late as half a century ago this part of the Balkans might have been called the "end of the world." Its *Kapetans,* public officials, were so many sovereign princes, and serfdom was still in flower. Here the big-wigs thought they were more pious than the Prophet himself, and rose against the High Porte because they considered the Sultan no better than an infidel. The province was isolated not only from the West, but also from the East. "Bosnia begins with the forest," the native proverb says, "Herzegovina with the rock." They have good land, poorly tilled. They have many minerals, including coal, iron, copper, chrome, manganese, cinnabar, zinc, mercury, besides marble and building stone. They could be made rich with money, but are poor because of lack of means to exploit their natural wealth. The Austro-Hungarian monarchy risked the World War when it annexed the two provinces six years before the great conflict. "Austria wants to sever our jugular vein," the Serbians shrieked; "the Bosnians are our kinsmen." But Austria did not care. She was so weak that she had to show her strength at every turn.

We resume our journey southeastward, as dark mountains push themselves between us and the Adriatic Sea. Albania lies behind those peaks, formerly a kingdom, now an Italian colony. There is no airway, railroad or even trunk road between Yugoslavia and Albania. The Austrians wanted Albania, not so much because of a deep-felt need, but because they had to bolster their prestige. The Serbians coveted her and so did the Greeks. Italy wanted her for the control of the Adriatic. Since all clamored for her, the best solution was to make her independent. Now she has lost her precarious independence which was maintained by a balance of power.

As we fly south, the Kara Dagh floats into view, and we are in another trouble center of the Balkans—Macedonia. This is the darkest part of the dark Balkans, inhabited by Slavs with an admixture of Vlach, Hellenic, Albanian, Turkish, Circassian, Gypsy blood. Here four nations—South Slavs, Bulgarians, Greeks, Albanians—crystallized along vague frontiers, overlapping and encroaching upon one another's lands. Here anarchy was the rule of the land because one neighbor could not or would not understand the other neighbor's tongue. The mountains are naked because the Turkish pashas found that trees were worse enemies even than Macedonian *comitadjis*. Robbery was patriotism and

323

the "gold wagons" of the pashas, full of tax money, could be more easily raided in dark forests.

Turkish justice was worth its weight in gold, and the natives organized an outlaw government of their own, which, however, had no means of running schools, hospitals or jails. But they could run nocturnal tribunals in forest clearings. If the defendant was found guilty nobody bothered about a court of appeals. There were enough trees in the forests in those days; they served their purpose as well as the most elegant gallows. If the accused was not present, the tribunal found him guilty anyway, and later a bullet did the duty of the rope, whether he was king or peasant. How many were killed in such a way, no one can tell. King Alexander II, who was shot at Marseilles, was one of the most prominent victims of this lawless law.

If we fly low enough we may see the barbed-wire entanglements which the Yugoslav police set up to keep Macedonian raiders out of neighboring Bulgaria, where at one time they controlled the government and organized a reign of terror. We may also see the wolf-traps, made for man and not for beast. A few more minutes, and Yugoslavia is behind us.

A village in the heart of the South Slav Kingdom does not look much different from a village in the mountains centuries ago. Its uneven wall of mud tries to keep together its straggling houses around a spacious clay mansion which once belonged to the *Beg*. The village is built with the native earth, blending into the landscape, probably in the hope that marauders may overlook it. The slender minaret of the mosque, if it is a Moslem village, stands out incongruously, not because it sought to betray the village, but because Allah must be given his due. Besides, ma-

324

rauders, usually faithful bands of Mohammedans, might take mercy on a village of such piety.

The streets are unpaved and unlighted. After a rain, carts sink into mud axle-deep. It does not matter, since the streets lead nowhere. Not all villages are as backward as this, and the closer we move to the Danube the nearer we come to civilized life. One radio in a village and one movie in town can accomplish more than centuries of uplift, even though the air transmits merely jazz and the screen a masterpiece of imbecility. They bring the mud-village closer to a wider world in which even gangsters eat with forks. They arouse the imitative instinct of man, not so much for murder, with which they are surfeited, as for the comforts of which the Balkans had never heard.

It will take some time, however, before the Balkan village reaches the Hollywood level, if we judge by the stock of a general store in the outlying parts of the Yugoslav Kingdom. You cannot help recalling that a New York store boasts of having some 400,000 separate items in stock (exclusive of color and size differences). Forty "items" seem to be sufficient for a Macedonian village. A measure of wood is dragged to the community scale, where crude stones serve as weights. If the village is on the railway, part of the population meets the daily local, staring wide-eyed at it, as if it were the miracle of the age. When the guard hands over the day's mail to the station-master—one letter—the village wonders whether it has brought word of birth or death.

At festivals you can see the Serbians as they would like to live. Men wear a long smock of homespun linen, beneath red or blue waistcoats with trousers of white frieze. The women's dress consists of a similar smock, a zouave jacket of embroidered velvet and

325

two brightly colored aprons tied over a white skirt, one in front and one behind. The headdress is a tambourine-shaped red cap, and strings of coin are coiled in the hair or worn as necklaces. "In this manner a farmer's wife will often decorate herself with her entire dowry. . . . During the cold months, both sexes wrap themselves in thick woolen coats or sheepskins, with the fleece inwards; both are also shod with corded sandals, called *opanke*. In the more backward parts, Serbian women wear their children in canvas bags."

At festivals they form a single serpentine line and dance the *kolo,* sometimes performed by as many as a hundred men and women. Their national instrument, the *husle,* a roughly fashioned, single-stringed fiddle of wood and ox-hide, furnishes the music. A rustic bard intones endless romances, listened to by a crouching audience in front of the wine-shop. The patron saint's day is a special occasion for rejoicing.

Weddings and funerals are events in the village long remembered. The gypsy fiddler shares the coachman's seat and plays music, sad and gay, as the jerky vehicle takes the newlywed couple home. During the Sultans' rule arms were often hidden in coffins, which made the Turks issue orders that they should be left open until the last moment. This custom is still observed in many parts of the Balkans. The living are no more real to the peasants in the isolated valleys than the dead. Their world is peopled with vampires, werewolves, ghosts and white-robed spirits of the air, with goat-like hoofs and henna-dyed nails and hair.

One might as well try to lead a bucolic life on the rim of Mount Vesuvius as to live peacefully in the heart of the Balkans.

326

Nature Helps the Serbians

The history of the Serbians is an endless chronicle of wars. They are a Slavic nation. The two other main parts of the Kingdom of Yugoslavia—Slovenia and Croatia—are inhabited principally by Slavs. They are only incidental to our story because they had been for centuries only satellites of larger powers.

Some time in the third century, the Serbians were pushed out of the northern slopes of the Carpathian mountains, which are in Southeastern Poland today. Following the lure of the Danube, but repelled by it because of waves of barbaric invasion, they moved toward the Black Sea. From there they returned to the Balkan mountains, which afforded them the hilly protection they had been used to in the North. Nature helped the early Serbians to preserve their individualism. In every valley they had a miniature country of their own, the *zhupa,* headed by the *zhupan.* Members of the community were called brethren, *bratsva,* from the word *brat,* brother. When the Christian missionary wave struck the Balkans, the Greek and Roman churches clashed. As we know, geographic location was the decisive factor, and the Serbians fell under the sway of the Eastern church.

Early in the tenth century nearly all Serbia was conquered by the Bulgarians, a "dynamic" race, which believed in its mission to rule over the Balkan country and was undeterred by any fear of destroying it entirely. It is pleasant to record, however, that in an age when murder was considered the best part of valor, their Czar Simeon could not only kill but also discuss Plato's ideal State. He was hailed as "marvel of the world," like Emperor Frederick II of the Holy Roman Empire, not because he possessed the whole body of knowledge of physical science, which was little, but also because he was conversant with theology. Between his campaigns he wrote and encouraged others to write.

327

Much of the early history of the Serbians is admittedly mythology. For that matter, much of contemporary history is mythology, too, but we do not admit it. When Czar Samuel the Bulgarian captured King Vladimir the Serbian in battle, the captive wore his chains with such dignity that the captor's daughter, Kossara, fell in love with him, and the incident ended in marriage. Vladimir regained his country, but Samuel's heir could not resign himself to this loss and had the King murdered. Vladimir is venerated as a saint, his deeds perpetuated in sagas, all the more beautiful because their authenticity has never been questioned, nor corroborated.

When Count Raymond of Toulouse led his crusaders to the Holy Land, Serbia entered world history. The Black Death had decimated the army of the Cross on its way down the Danube and the Hungarians, who resented the high-handed deeds of the crusaders' camp-followers, did the rest. The Balkan mountains offered new obstacles to the fighting missionaries of faith. The natives saw in them a hostile army of the West, come to exterminate the faith of the East, and resisted them. The crusaders found the lean food of the hills not to their liking. They fought their way on, slaughtered by Christians, and in turn slaughtering them, and weakening the already undermined unity of the Serbians.

Nonetheless, under Stephen Nemanya, Serbia became united, after a fashion, in the twelfth century. His son, Sava, spent his days in prayer on Mount Athos, had churches and bishoprics built, and his name is blessed to this very day. But neither the churches nor the bishoprics seem to have made his countrymen less belligerent. The crags, impasses and issueless valleys invite adven-

328

ture. The Serb fought the Greek, the Greek fought the Serb, and all fought the Bulgarians.

Islam had already tried to force the front door of Europe open in Spain, but was repelled. Granada was still in Moorish hands, but Western Christianity was too strong for the East. Now Islam began to fight for admission through the back door. The conquerors marched along the Danube. The dissension in the Balkans was a challenge to the bearers of the Crescent. In the course of the fifteenth and sixteenth centuries the Danube became the lifeline of the Turkish Empire.

Individual heroism was not lacking when the Turkish hosts swept out of Anatolia. Milos the Brave crept up to the camp of the Sultan and slew him. But the Balkans lacked unity; the Turks had organization. Czar Lazar led his nation against Sultan Murad I, and both rulers died in battle. On the battlefield of Kossovo, on June 15, 1389, Christianity lost, Islam won and Serbia forfeited her independence. For seventy years she retained a semblance of power under native despots who paid tribute to the Sultans. Then for four hundred years, Serbia had no history. She was merely a Turkish *pashalik,* ruled by Albanians, Greeks, Roumanians, Bulgarians, who wielded the whip for the masters in Constantinople. *Divide et impera* was the Turkish motto. The tax collector was the hated neighbor beyond the hills, but the treasury was in Turkey.

The history of the Danube valley might have taken another course if America had not been discovered. In that case the Christian world might have been aroused to the danger of Islam. Another crusade might have united the Western Powers. But America had been discovered and the eyes of the West were

329

fascinated by the Atlantic, and not the Danube. While the Western world turned toward the setting sun, the rising sun saw the
expansion of Turkish power. Along the Danube the Janizaries'
horses beat a tattoo sounding like the doom of the world. They
were going to take Belgrade, then Buda and Pest, finally proud
Vienna. Once there, who could hold them back? "Whoever is
master of Vienna. . . ." The words had not yet been spoken,
but even then everyone knew the significance of that gap in the
mountains.

Some of the Serbians became Grand-Viziers, provincial gov-
ernors, hated by Albanian, Greek and Bulgarian. The Serbian
had no sense of nationality in those days. The peasant assumed
that it made little difference whether his master spoke Turkish or
Serbian as long as the taxes were crushing. Whoever gave com-
mands was obeyed. The Turks impressed many Serbians into their
Janizary élite. In the middle of the sixteenth century, a historian
says, nearly all Janizaries spoke Slav. Until the end of the seventeenth century the Sublime Porte used Serbian for its international
transactions, and its treaties with the Holy Roman Empire, for
instance, were all written in Serbian and Greek.

As long as taxes were forthcoming the Turk was not difficult
to please. But when the pest decimated the cattle and drought
parched the peasant's patch, he was aroused. As time went on
the fighting Turk became the sleeping Turk—too rich to work,
too fat to move. His exactions increased with the size of his body
and the extent of his harem. He became wantonly cruel, and the
mountain slopes were alive with grumbling resentment. At the
end of the seventeenth century, some 30,000 Serbian families
migrated across the Danube, seeking Habsburg protection. This
was the Great Trek of the Danube, paralleled only by the Great

Carmen Sylva

Trek of the Boers, more than a century later. Some of the Serbians sought to escape oppression by joining the oppressors. They embraced Islam and of them it was said: "A Christian become a Turk is worse than a real Turk." Others became bandit patriots, and started the Serbian tradition of guerrilla warfare.

> *With six hundred I went to the mountains,*
> *Six of them live and brought me hither.*

Turkish persecution increased. The churches were closed, and so were the schools; knowledge was a crime. As late as the beginning of the nineteenth century in the whole country only eight individuals could write. All were persecuted equally, except the renegades; hence there were no class differences among the oppressed. This was the Turks' unwitting contribution to democracy.

Napoleon brought nationalism to the Turks' very door. His realm collapsed, his message survived, and the Danube valley began to wake up. It was to become the lifeline of French revolutionary ideas, also the lifeline of reaction. The lesson of Rome was repeated on the Danube. Ancient Rome fell when her aristocrats spent more time in the *thermae* than in camp. The luxurious baths of the Turkish rulers kept them from the battlefields. Asiatic apathy and European virility clashed in the Balkans. The leaders of the Serbians' war of independence were swineherds, who had got around in the world and were affected by Western ideas.

Black George, bandit, swineherd and national hero, could not sign his name and only one member of his Supreme Council could write. Nevertheless, they were modern Serbia's founding fathers. He was the founder of the Karageorgevich Dynasty, which rules over the South Slav Kingdom to this very day. "Black" he was called not merely because of his dark skin but also because of his dark disposition. He started his career as a promising apprentice of Fazli-Bey, the Turkish bandit. Inadvertently he killed a Turk, instead of a Serbian, and had to flee for his life. He became forest-guard of a Croat monastery, joined the Austrian Army, fought the Turks, deserted his regiment, and lived a Dr. Jekyll and Mr. Hyde life, selling pigs by day, killing Turks by night.

A group of fellow-patriots, engaged in similar pursuits, was banded together, and they elected Black George their chief. The movement got started slowly because Islam's influence was strong and the executioner's blade sharp. But the fight caught the imagination of the shepherds and ragged peasants. The grand army of the have-nots launched its war against the pudgy Pashas. At first they were not nation-conscious and offered their country to the House of Habsburg, the powerful neighbor. The House of Austria declined the offer, for fear that the rebellious peasants might put strange ideas into their own subjects' heads.

Thrown upon his own resources, Black George continued his attacks on the Turkish Empire single-handed. His venture must have appeared as fantastic to his contemporaries as if little Estonia declared war on the British Empire in our own day. What followed was more amazing than funny. In every engagement Black George defeated the foe, and now the full extent of Turkish decadence was revealed. The Janizaries were swept out of the country, and the Turks' garrisons were pushed into a few towns. Black George demanded autonomy and, lo and behold, it was given to him. He thought things over, however, while the Sultan's grant of autonomy was on its way. The Sublime Porte had offered appeasement so quickly because it was weak, he reflected. The Turks were engaged in a war with the Russians, and Black

George took advantage of this by massacring the Sultan's troops in the towns. He no longer paid attention to the Porte, concluded a treaty with Russia, which thus recognized him as a sovereign, and had a hastily convoked National Assembly proclaim him hereditary *Gospodar,* Prince.

Black George ruled for more than four years in peace, as the word was understood in those days. He boasted of having killed more than a hundred men. He slew his father in a fit of anger and had his brother hanged in his presence, because of the infraction of a law. He had no sense of fear and was considered bulletproof. His sickly smile was appalling, but his ruthlessness was admired.

The war between Russian and Turk was over in 1812, and now the latter could turn all their attention to Black George. The supposedly "sick man" Turkey was healthier than he appeared, and the executioner's ax was no duller. The *Gospodar* fled from the advancing Turks across the Danube into Hungary and from there to his Russian allies. He resumed his old trade as a pig merchant and pensioned prince. But his restless blood drove him into new adventures. Hearing that his former henchman, Milosh Obrenovich, had become Serbia's Prince and the Sultan's faithful servant, he left his Russian exile, recrossed the Danube, and arrived at Belgrade, where his return created a great sensation. Prince Milosh reported him to the ruling Pasha who gave orders that George should be delivered to him, dead or alive. On a July night in 1817, George's head was severed from his body, while he was asleep, and delivered to the Pasha. In Constantinople it was carried to the Sultan's kiosk in a triumphal procession. Who was the perpetrator of the murder? Prince Milosh, no doubt. This was the beginning of the blood-feud between the dynasties of

Karageorgevich and Obrenovich, which have alternated in Serbia ever since.

The Obrenovich Milosh became Serbia's first hereditary Prince —a king in all but name. He looked more like a Tatar than a Slav, with high cheekbones, black eyes, and serpentlike moustache. Wearing a turban, surrounded by cushions on the floor, he lived like a Turkish Pasha. He tried to monopolize the swine trade, exacted taxes in good Austrian money, sent it to the Sultan in bad Turkish coins, and pocketed the difference. He forbade the working of Serbian salt mines, because he had a share in the Roumanian ones. He took what he wanted, and burned a part of Belgrade to build a new Custom House. "Am I not the chief," he asked, "and can I not do what I want with my own?" The murders of which he has been accused have never been proved, except for two. He killed an Archbishop and had another celebrity strangled. He was not unlike other despots in introducing certain salutary reforms. He gave land to the peasants, had roads, churches and schools built. His wife, Princess Liubica, is remembered to this day. She slew his sweethearts, and retired into the mountains, until he calmed down. She cooked his meals and washed his laundry. When his men hesitated to go into battle, she so infuriated them by calling them women that they rushed into the fray.

Prince Milosh paid a tribute of a thousand bags of gold to the Sultan and, in addition, sent him a gift of a thousand oxen. He kissed the hem of the Pasha's garments, and the Sublime Porte considered him a "safe man." He would, indeed, have been safe if he had been convinced of the Porte's strength. Since he was not, he engineered a plot against his masters, which turned out to be successful, and Serbia obtained full autonomy. But the

334

guard on the Danube remained Turkish. The Porte retained its garrisons in Serbia's forts.

All was well between Milosh and the Turks, but he forgot the Russians, who were beginning to take increased interest in their little Christian brothers of the Balkans and in the warm waters of the South. Russian influence gained the upper hand, and the Czar forced the Prince to abdicate. He was chased out of his house, and his arch-enemy, Vutcic, threw a stone after him, shouting: "You'll not return until a stone can float." "I'll die as Serbia's ruler," the disgraced Prince shouted back. Twenty years later he regained the Serbian throne, and the stone in the Sava was not forgotten. Vutcic was thrown into prison, where he died mysteriously, and the Prince refused the Turks permission to examine his body. A year later, true to his boast, Milosh died as Serbia's ruler.

His son, Michael, lacked the picturesque qualities of his predecessors on the throne, because he was neither an ex-bandit nor an ex-swineherd, but the first "European" monarch. He knew, what the world learned only after the World War, that the only remedy for the Balkans' troubles was international co-operation. His dream was a holy war against the Turks, in which Serbians, Greeks, Bulgarians and Albanians would chase the Half Moon out of the peninsula with Western support. The Great Powers had long denounced the "unspeakable Turk," but they did little about him for fear that any action might help potential rivals. Michael gave a new Constitution to his subjects. The Turks began to shell Belgrade from Fort Kalemegdan. Michael protested and sent his beautiful wife, Princess Julia, formerly a Hungarian Countess, on a diplomatic mission, which brought them victory. The Turks surrendered all their fortresses in Serbia to the Prince

335

in 1867. Serbia was now fully independent. A year after this victory Michael was killed by adherents of the exiled Black George Dynasty.

There was some doubt about the origins of his successor, Milan. "I want to see that man's birth certificate," a deputy shouted, when the ruler first met the legislature. He was supposed to have been the second cousin of the slain King, but popular belief held that he was not a Serbian, but the illegitimate son of a Roumanian Prince. Milan began his rule as the sovereign Prince, ended it as King. During his reign Serbia made its entrance upon the stage of history; events in his principality were the prelude to the World War. Because of Serbia, Russia went to war with Turkey. At the Berlin Congress, Serbia became a Kingdom and Austria-Hungary was given Bosnia-Herzegovina, which had belonged to Turkey. The Monarchy was given the right to occupy the two provinces, although the Sultan remained the nominal overlord. Serbia was never to forget that these fragments of Greater South Slavia should have been hers. King Milan did not object to the rape. It was found after his death that he had been in Austria's pay.

His dynasty had been in power too long and its rivals had little patience to await their turn. Plots were hatched to kill the King, but Milan took the wind out of their sails by abdicating. His son, King Alexander, was only seventeen when he took the crown. He was too young to know that he was sitting on top of a powder keg, nor did he have a premonition of his terrible fate.

At the foot of the Kalemegdan the Danube rolled its heavy waves toward the Iron Gates and the Black Sea. It was a quiet river around here, betraying no excitement. The silence kept the secret of the clashes of a half dozen imperial wills. Unknown to themselves, the leading nations were tuning up their diabolical instruments for the devil's symphony. The Russians' ambitions led them to the Danube, on their way to the South and warm waters. The Germans' aims urged them toward the Danube, on their way to the East and continental colonies. The Austrians' policy forced them to the Danube, on their way to the Aegean Sea and commercial expansion. England was everywhere, and France was suspicious.

Little did young King Alexander know that his capital on the Danube, which looked more like a Balkan village than a town, was cast for a leading rôle. Little did the lone policeman in front of the royal palace, the *konak,* know what tragic events were to occur there some years later. Now he watched the shadows of dancing couples on the second floor of the "castle," which was also its top floor. They were dancing the *kolo,* the national dance. The policeman did not know that the King was on good terms with Austria. Neither did he know that the Russian Minister, across the narrow street, held frequent conferences with a tall, broad-shouldered officer. The officer's black eyes were piercing and the ends of his dark moustache were brushed upward, which gave him a fiercely martial look. He was Dragutin Dimitrijevich, better known as "Apis," who was to play a vital part in a regicide. He was also to play a tremendous rôle in the events that led to the World War.

King Alexander married his mistress, an engineer's widow, and formerly his mother's lady-in-waiting. Mme. Draga Mashin was a woman of bad repute, described as the King's evil spirit. She was addicted to drink, and her shrill voice penetrated the street in their drunken quarrels. When he entered a café her brother made the bands play the national anthem and in his exu-

337

berance he fired his revolver into the air. Queen Draga was said to be plotting to have him proclaimed heir to the throne, since she had no child. The King knew he was unpopular and sought to gain prestige by an energetic foreign policy. South of Serbia the Turks still held sway, and the native population of Slavs was in revolt. Alexander wanted to regain this part of the Balkans— Macedonia—from the Sultan. It was also said that he considered divorcing the Queen. His enemies had to act quickly, before he could gain prestige. The Russians were interested in the *coup*, which was to oust a hostile family from a key position on the Danube. The Habsburgs, characteristically, were too indifferent to pay much attention to world-shaking events.

On the night of June 11, 1903, the plotters struck. They forced their way into the *konak*. "Apis" led the officers who were later to form the "Black Hand." The night was warm and the windows of the castle were open. The plotters found the King and Queen awaiting their fate. The short-sighted King, without his glasses, looked like a ghost in his long white nightshirt. The Queen put her arm protectingly around him. A captain fired and the King fell forward. "Don't shoot," the Queen screamed, and flung herself on Alexander. She was shot by a bullet from another revolver. The two twitching bodies were dragged out of the bedroom into the yellow drawing room. Revolvers crackled and the nightshirts were drenched with blood. Then the officers seized their swords, thrashing and piercing the bodies, stepping on them with the heels of their boots. The conspirators raised the two mutilated bodies and threw them out into the garden.

"Soldiers! There is your tyrant! Serbia, there is the whore who has brought disgrace upon you!"

In the morning a bearded gentleman in an impeccable cutaway

338

was walking up and down in front of the *konak,* muttering in a nervous voice: "Most unfortunate, most unfortunate, they were drunk and killed each other." He was Nicholas Pashich, the living symbol of Serbia for a generation.

A fortnight later a nervous little man entered the capital and was hailed as King Peter I. Again a descendant of Black George occupied the throne. Again it was a bloody event that paved the way to a change of dynasty. As a young man, an exile from Serbia, Peter was fighting the Prussians on the side of Napoleon III. A few years later he took part in Bosnian guerrilla wars. He retired to Zurich and translated Mill's treatise *On Liberty.* He married the daughter of "Nikita," the King of Montenegro. Princess Zorka was one of several beautiful sisters for whom the demand on the royal marriage market was large. In Switzerland, Peter lived as a minor national idol, and as years passed on he became known as "Old Uncle Pete." The usual stories were told about him, including the one about the grocer who refused to extend him credit. He was sixty when he entered Belgrade. Not many foreign envoys greeted him when he ascended the throne, and the English broke off relations with his Court. The country was heavily in debt; real power was in the hands of the murderers, headed by Queen Draga's brother-in-law. King Peter's arrival coincided with a complete change of Serbian foreign policy. The Kingdom turned its back to Austria and began to march with Russia.

Let us leave drab King Peter and turn to the man whom we last heard muttering in front of the Belgrade royal residence. Nicholas Pashich was the statesman of pre-War Serbia and post-War Yugoslavia and one of the really great statesmen of the Balkans. It was he who had to make the momentous decision about the

339

ultimatum which Austria sent his country after the assassination of Franz Ferdinand in Sarajevo. Would the world have been spared the holocaust if he had accepted it fully? Today we are inclined to believe that the World War would have exploded anyway, perhaps a little later.

When the murder of King Alexander was committed, Pashich was almost sixty, the best part of his career ahead of him. He was patriotic and unscrupulous, dynamic and shrewd. He performed remarkable feats and committed great mistakes. In his early life he was seeking truth in many ways: as anarchist, as patriot and as the sworn enemy of Socialism. The Turks were still in Belgrade's Kalemegdan Fortress when he fell under the spell of Prince Bakunin and his anarchism. At home he had seen authority at its worst and conceived a deep hatred for it. *"Le gouvernement, voilà l'ennemi."* He saw it as organized violence, greed and evil. He continued to be the spirit of eternal negation even after the Turks had left the Danube. He rebelled against despotic Milan. He had to cross the Danube on his way to exile. If he had been caught before reaching the river, another man would have rejected the World War ultimatum. In his absence he was sentenced to death. A dead man legally, but completely alive physically, he began to lead a strange existence, the proper setting of which was the fantastic Balkan range. Within a few years he had been a convict and Prime Minister. He was sentenced to five years in prison on absurd charges, but was pardoned on the condition that he leave the country.

Pashich became the power behind the throne after King Peter's accession. He was Premier during the crises leading to the World War, during the War, at the time of the Peace Conference, and after. More than any other human being, he was the creator of modern Yugoslavia, with all her faults and virtues. This master of political horse-trading cut a sorry figure on the speaker's tribune, apart from his patriarchal beard, which inspired confidence. Often he was inarticulate, a defect which he turned into an advantage. Stroking his long beard, he confounded his foes by disregarding feverish expectation and uttering incoherent sounds.

A peasant deputy once expressed interest in a Foreign Office secret fund. "Well, well," Pashich began, as Henry Baerlein, author of *The Birth of Yugoslavia,* tells the incident, "as to what our friend has told us . . . the . . . how should I say? . . . Well. . . . It isn't altogether wrong . . . in a way . . . the . . . what was his name? . . . When you examine the matter from all sides . . . there is . . . I forget the word . . . in a way . . . these public matters, you know. . . . How should I say? . . . It's best . . . how should I say? . . ."

"Are you satisfied with His Excellency's answer?" the Speaker asked, and the peasant deputy was satisfied.

Once another political leader, whose name was also Nicholas, expressed his opposition to Pashich by pulling his beard in a busy street of Belgrade. The Premier waved the detective aside, took his assailant by the throat, beaming at him sweetly:

"Darling Nikky, let's not quarrel. It makes a poor impression, my friend."

Although the Premier was past sixty, it took "Nikky" several weeks to recover.

Pashich owned half the stocks of some important copper mines, the value of which had risen from 500 to 80,000 dinars apiece. "Ah, well," he said in his deep voice, "my wife brought them to me . . . you see." Another time, a farmer "persuaded" him to buy a meadow from him for a few dinars. Lo and behold, soon an abundant spring of mineral water was struck on that very meadow.

Just the same, the peasants drank a toast for him and not for King Peter: "May God bless our dear old brother Nicholas."

He was pro-Russian and anti-Austrian. How could it be otherwise with Austria pursuing the policy she did? The Russians had taken a beating from the Japanese in the Far East. Youth was revolting in Turkey. In 1908 Austria took Bosnia-Herzegovina as legally her own. Pashich was Prime Minister when his neighbor across the Danube took this fateful step. The Serbians were shouting for war, but none of the Great Powers was ready for a showdown. Four years later the fever line shot upward; the Danube valley was at war. The Turks were on one side, and the Balkan nations on the other. Was the "sick man" of Europe to become its "dead man"? The small Balkan countries scored against the Eastern giant: Macedonia and Albania were free. The victors could not agree on the spoils, and the Balkans had still another war. Discontented Bulgaria was beaten and Serbia received a larger share of the newly acquired land. Flushed with victory, the Kingdom of Serbia was preparing itself for a showdown with Austria. If the leaders of the Habsburg monarchy could only have seen the danger! Yielding to the pressure of Hungarian land barons, the monarchy restricted the import of Serbian pigs. This would not have been of world-shaking importance in a country with hundreds of export articles, but Serbia was not such a country, and pigs meant sustenance to her.

Nerves were on edge. Young Yugoslavs saw Austria as a monster. On June 28, 1914, Archduke Franz Ferdinand, heir to the thrones of Austria and Hungary, and his wife, Duchess Sophie,

342

were assassinated in Sarajevo, the capital of the very Bosnia which the Serbians demanded as theirs by right and nationality and which the Austrians had annexed. The visit of the Archduke to this center of South Slav agitation was considered a provocation. The Vienna government accused Premier Pashich and his government of complicity. The crime was perpetrated by two Bosnian students, Princip and Cabrinovic. They had been in conference with "Apis," and had received hand grenades and revolvers from his henchmen, the Serbian Major Tankosic and the *komitadji* "Black Hand" leader Ciganovic. They had been smuggled out of Serbia into Bosnia across the river Drina. The Vienna government demanded that the "Black Hand" and other organizations should be dissolved and that Austrian officials should take part in the finding of the mastermind culprits and the suppression of subversive movements. Premier Pashich accepted all points, except those referring to Austrian participation, which he rejected on the ground that they were incompatible with Serbia's sovereign rights. A quarter of an hour before the ultimatum expired, at 6 P.M. on July 25, 1914, Pashich handed his government's answer to the Austrian Minister, who did not even open it. He handed Pashich a fresh note, announcing the rupture of diplomatic relations.

Emperor Franz Joseph had seen so much bloodshed, was so old and tired that he felt reluctant to sign a declaration of war. But the Vienna Foreign Office was in a hurry and in the war-declaration submitted to him it was stated that the Austro-Hungarian monarchy went to war in defense of its rights, since Serbian soldiers had already attacked the imperial and royal forces on the Danube (at Temes-Kubin). After the Emperor had signed

343

the declaration, the Foreign Minister struck out the reference to the attack. It is well known now that the fight at Temes-Kubin never occurred.

Serbia was at war, and Pashich organized her resistance. Old Peter withdrew in favor of his younger son, Alexander, who took the Regency. His older son, Crown Prince George, was confined to a lunatic asylum—called by a more polite name—after he had killed one of his manservants. The bullet fired at Sarajevo caused a detonation heard around the world. One country after another joined the growing ranks of belligerents. At the outset, Serbia scored several remarkable victories. Again it was a David-and-Goliath story which should have opened the Austrian leaders' eyes. An epidemic ravaged Serbia, killing hundreds of thousands. After the Austrians had failed, the Germans took matters in hand and their steamroller passed over the Danube frontier. In a few months all Serbia was wiped off the map.

The Serbian army could have surrendered, but it did not. In the dead of Winter it began its heroic trek across the mountains of Albania, until then believed impassable to all except mules. They had little food, no medical help and not enough grave-diggers. Their route was strewn by the dead and the hopelessly ill. The old King himself was sick, carried in a litter by his soldiers, sometimes propped up in a bullock cart. Their exploits put the march of Xenophon's Ten Thousand to shame. Finally, they reached the Albanian sea coast. Allied ships conveyed them to the Greek island of Corfu. Serbia was no more; her army was in exile. Her neighbor, Bulgaria, solemnly declared that Serbia's reconstitution would never be permitted.

Seventy-one-year-old Pashich, Premier of a non-existent country, did not give up the struggle. In the darkest hour of his nation's

344

life, he thought only of victory. On alien soil he agreed with the representatives of the Croats and Slovenes on the main policies of post-War Yugoslavia. The three of them were to unite under the dynasty of Black George. The Declaration of Corfu is the birth certificate of the South Slav Kingdom of the Serbians, Croats and Slovenes.

Pashich carried on as if his country were in existence. He even found time to stamp out opposition to the ruling family. Was he responsible for the execution of "Apis," legendary leader of the "Black Hand"? Is it true that this restorer of the Black George dynasty had turned against it? Plotters of this type have conspiracy in their blood. It was on the Salonika front, partly held by the Serbian army, that the end of the World War came. The Allies forced open the rear door of Central Europe, and now they were on their way to the Danube. Bulgaria gave up the fight, and Austria-Hungary followed suit. The country of the Serbians, Croats and Slovenes—Yugoslavia—became now a reality. Peter died as King of the South Slav Kingdom. Pashich led his country's delegation to the Paris Peace Conference.

What form would Yugoslavia take: a unitary or a federal country? Slovenia left Austria, and Croatia left Hungary. "The forces of evil had been scattered," the Croat peasant-prophet Stephen Radich proclaimed. "Millennium is here! We are the instruments of a miracle-working God!" The interests of these two provinces were linked up with the West, they were Roman Catholic and wanted to have a federal State and equal rights with the Serbians. Pashich took a different view. Serbia was the Belgium of the Danube valley; she fought and was bled white in the War. The Slovenes and Croats, on the other hand, had been forced to share the enemy's trenches. They had been so long

345

under alien rule that they lacked the real South Slav approach. History and her heroic rôle predestined Serbia to take the lead. The Croats set up a rival government. Stroking his patriarchal beard, Pashich approved of the Zagreb Cabinet, knowing well that the National Assembly, which he controlled, would put it out of existence. Yugoslavia became a centralized State.

Meanwhile, a diplomatic war was raging in Paris. In a secret treaty Italy had been induced to join the Allies with the promise of obtaining certain territories, including a large part of Dalmatia, the narrow coast on the Adriatic Sea. The Italians wanted it on historical and strategical grounds. The lions of the Queen of the Adriatic, Venice, had stood guard over this mountain-locked land. Dalmatia had been a treasure colony of the Doges, a link between the canals and the Orient, a beneficiary of Venetian culture. The sea of Dalmatia is crowded with small islands, well supplied with harbors. The Italians professed concern that the indented coast would fall into the hands of an unfriendly power. Their own Adriatic coastline is flat. The Yugoslavs, on the other hand, claimed Dalmatia on the ground that its population was South Slav, that they needed the harbor of Fiume, which would be their only access to the sea with a railway connection, and that the inhabitants themselves demanded the union. These were the days of "self-determination of nations." Italian troops were moving upon Ljubljana, which Rome demanded as a strategical town. Italy's soldiers were marching upon Fiume, too, and so were the Croats. It looked like a miniature second World War on the Adriatic.

The demigods of the Paris conference thundered their orders, but the land-hungry belligerents paid no heed. The South Slavs

346

Nicholas Pashich

took Ljubljana and refused to relinquish it even in the face of threats. American troops were dispatched to maintain peace at Fiume. Italy's spokesman, Baron Sidney Sonnino, produced the signatures of England and France, covenanting their word on Dalmatia. For good measure, he also demanded Fiume. The representatives of England and France, "Tiger" Clemenceau and wily Lloyd-George, although recognizing their own signatures, pointed to Woodrow Wilson, who had descended from his Washington Olympus to let justice prevail in Europe. When the Allied Powers had accepted his Fourteen Points as the basis of the Peace Treaties, they tacitly dropped secret agreements. He said that the United States had not been told of the secret understandings and could not honor the pledge, which was not hers. The President was indignant; both justice—mostly abstract—and his prestige—annoyingly concrete—were at stake. He did not want to start his career as peacemaker of the world by having his Fourteen Commandments violated. He issued a strong manifesto, in which his indignation was expressed in elegant periods. The Italian spokesman retired; the French and English were at sea. Would the conference be torpedoed because of a side-issue? Wilson ordered his ship, the *George Washington,* to stand by.

Stroking his beard, Pashich was beaming at everyone concerned. He pretended to be hard of hearing when he did not wish to hear. He pounced upon the enemy's weakness with breathtaking rapidity. He had to give the impression of great strength behind him, fighting, as he was, the claims of a Great Power with the resources of a disorganized country. Finally, he got Dalmatia for Yugoslavia, except for the town of Zara, ceded to Italy. The Italians got Fiume too, after a romantic incident, when the poet

347

D'Annunzio took the port at the head of his equally romantic irregulars. As a compensation, Yugoslavia was given the Porto Baros of that city.

The question of State unity was still to be solved. The Croats took up the cudgels on behalf of the Slovenes. Their leader was Stephen Radich, who carried on a remarkable war against the perennial Pashich. Radich was impulsive, spontaneous. He was also an admirer of India's Gandhi, and subject to fits of doubt in himself. The name of his "Croat Republican Peasant Party" was a program in itself. "He spoke a language that even the most illiterate could understand. He was always like a father telling fairy stories to his children," says Stephen Graham, author of *Alexander of Yugoslavia*. He was not a great statesman, not even a politician; he lacked a consistent line of conduct and a will strong enough to pursue his aim to the end. He owed his fame to a gift for sentimental oratory. Next to Pashich, he was the key-man of the first decade of Yugoslav history. The peasants knelt in his presence, sang songs about him and placed him next to Jesus.

A plump little moon-faced man, always smiling, not Balkan in appearance but recognizably Slav, he was forty-seven in 1918. He was one of eleven children of poor peasants on a seven-acre farm near Sisk. He and his brother Ante went to school in Zagreb; the others stayed on the land. Stephen's political troubles began when he was sixteen. His Croatia was then an autonomous province of Hungary, which was represented by the Governor. "Down with the Governor!" he cried out in a theater, and was sent to prison. Free again, he was a hero among his schoolmates. His principal told him to keep away from school for some time lest the authorities demand his expulsion. He went to Russia, home of the Pan-Slav. There he learned the language, and, after his return to Zagreb, he began to give Russian lessons. The police watched him as a man suspected of being a Russian spy. He acted so strangely that he was committed to a lunatic asylum. Three doctors had certified him a harmless madman. He was released and sent to his father's farm, where he talked with the peasants, continued his studies. Next year he passed his examinations with distinction.

He entered Zagreb University and began to organize a student movement; he also edited a patriotic paper. He was arrested and put in jail for four months without as much as a mock trial. He learned Czech in prison and went to Prague after his release. There he was arrested, released, expelled, and went to Budapest, where he was not arrested. He entered the university and learned Hungarian. Going home on his vacations, he quarreled with the conductors because his ticket was printed in Magyar and not in Croat. When he did not quarrel, he played the village guitar, *tamburitsa* and sang folk-tunes. He demanded a Croat king, but was not interested in bombs and firearms, nor in Russian terrorists and nihilists. He never engaged in fights, but organized student demonstrations to burn the Hungarian flag. For this he was re-arrested in Zagreb, now by the Hungarian police, was tried for sedition and sentenced to six months in jail.

Each jail term increased his popularity. Out again, he went to Moscow, where he conspired with Nihilists, and to Paris, where he plotted with Socialists. He concluded alliances at four in the morning and forgot all about them at four in the afternoon. His dynamic energy generated vast floods of words which left people wondering whether he was an elemental force of nature or just a windbag. When not in jail, he was organizing the Croat Peasant

Party. The police arrested him every time the young people of
Zagreb disturbed the burghers' sleep. He hailed the World War,
and wrote eulogies of Emperor Franz Joseph because he had
caught the war fever. He wept over the dead body of the Emperor,
whom he called a martyr and father of his people. He foresaw a
remodeled triune realm of Austrians, Hungarians and Croats.
The latter would annex Serbia and make "Great Croatia" a reality. His ardor for Austria's war subsided in proportion to the
Allies' diplomatic victories.

The World War over, Radich appealed to President Wilson
for his help in setting up a peasant republic in Croatia. Pashich
had him arrested and sent to jail for eleven months. This was the
Croat tribune's first experience in a Yugoslav prison, and we do
not know whether he liked it better than all the others. Some two
hundred thousand peasants appealed to the American President
on behalf of their idol. When Radich was released, Croatia was
part of united Yugoslavia. Thanks to Pashich, he had a martyr's
halo. Radich tried to pacify the old Premier: "We are opponents,
not enemies." But he himself was not quite sure, and so he slipped
out of the country and went to England. President Wilson had
sailed home, defeated in his diplomacy and sick. In the early
twenties England's name stood for strength in the Danube valley;
her prestige was untarnished. Downing Street refused to lend ear
to the fantastic Croats.

Radich went to Moscow, and told the Bolshevists that bolshevism was wrong and that they should set up a peasant republic.
He was in his element, because he could have talk-marathons
with the Russians. He returned home, less Left-wing than before
and readier to compromise. The Moscow trip gave Pashich an

Stephen Radich

excellent reason to outlaw the Croat Peasant Party. The police called again for Radich, but he hid himself in a recess behind racks of his bookshop. He was found and sent to jail again. "He was more at home in prison than out of it," Stephen Graham writes.

Pashich kept on stroking his patriarchal beard and smiling at the dreamy Croats. Radich issued a proclamation in jail, recognizing the monarchy and the Constitution. He had fallen even more under Gandhi's influence and now expressed horror at violence. "Well," the old Premier said, "in politics as in life you cannot go on fighting a man who ceases to strike back." Too much jail impaired Radich's eyesight. Although he became more and more fantastic and talked too much, the Croat masses kept on following him as their Messiah. King Alexander took a great liking to him. From prison, Radich was driven to the King, who entertained him at lunch. The Queen was attracted to the peasant tribune by the magnetic power which made millions follow him. "You know," she told Stephen Graham, "he had become almost blind. He really could not see his food. Often when he came to lunch I would take his plate and cut up his meat for him so that it would be easier for him. He was often with us, and my husband and I were very fond of him."

Radich was made a Minister of the Crown, a Cabinet member. Nevertheless, he continued to make converts to his peasant democracy. "Christ was born in a village," he said; "He was crucified in a town." "God made the country; the devil made the town." Old Pashich represented the town, which was corrupt, and democracy became synonymous with crookedness. Radich accused the Premier's son of corruption, and Old Pashich resigned. A year later he died, more than eighty years of age, bewailed as the Grand Old Man of the Balkans. His life spanned the ox-cart and the airplane, Turkish rule and Great Yugoslavia.

Was Radich the man of tomorrow? "If he says so it must be right," his peasants said, and King Alexander liked him. But not so the politicians of the underworld. They hated him because he dramatized the people's fight against corruption and because he was a Croat. They accused him of being a Communist, atheist and traitor. A Belgrade newspaper declared that he should be murdered for the country's good.

Again blood flowed on the Danube's bank. A savage Montenegrin deputy, who identified honesty with atheism, shot him and others in the parliamentary sitting of June 20, 1928. The King rushed to his bedside, we are told, and tried to improve his spirits by offering him the Premiership. Radich could not be saved, and he died a few weeks later. Hundreds of thousands filed past his bier in the Peasant Party Assembly House, where his body lay in state. His burial place at Zagreb is a shrine of Croatia.

Half a year later King Alexander proclaimed himself dictator. Until his assassination at Marseilles in October, 1934, he was the Kingdom of Yugoslavia. Much has been written about him, good and bad. Louis Adamic depicted him as a sinister despot, plotting at every turn, incapable of intellectual honesty. He was described as the most expensive monarch of Europe, a king who drew upon State secrets to further his business deals, a parasite. Stephen Graham, another biographer, has described him as a martyr-king, modest and thrifty, a democrat on the throne. Whichever version is correct, Alexander has become a historic figure.

He was brought up in Geneva as an exile, going to school with merchants' sons, eating enough when the family had money and little when it ran out of funds. He shone in mathematics, we are told; his mind grasped the limited and defined, but he had no flights of fancy. From Geneva he was sent to the Russian *École des Pages* in Petrograd. The Czar's Court paid close attention to Black George's exiled family. Young "Sandro" might one day occupy the throne of Serbia, a key-country of the Danube, they believed.

When King Peter took the Crown, their mode of life did not change much. The royal household was democratic. The King liked to sit in a café or public restaurant. Sandro was only a second-lieutenant when he became heir to the throne, and a colonel when the Balkan war broke out. But soon he was appointed Commander of the First Army. He distinguished himself in the second Balkan war—as royal scions usually do—and returned home a young hero. His Petrograd education had made him deeply conscious of Slav solidarity.

Sandro was ambitious, and King Peter felt older than his sixty-five years. About a fortnight before the Sarajevo murder, Alexander was invested with a Regent's power, and the King retired to the background. The story of the War has already been told. Alexander tried to convince the Allies to force open the Salonika door. "Alexander has to convince them that the offensive there would help to win the War," General Dimitrievich, the Serbian military expert, wrote. "It is difficult. The British Higher Command and the specialists cannot see it. The Regent's plea is that a successful blow struck from Salonika into the center of Serbia would relieve the pressure on the other fronts. The British position on the Western Front is not too bright. They are hard pressed. At length they agree that there is something valuable in the Salonika plan, not only for Serbia, but for the whole Allied cause."

Regent Alexander led the triumphal entry of his troops into Belgrade. His father stayed behind in Greece, grew a long beard, returned to Serbia a year after the War, lived in a small-town hotel with no running water and then in a small villa of the capital. He died in the Summer of 1921, when his son was in Paris. He was buried in Alexander's absence. Critical biographers say that the old King was too easy-going and his son too ambitious, while friendly biographers merely point out that the house of Black George had never been clannish. Father and son embodied the passive Balkans and the restless West.

The love-life of kings is subject to etiquette and protocol. The smell of Queen Draga's blood was still in the nostrils of eligible Princesses. The World War had decimated royal families. It was Pashich's idea to link together the two major countries of the Lower Danube by marriage. The daughter of King Ferdinand of Roumania and Queen Marie was beautiful and accomplished. Princess Marie was used to the metropolitan life of Bucharest, and Belgrade was still an overgrown village. But the number of royal courts was small and the diplomatic advantages of such a marriage obvious. After the marriage, the King could devote himself more fully to State affairs. In those early days of his rule, Alexander II lived in the shadow of Pashich's beard. The perennial Premier was a national institution, the depositary of wisdom in statecraft. The King sought to dislodge the bearded patriarch by favoring Radich. It may have been he who tipped off the peasant leader about the alleged corruption of the Premier's son.

Now the King became the dictator of Yugoslavia and things

354

began to happen on the Danube. The Serbian peasant is a born democrat; he likes to talk politics and hates to be muzzled. The Slovenes and Croats suspected that one of the purposes of the dictatorship was to weld the triune Kingdom into one with strong-arm methods. His people could not get enthusiastic about Alexander. "In Serbia men with hirsute faces are always popular," Stephen Graham writes. The King looked like "a college professor from the Middle West." He grew no beard or side-whiskers, and shaved off his little black mustache. He was a "European," and the Serbians have made a virtue out of necessity by being proudly Balkan. The King took up his Summer residence at Bled in the Julian Alps, where hotels have running water and bedbugs are rare. That, too, counted against him because it made him appear soft.

The King began to control public opinion. He had a new Constitution drafted and Ministers became responsible only to him. The ballot, formerly secret and voluntary, became open and obligatory. Only the officially designated party was allowed to take the field at the general elections. All other parties were outlawed, their leaders jailed. The King placed the press under police control and had newspapers confiscated. In a short time he became the government of Yugoslavia.

But the Serbian peasants, long used to the democracy of the oppressed, could not learn to look everywhere for spies. Although they did not want to hurt their ruler's feelings, they continued with their political discussions. The press discovered a way which meant compliance with all laws and yet made censorship distasteful to its wielders. Day after day they reproduced the pictures of the King's henchmen, repeating fulsome eulogies. The victims winced but could not forbid the publication of their pictures.

355

Opposition intensified the King's zeal. He dismissed Parliament altogether and ruled by decrees. Then he took a decisive step in dealing with the nationality problem. The names of Serbia, Croatia, Slovenia and of the Kingdom's other component parts were abolished, and the country was divided into nine *banats* and Belgrade. They were named mostly after the rivers of the Kingdom: Danube, Drava, Sava, Morava, Vardar. These *banats* were masterpieces of gerrymandering, so shaped as to cut across ethnographical frontiers and to contain large "loyal" elements.

A few days after the King assumed dictatorial powers the secret society of the Croat Revolutionary Organization, *Ustasha*, was founded by Ante Pavelich, a lawyer and ex-deputy, who had been sentenced to death *in absentiam* for high treason. It was the *Ustasha* that killed the King at Marseilles in 1934. The investigations of Stephen Graham seem to show beyond a doubt that this organization acted with the help of Fascist Italy.

Mussolini had been in power years before Alexander began to copy his methods. Il Duce knew that a dictator could maintain himself in power by saving his followers every day. "A danger a day keeps democracy away." He had a large stock of such dangers on hand, and they were judiciously selected, according to his country's means and needs. When Italy was still weak, suffering from the post-War political turmoil and dislocation of trade, the enemy was Yugoslavia, shell-shocked victim of the great conflict, rent by internal dissension. From time to time the Leader of the Fascisti would rattle his saber, announcing loudly that Italy's patience had come to an end. To vary the fare, he appointed Germany and Austria his country's official foes at a time when the two nations could hardly move because of their war-time loss of blood. As years went by and Italy's military power increased,

Mussolini thought of bigger game. He had refrained from arousing the Gallic cock and British lion until their strength was tested and found wanting. But at the time King Alexander assumed supreme power, Yugoslavia was Italy's enemy.

After having been sentenced to death in July, 1929, Ante Pavelich fled to Italy, where he saw leading Fascists. He evidently made a good impression because he obtained an Italian passport, with which he undertook mysterious journeys and was given a villa at Pesaro. It is believed that he began to enroll a detachment of volunteers in Croatia, whom he smuggled into Italy. His men began to appear on Lake Garda, at Brescia, at Trieste, Turin and in the so-called Bulgarian village of Borgotaro. It is possible that some of them were Macedonians, from the Southern part of the Yugoslav Kingdom and from Bulgaria. At Borgotaro Pavelich was often seen with Vlada the Chauffeur (also known as Chernozemsky, Dimitrov, Giergiev, Kelemen, Kerin, Stoyanov, Suk, Velichko), a mad killer, credited with some thirty murders, for profit and pleasure. He looked like a Tatar and acted like one. He was a man of greatly limited intelligence, good at nothing except the trigger, and was proud of his prowess as a gunman. He was childishly impressionable and liked to consider himself a patriot, killing for the good of his country, which was probably Macedonia. Pavelich hired Vlada the Chauffeur to kill the Yugoslav King. "We condemn Alexander the Last," Pavelich wrote in one of his newspapers. The King was to pay a State visit to the French and was to disembark at Marseilles, where Vlada was to kill him. Should Alexander escape with his life, he was to be murdered at Versailles. The pistols and bombs were smuggled into France, since it would have aroused suspicion to buy them there.

357

The royal party took a small destroyer of the Yugoslav navy, and on the way to France stopped off at a watering-place in Dalmatia. The sea was rough, the land inviting and the King was apt to suffer from seasickness. In the last moment, he drafted an alternative plan of going to France by land, but seeing the disappointment of the ship's commander he decided to follow the original itinerary. In Marseilles the King was given an indifferent reception. The official car which picked him up on the pier was seven years old. "This car is more like a hearse than an automobile," its French policeman-chauffeur said. Before starting off, news photographers took pictures of the King; they show that he was mortally afraid. He tried to smile and produced a grimace. The deafening noise of airplanes and harbor craft, the surging crowd, popping flashlights bewildered him, and he was still dizzy from the long sea trip.

The people of Marseilles are notoriously absent-minded, and their police in 1934 were disorganized. They were not greatly interested in the King of a Balkan country, and wanted to get through with their work quickly. They took the man who leaped on the running-board of the King's car for an aggressive cameraman. It was Vlada the Chauffeur, his finger on the trigger. The French Foreign Minister, Louis Barthou, shared the car with the Sovereign. Vlada fired. The King slunk back, and an artery of the Foreign Minister was severed. The police still did not know what it was all about. Vlada killed a policeman, murdered two women as he turned to fight his way out of the crowd. An accomplice was to hurl a bomb at the populace, to divert attention from Vlada and help him get away. But he got cold feet in the last moment and decamped, leaving Vlada to his fate. The gunman was cut down, shot at, trampled underfoot. King Alexander and Barthou were dead. At the terrorists' trial in France the defense-lawyer pictured his clients—Vlada's accomplices, who were to hurl the bomb or kill the King at Versailles—as noble-hearted patriots. "Ah, gentlemen of the jury," he closed with an eloquent plea, "when I recall this long series of murders I say to myself that the beautiful blue Danube is the beautiful red Danube."

The French jury found Pavelich guilty of having been author of the murder and sentenced him to death. He was safely in Italy and Il Duce's government refused to extradite him. New problems arose. The enmity between Yugoslavia and Italy did not last long. Mussolini found a more convenient enemy in the barefoot warriors of Ethiopia, whom he blasted out of their strongholds with airplanes and high-pressure instruments of mass-murder. The dictator was committed to a succession of wars. Fake enemies and saber-rattling without the orchestration of bombs and shells would no longer do. "The miracle-man" was forced to perform miracles, willy-nilly. The dictator's monomania turned out to be a mortal affliction. Living in an enchanted world from which the voice of critics is forever banned, he rose to the highest peaks, in his own estimation. Hitler made him see the democracies' weakness, and now he had to turn his fire on real enemies. Gibraltar . . . Suez . . . Tunisia . . . Corsica . . . Savoia . . . dreams of Caesarean power. The sky of Rome inspired the great of ancient times. Its deep blue and black shadows form the background for grandiose delusions. Behind Gibraltar lies Spain, and behind Suez lies immortality. Italian armies fought Gibraltar in the guise of "anti-Reds." The masters of Gibraltar closed their eyes, and the Italian dictator knew then they were weak. "I am invincible," Mussolini kept saying to himself, "because you are even weaker than I." Yugoslavia became a side show.

Napoleon tried to reach Suez and failed, but Mussolini would win, he was sure. He saw the Mediterranean as a Roman lake, and his ambition soared. He made his peace with the Yugoslavs. The Danube saw another strong man for a few moons. A bold ex-financier, Dr. Milan Stoyadinovich, Premier of Yugoslavia, was ready to play for high stakes. The King's son, Peter II, a boy of eleven at his father's death, was given the crown under a Regency of which H.R.H. Prince Paul, the late ruler's cousin, became the head. The press chiefs of Italy and Yugoslavia directed the newspapers to be friendly toward their neighbor. Rome's man-in-the-street no longer shook his fist at his Yugoslav neighbor. The dictator designated the French and English as the official enemy. The "mass man" spoke up in street and legislature. "Right or wrong, my Duce!" The man with the whip became the symbol of strength of the mass man. The less he had to say the prouder he grew, disguising his cowardice by calling it strength.

Hitler took Austria and Czechoslovakia. The Danube became the lifeline of the German Empire. The Little Entente was disrupted, and Nazi influence was on the march. Raging inwardly, Mussolini hailed *der Fuehrer's* feats across the Alps. The two of them proclaimed their will to march together, but said nothing about the ultimate outcome of their friendship.

One gangster does not make a gang. Hitler and Mussolini intimidated the Danube valley. Stoyadinovich was succeeded by another Premier. His name is of no importance. The Yugoslav flag was still reflected in the Danube, but the Fascist ideology was in the ascendant. The Danube had long taken its orders from

Vienna, and the world was puzzled. What will the next step be? Will the two Fascist countries corner the market and make Europe safe for autocracy? Italy took Albania with airplanes against bare fists. On all fronts but one Yugoslavia was surrounded by States of the Berlin-Rome axis. Only a small part of her trade went to other countries. Czechoslovakia's example served as a deterrent to Belgrade. Yugoslavia felt she could not depend upon the help of the Western Powers, and the dictators' mailed fists banged the diplomatic tables. Yet the memory of the past is not obliterated, and youth has a way of making its voice heard.

Yugoslavia listens to the whisper of the Western breeze. The Seine is trying to transmit a message to the Danube. Will the whisper of the West ever become thunder, and will Yugoslavia ever be able to follow the voice of her heart?

2. Roumania—The Danube Meets the Sea

I am the immense Danube,
Beware of my wrath.

In Roumanian the Danube's name is Dunarea, and "rea"
means "bad."

In good and bad times,
The Danube brings me only evil.

The Roumanian is "as furious as the Danube." To the gypsy
the river is "the dustless road." The Danube is a vital part of
Roumanian life, and its importance is reflected in language and
folklore. It helps her abundant produce to reach all parts of the
world, and brings her closer to West and East. Roumania is a land
of contrasts even more than Hungary. In most of Hungary the
Danube follows a course from north to south, flowing through
identical strata of culture. But a river flowing from west to east

Where the Timok Meets the Danube

is laden with problems because its waters reflect the regressive phases of civilization. The Danube's direction explains the ambiguity of the Roumanian soul and the nostalgia of the capital, Bucharest. That is why her elite attempts to appear more Western than the French.

The Danube flows between Roumania and Yugoslavia and, for a longer distance, between Roumania and Bulgaria. Frontiers in these parts are ends of the road over which deep silences brood. The Carpathian Mountains are behind us and the last lap is across the plains. Near the frontier a piece of the wall of Apollodor's bridge is still standing. Trajan crossed this bridge in the year 101 A. D. to plant the Roman eagle. The ruins of a Roman fort attest the craftmanship of the legionnaires from all over the world, *ex toto orbe terrarum.* Altars still stand to gods from far and near, and weeds shroud the blocks of stone whose inscriptions tell of the death of a centurion and the sorrow of two children lamenting the loss of their mother. Where the Timok meets the Danube the common frontier of Roumania and Bulgaria begins for a distance of 284 miles, as far as Silistra. To the north, marshes, looking like lakes and arms of the river, accompany the Danube. Beyond them lie the fertile fields of Oltenia. If our eyes had the magic power of piercing the light mist and spanning the sights of many scores of miles, we could see the Alps of Transylvania. Huts of fishermen hem the river, and, hugging the shores, silent craft ply an ancient trade, smuggling. In the evening the horizon is filled with nocturnal sounds, in which the bullfrogs carry away high honors. The soprano of a bird of prey blends into the rhythmic splashing of the river as it beats against the restless reed. A darkened motor craft detaches itself from the southern shore and suspiciously glides after a heap of dark-

363

ness. Frontiers like the night and boundary guards make their best catches after the sun goes down. Smugglers live the lives of owls, and the Danube sentinels are on guard.

On the Bulgarian shore, to the south, the Danube is followed by hills, decorated with blinking stars, as a town floats into view. The names of Lom Palanka, Rustchuk and Silistra are remembered from history. They were witnesses of Balkan tragedy. There the Turks and Russians clashed; there, too, thousands of Bulgarians suffered martyrdom. For many years these two shores were at war, in the Second Balkan conflict and in the Great Disaster. They have never been on good terms since.

Yet the two shores would like to return to normal life. A town on the Roumanian shore has a corresponding town on the Bulgarian side, but ferries are extremely rare. Here the river limits rather than extends life. Now the south bank arrests our attention. Hills lend themselves to adventure and defense. The ruined walls which follow us on our way vanish, then re-appear from nowhere. They are dark and forbidding, built for use and not for beauty. If we had time to investigate we would find that some of them reveal the peculiarities of Roman architecture. They were built in an age when the Danube was a lifeline of the *Urbs*. When it became the lifeline of the Turkish Empire, Islam superimposed its forts upon the Romans'. The Tower of San Giorgio, the ruins of which still stand in the Roumanian town of Giurgiu, were built by the Genoese, who plied the Salt Route from their sea-coast town all the way to Bucharest and to the Black Sea. They carried not only salt, but also the treasures of the Transylvanian Mountains which we can fancy but cannot see from here. Giurgiu gets a part of the oil from the fields in the shadow of the mountains. Her harbor is busy, and the ships at anchor fly the flags of

364

many nations. The contrast of the countryside is dramatic. The white villas in a setting of vapor-laden lawns appear out of place in the company of the needle-like minarets. It looks as if an absent-minded stage-manager had thrown together the scenery of a French farce and an Oriental tale.

At Silistra the body of the Danube grows enormous, swollen by flood-waters on both sides. Bulgaria is behind us, as the Danube turns northward before it reaches its Delta in the east. In front of us lies Dobrudja the mysterious, parts of which are as far from civilization as Tibet and others as close as Cannes. As if the boundary line had subdued the Danube, it now assumes a livelier air. Boats of all sizes are tied up at small-town docks or are on their way up- and down-stream. Here the Danube is Roumania's own, and she is proud of her river. The name of King Carol I is magnificently displayed on the Cernavoda Bridge, across which the "Blue Danube Train" connects Bucharest with the Black Sea port of Constanza. As we approach Braila, the Danube is so wide that we cannot see across. The pilot must beware against running his ship onto a moving island of mud. These are treacherous waters, and little has been done to regulate the river.

In a short time we reach Braila, where the sea air strikes our nostrils. Seagoing vessels come this far up the Danube, and a score of big steamers may often be seen. From here down to Sulina, at the mouth of the Danube, the river was placed under the "European Commission" after the Crimean War. In addition to the river States, France, Great Britain, Prussia and Sardinia obtained representation on this Commission by authority of the Treaty of Paris of 1856. They were to dredge the mouth of the river and the adjoining sea. The European Commission has been doing good work and is still in existence, although its composition has changed.

Braila greets the visitor with gay but not too tidy streets, spreading out like a fan from the center. Every time some change occurred in the Danube valley, Braila was burned down. Hence the town is young, although it was a trading post in Roman times.

The mountains of the Dobrudja blend into the Eastern sky like clouds that greet the sun. The concert of water fauna is pitched higher; the fen teems with half-wild swine and waterfowl. Galati, or Galatz, takes refuge from the mosquitoes on a slight eminence. In this port as well as in Braila, much of Roumania's timber, wheat and oil are shipped to the outside world. Roumania today is the fourth largest oil-producing country, preceded only by the United States, Russia and Venezuela. That is why so many of the flat tankers and grain boats at Galatz fly the German swastika flag.

Beyond the harbor the river Pruth brings to the Danube the breath of the steppes. Until the end of the World War, this was the Russian frontier. As the Danube turns East, Bessarabia is on the left bank. The bulbous Orthodox churches and the wooden houses, the knee-length boots of the peasants, their *rubashkas,* jackets, and their heavy fur caps serve as additional reminders that not long ago this was part of the realm of the Czar of all the Russias. Farther than eyes can see is the city of Kishinev, which acquired a sad name under the Russian rule as the scene of the bloodiest pogroms against the Jews.

And now we are well on our way into yesterday. Here it is hard to realize that Vienna and Budapest are on the banks of the same Danube. Villages on the left bank are shrouded in the fine dust of the steppes. Some of their inhabitants may have never

366

seen a movie, never heard a radio. To the right, the hills of Dobrudja have caught up with us, concealing their deep mystery in a conspiracy of silence. If it were not for the boats puffing up and down the Danube, one might say that this was the end of the world. Here are to be seen a conglomerate mass of people who come up to the river in a fantastic assortment of costumes, colorful and dull, clean and not so clean. Some of them wear the Turkish fez and turban, others appear in garments which their crusader ancestors must have brought from the West. They worship God in all forms, even with vestiges of pagan rites. They are fishermen and hunters in the Danube delta, bargers and artisans. They live closer to nature than the inhabitants of any other part of the Danube. When they wake up, the sun rises out of the heavy waters of the river, and every hour of the day they can listen to the waterfowl and insect concert with a different counter-point. Animal life seeks such vast bodies of living water and this is the hunters' and fishermen's paradise.

At Tulcea the Danube delta forms several branches, of which the Kilia, Sulina and St. George are the most important. The Kilia is the northernmost one and it discharges twice as much water as the two others combined. Although the middle branch, Sulina, is the smallest, it carries the burden of navigation, because it is the deepest. St. George is the southernmost branch. Before reaching the Black Sea, they break up into several smaller arms, which carve a channel in the soft mud one year and desert it the next. The Danube delta is a wilderness of bars, islands, shoals, bends and sharp curves. In one year before the delta was regulated, about two score vessels were wrecked. The European Commission has done much to avert naval disasters by building channels and marking them, widening the known routes.

The delta is overgrown with rank vegetation; some of it is poisonous, some useful. It bars the way in places even to the most intrepid hunter. There are islands, not anchored to the soil, but floating in muddy waters. On peaty substance rank vegetation revels, enriched by its own waste. Plant lives on top of plant, undisturbed by man's hands. The waters teem with salmon and sarda, pike, sturgeon and other fish. Here pelicans and coots, herons and storks, wild geese and plover are at home. Broad expanses of willows, reed and tamarisk flank the channels. In the forests wild boars engage in screeching battles with wolves. This is an enormously large sea, known as the *plauer,* the bottom of which is six feet below the level of the Black Sea. For that reason dams cannot transform this empire of reed and wild fowl into Dutch *polders.*

Each year the Danube extends its domain into the sea, which it reaches at the end of a long journey. It has seen a greater variety of peoples, customs and history than any other river. Behind the Danube is all Europe, with its hopes and despairs, its wars and dreams of peace. Behind it, too, is the history of thousands of years—the history reflecting the fate of all mankind. Indifferently, the waters of the Danube—neither blue nor green—roll toward the Black Sea. For miles they can be distinguished from the sea waters, as if here, too, this fighting stream was making a last stand against grim destiny. Then nothing is seen of the powerful river—only the lights of the boats, headed for the delta.

Roumania's destiny is the Danube. It brought her the Romans' culture nineteen centuries ago, exposed her to the influence of

Byzantium, then opened the way to Turkish rule. The river helped Roumania win the peace after the World War. The Danube today shows the way to Germany's expansive ambitions. It is a country of mountains and plains, of torrential Alpine brooks and sedate rivers, of sea and marshes, of oil and grain, gold and ore. It is the country of refined culture and of primitive nomads. Its capital has been dubbed "eastern Paris" and some of its villages lag two thousand years behind our times.

The two Danubian principalities, Walachia and Moldavia, stood guard on the Danube and at its delta. From the Danube to the mountains, where the river turns east on its way to the sea, the plains and oil wells of Walachia have attracted greed. The flat monotony of Moldavia in the northern part of the Old Kingdom extended the reign of the Russian steppes as far as the Carpathians. By conquest in the Balkan and World Wars Roumania more than doubled her size to 122,282 square miles. She gained land from Hungary and Austria, Bulgaria and Russia. Hungary had to cede her fabulous Transylvania, with its old towns and high civilization, also the Bánát, "granary of the Danube." Austria lost to her Bukovina, the capital of which, Czernowitz, used to boast of being the Eastern Vienna. From Russia, Roumania took Bessarabia, a land of rich wheat and deep ignorance, of Arctic colds and torrid heats. Before the War Bulgaria had to yield her part of Dobrudja, rear door of the East. A bird's-eye view of the various parts of the Kingdom helps us become acquainted with an obscure part of the Old World.

A visitor anxious to meet Roumania through the Foreign Office press department—as many visitors do—finds it manned by the most enchanting people, who speak Sorbonne French and Oxford English. Journalists from the West are treated with a deference

369

which other countries reserve for crowned heads. The Roumanian capital looks up to the West and hopefully considers all visitors ambassadors of good-will.

The visitor need not waste his time by asking his accommodating guides to show him the countryside. If he does so, he is taken to the ethnographical museum at a beauty spot in Bucharest, where he can look at windowfuls of peasant sleeves, embroidered aprons and other native handicraft. A diorama shows him the Danube delta, with its amazing flora and fauna, watched over by a crouching wax Nimrod and his brood. To supplement his knowledge of the countryside, he is taken to an exposition of the Roumanian village in a beautiful setting of flowers and an artificial lake. There he finds the exotic steeples of Oltenia, reproductions of the exterior frescoes of the Voronet Monastery, bulging pillows piled as high as the ceiling in the large beds of Transylvania, a Bessarabian farmyard, a Danubian homestead, surrounded by a willow-plaited palisade fence, reproductions of fortified churches, young Saxon girls in wax. The visitor cannot help noticing that most of the exhibits are from the younger parts of the country and not from the *Regat,* the core of Roumania. He also notices the reluctance of Roumanian officials to conduct him into the country. Should he go himself he will see the reason for this reluctance.

Intellectual Roumanians are so jealous of their position in the cultural scale that they cannot bear the thought of disappointing a visitor. They know that on the outskirts of their very European capital Asia begins. And Asia haunts them like a nightmare. Of course, every visitor knows that his self-conscious hosts are not responsible for this state of affairs. Roumania is what she is because of her geography. Turkish land is near by. The Danube has kept the door open to aggressors. The Roumanians had no time to settle down.

Walachia is best seen from the Alpine heights of the Carpathians. "A multicolored carpet spreads out endlessly," wrote the late Premier and poet, Octavian Goga, "astonishing one's eyes with the eruptive magnificence of that black soil overwhelmed with vegetation." The farther one goes along the banks of the mountain rivers, the vaster grows the horizon. Contours flatten down and the eye wanders across the vastness of that plain without discovering a point upon which to rest. This is the Canaan of Roumania, a country of rich humus, with a seemingly limitless abundance. An old Roumanian legend says that the Lord, after creating the world, was striding about the sky in the process of sowing the earth when suddenly his sack burst and all the seed poured out from it upon this place.

"Through hot Summer days vast areas of golden corn sway beneath the blazing sky, the maize rustles its metallic leaves like a forest of shining swords, rapeseed squanders its drowsy aroma on the air, from every crevice life is throbbing as though the sap of being was ready to burst in fruitfulness at the slightest touch. Herds of cattle roam these happy pastures, wild horses graze beside the tall-armed well, to gallop away in boisterous alarm, flocks of well-fed bustards rise from their hiding places and beat the dust with their wings as they take flight. Hours, entire days one may wander in the face of a warm breeze which carries along with it like skeins of flax the sparkling silver threads that some trees weave. Now and then the walls and towers of some imaginary castle appear and disappear again, as in a fairy tale, for it is a country where solitude is peopled by strange fancy.

371

Wandering in this way, you may find yourself quite unexpectedly upon the banks of the Danube, which great river, folded as it were in plates of shining steel, wraps itself around the province of Walachia." Thus the late Premier Goga paid lyrical tribute to his country.

The southern declivity of the Carpathians was the show place of the old Kingdom. It is the land of churches and old monasteries. The German Renaissance style of Castle Pelesh at Sinaia attracted the "Woman in White," Queen Elizabeth, known to poetry-lovers as Carmen Sylva. Prince Brancovan the Decapitated had the Horezu Monastery built for his dead body. He lost his life in distant Constantinople, and his grave and coffin have never met. The rich stone ornaments and frescoes showing saints, prophets, philosophers and kings, the characteristic vestibules, are native art influenced by East and West at the crossroads of many cultures. The peasant houses of the plain reveal great variety because of the many influences exerted by the Danube. The roofs of some of them are supported by struts; others have wooden galleries with overhanging roofs or verandas and covered balconies. The heavy, broadly set church tower is characteristic of the plains villages. The wayside and sepulchral crosses are features of the countryside. In certain Northern cemeteries the crosses are under fruit trees, the first fruit of which is sacrificed as a symbol to the souls of the dead. Some of the crosses are of wood carved in one piece, others are hewn in stone and painted with Biblical scenes and saints.

Passing Sinaia's royal splendor the international highway connecting Paris with Bucharest spirals down from the heights. The morning vapor is lifted from the plains as we reach the last spur. The moist air of the heights meets the heated plains. The scene

Moldavia's Waving Wheat

in front of us may have been cut out of Texas. The town of
Moreni has the greatest number of petroleum springs in Roumania, which takes first place in Europe's oil production. The
derricks are close together, and the petroleum, ready for dispatch,
is pumped into the huge pipe system to Giurgiu on the Danube
or Constanza on the Black Sea. The machinery here used is "Made
in the U. S. A." or "Made in England." "Made in Germany" is
also frequently seen. In the "canteens" of Ploesti's oil buildings
New Yorkese and London cockney are familiar sounds. "Anglo-
Saxon noses are attracted by the sweet smell of oil," critical
Bucharest says.

Northward the panting sea of grain curves, as the Danube seeks
its end in the delta. Moldavia is the more northern Danubian
Principality, part of the Old Kingdom. Here the villages are far
away, and as the fields often extend over huge districts, the laborers go out to them with a score of carts, which often serve as
lodgings and form a peculiar, movable village. Sometimes the
wagon tilt is set to the ground and serves as a tent, and in some
cases cottages of clay, straw and reed-grass are erected. The fire-
place is dug in the ground and protected by a windscreen. The
introduction of machinery would lighten the burden of work, but
the peasants are attached to the past, no matter how cruel. The
roads are lost in a sea of mud after a downpour. Waving fields of
wheat are sprinkled with blue cornflowers and red poppies. The
ox-carts move as if they had an eternity to reach the village.
Myriads of dust particles dance a wind-swept pirouette as the
cart halts on the square. Wearing his tiara, the village pope with
the venerable beard makes the sign of the cross. The acrid smell
of the tavern brings tears to alien eyes. At the sight of a stranger
the children run away, as if they were still afraid of the bamboo

373

stick of the Turkish tax-collector. Fear is a hereditary disease and civilization is far removed from the Moldavian village.

"From the Dniester to the Tisa," the Roumanian poet sings. *Dela Nistru pin la Tisa.* Roumania realized this dream at the end of the World War, when she obtained all the land from the heart of Hungary all the way to the Russian Ukraine. This is new Roumania, rich in lore and natural treasures, rich in history and tribulations. The waters of these lands drain into the Danube, the fate of which they share. For the better part of ten centuries the destiny of Transylvania was linked with Hungary's, although the larger part of her population has been Roumanian. But in the heart of Transylvania there live more than a million *Székelys,* frontiersmen in the Turkish language, who consider themselves as good Hungarians as the inhabitants of the *Alföld.* The population of the towns is predominantly Magyar, their culture is German in many cases, and their hinterland is Roumanian. Other towns are populated by Swabians and Saxons, whose ancestors migrated to these mountains seven centuries ago.

Here you have the core of the Danube problem in its tremendous complexity. These parts have not one history, but two histories, sometimes even three. Who were the first inhabitants of Transylvania? Were they the descendants of Trajan's legionnaires or were they the conquerors of legendary Árpád? If it was the former, then this is ancient Roumanian soil, but if it was the latter, then the Roumanians are descendants of later immigrants. It makes little difference which of the two versions is true. Even if the Hungarians had found that the Roumanians had prior rights, they would not have evacuated Transylvania while they were her masters. Conversely, even if the Roumanians were to find that the Magyars were the earlier comers they would not

374

yield their rule. The contest rages around Transylvania. "We shall never give up our rights," Hungarians declare, and the intensity of their belief is a powerful weapon. The Magyars look down upon the Roumanians, call them "slippered Walachs," which is supposed to be something terrible, judging by Roumanian patriots' reaction.

Transylvania lives on a higher plane than most of the country around her. The old patrician houses with the fine courtyards in the medieval style would not be out of place in richest Germany. The narrow, winding streets with their gabled houses have preserved the old German character of the towns, reminders of their founders from the Rhineland as early as the thirteenth century. The Teutonic Order of fighting monks, many of whom settled here, left their mark upon the fortified churches at the heads of mountain passes and approaches to strategic valleys. These towns had to fight for their rights. The famous "Black Church" of Brasov is scorched because of the fire which nearly consumed it at the time of the Turkish wars.

Customs die hard in the mountains, and women's wear is the best evidence. They wear dresses designed centuries ago, indicating their attachment to the past and the thousand miles that separate them from Paris. The young girls of a Saxon village in Transylvania wear aprons embroidered with their names, over white, loose frocks. The silver belts are often decorated with stones, holding a silk cloth embroidered with gay colors. On the breast, suspended on a chain, the *heftel* is worn, a round richly decorated metal plate with stones. On the head the *borten* are worn, high, black velvet hats, open on the back, richly embroidered; many broad, multi-colored silk ribbons flow down from it, most of them reaching down as far as the hem of the frock. In many Saxon villages the bouquet of flowers is a requisite for the procession to the church. Each age and sex has its fixed place in the houses of worship; the young girls sit in the apsis, the oldest men in the stall. In some villages the embroideries are geometrical black designs; in others a broad brocade ribbon is bound over the veil cloth, to which the long velvet and silk bands are attached. The hood is held by the so-called buckle-needles, which are often very valuable. Who could enumerate all the picturesque costumes of Transylvania, of which there are almost as many as there are villages?

The mountains of Transylvania have fostered the growth of a higher culture because of the protection they afforded against the Turks. They gave the world some of its great religious fighters: Bethlen and Báthory; the "Turk-Beater" János Hunyadi and his son, King Matthias the Just; the Oriental explorer, Sándor Körösi Csoma; the mathematician, Farkas Bojay and some of Hungary's most gifted authors.

Over the mountain lies Bukovina, "the land of beech trees," a little Babel, inhabited by Ruthenians, Roumanians, Jews, Germans, Poles, Hungarians, Russians and Armenians. These nationalities deposited here long ago, when the East came in search of the West; they were deflected by the Danube and turned into a human overflow. Before the War this was the last outpost of Austria, the "Siberia" of the imperial and royal army.

The capital, Czernowitz, now Cernauti, invites the eye on its hilly perch above the river Pruth which seems to be in a great hurry to reach the Danube. Not in vain was Czernowitz called "Eastern Vienna." Nowhere else was the waltz sweeter, this year's wine, *heuriger,* more sour. Although the Austrian capital was only four hundred miles to the west, officers of the army felt homesick for the metropolis on the Danube and tried to re-create its atmosphere on the river Pruth. The Czernowitz cafés were perfect replicas of their originals; they dulled ambition with smoke and music, but made life pleasanter for the exiles from the West.

Crossing the Pruth we are at the end of the Danubian world. This is Bessarabia, and if we go farther east, we reach the river Dniester and Soviet Russia. Long ago it was the highway over which the East was streaming into the West, migratory tribes chasing one another, stampeded by the fear of hunger caused by a cataclysmic drought in Asia. This was the historic Atel-kuzu, the land between the waters, where the original Cimmerian and Scythian inhabitants were crushed by the elemental force of successive waves of migratory tribes. Among the victims were the Bessi, a Thracian horde. Tibetan Lhasa could not be farther from the world than parts of Bessarabia, although Paris is slightly more than a thousand miles by air. Bessarabia's ruined fortresses and the remnants of the Roman earthworks are reminders of her rôle as a frontier land. This was Imperial Russia's way to the South. Here the Czar's and Sultan's forces wrangled for the Balkans' soul. Russia got her finally, but did little to improve her.

Much of Bessarabia is rich black humus, while part of it is cattle-grazing steppe. This is Babel, too, with a population of Moldavians, Little Russians, Bulgarians, Germans, Gypsies, Greeks, Armenians, Tatars and Albanians. The Kishinev massacre of the Jews is remembered with the same horror as the slaughter of the Armenians. Orders came from high quarters to slay the Jews of the Bessarabian capital. The Czar's rule was corrupt, and discontent was in the air. The peasants' attention was

377

diverted by concentrating it on the eternal minority—the Jew— whom Providence seems to have created for the rôle of the chosen people—chosen for sacrifice.

In Bessarabia the landscape is dominated by the bulbous top of Greek Orthodox churches. So large are two of them in a village near the Danube delta that the entire population could find shelter in them. Six priests minister to the religious needs of fewer than a hundred families. The ikons dazzle the eyes, the organ delights the ears, and the village priest's chanting insistence upon other-worldly reward and punishment satisfies the peasant's sense of justice. Time was when the church provided the only escape from tyranny. The mystic fragrance of the censer brought ecstasy to the believer. When Sulina reported the approach of enemy craft, the inhabitants crowded into the churches, invoking heaven's intercession. When the pillaging hordes were deflected to the south bank, paeans soared heavenward. Should the pagan's wrath fall full force upon the village, God's punishing hand was seen.

When the Czar visited nearby parts the priests announced that the life span of all who cheered him on his way would be extended ten full years. Russian Communists say that at one time it was a practice here to sell seats to peasants who wanted to be close to God in after-life.

Roumania took Bessarabia from Russia at the end of the World War, probably because it was the fashion then to take things from the Soviets. The Communists objected and did not recognize Roumania's rule over Bessarabia. Traffic was suspended between the two countries and the Dniester became the dead river of a dead land. It was only in 1937 that railway connection between the two countries was re-established. Bessarabia is still sunk into

378

Autumn mire and all-year ignorance. The government is concentrating upon the improvement of conditions in Old Roumania. Newspapers, radios and movies are still strangers to the backwoodsman, but change is in the air.

Our attention is attracted by the south bank of the Danube, where mosques stand out in a crystal clear air against the outlines of violet hills. Bessarabia is backward; so is Dobrudja, but it is also picturesque. It is a different world, this strip of land between the Danube, the Black Sea and Bulgaria, and on it the Turks left their mark. Parts of this district hardly look as if twenty centuries had passed by since Ovid wrote his epistles from his exile in Tomis, now Constanza, Dobrudja's most important town. The lack of wood makes it necessary for the poor population to build their cottages of reed and clay. Shelter against the heavy Winter storms is secured by caving out the cottages, cellar-like, so that the roof reaches the ground. Although many Turks have left, some have remained and they are beginning to move with the times. The women no longer cover the entire face, but only the lips. Dobrudja is famous for its wells, and the Turkish Sultans formerly had water carried from here all the way to Constantinople. Of the district's many sights the Rock of the Forty Girls usually attracts attention. Here, according to legend, two score girls were pushed into the sea by order of the Sultan. The Mausoleum in Teke contains the grave of the Mohammedan saint Hafus Kahalil Baba, and is a famous place of pilgrimage for the Turks. The tombstones are without form or inscription; a turban or fez denotes a man, and a flower denotes a woman. Some of the Dobrudja windmills use canvas instead of vane. In some villages a *sapkali,* a man wearing a hat, is still the object of derision. Long isolation has created a patriarchal democracy

379

among the inhabitants. They crowded around the late Queen Marie's car, engaging her in conversation, addressing her as "thou." She was an acquaintance of a childhood thronged with fabulous characters of Oriental lore.

Here a road is an event, even the ox-path is rare. Dobrudja, on the shore of the Black Sea—a dead sea—is cut off the main highways, accessible only through the Straits of the Dardanelles. Czarist Russia occupied two-thirds of the shores of the sea, some of them sub-tropical, and yet she was perennially craving for warm waters. Black Sea it is indeed because its surface waters are devoid of life.

Constanza is the antithesis of Dobrudja—gay and busy—a combination Deauville and Rotterdam on a smaller scale. The elegance of tea-terrace guests on its beach named after Carmen Sylva reveals social distinction. The restrained gaiety and subdued laughter bespeak congenital aristocracy. A yacht trip by night brings back memories of the *Côte d'Azure* of France. But you need not go far to see that, like the Prophet's coffin, Constanza floats in mid-air because it lacks a link with the rest of the world. Its hinterland is primitive, Asiatic. Constanza is the end of an oil pipeline, and since she is open to navigation all year, she is Roumania's greatest port of timber and grain.

It will take time before Bessarabia and Dobrudja can be geared to a faster tempo. Although the Danube washes their banks, it has not increased greatly their desire to catch up with the Western world. The fatalism of the Orient lies heavily on them. A man of culture could find little joy in satisfying merely his animal tastes as so many of the natives do: eating *mamaliga*, corn-bread, sharing the sty with the pig. But here the Orient is a great stabilizer, and most people lack the strength to break their bonds.

Since New Roumania consists of such varied elements, how are they to be adjusted? Because of her geographical position and history, Transylvania is in the van, and Bessarabia and Dobrudja are in the rear. The two Danubian Principalities, known as the Regat, the Old Kingdom, are somewhere in the middle. Visitors are apt to be misled in this regard. In Bucharest they find an intellectual élite of the highest order. It is well informed, well read, balanced in its judgments, often dazzlingly brilliant. The art of conversation is cultivated. Roumania has an intellectual aristocracy.

Judging by its intellectual élite, Roumania should be in the forefront of progress. But this élite is the first one to admit that such is not the case. Again it is geography and the Turks that are to blame. Every effort is being made to elevate the cultural level of the country. Young people are teaching the village with the same religious zeal which characterized the work of the followers of Tolstoy in pre-War Russia. Yet even today more than a half of the adult population cannot read and write, and before the War some 65 per cent were illiterate. It is too early to pass final judgment on Roumania's rôle as a cultural force.

The strong and the weak have fought their battles on the Danube as elsewhere. The strong have won nearly always, but time works for the weak, because it wakes them up and without them the strong would perish. The people of New Roumania are familiar to us. We have seen them on the German Danube, then on the Danube of the Hungarian *puszta*. We have seen them in the villages of Yugoslavia. But the core of Roumania— the two Danubian Principalities of Walachia and Moldavia, as they were known—has produced types we have not met so far. The boyar is the strong and the peasant is the weak. In recent

381

years the boyar has lost much of his strength, and the peasant has been trying to steel his muscles.

The boyars were the owners of the vast estates, the retinue of the Sultan and the Princes, the courtiers of kings, the descendants of exalted highway robbers. One of the boyars owned one-third of the Roumanian capital. Others were high officials, mostly corrupt, because being honest was considered dishonest. Many of them lost their estates when the mute weak demanded land after the World War. Many lost their offices when the royal dictatorship took power. The remnants of the boyars still live in their country mansions and city villas. They may be doomed to extinction, but they were a great historic force and cannot be overlooked.

The name reached Roumania via Old Russia, where the *boyarin* was an intimate adviser and confidential official of the Prince. He had money and was described as belonging to "the best people." The Roumanian boyar could be distinguished by his haughty mien and erect stature among his inferiors. He wore a long kaftan of the heaviest silk and vied with his fellows in growing a long beard, which was a sign of high caste. The taller the peaked cap of the boyar the greater was his importance. And so the caps grew enormously. It was only in the middle of last century that they discarded the long robe for ermine-hemmed Russian suits, and, later, for English clothing. Their wives, however, kept on dressing like princesses of the Thousand and One Nights. One of them affected inability to lift her finger to be kissed, a traveler tells us, weighted as it was with heavy rings. Another boyaress kept her couturières in virtual captivity, so as to assure their exclusive services. Not even her best friend was to have as good a dress as hers. The richest of them tried to bribe Empress Eugénie's official dressmaker to desert her mistress.

In dealing with inferiors, the boyar recognized no rules. The story is told about a boyar's son, who not long before the War took his first trip abroad. Passing through Austria, he pulled the emergency brake for fun. The train conductor called him to account and wanted to make him pay a fine. "Tell him who I am," he ordered his escort.

The colors of their robes and their posture in the presence of the Prince in Turkish times distinguished three classes of boyars. The Grand Boyar of the Divan had the right to harness four horses and to squat in the Prince's presence. The middle boyar had to stand at the door, while the small boyar had to bow in the exalted presence. Each class paid the same obeisance to the higher class it paid the Prince. There was no greater attribute of high dignity than to comb one's beard slowly.

The Grand Boyar had the right of life and death over his subjects. Sitting on the veranda of his mansion, smoking his three-foot pipe, he passed sentence on peasants who crawled abjectly before him. One complained about the trespasses of the neighbor's hen and the other had a grievance against an enemy who had done him injury. The boyar's powerful guards dragged away the guilty one, laid him out on the whipping bench and soon his screams filled the court. Women were beaten with straps.

Some of these grandees were immensely wealthy. One can still see the map of the estate of a famous boyar, which he had prepared to show the names of all his villages, the number of their inhabitants and their possessions, which were his by right. Some of these boyars had garments costing as much as 150,000 gold francs and wardrobes worth hundreds of thousands of dollars. They gambled tremendous sums and had countless parasites in their retinues. Many of them had no budgets at all, nor any idea of their revenue. The loss of wealth usually entailed the loss of caste. Hence many boyars went any length to maintain their income. A Grand Boyar of Walachia sold his daughter to a Russian General to get a lucrative treasurer's post, and the Vice-President of the Legislative *Divan* "loaned" his wife to General Mikhail Kutuzov, the man who had measured his strength on Napoleon.

Being a boyar had its disadvantages because they were like dust to the ruling Prince, even though they were gods to the serfs. The boyar's sons lifted the Prince from his carriage when he paid a visit, carried him across the muddy street and deposited him with the warning: *"Prag, Maria Ta,"* Threshold, Your Highness. The boyars lifted the ruler like a doll and carried him to his throne. They paid him their morning obeisance by touching their beards and foreheads, bowing their heads, which were completely shaved except for a tuft of hair for the ruler to seize in his anger.

The boyars' lives were as precarious as their fortunes. They were perennially sad, a French traveler remarked, always expecting the fatal rope which the Turks sent to those who fell from favor. "Here my father was killed by order of the Porte," a boyar told a visitor, "and here my sister was killed by order of the Prince."

Tremendous wealth, the uncertainty of tenure and constant fear produced many eccentrics among the boyars. Prince Sturdza was called "Sturdza the Calf" because he kept fit by taking his morning walk with a calf slung over his shoulders. He did not discard the calf until it grew into a full-weight cow. It was said of him that he received his guests at the head of the stairway: "The buffet to the right, the Princess to the left."

Prince A. was madly jealous of his elderly wife and in order to insure her honesty locked the end of her long hair in the drawer whenever he attended a session of the Senate of which he was a member. One day a servant of his household rushed into the Senate screaming at the top of his voice: "Fire, fire! Your Highness, the key!"

Prince G. fired his pistol out of the window to welcome a friend, fired at the door to summon his valet and fired at the wall to kill a bedbug. Prince R. was surrounded by thermometers in his country house, which he never left. His servants informed him about weather changes as a check, and in accordance with this information he put on or removed undergarments. Prince M. was head of the national police and had all country commissioners under his orders. Whenever a police officer was to be disciplined he called him to the phone of the town hall, and instructed the mayor: "Slap his face!" A second later he said: "I've heard nothing, slap him harder. . . . Now I've heard it. All right."

It is a long step from the boyar to the peasant, but we shall see the intermediate types in the chapter on Bucharest. The Roumanian peasant of the Old Kingdom is a mixture of many traits. Slav or Latin, Avar or Hun, he has been a peasant for centuries and cannot deny his origin. His appearance itself reflects the past. The astrakhan tiara-cap he wears was worn by priests of the Persian god Mithra, venerated on the Lower Danube two thousand years ago. At Christmas time he trundles into the neighbor's court disguised as a bear or joins with his friends to make a pack

385

of wolves. In some parts of the Kingdom the new moon is celebrated with voodoo rites. The hunters of the Danube delta meet for animal dances, imitating the fowl they want to shoot. When hot winds sweep the land and drought parches the seeds, naked gypsies dress themselves in leaves which peasants water, thus showing an example to heaven to give them rain. The peasants bury their dead with a coin in hand—Charon's ferry fee. Girls bury clay statuettes in the Spring, perpetuating the cult of Adonis and of fertility. In the very heart of the capital women of all ages thrust scraps of paper into the hand of the priest, imploring heaven to give them the beloved man.

On church holidays young and old meet in the village square, where the steeple and the well symbolize the needs of the spirit and the body. A deeply unconscious craving for a higher plane thrusts the church-tower skyward, and life springs from the well. The bell rings out the Angelus, to which they listen on bended knees. They hardly stir before the sun sinks behind its veil of dust. The cries of the romping children are subdued. A few slaps put them in their places. The blows are hallowed tradition, informal education transmitted from parent to child. As if afraid of the envious god looking at them from the steeple, not a lip smiles.

Night falls and the darkness is accentuated rather than relieved by the oil lamp of the tavern. There is light, too, in the house of Rich Juon—he has a team of oxen—who shows off by lighting a lamp. He nurses a gouty leg, which is another luxury that only men of means can afford. A peasant is on his way to a blissful bender in the tavern.

The village people sit around the well and on low benches before the huts. The drudgery of a long week of work is behind them, relieved by the hope of nocturnal merry-making. On week-days, only *mamaliga,* corn-bread, is the reward life offers. One must have luck and ruthless will to be as rich as Juon with his team of oxen. Yet the road they travel toward the churchyard does not dismay them. No views are exchanged about life and the futility of it all.

These peasants are not unhappy, but they cannot smile while the sun is up. As silence deepens, their faces soften, and they listen to the western breeze, sent to them by the dying sun. The children break into a caper under the cloak of darkness. A young woman's high soprano starts the gossip. Woe befall the unfortunate creature whose tryst is detected in the clump of bushes at the mill. Lashing tongues are dipped in poison. Being stripped of her clothes, put on a donkey's back and whipped across the village would be a light penalty.

The older women's alto responds to the girlish chatter. The men are better at the scythe than at the well, and are at first reluctant to talk, but the intoxication of voices draws them in. The hesitant tenor of the lads mingles with the sopranos. The peasants' baritone obtains support from the basso of the elders, the last to join the Babel. Now the entire square is alive with chatter, and even gouty Juon cannot hold out any longer. The women talk about one another, and the men talk about the harvest and, sometimes, about politics. They scan the sky for happy omens and cast sheepish glances at the church. The ikons at the altar may avert the worst, even if they talk about hail. A May rain is the object of their half-pagan prayer. Many think that politics should be left to the boyars to worry about. In the days when elections were still held they were rounded up and sent to the polling booth, where most of them voted as directed. What

387

difference did it make which political party skinned the peasant? When the King took over dictatorial power in 1938 they were freed of their worries about politics. The royal dictator merely expected them to approve his steps.

Meanwhile groups of young men and women have drawn closer. They all know the meaning of that suppressed scream trailing off in a giggle. Darkness has tempted a young lad to squeeze a shapely leg, and it will probably end in marriage. These are the village ways of courtship. The sopranos and tenors now intermingle freely, leaving the altos, baritones and bassos to themselves. A shepherd's flute appears, its thin tones lost at first in the turmoil. A circle forms and the young ones swing into the native *hora,* holding tingling hands. They fall under the hypnotic power of mass movement, swaying rhythmically, sadly, yet happily. The darkness kindles fires in the eyes; Nature provides for a future generation around the well. Now the dancer's humming, blended into the voice of the flute, changes the nocturnal orchestration. The croaking of the frogs and chirping of the crickets form Nature's background. The western wind from the mountains sends a shudder through the trees, gets entangled in the steeple, where it beats the rope against the bell. Superstition listens to its whisper. Does it mean marriage to the lad whose hand the maiden holds?

At the height of the social excitement the baritones retire to the tavern. The acrid air and wheezy harmonica help to numb the senses. The *tsuika* drink is strong and its warmth blessed. It removes week-day inhibitions and men dare to become themselves.

An other-worldly smile is fixed on lips, as if a pagan-heaven of blissful intoxication had been opened. A hirsute peasant kisses his neighbor, vowing him eternal love, while tears flow down his cheeks. Another one gets aggressive, blurts out insults. Two knives clash and blood spurts. The combatants are separated. Others break into a song and voices are raised.

The deep bassos have left the merry-makers on the square and as the hour draws late, deep-voiced women cry warnings to youth to clear out. The dawn of tomorrow brings another back-breaking week. The flutist takes up a collection, which he spends on a glass of *tsuika.* A couple has a last-minute whispered chat on the bank of the brook. At ten o'clock the village is asleep under the clear sky except for the frogs and crickets. The carousing wind tugs feebly at the church-rope and the peasants make the sign of the cross.

"There are three classes of Roumanians," a French observer said, "the poor ones, very poor ones and excessively poor ones." Most of the peasant's time is spent, of course, at work and not on the village square. He works hard on the best soil in Europe and has little to show for it. He was given land after the War from the boyars' large estates, but the compensation he had— and still has—to pay is high. He had no equipment to make his ownership real, and fell into the hands of village usurers who made him pay as much as 40 per cent interest on his loans. The State gave him the land and is taking it back in the form of taxes. Many of the former owners turned to the government and were given political positions, thus swelling the tremendous bureaucracy. It was a corrupt officialdom, which expected tips, *bakshish,* at every turn. This was a heritage from Turkish times and its prevalence should not condemn all Roumanians. What the boyar had lost on his land, his son recovered in government service.

If the peasant were more progressive, he might be able to make a better living, but the East is too close and its breath is deadly. The Roumanian farmer has not yet learned to use the machine. His hands have merely learned how to swing the scythe. He loves the cruel soil with mad affection; the machine would keep him away from it.

He could have helped himself, probably, by making his country a real democracy. The parliamentary machine was there, and Roumania was young enough not to fall into the errors of older nations. But democracy in Roumania was a farce. The government always won the elections, and the peasant always lost. Peasants occasionally tried to stand up for their rights, but were prevented from leaving their houses for the polling booth. It happened more than once that the military shot at groups of peasants trying to reach a polling place. Failing these precautions, a convenient fire destroyed the urn for votes. Their registration was in the government's hands, and it announced the result it saw fit.

This part of Europe had too long lived under despots to find much pleasure in a different way of life. Roumania's parliamentary system was worse than a failure because it covered unsolved problems with a veneer of legality. Turkey and Russia have shown that the Oriental mind breaks into a trot toward progress only when it hears the crack of the whip.

Roumania has two histories, depending upon its writers. According to one history, the Roumanians are of Roman origin, while according to the other, they are a mixture of Slavs, Greeks and Turks. Professor R. W. Seton-Watson is the best-known

Two Histories

interpreter of the former history; Hungarian scholars expound the second view. The battle of historians has a practical background, not merely national pride. If the Roumanians are descendants of Romans, they preceded the Hungarians in the Lower Danube valley. In that case they have no claim to Transylvania and several other sections they now possess.

The Roumanian peasant of today looks very much like the Southern Italian. The Sicilian immigrant of New York's Little Italy does not look like the haughty descendant of the Caesars any more than the Roumanian peasant of Walachia. The Roumanian calls himself "Roman," "Romen," "Rumen" and "Aroman." He gets indignant when an outlander calls him "Vlach," or "Oláh," as the Hungarians do, "Vlachoi" in Greek, "Volokh" in Slav and "Ifflok" in Turkish. He considers these designations a denial of his Roman origin. He would be less indignant if he knew what these names meant. They are, in fact, varieties of the names the ancient Germans gave to the Romans, signifying people who are different, outlandish. They are synonymous with the word "Welsh" or "Walloon" in Belgium. This, by the way, was the name given to non-Teutonic races, particularly to the Latins, by the Germans. By the testimony of the names alone, the Roumanians are really of Roman origin. But if we bear in mind that the Lower Danube was the great highway of world-wide migration, down which wave after wave of barbarian tribes swept on their way to the Eastern and Western Romes, the Balkans and the West, the mere evidence of names is weakened. This becomes apparent when we consider what the Slav invasion did to the Lower Danube.

The earliest known ancestors of today's Roumanians were known to the theatergoers of ancient Greece as "Davos" and

391

"Geta," comic slaves. "Dacian" was the name of their tribe in Greece, and the Romans knew them as "Getae." Theirs was a large part of the Danube valley as far as Buda in the west and the river Dniester in the east. "The Dacians had not been a mere collection of barbarous tribes," Seton-Watson writes in his book *History of the Roumanians*, "but had a rudimentary culture of their own, and a well-marked social and economic structure." They held the souls of the higher castes immortal and welcomed death as a more exalted form of life. The King had to bow to the Chief Priest, who was the incarnate will of God. Members of the privileged classes had a right to wear a felt hat, while peasants, shepherds and common soldiers were compelled to wear their hair long. The power of tradition in the Danube valley is shown by the fact that many of these customs still prevail.

The Dacians were not awed by Rome's reputation and often crossed the frozen Danube. Their ruler, Cotiso, was a barbaric Napoleon, so powerful that Emperor Augustus wanted to marry his daughter. When the match fell through, the Dacian nearly became the Emperor's son-in-law by betrothal to the latter's five-year-old daughter, Julia. Decebalus the Great covered his barbarian court with glory and established a name for himself as a chivalrous foe. After having beaten the Roman outposts beyond the Danube, he returned the prisoners hale and safe, even restored their captured arms. Emperor Domitian gave him a king's crown wrought by Syrian masters. The gift pleased the Dacians; gold, however, pleased them even more, and proud but decadent Rome had to buy peace from the barbarians.

Rome was still strong enough to command respect for her name, and the Dacian chieftain was beaten by Trajan. This was the greatest event on the Danube for many centuries. Roumanians

392

date their national history from this campaign. It was responsible for a great engineering feat of classical times, the remnants of which we saw near the Iron Gates, higher up the Danube. It was also responsible for the erection of Trajan's triumphal arch, one of the prides of Rome today and a symbol of the importance the Romans attributed to their victory. Remembering the Dacian's chivalry, the Emperor let him keep his crown, but gave him a Roman adviser, thus establishing a precedent for a "protectorate" in the Danube valley. Decebalus was no man to be advised, and no sooner was Trajan out of sight than he called his men to war. Once more he was defeated, but escaped in a shepherd's tatters. The indomitable King now led a guerrilla warfare, assisted by the mountain woods. A woman betrayed him, so legend says, and Trajan took him prisoner. He was to be taken to Rome in Trajan's triumphal procession; he committed suicide to escape the shame. Trajan's Column in Rome shows the victorious legions and the Dacian captives.

Rome had gone into the Lower Danube valley for several reasons. It had then the fame of an Eastern Eldorado because of its gold, minerals and soil. Besides Rome felt that this gap in her protective system had to be filled if the barbarians were to be kept in check. The shores of the Black Sea were the end of the world. Her dynamic energy drove the Eternal City into over-expansion. Her legions were settled on the conquered land. The Roman high command strengthened them with colonists from less favored provinces. The survivors of the older tribes ventured again into the Danubian plains and were absorbed by the new settlers. They learned the Latin names of months and days; Latin *strigae,* witches, displaced the barbaric ghosts, and the festivals of *Kalendae* were celebrated. Writers of the second type of history maintain, however, that these legions were Roman only in name and that in reality they were a classical anticipation of to-day's Foreign Legions in which Romans merely held the command, while the rank and file consisted of foreign adventurers. These critics hold that the supposed Romans were a motley crowd of Latinized barbarians who spoke a corrupt Latin as the *lingua franca* of the Danube. Where are the Roman temples and baths, where are the circuses and theaters? they ask.

The Lower Danube was then the Siberia of Rome to which the politically undesirable were banished. Ovid, trying to warm up his numbed fingers at the dying fire, wrote his *Tristes* in this colony. He did not foresee, nor did anyone else, that Rome's enemies would rise in those endless plains from which the cold winds swept into his uncouth hut. In the center of Asia, somewhere on the confines of Mongolia, on the Pamir and between the Caspian Sea and the Ural mountains, an entire world was set into motion. Was it a series of catastrophic droughts which transformed Mongolia's pastures into the Gobi desert? Was it a warlike foe which wanted greater living space for himself? Or was it merely the fabulous tales which penetrated to the Far East about the wonder-world of the West? Never did history see such a stampede; Asia began to pour into Europe. Across the parched steppes the Old World began to move, responding to the irresistible call of pasture. The Goths swarmed into the Lower Danube region, and under Emperor Aurelian the Roman legions crossed the river, retreating southward.

Endless controversies have been aroused by the historian's words: "Aurelian retired the army and the provincial population, establishing them in Moesia" [south of the Danube]. Were the Latinized settlers evacuated altogether? The Roumanians assert

394

that the Romans took only their legions, officials and wealthy colonists across the Danube, while the common people remained. Let us not argue with Roumanians about this question. There are no documents left to prove or disprove their contention.

The Sarmates followed the Goths, pressed hard by the Ostro-Goths, who were chased by the Huns, upon the heels of whom came the Avars. The Slavs were spreading everywhere, pushed westward by the "rat-eating Mongols." From the Volga came the Bulgarians, the Finno-Hungarians. The name of the Petche-negs is all but forgotten today, but then theirs was as formidable a name as the Magyars'. The pageant of pasture-seeking bar-barians continued with the Kumans, later absorbed by the Hun-garians. The stronger tribes usually vanished without a trace, because they offered a bold front to the tidal waves, and the weaker often survived, because they awaited the subsidence of the storm in mountain retreats. The Slavs were among the latter, serving the strong and watching them pass by. They had joined the Daco-Roman shepherds in the mountains, and then returned to the plains after the invasion had blown over. "There is no other Roman province where so many important towns so com-pletely lost their former character and even name," says Seton-Watson.

The Slavs lived under their village chiefs, the *knezes,* and the district leaders, *voyvods.* They mixed with the remnants of the original population. Let us call the mixture Roumanians, a name which became popular much later. The great missionaries of the Slavs are thought to have been responsible for the Roumanians' conversion to Christianity. Roumanian liturgical books were printed in Slav characters until the middle of the nineteenth century. The heaven of the old Roumanians was peopled by ancient and modern gods. Pagan rites blended with primitive Christianity.

For a full thousand years the history of Roumania is a blank page. The records, if any, were lost in the *Voelkerwanderung,* migration of the barbarians. Roumania was "the enigma of the Middle Ages." Her history begins in the thirteenth century, and for the following five hundred years the country was divided into Walachia to the south and Moldavia to the north. Both of them had distinct histories. They were for the most under the over-lordship of the Turkish Sultans, who adopted a uniform system of administration for both of them in the eighteenth century. It was only then that they became Danubian Principalities. Independent Roumania was founded in 1859.

At the end of the thirteenth century the barbarian invasion was almost ended and the Carpathian mountains disgorged the refugee tribesmen. The Black Prince, also known as Rudolf the Black—*Negru Voda*—was the founder of Walachia, if tradition may be trusted. His mountaineers beheld a land of weeds and malaria. The rich soil feeding the weeds had tempted the hill folk, whom the Hungarians were constantly pushing from the rear. The soil had to be watered with sweat, but its yield was rich. The workers had no time to accumulate wealth, and those who did, had no time to work. Rapidly society became stratified. The "haves" had the arms and authority, and the "have-nots" became heretics and traitors if they tried to rise against tyranny. Tragedy came to stay in the Principalities on the Danube. Privilege cowed the masses, so that when the Turks came they were unable to defend themselves against the Oriental danger. The election of the rulers was also conducive to misfortune. All the sons of the native ruler, *voyvod,* were eligible to succeed their fathers. The bastards

396

were not excluded. A woman spent a few months with the Prince and would claim the throne for her son. A council of boyars and priests, *divan,* elected the Prince and presented him to the crowd for its approval through acclamation. The boyars' enthusiasm for a candidate cost money, and the help of Hungary and Poland was often invoked.

Then came the Turks. They reduced the two Principalities to the position of vassal States. The Sultan gave his approval to the highest bidder. Since each of them came with wagonloads of treasure, it was in the Sublime Porte's interest to speed up the turnover. Princes were executed or assassinated. The native ruler, on the other hand, had to recoup his investment and even more. He pillaged the rich, oppressed the poor and applied high-pressure methods to feather his nest before his short day was over. Six years was the average reign of a prince. Their quality was poor, barring few exceptions. The names of some of the rulers, such as Alexander the Good, Stephen the Great, Michael the Brave, reflect contemporary opinion. One of the "good" Walachian Princes was Mircea the Old. The great cataclysm which decided the fate of the Danubian Principalities struck the country during his reign. The Turks had begun their march in response to a *Drang nach Westen.* They penetrated into the Balkans, defeated the Serbians, crossed the Danube and appeared in Walachia. When Mircea was buried, Walachia's independence was carried to her grave.

When Constantinople fell to the Turks, the superstitious medieval mind was terror-stricken by as elemental a force as the Black Death itself. The "totalitarian" war carried on by the Sultan's hordes was all the deadlier because the countries of the West could offer no resistance. The Middle Ages had led West-

397

ern mankind into a blind alley. Instead of building up a world of Christian love, the Crusades had perpetuated warfare. The *Landsknechte* transferred their hatred from the Turk to the Christian neighbor. Religion became the institutionalized church with its awesome power, and corruption weakened its hold. The flame of the stakes drove fear into the thinking man's heart and prevented him from pursuing the mysteries of life. Western Europe was sunk into a mire. The Danubian Principalities were crying for help, but their voice went unheard. The Holy Roman Empire devoted itself to prestige and gold. Rome was preoccupied with the souls of heretics. It had no time for the Turks. The rich Italian cities were dismantling one another, and France was liquidating the Hundred Years' War. Hatred was smoldering in the embers of the stake, and the West was completely paralyzed. It was then the Turk took the Eastern capital of Christendom. The way was open to the Middle Danube.

Walachia was helpless in the face of an elemental force, and she signed a treaty, *hatti-cherif,* with the Turkish Sultan, who became her suzerain "protector" for the modest payment of 11,000 piastres, 40 falcons and 40 horses. The Sultan was not to interfere with the Prince's election, build mosques or colonize Turks in the land. He allowed the Danubian Principalities to ring their church bells—a rare privilege.

Some of the Princes tried to assert a measure of independence. One of these was Vlad the Impaler, whom his contemporaries called *Dracul,* Vlad the Devil. He had the Turkish envoys' turbans nailed to their heads and had them impaled on high stakes, "to honor them." The Sultan dispatched the Pasha of Vidin to depose him; Vlad impaled the Pasha. The Sultan led his army against him and found a forest of pales with the bodies of

398

men, women and children. Vlad liked to feast in the company
of his impaled victims, whose wounds he had salted. Not only
the innocent but also the guilty felt his wrath. Highway robbers
and thieves were punished mercilessly. It is recorded that in his
days it was safe to leave doors open in Walachia.

Candidates for the throne submitted their petitions to the
Sultan, along with the precious pearls of the Indian Ocean for
the sovereign's harem. Since the chief eunuch had the ladies'
confidence, he was not forgotten either. Now the Grand Vizier—
whose position corresponded to the Premier in an autocracy—
could afford that new Summer palace in suburban Constantinople.
What present would be given to the Sultan himself? The granddaughter of Peter the Great, wily Kiajna, wife of Peter the Shepherd (the one who supplied the Sultan with lambs), had seven
hundred thousand ducats distributed in Constantinople to chase
a rival from the Walachian throne. This was Peter the Ear-ring,
ousted in favor of Mihnea, her son. Kiajna's gold to the Sultan
was carried by 600 horses; Peter was thrown into the Bosporus
and Mihnea got the job.

All was set for the investiture of the new Prince by the Sultan.
Prince Nicholas Soutzo has left us the details of the elaborate
ceremony. The would-be ruler rode to the Grand Serail on a
richly caparisoned horse. Entering the court of honor he would
cast an awed glance at the shining scimitars of the Janizaries.
Dressed in the princely kaftan, he was received by the Sultan who
gave him the royal bonnet (decorated with aigrettes and ostrich
feathers), a pelisse of Siberian marten, reserved only for the
highest dignitaries, the banner with the horse-tail and the steed
of honor. The Sultan also gave him his certificate of appointment,
firman, which the Prince held to his chest, and then backed out

of the hall. He now had the right to declare war, conclude peace, coin money, impose taxes, pronounce death sentences and to pardon.

The *voyvoda* was now on his way to his capital, Bucharest, traveling in a wagon of red and yellow. He timed his journey so that the caprices of the Danube would not retard him unduly. Today the distance can be covered in three hours, but then it took several weeks, even more when the Danube flooded the low-lands. It was considered a good omen if the cold *crivatz* of the North froze the Danube. Across the river, he was in his own realm. He put on his golden helmet and organized a procession, headed by the *timbalier,* behind whom stalked a saddled horse, carrying the Sultan's present, a silver coffee-pot. Members of the court followed in the order of their rank: the chief of the boots, guardian of the pipes, chief of the *sorbets,* the grand tambour or chief of music, the head saber-holder, the grand-cafetier and standard-bearer. Ringing of the church bells accompanied the solemn procession of the Prince. Wearing *kalpaks* of tremendous height, wrapped in the finest silks of the Orient, the boyars paid him their respect. Priests with immense beards offered him bread and salt at church doors. Peasants prostrated themselves in his presence.

The new Prince rewarded those who pleased him and impaled those whom he disliked. He collected a group of loyal boyars and paid cash for their loyalty. Some of the Princes divided the country into fiefs and entrusted the collection of their taxes to favorite boyars, who retained their share and turned the rest over to the ruler. Often the Prince had bought his throne on the installment plan, and then he was particularly ruthless in the collection of taxes. In any case the peasant had to pay and was tortured if the drought or Danube flood had destroyed his harvest.

The Prince was particularly anxious not to antagonize the ruling race of Turks. One of them was so eager to please the real sovereigns that he issued orders to his prefects to have Turkish assassins and thieves shackled "with the utmost kindness." A slight to Islam was likely to be paid for dearly. The Prince had left his representatives at the Serail, and another one in the entourage of the Grand Vizier. He saw to it that the disloyal boyars' complaints to the Supreme Master in Constantinople should be intercepted.

If the Prince could no longer pay his installments, if a higher bidder came along, if Serail intrigues led to his disgrace, or the Grand Vizier was promised more money from a candidate, the *voyvod* lost his position. Bad administration was never valid grounds for dismissal; good administration which did not take all the cream of the land was penalized. Some of the dismissed Princes were merely exiled, enslaved, reduced to a commoner's status. Their families were sold as Serail slaves. One Prince had his nose and ears cut, and his successor had to redeem them from the Sultan. Since dead men do not talk, and the Seventh Heaven is closed to heathen dogs, *voyvods* were often killed. Alexander the Bad of Moldavia was crowned with a nightpot, then paraded in his princely garb to the square, where he was hanged. Prince Hangerli also died under curious circumstances.

One day the Sultan's delegate appeared in Bucharest, accompanied by a burly Negro, "grand and terrible," an adept at slashing throats. The princely chief of beds, *postelnic,* saw the two pass the threshold and implored his master to pretend sickness and refuse them admission until ways could be found to get him out of danger. Hangerli, however, was so paralyzed by fear that he received the delegate without delay. No sooner were the Turk and his escort in the throne room when the giant Negro lassoed the Prince and threw him to the ground. A strong man, he put up a terrific fight to save his life. The din attracted the boyars who were to attend on the Prince, and they were so numerous that they could have easily saved their master from the two. The Turkish delegate shouted: *"Dur, dur, firman,"* "Halt, halt. Imperial Orders!" and the boyars looked on, paralyzed, while the delegate stabbed their Prince to death. The Sultan's power was so great, the contemporary historian Xenopol said, that the Turkish delegate and his Negro could have the entire population of the capital put to death merely by uttering the magic word *Firman!*

The hero about whom fishermen of the Danube delta and shepherds of the Carpathians weave naïve sagas lived at the turn of the seventeenth century. He is a demigod of legend, who fired imaginations and gave ambitions an object for centuries to come. His equestrian statue is a sight of the capital, and the highest Roumanian decoration, Michael Vitzacu, is named after him. He was Michael the Brave, "Voyvod of Walachia, Councilor of His Most Sacred Imperial Royal Majesty and his Lieutenant in Transylvania." The Roumania he controlled was almost as extensive as the Roumania of the post-World War days. He fought the Turk with the help of the Emperor, and fought the Emperor with the Turk's help. He secured his appointment by a loan of 200,000 florins, part of which the English Ambassador at the Sublime Porte had helped him to obtain. "Yet," Seton-Watson says, "almost his first action was one of revolt against the Turkish creditors who were settling like locusts upon Walachia, accompanied by tax-collectors on their rounds and thus extorted all sorts of illegal contributions, in addition to the monstrous sum already extracted." The Turks, thereupon, imprisoned him in his own palace, but he escaped unnoticed. His captors continued to guard the empty chamber. When they were all in the building he burned it to the ground and besides had the Turkish settlers massacred. The Grand Turk considered the "Walachian Vespers" a declaration of war. Michael's soldiers crossed the Danube, invaded Turkey proper, dispersed the Turkish army, slew Mustapha, its commander, and captured the Prophet's Green Banner. The enraged Sultan dispatched Sinan Pasha the Renegade to invade Walachia with a host of a hundred thousand men. Michael retreated into the hills. Sinan took the capital and massacred its people, but Michael relieved it and chased the Turkish army into the Danube. Sinan died of "a broken heart" shortly afterward. The Sultan sent Michael the red flag of reconciliation. Now he schemed with the Sublime Porte against the Emperor, then plotted with the Emperor against the Sultan. Finally the imperial commissioner, General Basta, made him prisoner and had him disemboweled by his own subjects.

A period of profound darkness followed Michael's reign. When the Sultan besieged Vienna late in the seventeenth century, Walachians built the Danube bridges that were to help him triumph over the Christian world. It is true, too, that they found means of warning the Habsburg capital of the approaching danger. Some of the Princes were little more than the Sultan's messengers. Their methods were as cruel as those of the Turk. Prince Stephen Tomsa combined business with pleasure—the business of robbing the boyars with the pleasure of executing them. His victims were herded in the council chamber and the

403

gypsy executioner announced, prostrate at the foot of the throne: "My august master, the rams are fat."

The last native ruler of Walachia was Brancovan the Decapitated, whose name tells his sad tale. His portraits show his big eyes dominating his long face. His turned-down moustache half concealed two heavy lines of his smiling face. His fleshy lips revealed a man who took his motto to heart: *Carpe diem.* His escutcheon depicted a crow holding a cross in its beak, flanked by the sun and moon. The crow turned out to have a deeper meaning. Brancovan tried to appear an Occidental ruler in his stiff gold robe and *pelerine* mantle held together by a diamond clasp.

It was Brancovan who had the capital's famous street built, the Calea Victoriei, then merely a country road connecting his farm with his town mansion. Roumania's "Broadway" is crooked to this very day because the Prince wanted to keep away from the estates of his kinsmen and enemies, the Cantacuzenes.

An empty throne, facing his own, reminded him that ultimate power on the Lower Danube belonged to the absent Sultan. Brancovan's diplomacy was as tortuous as the road he built. When the Sovereign visited the principality he held his bridle and lay prostrate as he passed. No sooner was he out of sight than he concluded a secret pact with Russia's Peter the Great, who, later, offered to lead a crusade against the Turk. It was then that the Russians took their first halting steps toward the warm waters of the South, the *Drang nach Sueden,* which was to become their guiding policy.

In Constantinople, Brancovan was known as the "Golden Bey," and, indeed, the gold of the Argesh river and of Transylvania was to keep him in the good graces of the Sultan, the reigning Sultana, the Sultana-Mother, the ladies of the harem, the eunuchs and their mute slaves. The more he gave the more the Porte suspected him of hiding. The Grand Vizier drew up an indictment in which he was accused both of treasonable ambition and treasonable lack of it. He was arraigned for having been in correspondence with the Czar, the Emperor, the King of Poland and the rulers of Venice. He was found guilty of having acquired palaces in Transylvania and having minted coins with his own effigy. One day the Sultan's delegate appeared, attached the fateful black chiffon to the shoulder of the Prince and declared him *mazil,* deposed. Brancovan sent six wagons of gold to the Porte to ransom himself, but could not have convicted himself more effectively. Now the legend of the hidden treasures became a firm conviction. He and his family were thrown into the Seven Towers prison of Constantinople, and subjected to torture. In the presence of the Sultan he and his two sons were beheaded.

The contrast between the wealth of the boyars and the misery of the peasants shocked even that age. A relative of the beheaded Prince owned 12,000 heads of cattle, 4,000 pigs and 1,500 gypsy slaves. A Florentine traveler gave a vivid impression of the countryside, in which half-starved peasants lived in a land of plenty. It would have been blasphemy to suggest that these miserable creatures were created in God's image. Procreation and drunken sprees were their only joys. The fruit of their work went to the boyars who had nothing but contempt for them. Only the peasant's ability to stand no end of torture distinguished him from the cattle. There were so many beggars and they were so wretched that they had to organize themselves and live in a self-governing syndicate under the rule of the *starost,* the beggars' chief. Their shacks extended all the way to the princely mansion of Bucharest. The streets of the capital were lakes of mud and the houses were of wood, which could be abandoned without heartache when the purple horizon signaled the approaching foe.

The boyars not only oppressed the peasants but also fought one another. In their letters of complaint to the Porte they denounced their fellow-boyars for the most outrageous crimes. These letters were dripping with the most abject expressions of loyalty to the Turk. If they had not exhausted themselves in domestic strife, they might have been able to offer resistance to the Sultan.

The beginning of the eighteenth century would have been auspicious for the Lower Danube to break away from the Turk. The walls of Vienna saw the decline of the Sultan's star, and the myth of his invincible power was dispelled. Soon the Turk was chased out of Hungary. The *élan* of the Turkish invasion had spent itself. Europe had poisoned the warlike Ottomans. In war they were dynamic, in peace they were static. Having amassed vast treasures they yielded to their Oriental nature; to do nothing was bliss. Unlike the Balkans where the Turks had their garrisons, the Danubian Principalities were not effectively occupied by the Sultans. Only an effort might have shaken off the semblance of Turkish rule. But who would have rebelled? The peasants were trained in the virtues of obedience and not of rebellion. The boyars were busy fighting one another. Time sanctified oppression, and it would have been sacrilege to rise against it. Myths are stronger than realities. If an analytic intellect had looked behind the scene it would have found that the Turks' power was a fiction. But no one thought of contesting myth. The medieval tradition was strong. *Credo quia absurdum.* . . . I believe in it because it is unbelievable. The hold of dogma was strong.

The Lower Danube region was completely demoralized. For some time the Sultan considered transforming the Principalities into Turkish *Pashaliks,* such as the Bulgarians, Greeks and Serbians had. Instead, he turned to the method of *divide et impera.* For nearly a century Roumanians were governed by Greeks from the *phanar* lighthouse section of Constantinople. Hence this is known as the *Phanariote régime.* The rich Greeks of Islam's capital were easy to recognize, since minorities in the Empire were compelled to wear distinctive clothing. The Greeks' furs were otter or marten, and their dresses had to be blue, to distinguish them from the Armenians who had to wear red, and from the Jews, whose color was black. The Greeks were extremely unpopular, but nonetheless rich and powerful. When they ventured into the popular quarters of the Turkish capital, the natives spat at them. Their windows were shuttered to keep out unfriendly stones.

The *phanariotes* occupied some of the highest positions of the Turkish Empire. Several Sultanas were of Greek origin, and their influence in the palace was great. Wealth did not turn their heads; hashish or opium did not enslave them. *Phanariote* Greeks were placed in key positions while the Turk kept in the background. "Let the accursed *giaour* kill the *phanariote* dog," the Turk said. After the extinction of the native Princes, the thrones of the Danubian Principalities were sold to the *phanariotes* without as much as the semblance of an election or the need of acclamation by the people.

"The entire lighthouse district is here," a Greek of Bucharest wrote to his kinsmen in Constantinople. All of these Greek Princes were tyrants, some of them good, most of them bad. The good ones founded schools, hospitals and churches. Roumanian replaced the old Slavic tongue as the language of liturgy under their rule. Most of the rulers were interested in feathering their nest and returning to Constantinople. In Bucharest they missed the luxuries of the capital of Islam.

The Princes conceived ingenious ways of plundering the people. One of them prohibited the importation of certain goods, so that he could smuggle them into the country himself, reaping a rich harvest. When the Sultan issued the order to levy a special tax, the Prince raised it fivefold and retained the balance. The most popular tax for the Princes and the least popular for the peasant was the *vakarit* on horse and cattle. Sheep and smoked fish, bees and wine, pigs and tobacco, cloth and chimneys were also taxed. That is why a chimney is still a luxury in parts of the Danube valley. In order to escape the tax-collector, the peasant drove his cattle into the mountains. If it happened to be mid-Winter the cattle were decimated by the cold. The hoofprints often betrayed the peasant, and then he was flogged.

"All posts from the highest to the lowest," the Austrian consul wrote, "not only bring in good income, but carry with them the right to plunder the people." "Plucking the hen without making it cluck," is a Roumanian proverb, the truth of which is deeply felt. Instruments of torture suppressed the clucks. So great was the pressure that the population was seeping into Turkish and Hungarian lands. In the middle of the eighteenth century the number of tax-paying families decreased from 14,000 to 7,000, and in a few years the number of peasant families fell from 147,000 to one quarter of that number. At the end of the century, Roumanians were worse off even than the completely subjected Bulgarians and Serbians. "When the masses murmur," it was said, "the Prince makes a bonfire of their petitions and sends out the Albanian guard." When despairing protests were made to a Prince before his palace—a most unusual event—he appeared at his window and called out angrily: "Pay the taxes and you won't be killed." The turnover on the throne was so great that the average rule was reduced to two and a half years. "The Prince changes," the proverb said, "and madmen rejoice." The despotism of the *phanariote* rulers surpassed all bounds and now they turned not only against the peasants, but often also against the boyars. An Austrian traveler saw a boyar make the sign of the cross before being admitted to audience by the Prince. "What is remarkable about these despots," a contemporary wrote, "is that all their riches, money, jewels and furnishings are always in trunks and traveling coffers, as if they had to leave at any moment."

A special niche in the Hall of Fame should be reserved for Constantine Mavrocordato, whose large eyes look at posterity from under a vaulted forehead. He made a discovery with which he was a long way ahead of his time: "You should not kill the goose that lays the golden egg." The boyars and clergy could not understand him and considered him "godless" for sparing the poor. They should be content with their place of honor in heaven, they believed, and should not want to have the good things of the earth as well. Constantine instructed his tax-collectors to go easy, and the peasant at least had a chance to live. Under his rule ten piastres bought the serf freedom, and this was considered a bargain. Constantine also tried to raise the standard of the clergy, demanding that they should at least be literate.

409

The life forces of Turkey were ebbing while those of Russia were swelling. St. Petersburg found herself the capital of a vast continent. At last the Asiatic tribesman reached his goal. Peter the Great translated the ideals of Attila the Hun into a modern tongue. The gigantic landlocked country continued its search for an access to the world, moving irresistibly west and south. Russia scored in the west when Poland was dismembered, but there she exhausted herself while trying to overcome the resistance of the victims, who were strong enough to make Russia waste her strength but not strong enough to stop her. The virility of awakened Prussia was another bar. At first the route to the south was barred by Turkey. Missionaries had taken Greek Orthodox religion from the capital of the Eastern Empire to the steppes of the Volga. That was also the faith of the Balkans. Russia was a country of Slavs and so were the Balkans. She was the logical defender of the Lower Danube and of the mountains beyond.

Many times her armies marched across the river valley and more than once they were within shooting distance of Aja Sophia, the pride of Constantinople. Roumanian nobility kissed the footprints of Catherine the Great. Some of the boyars favored Russian rule, but the Slav giant had to move cautiously because of his friends and enemies. "On to Byzantium" was written on the triumphal arch in honor of the Great Catherine. Peter the Great had styled himself "Monarch of Russo-Greeks" and the splendor of his camp at the Moldavian capital, Jassy, was designed to impress even the pomp-loving boyars. At the great feast, to which only nobles of princely blood were invited, the boyars tasted champagne for the first time in their lives and drank it like water, deceived by its smoothness, and soon were rolling under the

410

tables. Their Russian hosts robbed them and returned home in triumph.

Russia acquired the treaty right to make representations to the Porte in favor of the Greek Orthodox church in territories controlled by Turkey. If the peasants were sighing for a less cruel Christian oppressor—they knew that there must be oppression—they were disillusioned.

Let us now cast a glance at the more northern of the two Danubian Principalities—Moldavia. There the Pruth and Sereth drain the highland waters into the Danube. In the west the massed ranges of the Carpathians look at the plains, lost in the haze of the steppes—Russia before the War. Of industries we see little and life moves at a slower tempo than in Walachia. The capital, Jassy (Iasi) is carrying on a bold fight against ignorance.

Do not blame the historian for the paucity of knowledge on Moldavia. Much of her story is legend, and much of it is the boasting of the wayward and the weak. For centuries this had been the end of the world, and ignorance was so abysmal that not even the clergy could write. Impartial history was impossible since Roumanians, Hungarians, Austrians and Russians had a large number of axes to grind, while the destructive Turk applied the torch to the records of the *giaour*, Christian dog.

A mountaineer, peasant and prince, Dragosh, who lived in the thirteenth or fourteenth century—the legend itself is vague—was chasing an aurochs—the European bison—when his dog, Moldova, perished in the river. Hence the name of the Principality. The aurochs is on the escutcheon of Moldavia. Dragosh had come from the mountains. He and his followers settled in the plains. The Roumanians say there is no difference between

Walachians and Moldavians—the Russians say there is. In such a primitive country, where even today roads are bars rather than links, differences are bound to develop even among kinsmen, especially if fostered by jealous neighbors. Communist Russia has a Moldavian Republic on her side of the river Dniester, to show the Roumanian Moldavians how much better off they would be under the hammer and the sickle.

In her uncertain history Moldavia had several rulers who were either heroic or made so by legend. Stephen the Great established a record by ruling for forty-eight years and by defeating Hungarian, Pole and even the paramount Turk. He spanned the fifteenth and the sixteenth centuries and gave Moldavia a national hero. His portrait in the fresco in the Putna monastery shows a handsome round face with regular features. On his knees before the Virgin, the potentate looks at the holy image with one eye and at an invisible audience with the other. This pose suggests his historic part as the "Judas Maccabaeus" of the Christian cause. Although deeply religious, Stephen had a flair for showmanship.

Pope Pius IV called him the athlete of Christ, *Athleta Christi,* and honored him with a carved ivory cross supposed to contain a fragment of the true cross. Stephen was urging the Western Powers to help him "cut off the pagan's right hand," and thus publicized his achievements to the Venetian envoy: "I have fought thirty-six battles since I am lord of this country and of these won thirty-four." He entered into alliance with Powers as far apart as Venice and Persia in an effort to organize a grandiose coalition against the Turk. He pitted one neighbor against the other. In his domestic policies he was a Dr. Jekyll and Mr. Hyde. "Often at meals he would order people to be put to death without legal

412

sentence." He built forty stone churches in different parts of the country, and in the words of a contemporary chronicler: "The Moldavians think of him with the veneration one holds for a saint in religious honor."

Bogdan the One-Eyed, his son, was not of heroic stature and under him Moldavia sunk so low that the Turks changed its very name to Kara Bogdan, in honor of their first vassal. Sultan Suleiman was to receive a *bakshish,* poetically called a tribute, of 4,000 ducats, 40 horses and 25 falcons, also a thousand men. But Stephen the Great's heroic stature was clearly discernible in his granddaughter Kiajna. Had she not been disqualified by her sex, she might have excelled as a warrior. She was the "mother of the Danubian Principalities," a genius of diplomatic intrigue. She bribed the ladies of the harem, from the Sultanas downward, knowing of their great influence at the Sublime Porte. She bought a throne for her elder son, Peter, and, when he was overthrown, re-purchased the same throne for Alexander, her younger son. She also bought a place in the harem of Murad III for her daughter. The throne of Moldavia was then occupied by John the Terrible, so strong that he "could lift a cannon with one arm." He had started his career as a Constantinople jeweler. The annals do not reveal whether the Sultan traded an empty throne for overdue bills for diamonds and emeralds. It was then that Kiajna trumped John's bid for an annual tribute and offered the Sultan a larger sum in the name of her son, Peter the Lame. John must have thought that the whole Principality was not worth that much money; an army would be cheaper. He tried to resist the Turks and found himself deserted by his many friends. His own boyars surrendered him to the Grand Turk, who broke him on the wheel with four camels. Kiajna was triumphant, and Peter hobbled up the steps of his throne. He ruled over a hungry country, from which constant civil wars had exacted their toll. When Transylvania's ruler passed through his realm, the most precious present Peter could offer him was a loaf of bread.

Peter the Lame was so unpopular that Kiajna had to replace him by John the Saxon. When John the Saxon could not fulfill his part of the bargain, she replaced him with Peter the Lame, and so on. Now she was selling thrones to the highest bidder, in business for herself. The Turks considered her a hobgoblin in a woman's guise. When the Sultan's executioner appeared near the palace she would hide among the hucksters. Native folklore is rich in stories about the royal witch with the evil eye which made the cattle lame and brought on the plague. The poison potions which extinguished several exalted lives may have been brewed in Kiajna's caldrons.

Chaos into which Moldavia was plunged gave birth to a breed of adventurers, half-heroes and half-criminals. None was stranger than Bazileus (also known as Jacob Basilicus). Even Dr. Faustus could not have been more versatile. A Greek by birth, he spoke with false modesty of his adoptive father, the despot of Paros and Samos, islands of the Aegean Sea. He succeeded the despot of this tiny realm. He revived the Olympic games, and donning the ancient philosophers' garb he crowned poets with laurel wreaths. He turned up in Constantinople one day and dazzled the Greeks' *phanariote* quarter with a pedigree all the way back to Hercules. He traced an illustrious line of rulers century after century, generation after generation, down to his own day. Centuries before, his records showed, his family had strayed into the Danube lands and had given Serbia some of her rulers, through whom he was related to the Moldavian Princes. Next he turned

414

up at the Court of Emperor Ferdinand in Vienna, where he produced papyrus and parchment to prove his claims. Radiating the distinction of high birth, cloaked in mystery, he paraded his royal modesty in the highest circles. Now he became also known as a scholar of note. As an astronomer he was conversant with the secrets of the sky, and as a historian he excelled in interpreting ancient records. The great men of the age deemed the time well spent in the company of the young Greek in whose eyes the fire of knowledge burned. The more he penetrated Nature's secrets, the more ardently he pursued the mysteries of man's mind.

The Emperor himself was impressed, and succumbed to his guest's uncanny eloquence. He gave him a well-trained cavalry corps of 1,600, with which Basilicus routed the forces of the then ruling Prince of Moldavia. With his high Constantinople connections Basilicus bought himself a confirmation as the ruler of the Danubian Principality. The *firman* was given to him at a cut rate.

As the Prince of Moldavia, Jacob Basilicus did some curious things which raised the question of his sanity. He had a school erected, filling it with children from all over his country, who were studying at his expense. He collected a library, which his subjects found even more incomprehensible than the school. He carried on a crusade against bigamy and divorce, thereby antagonizing the higher classes, while the lower classes abhorred the tax of a ducat per family which he imposed. The people rose against him and slew him, together with his schoolmasters, librarians and foreign guard.

Prince Aaron, a converted Jew, was another remarkable ruler. He bought the country on a "shoe-string," by promising 400,000 ducats to the Sultan and 200,000 ducats to the high dignitaries.

The ladies of the harem were to receive emeralds and brilliants of great value. In order to insure his integrity and prompt payment, his princely retinue contained a large number of creditors' spies, who made themselves at home in Moldavia and harried the tax-collectors into action, witnessing the tortures to which slow-paying peasants were subjected. The boyars, too, had to bear the increased burden, and they rose. Aaron was recalled to Constantinople by the Sultan, but he found the money to buy his crown anew.

Had the peasants nothing to say about their cruel treatment? The records speak only of infrequent outbursts in the Danubian Principalities, but not of organized rebellions. The peasants were too ignorant and resigned to revolt. The only organized peasant war broke out in Transylvania, then linked to Hungary. Since its participants were Roumanian peasants, the story is part of this chapter.

The throne of Austria-Hungary was occupied by that "Imperial Jacobin in the palace," Emperor Joseph II. He traveled all over the country, including Transylvania, where the Vlachs, *oláhs,* as the Magyars nicknamed them, fell on their knees as the royal carriage passed. God and His Imperial Majesty were residents of the same heaven and he brought the Roumanian peasants the promise of a new day. He permitted the serfs to marry, dispose of their property. He forbade the imposition of excessive taxes; it was all like a dream. The Emperor introduced military conscription. Word spread in the Transylvanian mountains that all serfs who were accepted for service in the army would be freed and given land. Village people began to flock to town and recruiting officers worked overtime.

Emboldened by the kindness of the Sovereign, Ion Ursu, whom

416

history knows as Horia, called upon him in Vienna. It was nothing short of the miraculous for an uncouth *oláh* to be received by the head of the Holy Roman Empire. We do not know what took place between the Emperor and the peasant, but we do know what Horia thought had taken place. Evidently the peasant had been so dazzled by the imperial presence that he read his wish-dreams into Joseph's words. He returned to his Roumanian neighbors with the glad tidings that the Emperor had consented to the abolition of serfdom. His friend, Closca, understood him to say that the Sovereign had granted the right to the peasants to take arms in defense of freedom. Horia and Closca called a meeting. Its peasant participants, carried away by their enthusiasm, jumped to the conclusion that if the nobles resisted they should perish by the sword. In this tragedy of errors one misunderstanding led to another. Casual words were taken for promises. They in turn were interpreted as encouragement to rebellion.

In a frenetic outburst the repressed hatreds of centuries found vent. Horia sent the nobles an ultimatum, demanding that they pay taxes, surrender their lands and titles. His peasants swept the Maros valley, killed a hundred nobles and sacked two hundred castles. The government moved against the rebels. Joseph called upon them to lay down their arms, promising amnesty for all except the leaders. The nobles captured Horia and Closca. They dealt with Closca more cruelly, considering him more dangerous. Horia was merely executed. Closca was first given twenty strokes with the whip, then was disemboweled alive and finally broken on the wheel in the presence of thousands of peasants. Thus the nobles took revenge on misery. In vain the Emperor pleaded with them "not to seek safety in wheel and pike alone."

At the end of the eighteenth century the two Danubian Princi-

417

palities became practically one. The Russians' interest increased, and periodically they occupied the land, extorting concessions from the Sultan and often exercising supreme authority. The Turks continued to be nominal rulers for a century and a half, but if it had not been for the opposition of the great Western Powers, the Russians would have occupied the Lower Danube region, just as they had annexed Poland and the Ukraine. "The Russians and French employ one half of the town," an early nineteenth-century British confidential report on Bucharest read, "to spy upon the other; it is hell's own police." Napoleon was too busy with his plan of reaching India via Moscow to bother much about the Lower Danube. If he had not been chasing the mirage of the Russian steppes, history might have taken another turn. He was defeated, not by the superior generalship or numerical strength of the Russians, but by the mud of their country, which mired his heroic resolve.

For six years the Russians held most of the Danubian Principalities, "saving" the little Balkan brothers from the Turk. Incidentally, they requisitioned the peasant's food, forced him into compulsory labor, debased the currency and exacted high fees for the most normal services of the government. Replying to appeals for leniency, General Kutusov, "Grand Old Man" of the Napoleonic campaigns, answered: "I'll leave them only eyes to weep." It was under Russian rule that the Roumanian system of *bakshish,* corruption, took deeper roots. The peasants developed resistance against exactions. "The genuine Walach scarcely ever pays a para," an English consular report reads, "without having previously submitted to as many blows as his posterior can endure." The Turks beat only his soles. A French diplomat reported that the population of the Danubian Principalities was "entirely

418

Roumania Awakes

Greek," hence ought to belong to Russia rather than the Porte. He was not to blame for having failed to be aware of the Roumanians, since the higher social classes consisted really of Greeks. Anyone suggesting that the majority of the people should also be considered would have been called a madman or a Jacobin.

A hundred years ago nationalism in the Lower Danube region was so languid that Roumanians themselves thought that they were Greeks, mistaking their rulers' nationality for their own. They remembered the glory of Byzantium and thought of redeeming Constantinople. They went to battle for "the triumph of the cross over the crescent." In the Russian seaport of Odessa many Greek merchants had made money in grain during the Napoleonic war, part of which they were willing to spend for the promotion of the "Society of Friends," *Philike Hetairia.* Its aim was a Greater Greece between the Carpathians and the Danube and all the way down to Constantinople. The Russian government was probably not averse to this movement. It is a safe guess that "Greater Greece" would have been absorbed by the Czars.

Not even the Lower Danube could resist nationalism, which began its victorious march on the barricades of Paris, when Louis XVI was king. It had taken half a century for this idea to reach the Lower Danube. In 1848 revolution was the thing, and the two Principalities contributed their share. A group of intellectuals drew up a manifesto, read from altars with lighted candles. The rebels took oath upon the Gospel. "Have no fear save the fear of the Lord," the manifesto read, "and then you can sing without blushing: 'The Lord is with us.' Rise in his name, and the angel of heavenly justice will crush every enemy, will overthrow the rider and his horse, his chariots and arms will be scattered into dust, his projects will be dissipated like smoke. To arms, Roumanians, to the arms of salvation!"

The revolutionists demanded an independent country, a Prince elected for five years, Parliament and equal rights, free press, the abolition of death penalty, the emancipation of Jews and gypsies. "If the boyar could have laid his hand on the sun," a peasant deputy said in an indictment of the ruling classes, "he would have seized it and sold to the peasant for money the light and heat of God." At last the Turks and Russians agreed on an issue: the revolution must be crushed. The peasants lost again, since nothing but right was on their side. The Turks denounced the revolution as "inspired by the spirit of Socialism," and they occupied the capital. The troops of both neighbors were to hold the country until it would be fully pacified. When the Czar's soldiers evacuated the Principalities he demanded indemnity for the expenses of the occupation which the country had neither invited nor desired.

The despotism of the East aroused a craving for the West, and many young Roumanians adopted France as their spiritual home. The greater the contrast between the Seine and the Lower Danube, the greater was their love for France. While at home the gypsy slave stuffed the young Roumanian's *chibuk;* the second one lighted it; the third one brought it in; the fourth one saw that the fire did not go out; the fifth one brought a glass of water to his master. In Paris, however, the Roumanian aristocrat went in for democracy. He wanted no gypsy slaves, and besides could not afford one. The spirit of revolution filled him with enthusiasm. He threw himself on the writings of progressive authors, and watched French political intrigue with breathless interest. The French culture of Bucharest was largely due to his influence. Roumania was to become "Danubian France." "The world is a Sahara and the only oasis is Paris." At home such young men were called *bonjourists,* because of the way they greeted one another.

One of these young men and his family were to play a leading rôle in the liberation of Roumania. He was Ion Bratianu, a youth with charcoal eyes. One day he succeeded in being received by the French Minister of Foreign Affairs, M. Bastide, to whom he confided his plans.

"Pardon, Monsieur," Bastide asked, "what's the name of the capital of your country?"

"Bucharest, Excellency."

"Ach, Buchara? Buchara, you say. Proceed, if you please."

In those days the best way to arouse interest for a country was to throw a bomb at Napoleon III. An Italian patriot had done it, and his deed made a strong impression upon the French Emperor, who helped shape United Italy. Roumania never got so far as to hurl a bomb at the ruler himself, but her young men managed to throw a few infernal machines. Bratianu's house was searched; a printing press and pamphlets were found. The French sentenced him to three years in prison for belonging to a secret society. This, however, did not abate the ardor of the Roumanians for France. "Whether she accepts or repudiates it," the French consul in Bucharest wrote, "France has an inevitable clientele on the banks of the Danube, which attaches itself to her as the head of the Latin nations, and as its political metropolis, and which tries every day to assimilate her language, legislation, literature and even her most futile fashions."

The *bonjourists* and romantic bomb-throwers finally did succeed in calling attention to the Lower Danube. European Turkey's sickness was diagnosed as a deadly paralysis, and the Czar made ready to take the Danubian Principalities. Russia challenged the Western Powers. The challenge was accepted by a coalition of Britain, France, Sardinia and Turkey. The Crimean War broke out. Russia was defeated after a bitter struggle. The loser had to pay the price. Napoleon III had his uncle's passion for changing maps, and the Great Powers acted on the Danubian Principalities in 1856, at the Conference of Paris. They undertook to guarantee the "existing privileges and immunities" of the two vassal Principalities. Turkey retained nominal suzerainty, but she no longer counted. The treaty was a huge "exit" sign for Russia. Roumania was on the way to becoming wholly independent.

Who should be the ruler? A foreign Prince would have looked impressive, but the competition for the crown was not keen, as memories of Brancovan the Decapitated still haunted the Bucharest throne-room. The assemblies of both Principalities finally decided upon a son of the river basin, Alexandru Joan Cuza, who was born at Galatz, on the Danube. In his youth he joined the revolutionists because that was the fashion of the day. He had no strong political convictions. He had failed at his examination at the Sorbonne, but acquired that levity which is often taken for French *esprit*. In January, 1859, he was elected ruler of Walachia and Moldavia with the title of Prince. "Gentlemen," he said at his election, "I fear you will not be satisfied with me." He was not far from the truth. He freed the peasant serfs, instituted free education and slowly moved toward progress. Gradually the separate institutions of the Principalities of Walachia and Moldavia were abolished. Two years after his election, Roumania was united.

Prince Cuza was too indolent to take deep interest in honest government. Corruption was rampant, public office meant legalized bribery, droves of foreign firms descended upon the indus-tryless country, selling inferior products for superior prices. The Prince lived with his mistress, who gave him several children, while his own wife, Elena, led a life of enforced saintliness. The rule of the first native Prince of united Roumania did not sug-gest the expected Eldorado. Several high officials of the palace staged a miniature revolt, dragged the Prince out of his bed, while his mistress was hiding behind a screen. Cuza scribbled his abdication on the back of an officer, and was escorted to the frontier.

Ion Bratianu, one of the early *bonjourists* whom we last saw manufacturing infernal machines in Paris, knew the value of making kings. He picked Prince Charles of Hohenzollern-Sig-maringen as the future ruler. The Prince was a member of the elder South German and Catholic branch of the family. He was also a cousin of Napoleon III. He was related to Napoleon the Great through his paternal grandmother, a niece of Prince Murat, and his maternal grandmother, a Beauharnais.

Bratianu called on the Prince, who did not appear to be greatly interested at first. He wanted to know what Roumania thought of him. Popular opinion was consulted in a plebiscite, in which 685,969 electors voted for and only 224 against him. Napoleon III said he was gratified with the result, but his face registered no joy. He was thinking of the inevitable struggle with Prussia and knew that the Czar, whose help he wanted, would dislike this solution. King Wilhelm I of Prussia, who a few years later was to become the German Emperor, also said he was glad, but he, too, was worried about the Russians, whom he wanted to keep quiet. He knew—what the rest of the world did not know—that in a few weeks his armies would be on the march against Austria in a final showdown between Habsburg and Hohenzollern. At such a time he could not afford to antagonize the Czar. The ruler of all the Russias did not say that he was glad, mainly because he did not even know what was going on behind his back. The Turkish Sultan would have definitely said that he was not glad to see the Prussian Charles on the throne of a country which was nominally still Turkish, but nobody asked his consent.

Charles' first problem was to get to Roumania without getting into trouble. The shortest route would have been across Austria. But he was a Prussian officer and war between Austria and his own country was only a question of days. He would not have enjoyed beginning his career as a prisoner of war. The alternative route would have taken him to Russia, but surprises were everyday affairs in that country. Who could guarantee that a Prince who started a trip would also see its end? The sea route would have taken him past Constantinople, where surprises were even more frequent. Besides, it would have taken three weeks, and he had just heard that in a magnanimous mood the Italians had offered Roumania to the Austrians in exchange for Venetia.

In Zurich the Prince obtained a forged passport in the name of "Karl Hettingen," a drummer, bound for Odessa in Russia to join an orchestra. He traveled across Austria-Hungary, where the trains were already crowded with mobilized soldiers. In order to avoid detection he wore goggles and stayed up nights in unclean second-class coaches. He heard an Austrian officer tell his comrade that their fellow-passenger looked very much like Prince Charles with whom he had been fighting the Danes in Schleswig, when Austria and Prussia were on the same side of the fence.

Finally, he got off the train at Bazias and, still on Austrian territory, had to wait two full days for the Danube boat, which

424

the mobilization had delayed. Then his trip on the Austrian Danube began. The reception committee, which could not recognize the Prince without exposing him to danger, traveled first class, while Charles was in the second class. At the first Roumanian station, Turnu Severin, Charles rushed down the gangplank. Bratianu greeted his Sovereign on Roumanian soil. It took them two days to reach Bucharest in a carriage drawn by eight white horses. When the trip was over the ruler looked white, too, because of the dust on the drought-ridden land. Just as they arrived in the capital, a thunder-shower broke the three months' drought—a good omen in a peasant country—and he was drenched. The carriage stopped in front of the future princely residence, which had been a boyar's mansion, school and barracks. The mayor met him with the traditional bread and salt. Scratching his big nose thoughtfully, the Prince asked: "Where is the palace?" He could have asked, Paul Morand suggests, "Where is the capital?" Fire, floods, cholera, Russians, hunger, bandits, Turks and plague had destroyed three-fourths of Bucharest.

Had the Prussians not beaten the Austrians while Charles was furnishing his residence, the money for the trip would have been wasted, because neither the Austrian Habsburgs nor the Russian Romanovs nor the Turkish Osmanlis would have tolerated an ex-Prussian officer on the Roumanian throne. Prussia's victory changed the history of the Danube valley. Now Hohenzollern Princes were the rulers of the countries, at both the source and mouth of the Danube. Thus Prince Charles of Hohenzollern became Prince Carol of Roumania.

Now that the Great Powers had tacitly approved of his presence, he paid a visit to the Sultan, which consumed as much time

425

as it would have done three centuries before, since Roumania
had no railways. The Sultan was friendly. The days were past
when he could have the Princes of Roumania hanged. He yielded
to him on many points on the condition that the country should
remain nominally part of the Ottoman Empire. Charles, now
Carol, then paid his respects to Europe's crowned heads and returned with Princess Elizabeth of Wied as his wife. To the world
she was to be known as Carmen Sylva, the poet. A big woman,
red-faced, she caused world-wide commotion by having her black
hair bobbed. She was a familiar sight to shepherd and peasant in
her long white robe. She looked like a druid priestess. Their
daughter was seven when they lost her, and thenceforth the
Princess devoted her life to poetry and the poor. She was a woman
of great intellectual curiosity, endowed with an unusual gift of
self-expression. Few marriages in the palace of Bucharest were as
successful as that of Carol and Carmen Sylva.

Carol had the missionary zeal of a Teutonic Knight of the
Cross and the educational frenzy of a Prussian schoolmaster. He
wanted to raise his country to the level of the West, but Turkish
tradition, indolence and *bakshish* thwarted him at every turn. His
efforts to open the gates of the West were denounced as un-
patriotic. He offered to resign several times, but the politicians
could not agree on another Prince and knew that foreign countries were lying in ambush.

The nineteenth century was drawing to its close and great
changes were impending along the Lower Danube. In a desperate
attempt to break through the steel blockade, Russia lashed out
furiously at Turkey. She passed the Balkan range, and nothing
halted her until she came within view of Constantinople. Did
nothing halt her? Not the Turk, at any rate, but the Great Powers

426

King Carol of Roumania

of the West anxious for the road to India, the balance of power and prestige. The Russo-Turkish War of 1877-1878 revealed the weakness of both victor and vanquished. Turkey was definitely on the way out as a major power, but Russia certainly was not in.

The army command of Grand Duke Nicholas sent a deputy to Prince Carol to negotiate the passage of his army through Roumania. At the same time, the Sublime Porte dispatched cunning Ali Bey to insure the loyalty of the Prince. Carol overreached himself in hospitality to the wise man of the East and broached the question of additional privileges for Roumania. Assuming that this meant common action against the Russian, the Sultan consented to the reforms. At the same time, Carol concluded a secret treaty with Russia, assuring her free passage in return for certain favors. Not to antagonize the Turk too much, the Roumanian army pretended to make a stand against the Russian army as it began its march across Roumania, then withdrew without firing a shot, and placed its stores at the Russians' disposal against payment in gold. Making common cause with the Russian unofficially, the Roumanians joined in the pursuit of the Turks, still their nominal rulers.

Roumania won the war without entering it. In the future she was to excel at that game. The territorial gains she has made in the last half century have been largely due to her brilliant diplomacy, acting upon the principle that in foreign relations honesty is crime. Roumania became an independent kingdom. On May 22, 1881, Carol's coronation took place. The royal crown was made of the steel of captured Turkish cannon.

Now Roumania set out to build her house. There was much to be done, many problems to be solved. The country was rich in natural resources, but poor in equipment. Millions of Rou-

manians beyond the Kingdom's frontiers were clamoring for
liberation. Too weak as yet to pursue an independent foreign
policy, Roumania had to decide whether to join the Central European
powers of Germany, Austria and Italy, or the combination
of their opponents, later to be known as the Triple Entente.

Two parties alternated in office, the Liberals and Conservatives.
For years Ion Bratianu was virtual dictator of Roumania, and his
power descended to his heirs, who played vital parts up to a few
years ago. The heritage of Turkish and Russian corruption became
deeply imbedded in the Roumanian political system. From
the highest to the lowest, public officials demanded their share of
profit and even more. They were not public servants but public
masters. From time to time they made half-hearted efforts to
alleviate the lot of the rank and file. These were mere alibis.
The elections were corrupt and availed so little that it would have
been more honest to abolish them altogether. In this Promised
Land of the Danube the peasant was poverty-stricken. Rickets,
tuberculosis, pellagra and all diseases of undernourishment had
an appallingly high rate. In 1907 the peasants rose against the
Jews, who were in many cases the front-men of exploiting boyars.
The manufacturers of public opinion fanned the flame of hatred.
But the peasants were not as dull as they appeared to be, and
from the Jews their wrath turned against the boyars. It took some
150,000 soldiers to crush the revolt. It was a lesson to the masters
that even the meekest peasant's patience had its bounds.

Roumania became a silent partner of Germany and Austria.
King Carol I could never forget his German origin, and his country
was blocked by the solid mass of Central Europe. Russia,
another neighbor, did not appeal to the Roumanians who had ex-

428

perienced the heavy hand of the Czar's affectionate care. When
the Balkan War broke out two years before the World War, Roumania made no attempt to get into it. But she did get into the
Second Balkan War, started by Bulgaria, which was dissatisfied
with her share of the spoils. Roumania got the southern part of
the Dobrudja from Bulgaria.

When the World War broke out, Roumania was still an ally
of the German and Austro-Hungarian Empires. King Carol I died
a few months after the outbreak of the War. The Germans' on-
rush was halted by the French on the Marne. Stronger than the
treaty of alliance was the call of the oppressed brothers across
the Transylvanian range. Public opinion was on the side of the
French and English, who made even the Russian alliance palata-
ble. The Roumanians could have got little from the Central European Powers, but much from the Entente, which promised them
almost half of Hungary, should they throw in their lot with them.

The horizon was overcast for the Entente when Roumania declared war on Austria-Hungary in August, 1916. Now the traditional lines were drawn: East against the West in the Danube
valley. Across the mountain passes the Roumanian army marched,
supported by the Russians. Then the German steamroller started
to move, and the Roumanian army was pushed into the northernmost corner of the country. The capital, too, fell into enemy
hands. Before their retreat, the Roumanians destroyed most of
their oil equipment and the Germans got little from the wells.
But trains of wheat began to move toward the north. The royal
family clung to the last remnant of their Kingdom. Carol's successor, King Ferdinand, was a benevolent ruler, dominated by
the politicians. His wife, Queen Marie, granddaughter of Queen

Victoria of England, beautiful, brilliant and domineering, never gave up hope. But for a time the world wondered: would they ever recover their throne?

The World War was not decided in Roumania, but in the West. Almost overnight the vanquished became the victor. Roumania's territory was more than doubled at the Peace Conference. Beautiful Transylvania became hers, and millions of Roumanians were united with the Old Kingdom. Part of the Bánát was hers, with its rich wheat-fields. Bessarabia was detached from Russia, attached to Roumania. Austria was forced to give her Bukovina. Old problems were solved; new problems were created. Some 1,500,000 Hungarians lived in the land they were forced to cede to the Roumanian Kingdom. Russia failed to recognize the loss of Bessarabia. Nearly a million Germans now live in the country. At long last, the peasant was given land. The boyars lost their holdings, with the exception of 500 hectares, and absentee owners were completely expropriated. They were to get compensation in State bonds, the amount of which was not to exceed twenty times the value of the annual return. But how was the peasant to work his land without capital and machinery? He lacked organization and the ability to manage his affairs. Production decreased. The Danube valley was no longer the granary of the Old World.

Because Roumania had her eggs in several baskets she weathered the economic storm. Her Hungarian neighbor was restless, and Roumania was one of the Little Entente members to keep her quiet. Yet the great wealth of the country did not improve the standard of the people. With the addition of the new territories, Roumania became an ideal economic unit, as far as such ideals go in the dismembered Danube valley. Why were the peasants so poor in the richest part of the Danube basin? The curse of the

430

Turk lay heavy on the land. The workers were to have nothing, and the drones were to have all. The Bratianu dynasty continued its rule and politics was the greatest revenue-producer. A vast Tammany Hall took hold of the country, draining it.

A dynastic crisis convulsed Roumania. It was preceded by a change of government. "God forbid that the peasant should have to suffer to the capacity of his endurance," a Roumanian saying asserts. This limit of endurance was reached in the late twenties when the Bratianus were finally overthrown and an honest man, Julius Maniu, took the helm as Prime Minister. He headed the National Peasant Party, the leadership of which was recruited mostly in Transylvania. Then things began to happen.

Previously, rumors of dynastic changes in Roumania had reached the world. No other royal family had been as much in the limelight as King Ferdinand's. It was the darling of the popular press, always clamoring for "color" and "romance." If the royal family failed to provide its expected contribution to "copy" bright journalists drew upon their imagination.

The heir to the throne was Prince Carol, described as the "wild colt" of the Balkans. During the War he eloped with a commoner, Zizi Lambrino, and was married in Odessa. This was "desertion from the army," the Court decreed. If the lady had been of more refined birth, the young man's crime would not have been considered so outrageous. He was lodged in a fortress, where the sentries snapped to attention whenever he passed, but they did not allow him to leave. When finally he did get this permission, it was only to leave for a trip around the world, which would give him time to forget. When he returned, the "desertion" was forgotten, and his marriage to Zizi was annulled. Ready for new adventures, he met a titian-haired lady in the Military

431

Casino of Bucharest. Carol was not popular among the politicians. Nor was he on good terms with his mother. Persistent backstage gossip tells of a late return of the Crown Prince from a spree—where he had drunk more than was good for him—and his running into Prince Stirbey, allegedly Queen Marie's lover. The meeting took place not far from the door of the Queen's bed-chamber. The heir to the throne made a scandal, insulting the Prince. This envenomed his relations with the Queen even more.

Crown Prince Carol was married to the beautiful Greek Princess Helen, with whom he lived an unhappy life. She was cold to him, some say—to all men, other critics maintain. What was the main reason for Carol's leaving the country? The politicians made life hard for him, his mother made it harder, and his wife the hardest of them all. He renounced all his rights to the Crown in 1925, and his four-year-old son, Michael, became the King, assisted by a Regency council of three members.

What made him give up the Crown? His resignation was voluntary, the politicians said. It was forced upon him, the Crown Prince countered. He and the titian-haired lady he had met in the Military Casino now lived in exile, mostly in Neuilly, on the outskirts of Paris, and on the French Riviera. The ex-Prince visited England, but was told by the police to leave. Sometimes the couple had enough money for their daily bread and champagne and sometimes they had not. Three years after his resignation, Carol divorced the beautiful but cold Greek Princess Helen.

Little did the world suspect that the "playboy of the Roumanian Court" was preparing a coup. His worst political foes, the Bratianus, were out, and honest Julius Maniu was the head of the government. This was 1930, a year of many uncertainties. Economic crises rode the Danube valley, and the Roumanian

peasants were in a Messianic mood. A child-King made no impression upon them, and legend began to weave a fabulous tale
about the Prince Charming of their own, pining away in exile.
Carol and the Premier were in league, but the peasants knew
nothing about it. On June 6th, an unscheduled airplane descended
at the Bucharest airport. An improvised reception committee
welcomed Carol. Within a few days he had his son deposed by
Parliament and was proclaimed King of Roumania. Ex-King
Michael became heir to the throne under the name of Grand
Voyvoda of Alba Julia.

The Roumanian villages went wild with joy. Bands of ser-
enaders fought for the honor of doing the King homage. Windows of villages were illuminated; markets were crowded with
gaily dressed people, hastily assembled to make a royal holiday.
Resolutely King Carol II set to work. Out of a half dozen dis-
united nationalities he was determined to weld a united nation.
Foreign loans had to be obtained if the country's natural resources were to be exploited and its population saved from
catastrophe. He put down his foot on political corruption and
monopoly of power by political cliques. He made an effort to
improve Roumania's relations with her neighbors in the interest
of peace and the free flow of goods across the frontiers. He was
determined to liquidate the virtual state of war with Russia and
to make Roumania play a leading part on the international stage.

Then out of a dismal sky descended the whirling northern
wind. Hostile strangers, envoys of his political enemies, whispered into peasant ears in village taverns reports of a royal romance. The King was painted in dismal colors. What business
did he have to send away his beautiful Princess Helen? How could
a man inspire his country if his private life was not above re-

proach? Out of the mist of insinuations arose the picture of a Princess smiling through her tears at the faithful peasants who would punish an unfaithful King.

In this fog of gossip the picture of another woman took shape. Titian would have liked to paint the head of Mme. Magda Lupescu, the King's favorite. She was good to look at, the peasants were told, but her words were venom and her acts were danger incarnate for the country. There were sinister stories of an underground passage between the royal palace and the house of the woman. If the King wanted to marry her, let him and be happy; but then he should not retain his throne. The religious bias of the peasants was brought into play, and since Mme. Lupescu was born half-Jewish, anti-Semitic outbursts occurred. The peasants were told of the King's inordinate vanity. Look at what he was doing again! He had ordered the postal clerks not to deface his portrait on the stamps. The tale about the stamps and clerks was untrue—at least in the form it took—but the peasants heard only one side of the affair. Taproom visitors were informed of the King's fondness for military display. He was represented as standing in front of his palace, making the soldiers march in Hohenzollern goose-step, spending his time designing new uniforms to the neglect of important duties.

Discontent ripened. The peasants felt the need of change, but did not know what ailed them. On the night of December 29, 1933, a young Roumanian Fascist shot dead Ion G. Duca, the Prime Minister, as he was awaiting a train at the Sinaia railway station after an interview with King Carol. The murderer was a member of the "Iron Guard." He boasted that he had committed the crime because Duca was a friend of the Jews. Search of the "Iron Guard" headquarters brought to light a blacklist of the country's leading statesmen who were also to be assassinated. "Jesus, King and Nation" was the slogan of the Guard, headed by Cornelius Zelea Codreanu, a high-tension young man with a mania of grandeur and courage to kill. He was of Polish origin on his father's side—another illustration that super-nationalists are often of alien birth. Some years before he killed the prefect of Jassy "because he favored the Jews." The original name of his organization was "Guard of Archangel Michael." The pistol and crucifix were their emblems. They wore green shirts, Sam Browne belts, red brassards with blue swastikas on yellow ground—the Roumanian national colors. The movement attracted young people, always in search of the new, and many peasants, unconsciously groping for a change. If Communism had not been a capital crime, the peasants might have followed Moscow. The only available substitute seemed to be the "Iron Guard," with its venomous attacks upon Bolshevism coating its semi-communistic program, aggravated by aggressive nationalism. "The basis of our program is one hundred per cent anti-Semitism," a Guard leader declared. "The Jewish element is destructive of society and State."

"What would you do with the Jews if you came to power?"

"I would expel them all without exception."

The German Hitlerites had spent about thirty million lei in Roumania, the dependable French publicist, "Pertinax," charged in the *Echo de Paris*. He also made the charge that N. Jonescu, editor of a Bucharest Fascist paper, was often seen at Court, so that Roumanian students were under the impression that their movement was under the King's protection.

Hitlerism first found a fertile soil among the Germans of Roumania. The Saxons of Transylvania, who, according to legend,

435

had been lured into leaving their ancestral homes centuries ago by the magic tones of the Pied Piper, responded with alacrity to the Pied Piper of the Reich. They organized their own storm troop detachments, sat in awe before Nazi propaganda films, listened to Hitlerite agitators and transmitted to the Fuehrer the expression of their homage. The German inhabitants of Cernauti allied themselves with the local Roumanian and Ukrainian anti-Semites and plundered Jewish shops. The *Czernowitzer Post,* of the same city, began a period of miraculous expansion. Another German language newspaper, the *Scharfschuetze,* blossomed forth as the official organ of the German Leader. The *Sieben-buergische Tageblatt* in Transylvania joined forces with the Hitlerites. At the elections of the Saxon National Council the Nazis scored important victories.

After Duca's death, the government proclaimed martial law and promised a policy of the mailed fist. But the siren song of the Brown Reich continued to enthrall the Lower Danube. Nazism was the universal panacea. What was good enough for powerful Germany should be more than good for Roumania. Shirts of various political colors began to bloom in town and country, and posters proclaimed an impending doomsday. Years went by, miracle-waiters watched the political horizon. Parliament was discredited and the pageantry of "strong men" failed to reveal historical strength.

Then came the bomb-shell. In December, 1937, the King appointed Octavian Goga, romantic poet and amateur-statesman, Premier of Roumania. Goga was a Fascist—anti-Semite, anti-liberal, pro-Hitler-Mussolini, pro-war. Tables were cracking as he banged them with a fist more used to writing poetry than to saber-rattling. He introduced anti-Semitic legislation which drove busi-

436

ness underground in no time. In a peasant Roumania, the Jews were the middlemen and bankers; by eliminating them, the Premier would kill business. Conditions grew worse day by day. What had been the King's intention in appointing the head of a small Fascist group as the helmsman of the country? Mme. Lupescu was suspected of a plot. Goga had long been on friendly terms with her. She was an ardent admirer of his poetry. He was leader of the anti-Semites, and she Jewish on her father's side. But she did not consider herself a Jewess, since her father was baptized. She appeared to be leading the pack of wolf-hounds instead of being pursued by them. Was she diabolically clever?

"Lupescu" is the Roumanian version of "Wolff," which was the original name of Magda's father, whom the opposition called "junk dealer." In reality he was a commission merchant for foreign chemical factories. "My children," he would say, pointing to the photographs of the King and his unofficial Queen. Magda Wolff had an eventful youth. At the age of seventeen she had been married to Captain Tampeano of the Roumanian army. Later she eloped with a colonel but became reconciled with her captain husband. Mme. Lupescu was fond of relating that she and the King first met when she was 9 and he 15. She had accompanied her father to the Royal Court, where he had been called, presumably on business. The first meeting may have been imaginary, but the second one, in the Bucharest Military Casino, was real. It ended in love and in her sharing his exile.

French newspapers reported on one occasion that she had taken poison, and the Crown Prince too had attempted suicide. He returned home as King and she remained his friend. She was called head of the *Sinaia camarilla,* so named after the royal country residence. She was seen in the background, pulling wires, setting

437

up puppets, overthrowing governments. To the peasants she was described as a she-devil, and the political underworld circulated pamphlets in which her horrible death was foretold. "Remember King Alexander and Queen Draga of Serbia!"

The Fascist Goga government had made a mess of things and fell after forty-five days in office. Early in 1938 King Carol assumed dictatorial powers. Had the Goga interlude been Magda's plot to discredit politics, preparing public opinion for the royal dictatorship? It was a good plan, no matter who was the author.

When I re-visited Bucharest in 1938, I wrote the following account of my visit:

Down the winding Calea Victoriei of Bucharest the royal guard marches at a spanking gait, wheels into the courtyard of the palace, snaps to attention and the band begins its daily serenade of operetta tunes. The royal banner hangs limply atop the palace, the roof of which is sprinkled with water under the torrid sun. The King is in his palace, the country residence of Sinaia is orphaned, its hunting park deserted. The King now rules, not merely reigns. He has sent Parliament its reluctant way, has dissolved the political parties; the government meets under royal chairmanship. In the streets of Bucharest buttonholes are bare of party emblems, political uniforms have been shed and walls have been stripped of hysterical posters. The Café Capsa no longer echoes political formulas, and the press obeys government hints. "Not since the foundation of the Kingdom," a Minister of the Crown told me, "has Roumania seen such a change." In a royal proclamation the King gave an account of his stewardship: "The national budget has been balanced, the currency kept stable, exports have increased, education has been given a new stimulus, a road-building program carried out, fortifications built, a new flying field completed and the armament industry's speed has been accelerated."

438

The King Takes the Reins

"Guests are requested not to discuss their political views in public," notices warn in hotel lobbies. Newspaper offices flaunt the three monkeys of antiquity: "See nothing, hear nothing, say nothing." The red stamp "censored" kills unwelcome facts, but no blank space must betray the vigilance of royal eyes. Before the royal dictatorship swept vociferous public opinion off the streets, the walls of Calea Victoriei reminded one of Hitler's Germany. The posters of the Iron Guards outdid the *Stuermer* of the Reich in their maniacal attacks upon the Jews. In the movies Hitler's marching guards received an ovation, while Premier Leon Blum of France was hissed. Extremist newspapers extolled the "night of the long knife," the German name for purge. "Down with all except us!" was the motto of intolerance. Business was paralyzed and moderation feared hatred might flame into disaster overnight. Today the Café Grand, where tradesmen meet for midafternoon Vienna *Capuziner,* black coffee, is once more a merchants' paradise. Business is no longer subject to panicky fear. Germany's Fuehrer is no longer recognized publicly as the hope of Roumanian youth. The Reich's papers have ceased to monopolize newspaper kiosks. Bucharest's traditional affection for Paris is once more proclaimed. But still the Calea Victoriei tells the tale—even if it is in whispers— and reflects the public appraisal of the King's stewardship. He is seen as a man of high intelligence, widespread interests and great energy. In Bucharest, where people know everything about everybody—sometimes even more—he is known to spend long hours at his desk. He is no longer available to curious visitors or concerned with social duties. Having learned applied mass psychology from the dictators, he has set himself the task of killing Carol the Playboy and building up Carol the Creator.

Calea Victoriei takes stock of the situation. If the extremists had seized the reins, how would Roumania have fared? Germany needs the wheat of Hungary and the oil wells of Roumania, the politically critical in the Balkans agree. "Hitler started to play the game for the greatest stakes. There was a flood of propaganda. The Third Reich's trade rolled incessantly across our frontiers. If Hitler had

439

succeeded, it would have been the beginning of another Tatar invasion. He could have swept all Europe." The King turned Roumania from this course.

In domestic matters the King is writing the history of a new epoch. Centuries of oppression have left behind a system of corruption unmatched in Europe. Elections were bought, officials were bribed, State service and wealth were synonymous. Today one cannot enter a ministry for private palavers; all transactions must be made in broad daylight, and royal wrath is visited upon the heads of the unreformed. Reassured by the new masters, business is beginning to be its normal self. Steps have been taken to give the peasants loans for agricultural implements. And if Calea Victoriei likes to think itself metropolitan, it knows that in Roumania the source of wealth is land and that a poverty-stricken peasantry will keep the country far in the rear of human progress.

But the Calea Victoriei would not be its own self if it found nothing to blame in the King and his régime. Carol has been so long in the public eye as the wild colt of Southeastern Europe that his private life cannot all of a sudden be closed to public view. "He is over-ambitious, not always scrupulous in his dealings with former friends," is a recurrent criticism which has taken deep root in the public mind. The King is said to have been scheming for years for just such an opening. Yet the man who brought him back from exile in his plane is a prisoner for life, and the man who was his guardian angel when the stress was greatest cannot leave the country for fear his criticism might be too outspoken. The Premier who welcomed the Prince with open arms is in disgrace.

When no suspicious person is around the King is blamed for some of his friends. "Madame" has become a mythical figure, since newspapers are not allowed to hint at the royal friendship. But it is generally known she wields great power. At the same time, the King gets credit for a friendship which has lasted for more than fourteen years and which belies his reputation for flightiness. Magda Lupescu is now part of Roumanian history.

Moving into the regions of domestic politics, the Calea Victoriei

440

The Town Teaches the Village

wonders if the King's reforms are far-reaching enough? How is it that the richest soil in Europe produces on a square kilometer only one-third as much as Denmark's unfertile land? Why is it that the daily meat consumption of the Roumanian peasant is one thin slice of ham—nine grains? Why is it that 37 per cent of the rural families possess no draft animals and 46 per cent have not even sheep? These critics say that heroic measures are needed. Across the Dniester river, Russia's co-operative farms may be an example. The Roumanian peasants' strips of land are too small for intensive farming. What can the King do to break the village of its hoary customs? The peasant hears about the strong King in the royal palace and is impressed. But he has his moments of murderous energy and anger. The rulers must beware.

The King has intensified the campaign to educate the peasants, the modern rulers' masters. Graduates of universities receive their diplomas only after service in the village. "Royal groups," composed of college students and young graduates, are busy in the countryside, studying the peasant's problems, teaching him hygiene, crafts and the rudiments of the art of living. Cultural centers begin to sprout in the mire of the rain-soaked fields. A beginning has been made, although it is not expected that ancient habits in this land of tradition can yield easily to new ways. Meanwhile the Calea Victoriei keeps silent counsel and watches the change of guards before the royal palace. A curtain flips aside, and behind it may be seen a man in his best years, the dictator of the country, King Carol. From the lowest depths of exile he rose to the highest peak, and history has cast him for a leading rôle. Will his name be remembered as the savior of his country from a new danger which the Danube valley sees approaching from the West? . . .

Several months have passed since I wrote the foregoing lines. Every month was an epoch of history. Dictators were on the go, taking countries, proclaiming their right to a new distribution of the earth. The German dictator took the heart of the Danube

441

valley, and only Roumania separates him and his vassals from the Russian Ukraine which he had publicly proclaimed to be the object of his predatory march. Once more the Danube basin became the cause of the changed fate of man. Champions of nationalism, victory-drunk dictators deny the right to live to smaller nations. Rome could not stop expanding once she started the fateful march, and Napoleon's steps were beguiled into Russian mire by his sky-storming ambitions.

"Dynamism" knows no bounds and explodes in a succession of cataclysms. The German dictator made Hungary his vassal and the Magyars have a grievance against Roumania. They alone would be impotent to deal with the larger country, but Germany's help would make them strong until they, in turn, would fall victims to the dictator's inescapable fate. Roumania mobilized her troops, Hungary's were on a war footing and threats were exchanged across a burning frontier.

The Fascist Iron Guard continued its extreme course irrespective of the danger to the nation. Why should they be worried, the super-nationalists, since their hatred consumed the last traces of their love for the country which they professed to serve? The neighbor was the enemy, the saber-rattling alien was the friend. National lines were demolished and international fascism set out to organize the war of man against man. The leaders of the "Iron Guard" made an attempt to escape as they were transferred from jail to jail, and they were killed on the spot.

This was the Nazi language! Would the Roumanian Nazis heed its message? The world moved closer to a great disaster. The Great Powers of the West guaranteed Roumania's integrity against aggression. The pages of history are being written at a furious rate, and the Danube keeps its counsel.

Mme. Magda Lupescu

As THE plane dips down to the airdrome, Bucharest, the capital of Roumania, floats into view. Why should she not be on the Danube, fifteen minutes away, or guarded by the Carpathians, the peaks of which may be seen, or on the Black Sea, to the east? Strange, indeed, it is that Bucharest should not be on historic highways. Thereby hangs a tale, also a row of heads, reaching as far as Constantinople. The founders of Bucharest, it seems, tried to find a poor site for the capital, away from the Danube, from the sea and the mountains. The irrational setting has a rational explanation, accounting for the tragedy of Eastern Europe and the reputation of the Balkans. The early settlers preferred the worst location for their capital, so that the Turkish rulers should have no easy access to Bucharest. It took them about thirty days to reach the capital, and the longer it took, the better pleased were the inhabitants. The Turk always came bearing a sword. Their scimitars were sharp and necks offered little resistance, which accounts for the long rows of heads.

443

Although not directly on the Danube, Bucharest is the capital of a key Danubian country. She is a city of many contradictions, often called the "Paris of the East," because of her social aspirations and French suburban houses. "Here the Orient begins," tourists often say. But if filth is Oriental, Bucharest is no Eastern city. Whether East or West, this is a city of contrasts determined to be Western, but unable to break with geography. Bucharest's streets reveal the contradictions. Here you find some of the most fashionable women east of the rue de la Paix. The barefoot gypsy with the flat wicker-basket on his shoulders keeps step with the belle. The coachman on his high box belongs to the Russian sect of *skoptzi*, who mutilated themselves after the birth of a son. The chauffeur of the expensive car behind the coach is familiar with all the intricacies of the combustion engine.

Unless the mordant *crivatz*, the furious, wind blows or the hot *baltaretu*, the swampy, Calea Victoriei is athrob with humanity, as if all Bucharest's 700,000 inhabitants tried to crowd into it. On sidewalk terraces a discriminating public has assembled, eating *inghetata*, ice cream, or *mititei*, the native roast. Calea Victoriei is the capital's spinal column, its Fifth Avenue and Champs-Elysées. It is named "Street of Victory" after the battle of Plevna which the Russians won with Roumanian help in the seventies. The featured sights of the capital lie along this winding road: Hotel Athenée-Palace, headquarters of political intrigues for years; the Café Capsa; the royal palace; the Telephone building, a skyscraper in the suburb of Asia, erected in the New York style. The white stone of the palace reflects the bold blue of the sky. It is not large nor particularly impressive, looking more like a Legation than the royal residence. The combination café, bar, hotel and restaurant Capsa is only a short distance away. Before the

444

royal dictatorship, political debutants made their first bow in the café, rubbing shoulders with greatness. A whispered chat at marble-topped tables might have meant success or failure. Here the bearded Bratianu brothers framed their cabinets, made history.

What Walter Winchell, *Variety, The New Yorker* and the National Press Club do for the United States, Café Capsa used to do for Roumania. Here *bon-mots* were coined at the expense of the mighty, and the Queen Mother's *vie amoureuse* was discussed in intimate detail. Here an itinerant genius of leisure, too indolent to put pencil to paper, drew masterpieces on café napkins. Here the grapevine of high society was working overtime. A few whispered words made reputations, which no contrary evidence could destroy, and thus a legend about a "strong man" got its start. The Café Capsa may long remain a landmark, but the royal dictatorship eclipsed it. Dictators like whispers even less than caricatures.

The Athenée-Palace is not merely a hotel and when last seen a sign announced it was closed "pending alterations." Its specialties were the three disgraces: politics, commerce and diplomacy. Commerce had its headquarters there because of politics—the Siamese twins. Every fool could make a living with hard work, but no one wanting to make money would waste his time laboring. Although the hotel does not occupy more than a ten-millionth part of Roumania, at one time it was responsible for all her foreign policy.

An arch of triumph marks the end of the Calea Victoriei and the beginning of the Chaussée Kisilev, the show place of the capital, and the compensation for its French complexes. For a mile around one can breathe the air of Europe's West. A miniature Renaissance palazzo, trying to hide behind a row of twisted tree-trunks, is the home of the King's mistress. Another building belongs to an ex-Minister, a third to a money magnate. This district is the Utopia of pension dwellers, and here social life flourishes under the platanes; love and music thrive. In the evening Nature's breezes vie with Chanel No. 5. Ravishing beauties sway to the tune of the latest waltz. The neighbor at the next table is often an audience, and long-distance flirting is condoned. This is the echo of bygone times when life had to be lived fast if it was lived at all.

Paris has taught Bucharest to be self-consciously proud, but not of its river, the Dambovitza, which is no Seine. Its two banks are display grounds of rustic rug-makers. "The Dambovitza traverses the capital between two walls of rugs." The local ballad sings:

> *Oh, Dambovitza,*
> *Those who have tasted your waters*
> *Cannot leave your banks.*

"Because they die of rat-poisoning," ironic Paul Morand reflects.

Not far from the river is the 42nd Street of Bucharest, Strada Lipscani, so named after the city of Leipzig because its merchants received their wares from that city. It is a human beehive, where there are more salespeople than customers. With their entire business slung around their necks, peddlers try to hypnotize the bewildered country lout. *A la Ville de Paris* and similar inscriptions are echoes of the city's Parisian nostalgia. Strada Lipscani's shops are unlike the bazaars of Constantinople, the nearest capital to the east. After centuries of Turkish rule, you would expect the city to live in the shadow of Islamic traditions. Vainly you would be looking for a Turkish mosque. Turkey might just as well be a

446

thousand miles away; her rule was never in harmony with the
spirit of Bucharest. How could Islam hold these parts so long,
when it had so little to offer?

Who are the inhabitants of this city of contradictions? The
stimulating friendships one cherishes conflict in memory with
sights of degradation. Extremes are the heart and soul of the
Roumanian capital. Where are interests more varied, conversa-
tions more stimulating than in her homes? The intellectually
inclined speak perfect French, flawless German and good English.
The farther east you go, the greater the linguistic achievements.
The Roumanian language is no key to the Western world, although it is sufficiently Latin to make the learning of French
comparatively easy. Under Turkish rule there was an advantage
in a language spies could not understand. But language is not
knowledge. The educated people of the capital find compensation
for the physical absence of the West by immersing themselves in
its culture. Conversation reaches far beyond the headline news of
the day. Hitler, Mussolini and Stalin do not monopolize the spotlight of the Bucharest hearth. Here you can listen to a discussion
on the merits of the Panama and proposed Nicaraguan Canals,
and the latest in biology, medicine and synthetic chemistry. The
most recent fashion fads could not arouse more animated discussion than André Gide's recantation of his communistic faith. A
recent arrival from the West serves as the oracle of the moment.
With his eloquent help the merits of Toscanini and Furtwaengler
are compared; the plays of the Parisian boulevards are reviewed.
Chats of this nature are necessarily superficial, the critical-minded
say. Human knowledge cannot range over so wide a field. Such
beliefs are not confirmed by facts in Bucharest, where man is left
free to lead a life of culture, where excessive work does not take

the best out of him, and society is a stimulant. Music in Bucharest is still practiced in the old manner and not as wrist-turning exercise.

In Bucharest as well as elsewhere in the Danube valley the high society of birth is on the decline. Boyars and their hangers-on dominated the capital in the old days. The rich were proud of their *mossafiri*, parasites. It is said of one of them that he remained in the same house for eighteen years, sharing his host's cigars and meals, his champagne and wife.

Bucharest's streets are so crooked because they bounded the estates of the capricious rich. The twentieth century has brought them destitution, although their names still make ignorance stand in awe. Their place was taken by the public officials, whose motto was: "Public office is public plunder." "Why don't you vote for the Conservatives?" a politician was asked in the good old days. "They have nothing more to give me." The tax-money flowing through the hands of the political sachems got stuck there. One wanting to ship a carload of goods had to pay not only the freight, but also a bribe to the government for starting the locomotive. Industries had to conclude political alliances or starve. The banks were owned and operated by politicians through their financial experts. A high official would not think of refusing *bakshish* for his signature on an army contract. It was considered anti-national to touch the system. Anyone doing so might easily have been labeled a Communist. When the King assumed dictatorial powers a break was made with the past and the standard of public-service honesty was raised in a remarkably short time.

The Danube is a highway of anti-Semitism. We have seen on our trip downstream how it ruled Germany, then spread southeastward. Roumania is part of the Pale extending from the Dan-

448

ube all the way to Vilna in Poland and beyond. The hospitable Polish Kings attracted the Jews in the Middle Ages. Forced to make their living by commerce, they favored the rural East of Europe, where the peasants were kinder and the freedom of movement greater. These parts lacked the trading ability the Jewish newcomers possessed in such a high degree. The Turk shunned all but army work, and his religious prejudices were not strong. The Roumanian nobleman was like his Hungarian neighbor; neither had any taste for trade.

The Roumanian peasant met the Jew, who brought to him a higher type of life. Until then he was restricted to his village, giving his goods for the neighbor's produce. The Jewish merchant meant the wide world. He paid money and brought to the peasant huts the luxuries of the earth. Even if the farmer lacked the money to buy these marvels of distant climes, he at least could dream about them, seeing them displayed on shop shelves. The native noble took advantage of the serf on a large scale. The Jew became the village banker. When shrewd business sense comes into contact with ignorance, the result is a foregone conclusion. The Jew exploited the peasant less than the aristocrat, but he was the ideal scapegoat. He became the ideal target for the merchants of hatred, because he had no Foreign Office to protest and no navy to protect him. But the Roumanian peasant knows only too well that the Jew is as much an under-dog as himself. When the boyars worked the age-old scheme of deflecting popular wrath by substituting a helpless minority, the peasant refused to be fooled.

Bucharest would not be what she is without her gypsies. No restaurant would be complete without its *lautari,* musicians. At the age of four the gypsy's soul is full of music and his hair is full of lice. They grow up into born fiddlers, and under an impassive

449

exterior there burns a mysterious fire. Some hidden spring of beauty resides in them. They can play for hours, always animated, overflowing with poetry, gay and somber. Yet no creative fervor flames in their oxen eyes. Are they descendants of a unique sect, which worshiped its idols with the sound of tymbals? Has their genius for fiddling developed because music is a universal language which the changing hosts of the eternal wanderers understood? If their secret could be solved, the world would lose some of its romance. Only death wrests the bow from the gypsy's hand.

Suburban Bucharest still likes the bear-dancing gypsies, *ursari*, who catch the animals young in the Carpathians and teach them the clumsy steps called "dance." The tinkers, *lingurari*, may be found in nearly every Roumanian village. Where did these gypsies come from and who are they? Are they descendants of the ancient Egyptians, as their name indicates, or are they refugees from India? What makes them lead a nomadic life in settled Europe? Their dark color indicates a long stay in a warm climate; their nomadic habits have been formed by ancient traditions. They have a secret. Were they an outcast minority, forced to shun the sun? They may have been untouchable outlaws in their native habitat, pariahs or descendants of a criminal colony in the East. Post-War frontiers, where passports must be produced, have not been drawn for Romany's children. The Roumanian government tried to force them to accept collective passports, but it might as well have tried to induce the rain not to fall. The boyar's whipping posts may have been the only effective argument against vagabondage. As late as a century ago the Roumanian nobles counted their wealth by the gypsy slaves they owned.

In Bucharest as elsewhere, the majority of the people are not aristocrats or gypsies, but artisans and tradesmen, taxi-drivers and clerks, theater-ushers and waiters. Little interest attaches to their lives, since they are in a majority. In the morning they go to work, and on the way there some of them read their paper, which for many years was the *Dimineata*. It supplied them with news and also with their opinions on important events. It contained a *feuilleton*, a very short short-story with a blurred point, which had the advantage of being removed from reality and thus helped them forget life for a few minutes. The authorities forbade the publication of their favorite paper and then they read the *Timpul*, which contained many homages to the King and less pronounced editorial opinions. This was a hardship in one way: How was one to have an opinion of his own if he could not get it out of his paper? If this newspaper should be ordered off the streets tomorrow, as was the previous one, again there would be no revolution.

On his way to work the bank clerk does not get hot under his collar because of an excessive amount of government in his life. He does not think much more about it than he does about the sun and rain. Occasionally he swears at the heat, of course; but what man in his senses would take arms against it? The government, too, is a force of nature, just as the Danube and the hot wind of the steppes. It would be different if he were very hungry, because even the wolves of the Carpathians attack the villages when frost closes their forest supply. But the wolf is more impulsive than man.

Their work done, many take refuge from the heat in Cismigiu Park, where beer is cheap, romance seeks deep shadows and the band plays the latest swing. Others stroll down the Calea Victoriei, visit the movies, take their refreshments on the terrace of the Military Casino, where rainbow neon signs proclaim the superior virtues of an insecticide. But here as elsewhere in Europe, most of the people go home; the cheapest way to spend the evening. They would go somewhere far, if they could afford it.

The Roumanian, like the Russian, is a nomad, Paul Morand reminds us. He takes a train, happy to leave, obeying an atavistic instinct to flee the invader. But he stays home to read the evening paper, listen to the radio, discipline his children or caress his wife. Any normal person knows how little a human brain can contain. Besides, in times like these, thinking might get one into trouble in the Danube valley. Thinking leads to talking, and that is discouraged in a dictatorship. Here only life, and not liberty and the pursuit of happiness, is accepted as man's right.

Bucharest's elite has a high rate of intelligence, but her collective genius is not so high. Talking to these amazingly well-informed men and women, one would think Roumania leads the world in the number of Nobel Prize winners. That, however, is decidedly not the case. Bucharest probably suffers from her reliance upon French culture. The book-sensation of Paris is the hit of the Roumanian capital, and native talent has a strong handicap to overcome. Even now the best Roumanian poets write in French, and the same is true of the most popular prose-writers. The greatest stars of Bucharest grace the Paris stage. Carmen Sylva, the poetess Queen of King Carol I, Queen Marie, wife of King Ferdinand, and Princess Bibesco have made names for themselves in English and French literature.

Bucharest is often called the "City of Joy" because its name is derived from the Albanian word *Bukur,* meaning joy, in memory of a victory over the Turks. Legend makes Bucur, a peasant, responsible for the foundation of Bucuresti—Bucharest. Peasants had little else to do with the capital of Roumania. Although re-

Roumanian Gypsies

moved from the great highways, Bucharest was too close to the Turks, Roumanians found. Their first capital, Campulung, had the advantage of having no trunk road, not even a brook. Tall Carpathian pines stood guard over this clump of shacks. That would have been ideal for safety, but the Turk was too indolent to climb the slopes and forced the capital to move to more accessible parts. Then it was built up a few miles to the south, on a mountain brook of idyllic peace.

The Turk thought that Curtea de Arges, too, was far away and forced the capital to move to the foot of the mountains. At Targoviste the tax-collectors and executioners had less trouble finding the local chiefs. It was only after much killing and coaxing that the present site of Bucharest was selected. As late as the seventies of last century, Calea Victoriei was called "Mogosoia Bridge" because of the planks floating on knee-deep mud. Nine times the Russians took Bucharest in the nineteenth century. "The soil sighs wherever Russian armies pass."

The World War made Bucharest the capital of the largest country of the Balkans. She has been building feverishly ever since. The Bucharest of yesterday was an Oriental town; the Bucharest of today is a world metropolis.

◊◊◊◊◊◊◊◊◊◊◊◊◊◊◊◊◊◊◊◊◊◊◊◊

The Danube forms the northern boundary of Bulgaria. "We are not a Danubian country," the Bulgarian government told an American university which arranged a conference of the countries in the river basin some years ago. The two main rivers of the Kingdom flow into the Aegean Sea. The small streams emptying into the Danube are too deeply furrowed and too rapid to be of significance. "Old Mountain," as the Balkan chain is known to

453

the natives, separates the bulk of the country from the great river. The capital, Sofia, is far away. Bulgaria is a mountainous country which attracted isolated tribes pursued by organized violence.

Remnants of extinct groups still survive in valleys which could not be farther away from the world even if they were in Siberia. It is a country of hard-working peasants; the Bulgarians have a reputation for industry. They live longer than any of their neighbors; a peasant of a hundred years is not too old. Their features are Slavic, and so is the language they speak. Originally the "Bulgarians" were not Slavs but of Finnish-Ugrian race, related to the Hungarians higher up the Danube. They enslaved the Slavs and were in turn absorbed by their supposed victims. In the valleys of Bulgaria the prehistoric house-community, known as the *zadruga,* still survives. Large family groups, sometimes numbering several dozen persons, live under a communistic system, in which all earnings are turned over to the family treasury. No excessive wealth or poverty mars the lives of these communities.

Tragic memories haunt the valleys of Bulgaria. Several times in her history she seemed to be within sight of the peak and each time her hopes were dashed. "Bulgaria assumed a rank among the civilized powers of the earth," says Gibbon, "as early as the tenth century." "Emperor and Autocrat of all the Bulgars and Greeks" was the title of Simeon the Great. Twice in those early medieval times Bulgarians ruled over most of the Balkan Peninsula, from the Aegean all the way to the Adriatic Sea. They challenged the Byzantine Empire and exacted tribute from the heir of Rome. They were to fall from their high estate because of the Balkan curse. Brother slew brother, and the Turk triumphed.

In five hundred years even the memory of Bulgaria was extinguished. The higher classes embraced Islam and made common

454

cause with the enemy. At the beginning of last century the peasants of the valleys and mountains called themselves Greeks, and even students of Slavonic literature knew nothing about the Bulgarian race. One after another the Balkan countries liberated themselves from Turkish rule, but the Danube brought the Bulgarians no saving word. One of the worst massacres of Europe was perpetrated by the Turks on the Bulgarians toward the end of the last century, when in one district alone some 15,000 men, women and children were killed. Outraged Europe lavished sympathy on the Bulgarians, but rendered them little assistance, except for the Russians who did it for themselves and not for their wards. It was only in 1908 that Bulgaria became an independent Kingdom under the rule of a Saxe-Coburg-Gotha Prince. Again Bulgaria made a bid for all, and lost. She surprised the world with her military valor in the Balkan Wars, but her friends turned on her when she demanded her fee. Again she tried and lost in the World War, when she sided with the losing Central Powers. This time she lost the vitally important access to the Aegean Sea.

Bulgaria tried progressive democracy and failed. Then came the reaction, which was bloody and uncompromising. An undeclared war was raging against her Serbian neighbor, which got Macedonia, sore spot of the sorest part of Europe. The Bulgarians demanded Macedonia on the ground of kinship, language and the self-determination of nations. Embattled patriots raided the neighbor's backyard and blood flowed in the streets of the capital as warring Macedonian factions executed illegal death sentences.

Politics and murder were synonymous terms in the heart of the Balkans. The country grew tired of murder as an instrument of

455

national policy, and a government which repressed terrorism found public support. King Boris III began to loom as the "strong man" of the country, although he exercised his authority through Premiers and governments. Bulgaria conceived the original of the American CCC and the German labor camps for youth. When Hitler began to move down the Danube, Bulgaria seemed to become a pivotal point of the Fascist axis. About three-fourths of her trade went to Germany and Italy. Smarting under the treaty, Bulgaria has never made a secret of her wish to make another try to climb the heights. Although she turns her back on the Danube, Bulgaria cannot escape the fate of the river valley. Many times she has tried; many times she has failed. What does the future hold in store for her?

What, indeed, does the future hold in store for the whole course of the Danube? Will the entire Danube become a Nazi river? As an indication of its intention, the Third Reich has speeded up work on the Danube-Rhine Canal, to link up the Black and North Seas more effectively. Bearded King Ludwig of Bavaria, whom we last saw hugging a country wench of stone on the pedestal of his statue, had a canal built, *Ludwigs Kanal,* in the middle of the last century. Between Ulm and Passau, where the Bavarian wheatfields are at their best, it begins and meets the Rhine at Mainz, with the help of the rivers, Main, Altmuehl and Regnitz. The Canal was in poor condition and not large enough for modern vessels. By means of the new Canal, the Brown Danube is to serve the Brown Reich; the wheat of Hungary and the oil of Roumania are to see the Rhine. The question must be answered: shall it be the Danube of one country or of all the nations in its valley?

The International Commission

At the Peace Conference a step was taken in the latter direction. Navigation on the entire Danube system was declared unrestricted and open to all flags, on a footing of complete equality from the town of Ulm in Germany to the Black Sea delta in Roumania, according to a statute signed on July 23, 1921. This was in execution of Article 347 of the Treaty of Versailles. An International Commission was set to see to it that the flags of all nations were respected on the Danube. No ships were to be discriminated against, nor deprived of any facilities and privileges. The Danube became the property of all nations, as free to all as the open sea. Some of the Danube tributaries were also internationalized. But Chancellor Adolf Hitler tore up the Danubian Statute.

Epilogue

$\mathscr{R}$IVERS cannot speak a language understood by man. History makes the message of the Danube clear. The river builds and also destroys. It builds where the laws of its inner nature are obeyed and destroys where they are flouted. The Danube was to be the lifeline of the Roman Empire, but Rome misread the river's message and made it a frontier instead of a unifying force for the entire basin. The Danube's middle reaches became the lifeline of the Hungarian Kingdom and helped a friendless tribe hold its own where scores of others failed. To the crusaders the river was a highway for the conquest of the East, and to the Turks it was an ally to subjugate the West. What fate would have been Islam's if it had heeded the message of its waters?

The Danube became the lifeline of the Habsburg Empire for four centuries, and almost performed its real function toward the end of their reign. Under the black and gold banner of the House of Austria, supported by the red-white-green flag of Hungary, a monarchy was reared on the Middle Danube banks in which German and Slav, Latin and Magyar found a haven. But the Habsburgs could not see that it was not the river's nature to play favorites. Their Hungarian partners understood the law of the Danube even less. Slowly the river rolled down its appointed way, unable to warn, an unwilling witness to impending doom. One nation suppressed the other, and tinder was piled high in the Danube valley. A farrago of divergent creeds, political and social, divided a natural unit, and the lifeline of Central Europe became the deathline of the world.

The peacemakers of Paris knew nothing of the Danube's historic mission. If the river had a voice, it would have cried out when the wise men of the West cut to pieces the bleeding body of its valley. Granted that nationalism was in the air and that moderation is not the victor's virtue, the dismemberment of the valley should not have been considered an act of supreme statesmanship. The Danubian countries were left to their devices, to prosper or to starve, to erect sky-high tariff barriers, cut themselves off from their neighbors. "The neighbor is thy friend," is the message of the Danube; "the neighbor is thy foe," ignorance replied. Some problems had been solved and secular injustices corrected, but other and graver problems and injustices were created.

New frontiers barred the way, and the Danube lost its rôle as a lifeline. Gloom settled upon its valley; even the victors were uneasy. Political alliances were to answer unanswerable questions, as if parchment could keep the river from its appointed course. Deep silences settled on the frontier lands, while the bitter fight for bread went on. The race of arms began in the Danube valley

and wan lips trembled: "Are we headed for another great disaster?"

The Danube went on its way, deeply concerned but unable to
speak. Discontent on its banks was groping for expression. A dictator saw his chance and harnessed despondency to serve his purpose. The "Rome pacts" were to hitch the Danube to the Mediterranean—an impossible feat. They were to help the hardest-hit
river States, but the price was high. Despair was to help the
Italian dictator's will.

Then the brown wave struck the headwaters of the Danube.
The German dictator marched into Vienna. Rome and the Habsburgs have shown that whoever is master of that gate between
East and West, North and South, is master of the Danube valley.
The river became the lifeline of Germany—not merely Germany's
but that of an intolerant creed, believing in war for its own sake,
forced by its own nature to create havoc. The Danube could not
change its course to escape its fate. Again the lines were drawn
and man sought to destroy himself. Inevitably what is a natural
highway became the dictator's battleground. The present became
shackled to a dismal future.

Is there, then, no solution for the Danube problem? Along the
river live some 80,000,000 people—Germans, Slavs, Latins, Hungarians. They are factory workers and farmers, miners and fishermen, men and women of all occupations, representing every level
of culture. The differences between them are not basically great.
All share the common fate of the Danube. The river basin is a natural unit. It has the richest farmland in all Europe, abundant
pastures, industries of all types, minerals and metals, the largest
oil deposits west of Russia, water power, timber, mountains and

plains, access to the sea, moderate climate and vegetation rich and varied. These tens of millions of people could live happily and safely, instead of eking out a poor existence in the shadow of sudden death.

Nature made the Danube for life and not for death. Various nationalities are scattered all over its valley, and it is impossible to draw just boundary lines. If the nationality lines were at least as clear-cut as in Europe's West, the problem would be less baffling. But they are not, and have never been since historical times. Change the map any way you like; no division into conventional national states can meet the need. Always there will be large masses of people left within a foreign nation.

History may provide the solution and call it "The Danubian Federation of States." Its name may be "Eastern Switzerland," or any other name. Utopia or absurdity—there still is no other answer. All other combinations have failed. One village is German, the next is Roumanian, Serbian, Croat or Slavonian. Each village cannot have its own flag, government and army. The principle of nationality has been reduced to absurdity in the Danube valley.

Some men have heard the message of the Danube. In his Italian exile, the Hungarian patriot, Louis Kossuth, elaborated his famous program of a Danubian Confederation more than a half century ago. Only an economic and political alliance between Hungary and Roumania, Serbia and later Bohemia, he said, would be capable of guaranteeing the independence of these smaller States against Pan-German and Pan-Slav pressure and, at the same time, in connection with the solution of the nationality problem, to maintain efficiently the peace of Central Europe.

A bolder dream came to the late French Foreign Minister, Aristide Briand, who set his diplomatically trained mind the task of working for a United States of Europe. He knew that the national concept was a catastrophic failure in parts of Europe. A master builder of the future, he was not content with bewailing the past. Although the late Thomas Garrigue Masaryk was a founder and first President of Czechoslovakia, he knew that the establishment of the Republic was merely a step toward the realization of a higher ideal. His successor, Eduard Benes, made a profession of faith in the Danubian Federation and the European United States. A prominent Hungarian statesman and scholar, Oscar Jászi, has done his best to popularize the idea of an "Eastern Switzerland" in the Danube valley.

The Danube knows that, no matter how rational, such heroic deeds cannot be performed overnight. Nationalism had come late to the river valley; its impact was all the more elemental, overwhelming. The nation took the place of the Sun-God as the object of frenetic public worship, and to question it is worse than heresy. Stronger than vested beliefs are vested interests. The national boundaries had become the bulwarks of private privilege, and patriotism a synonym for exploitation. Behind the tariff barriers industries had become monopolies. Political job holders, too, are fearful of change in the Danube valley.

Under the Federation, nations would not be wiped out. Their energies would be converted to the ways of peace and not war. Native languages and national laws would not relinquish their hold. Common history has forged too strong a link to break. The Danubian Federation of States would make use of man's competitive nature, without provoking conflicts. It would give emphasis to the idea that the nation would perform its real function by serving constructive ends. The member-States of the Federation would co-operate with the Danube in making it what it really is— a natural unit. The States would co-ordinate their efforts in the economic and political fields, so that the Danube would give all it has to yield.

Such a Federation would have to comprise Bohemia-Slovakia— the former Czecho-Slovakia—Hungary, Yugoslavia, Roumania. Austria would be a logical part of it, and also parts of Southern Germany. A peaceful Reich would find it to its advantage to make common cause with the Danubian Federation. But if Austria were willing to remain with such a Germany, she would belong to a sufficiently large economic unit.

All this may sound like the Biblical lamb and lion lying down together, but the future may show that there is no other choice. Incredible events have occurred lately and today's dream may be tomorrow's reality. Faced with the great disaster, man may at long last take counsel with his common sense. A solution should not be ruled out merely because it is sensible.

History has taught us the lesson that when the political horizon is darkest the stars appear. The French Revolution swept away the ideological cobwebs of thousands of years. The Holy Alliance yielded its place to light. Man, who sends his voice around the earth in a second, who spans the oceans with flying boats, who is fighting death on all fronts, cannot be so perverse as to climb the peaks to break himself to pieces from a greater height.

The Danube valley had led the way to war. It would be logical for it to show the way to peace. The danger there is greater, the need for action imperative. The ultimate solution would lead to a co-operation of all European countries. The continent is too small to shelter thirty nations working at cross-purposes and contriving one another's destruction.

Onward the Danube rolls on its inscrutable way. It has brought life and destruction, is making history from day to day.

The Danube has a message; history has made it clear. From the Black Forest to the Black Sea it resounds through the centuries. Its banks may echo the funeral dirge of millions or may exult in the strains of the "Beautiful Blue Danube." Man must make the final choice.

Index

Aaron, Prince, 415-416
Activists, The Sudeten, 188
Ada Kaleh Island, 303-304
Adamic, Louis, 352
Addison, John, quoted, 24
Adriatic Sea, 10, 131, 172, 215, 216, 316, 322, 346, 454
Ady, Andreas, 280
Aegean Sea, 7, 305, 337, 414, 453, 454, 455
Africa, 9
Aggstein, Castle, 50
Alaric, 314
Alba Julia, Grand Voyvoda of. *See* Michael, King of Roumania
Albania, 305, 319, 322, 342, 344, 360
Albanian Guard, 409
Albanians, 307, 311
Albert the Great, "Albertus Magnus," 24, 37
Albert the Rich, 58
Albrecht III, Duke of Bavaria, 40

Alexander, Czar, 73, 76
Alexander II, Czar, 89
Alexander II, Regent of Serbia, King of Yugoslavia, 319, 324, 340, 344, 351-359
Alexander, King of Serbia, 156, 336-340, 438
Alexander of Moldavia, 413
Alexander of Yugoslavia, by Stephen Graham, 348
Alexander the Bad of Moldavia, 401
Alexander the Good, 397
Alexander the Macedonian, 3
Alföld, 215, 305, 316, 374
Ali Bey, 427
Alps, the, 54, 215, 270, 360; Tyrolean, 22; Bavarian, 119; Transylvanian, 302, 363; Slovenian, 314; Julian, 315, 355
Alsace, 15
Alsace-Lorraine, 258
Altmuehl river, 456

465

Ambassador Street, Regensburg, 33
Amber Road, the, 131, 142, 314
Americas, the, 4, 47; America, 61, 315,
    329; Americans, 282; American in-
    fluence in Skoplje, Yugoslavia, 310
Amur region, 232
Anatolia, 329
Anne of Hohenberg, 60
Anschluss, 104, 105, 191
"Apis," 320, 337-339, 343
Apollodor, 363
Aquinicum, 213
Aragosa, 315
Argesh river, 404
Argusa, 15
Aristotle, 10
Armenians, 376
Arnold the Bastard, 33
Árpád the Hungarian, 3, 167, 233, 236,
    288, 374
Armenians, the, 291
Arrow Cross, the, 268
Arumani, the, 311
Asch, 190
Aspern, 63
Atel-Kuzu, 377
Athleta Christi. See Pius IV
Athos, Mount, 328
Attila, 28, 287-288, 410
Augsburg, Bishop of, 26
Augustus, Emperor, 392
Aurelian, Emperor, 394
Auschwitz, 58
Ausgleich, 250
Austerlitz, 61
Austria, 38, 41, 45, 46-128, 144, 291,
    294, 332, 339, 340, 359, 360, 369,
    411, 428, 459, 463
Austrobolshevism, 111
Austro-Goths, 395
Austro-Hungarian Empire, 160, 226,
    309, 322, 336, 343 *et seq.,* 424 *et
    seq.*
Austro-Prussian War of 1866, 250
Avala, Mount, 320

Avars, the, 4, 160, 233, 288, 395
Axis, Berlin-Rome, the, 361

Baba, Hafus Kahalil, 379
Babenberg, House of, 56
Bácka, 255, 258, 299, 300
Badacsony, 215
Badani, Count, 177
Baden, Grand Duchy of, 11, 16, 17,
    18, 31, 80, 92, 94
Baerlein, Henry, quoted, 341
Bagdad-Berlin, 104, 309
Bakony mountains, 270
Bakunin, Michael, 340
Balaton, Lake, 225
Balkan War, 429, 455
Balkans, the, 6, 76, 105, 131, 156, 236,
    251, 298, 301 *et seq.,* 443, 454
Baltazzi, Herr Alexander von, 94
Balti, 235
Baltic Sea, 6, 131, 159, 235
Bamberg Castle, Germany, 37
Bánát, the, 242, 255, 258, 300, 369,
    430
Banse, Ewald, 191
Barthou, Louis, 358-359
Basilicus, Jacob, 414-415
Basta, General, 403
Bastide, M., 421
Báthory, 376
Bauernbund, 106
Bavaria, Kingdom of, 18, 28, 31, 314;
    army, 26, 37, 48; Bavarian wheat-
    fields, 456
Bazias, 424
Bazileus, 414
Bécs, 147
Beer Hall Putsch, 110
Beethoven, Ludwig van, 5, 81, 141,
    152, 153, 157, 273
Befreiungshalle, 39
Béla IV, King of Hungary, 235, 272
    275
Belgium, 8, 47, 76, 265

Belgrade, 7, 254, 272, 305, 318-320, 330 *et seq.*, 352 *et seq.*
Beli Grad, 318
"Bell-beaker" folks, the, 9
Bellerophon, the, 74
Benedictine friars, 28
Benes, Eduard, 123, 177-183, 198, 260, 462
Beograd, 318
Berchtesgaden, 23, 119
Berchthold, Count, 157
Berlin, 20, 55, 65, 101, 104, 124, 154, 168, 251, 281
Berlin Congress of 1878, 304, 336
Berlioz, Hector, 244
Bernauer, Agnes, 40
Bessarabia, 366, 369, 377-381, 430; racial minorities of, 377
Bessi, the, 377
Bethlen, 376
Bibesco, Princess, 452
Biography of a Bygone City, by Henry Dwight Sedgwick, 150
Birth of Yugoslavia, The, by Henry Baerlein, 341
Bismarck, Prince Otto, 55, 56, 94, 159, 186
Black Brigade, the, 238, 239
"Black Church" of Brasov, 375
Black Death, 33, 136, 291, 328
Black Forest, the, 5, 10, 11, 15, 464
Black George, 331-333
Black George Dynasty, 331-345, 353
Black Hand Mafia, 94, 320, 343, 345
Black Sea, 31, 32, 132, 237, 327, 336, 364, 367, 368, 373, 380, 393, 443, 456, 457, 464
Bled, 314, 355
Blenheim, 24, 25
Blériot, Louis, 155
Blue Danube Waltz, 133, 464
Blum, Leon, 439
Bogdan, the One-Eyed, 413
Bogenberg, castle of, 41

Bohemia, 9, 57, 58, 63, 64, 132, 147, 159-160, 171, 177, 185, 203; -Slovakia, 463
Bohemians, 38, 160
Bohemian Woods, 44
Bois de Boulogne, 225
Bojay, Farkas, 376
Bolzano, 53
Borgotaro, 357
Boris III, King of Bulgaria, 456
Borneo, 9
Bosnia, 313, 322-323, 339, 342
Bosnia-Herzegovina, 103, 336
Bosnians, 311
Bourbons, the, 24
Boyars, the, 382-385, 397, 400, 405, 406, 416, 428, 430, 448
Brahms, Johannas, 5, 23, 141, 142, 226
Braila, 365-366
Brancovan the Decapitated, 372, 404-405, 422
Brasov, "Black Church" of, 375
Bratianu, Ion, 421, 423, 425, 428; Dynasty of, 431, 432
Bratislava, 158, 159, 211
Braun, 29
Breitner, Hugo, 138
Brege brook, 16
Brenner Pass, 31, 41, 52, 53, 105, 109, 119, 128, 175
Brescia, 357
Brest-Litovsk, treaty of, 169
Briand, Aristide, 462
Brigach brook, 16
Brigance, 58
British Empire. *See* Great Britain
Brixen, 58
Bronze Age, 9, 10
Brown Reich, 436, 456. *See* also Germany
Brunswick, Duchess of, 40
Bucharest, 254, 354, 363, 364, 381, 400, 401, 405, 432, 438-441; 443-453; Athenée-Palace, Hotel, 444, 445; Calea Victoriei, 404, 438-441,

Index

444-445; Capsa, Café, 438, 444-445; Cismigiu Park, 451; Dambovitza river, 446; Grand Café, 439; Kisilev, Chaussée, 445; Lipscani, Strada, 446; origin of name, 452; Royal palace, 444; Telephone Building, 444
Buckow, 168
Bucur, 452
Buda, 238, 240, 241, 247, 270 et seq., 330, 392
Budaörs, 264
Budapest, 5, 45, 86, 154, 213, 215, 222, 225, 228, 247, 251, 256, 257, 258, 263, 270-294, 349, 366; Angel's Field, 270, 282; Angel's Quarter, 230; Café New York, 280; Chain Bridge, 275, 278, 293; "Chicago," 280; Coronation Church, 271; Corso, the, 277-278, 283; Danube Embankment, 276-278, 285; Elizabeth Bridge, 276, 277; Elizabeth Ring, 280; Fisher Bastion, 276; Franz Joseph Bridge, 276; Hare's Island, 275; Hüvösvölgy, the, 281; Kávéház, 279-280; King Street, Király utca, 283; Liberty Square, 277; Lord's Island, 275; Maidens' Island, 275; National Academy, 277, 292; Palace Hill, 273; Parliament Building, 276; racial minorities in, 291; Rákos Field, 292; Royal Palace, 271; St. Johannes Mountain, 271; St. Stephen's, the Holy Right, 272; Tabán, 274; Tonangeber, 282; Watertown section, 291.
Bulgaria, 233, 298, 305, 309, 320, 344, 345, 363-365, 369, 379, 395, 429, 453-456
Bukovina, 58, 102, 369, 376
Burgtheater, Vienna, 87
Burgundy, 234; Dukes of, 241
Byzantine Empire, 454
Byzantium, 306, 369, 419

Cabrinovic, 343
Cafesieder, Balázs, 279
Calea Victoriei, 404, 438-441, 444-445
Campulung, 453
Cantacuzenes, the, 404
Capek, Karl, 162, 166
Capri, 275
Capuchin Church, 49, 64, 81, 82, 136, 154
Carinthia, 58, 110-111
Carlyle, Thomas, quoted, 174
Carmelite nunnery, 93
Carmen Sylva, 372, 380, 426, 452. See also Elizabeth, Queen of Roumania
Carniola, 58
Carol I, King of Roumania, 365; as Prince Charles of Hohenzollern-Sigmaringen, 423-425; as Prince Carol, 425-427; as King Carol I, 427-431
Carol II, King of Roumania, 183, 388; as Prince Carol, 431-433; as King, 433-442
Carpathian mountains, 51, 131, 158, 204, 213-214, 233, 249, 302, 327, 363, 369 et seq., 396, 450, 451
Caspian Sea, 233, 394
Catherine the Great of Russia, 70, 168
Catholic Church (Roman), 41, 47, 106, 117, 145, 175, 207, 234, 274, 312, 317, 327
Cernauti, 376, 436
Cernavoda Bridge, 365
Cesarini, 237
Ceska Trebova, 161
Cetinje, 321
Chamberlain, Neville, 123, 193, 195, 198, 201-204
Charlemagne, 3, 33, 42, 125, 288, 320
Charles, Archduke, 152
Charles V, Emperor and King (Habsburg), 60, 61
Charles VI, 49, 62-63, 67
Charles of Durazzo, 288-289
Charles, Prince of Hohenzollern-Sig-

468

Index

maringen. *See* Carol I, King of Roumania

Charles the Little. *See* Charles of Durazzo

Childe, V. Gordon, quoted, 9

Christian Social Party, 106, 144

Ciganovic, 343

Cimmerians, 377

"City of Joy" (Bucharest), 452

Clemenceau, Georges, 347

Closca, 417

Codreanu, Cornelius Zelea, 435

Colmar, 75

Communists, 224, 268; in power in Hungary, 255-257, 287; 350, 378

Constance, Council of, 174

Constantinople, 31, 55, 232, 233, 234, 290, 329, 333, 372, 379, 397, 401, 404, 408, 419, 424, 426, 443

Constanza, 365, 373, 379, 380

Corfu, 90, 344

Corfu, Declaration of, 345

Correggio, 184

Corsica, 359

Corvinae, 238

Corvinus, János, 239

Cotiso, 392

Craco the Giant, 35

Cracow, 58, 102

Crimean War, 365, 422

Croat Republican Peasant Party, 348, 351; Assembly House, 352

Croatia, 58, 102, 313, 316 *et seq.*

Croatia-Slavonia, 312

Croats in Yugoslavia, 311

Croix, Jean de, Marquis, 265

Cromwell, Oliver, 247

Crusaders, the, 3

Csanád, 274

Csepel Islands, 285

Csikós, 217

Csoma, Sándor Körösi, 376

Curtea de Arges, 453

Cuza, Alexandra Joan, 422-423

Cyrillic script, 317

Czech National Church, 207

Czech University, 130, 207

Czechs, the, 22, 161-163

Czechoslovakia, 6, 22, 51, 102, 119, 123, 159, 160-208, 360, 462, 463; treatment of minorities, 164; Agrarian Party, 165

Czernowitz, 369, 376-377

Czernowitzer Post, 436

Dachau, 124, 127

Dacians, the, 4, 392 *et seq.*

Daco-Roman Shepherds, 395

Daladier, Eduard, 123, 201

Dalmatia, 58, 315, 346-347, 358

D'Annunzio, Gabriele, 348

Dante, 281-282

Danube Canal, 86, 133, 139, 145

Danube-Rhine Canal, 456

Danubian Federation of States, 254, 461-463

Danubian Principalities, 246, 396-397, 399, 406, 407, 413-427

Danubian Statute, 457

Danuvius river, 10

Dardanelles, Straits of, 10, 131, 380

Darius the Persian, 3

Darol-i-Jehad, 318

d'Auvergne, Latour, 26-27

David and Goliath, 24, 35, 107, 344

Debrecen, 253, 254

Decebalus the Great, 392, 393

Dedigne, 319

Deggendorf, 42-43

Délibáb, 217

Delta of the Danube, the, 365

Denmark, 441

Der Alte Kaempfer, 127

Der Kommende Krieg, by Ewald Banse, 191

Deus Abnobius, 11

Die Wacht am Rhein, 47

Dillingen, Countess of, 23

Dimineata, the, 451

Dimitrievich, General, 353

Dimitrijevich, Dragutin, "Apis," 337-339
Dinarides mountains, 215
Divide et impera, 59, 329, 407
Divine Comedy, Dante, 282
Djordj, the God-fearing Despot, 302
Dnieper river, 9
Dniester river, 374, 377, 378, 392, 412, 441
Dobrudja, 365-367, 369, 379-381, 429
"Doctor Universalis," 24
Doene river, 11
Dollfuss, Engelbert, 105-113, 126, 135, 139
Dollinger, Hans, 35
Domitian, Emperor, 28, 392
Donau river, 11
Donaueschingen, 15
Donaustauf, 37
Donaustauf, Castle, 38
Donauwoerth, 25, 26
Donava river, 11
Downing Street, 350
Dózsa Dezsö, 240
Dracul, 398
Draga, Queen of Serbia, 156, 338-339, 354, 438
Dragosh, 411
Drau river, 299
Drava river, 299, 312, 316, 356
Dresden, 162
Drina river, 343
DuBarry, Mme., 69
Dubrovnik, 315
Duca, Ion G., 434, 437
Duernstein castle, 50
Duna river, 11
Dunarea, 362
Dunarea river, 11

Ebrach, Black Friar of, 30
Echo de Paris, 435
Edison, Thomas A., 276
École des Pages, 353
Efferding, castle of, 109

Ekaterinburg, 320
Elba, 61, 74
Elbe river, 159
Eleanor, wife of Prince Cuza, 423
Elizabeth, Czarina, 66, 89-92
Elizabeth, Princess of Wied, 426
Elizabeth, Queen of Hungary, 288-289
Elizabeth, Queen of Roumania, 372. *See also* Carmen Sylva
Elizabeth, Empress, wife of Franz Joseph, 87-92
Elizabeth, Princess, 96
Elta, the, 20
Emperor March, the, Haydn, 141
England. *See* Great Britain
Erfurt, 72
Ernst, Duke of Bavaria, 40
Eschingen, 10, 16, 18
Esztergom, 159, 213
Ethiopia, 118, 121, 201, 359
Etzelburg, 288
Eugene, Prince of Savoy, 77
European Commission, 365, 367
Eugénie, Empress, 383

Fabvrier, Colonel, 75
Fadrusz, John, 272
Farinelli, 151
Fascist International, 269; axis, 456
Fata Morgana, 232, 313
Fatherland Front, 116, 120
Fatra mountain, 205
Faustus, Dr., 27
Fazli-Bey, 332
Feldkirch, 58, 114
Ferdinand I, Duke of Hungary, 243
Ferdinand I, Emperor of Austria, 154, 248
Ferdinand IV, ex-Grand Duke of Tuscany, 94
Ferdinand, Emperor of Austria, 415
Ferdinand, King of Roumania, 354, 429, 431
Ferdinand of Castile, 310
Festetics, Count, 225

Index

Fifth Symphony, Beethoven, 141
Finnish-Ugrian race, 454
Finno-Hungarians, 395
Fiume, 103, 346-347
Floridsdorf, 63
Forgács, Kálmán, 289
Fourteen points, the, 347
France, 16, 17, 24, 37, 144, 188, 291, 337, 358 *et seq.,* 365, 398, 420-421
Francis I of Austria, 68, 73, 74
Francis II, Emperor of Austria, 34, 60, 71, 78, 79, 136, 246
Francis Ferdinand, Archduke, 156
Franco, Generalissimo Francisco, 127
Franks, 38
Franks, Kingdom of the, 232
Franz, Emperor. *See* Francis II
Franz Ferdinand, Archduke, 98, 99-100, 137, 142, 340, 342
Franz Joseph I, 61, 82-92, 98, 102, 110, 114, 137, 154, 156, 248-249, 257, 272, 343, 350
Frederick Barbarossa, 56
Frederick the Fair, 58
Frederick II, the Great, King of Prussia, 62, 63-67, 70, 72, 169, 170, 244, 327
Frederick William III, 73
Frederick with the Empty Pocket, 58
Freiheitssender, 126
French Revolution, 78, 463
Friaul, 58
Froissart, Jean, quoted, 43
Fruska Gora, 300
Fuerstenberg, Princes of, 15
Fuggerhaus, the, 25
Funchal, Madeira, 264
Furtwaengler, Wilhelm, 447

Galati, 366
Galatz, 366, 422
Galicia, 58, 102
Gambetta, Leon, 258
Gandhi, Mahatma, 351
Garda, Lake, 357
Garibaldi, Giuseppe, 247

Gedye, G. E. R., 123, 124, 195, 201
Geissenberg, 29
Gellért Hill, 248
Gemuetlichkeit, 48, 133, 145, 157
Geneva, 104, 243, 352-353
Genghis Khan the Tatar, 3, 235, 236, 288, 308
Genoese, the, 364
George, Crown Prince of Serbia, 344
George Washington, the, 347
German minorities in Czechoslovakia, 164
Germania, Tacitus, 19
Germany, 5, 6, 11, 15-47, 63, 95, 103, 104-105, 158, 213, 239, 309, 359, 360, 376, 428, 435 *et seq.,* 456, 460, 463
Géza, Duke, quoted, 234
Gibbon, Edward, quoted, 454
Gibraltar, 25, 359
Gide, André, 447
Giurgiu, 364, 373
"Gloomy Sunday," 278
Glowworm, 264
Gluck, C. W. von, 151
Godesberg, 202
Gobi, 232, 391
Godfrey of Bouillon, 3
Gödöllö, 290
Godomin, 302
Goebbels, Joseph, 192, 196
Goergei, Artur, 248-249
Goethe, 27
Goga, Octavian, quoted, 371-372; Premier, 436-437
"Golden Bey." *See* Brancovan
Golden Bull, the, 276
Golubac, 302
Gorky, Maxim, 231
Goritz, 58
Goths, the, 4, 394
Gott Erhalte, 85, 253, 254
Gradisca, 58
Graham, Stephen, quoted, 348, 351, 352, 355, 356

Granada, 329
Grand Armée of Napoleon, 3, 17
"Grandmother's Tooth," 304
Graz, 112, 121
Great Britain, 20, 24, 121, 144, 332, 350, 365, 432
Great Trek of the Danube, 330
Greben Defiles, 302
Greek Orthodox Church, 312, 327
Greeks, the, 19, 307, 407
Grein, 49
Gross-Essing, 29
"Guard of Archangel Michael," 435
Guastalla, 58
Gulf Stream, 51, 215
Gunther, King, 28
Gypsies, 310, 362, 377, 444, 449; origin of, 450

Habsburg, House of, 4, 24, 46, 47, 48, 55, 56, 58-103, 131, 132, 134, 159, 176, 207, 223, 244, 250, 251, 308, 314, 316, 332, 423, 425, 458, 459
"Hadur," 234
Hafelekar Peak, 128
Hamburg, City of, 120-121, 227
Hamilton, Alexander, 225
Hangerli, Prince of Moldavia, 401-402
Hannibal, 76
Hawk's Burg, 57
Haydn, Franz Joseph, 141, 152-152, 153
Heiligenkreuz Cistercian Abbey, 93
Heimwehr, the, 107, 110-113
Heine, Heinrich, 31, 89-90
Heinrich the Lame and the Wise, 58
Héjas, Lieut. Ivan, 256
Helen, Princess, of Greece, 432-434
Helenenthal, 80
Hellespont, 236
Henlein, Konrad, 189-193
Henry of Kalden, 30
Henry the Proud, 38
Herzegovinia, 312, 322; Herzegovinians in Yugoslavia, 311

Hesiod, 10
"Hettingen, Karl," 424
History of the Roumanians, by Prof. R. W. Seton-Watson, 392, 395
Hitler, Adolf, 19, 45, 104, 105, 113, 118, 119, 120-128, 139, 146, 157, 169, 191-204, 211, 256, 259, 266-269, 286, 314, 359-360, 435-436, 439-440, 447, 456, 457, 460
Hlinka, Andreas, 205-206
Hodza, Milan, Premier, 201, 206
Hofer, Andreas, 105
Hohenembs, 58
Hohenzollerns of Prussia, 154, 250
Holy Alliance, the, 3, 73, 75, 76, 77, 135, 177, 249, 463
Holy Land, 3, 33, 45, 50, 328
Holy Roman Emperors, 47, 57, 136, 240, 291
Holy Roman Empire, 34, 117, 172, 288, 330, 398, 417
Horezu Monastery, 372
Horia, 417
"Horst Wessel Song," 19, 122
Horthy, Nicholas, 257-259, 261-263, 271
Hoyos, Count Josef, 92
Hradčany palace, 176, 184, 195
Huefingen, 15
Hundred Days' Rule, 74
Hundred Years' War, 398
Hungary, 4, 6, 9, 22, 51, 58, 59, 64, 102, 132, 147, 149, 158, 163, 205, 211-269, 299, 301, 348, 362, 369, 370, 391, 439, 442, 450, 458, 459, 463
Hungarian Gate, 49, 158
Hungarian minorities in Czechoslovakia, 164; in Roumania, 376, 411
Hungarian Plain, 159
Hungary and Her Successors, by C. A. Macartney, 258
Huns, the, 4, 38, 160, 233, 301, 314, 395

Index

Hunyadi, János, "Turk-beater," 110, 236, 237-239, 241, 272, 289, 376
Hunyadi, Laszló, 272-273
Hunyadi, Matthias, King, 237-239, 240, 275, 289-290, 376
Huss, John, 173-174, 207
Hussite wars, 175

Iasi, 411
Illyria, 58
Ilz river, 45, 46
Immendingen, 19
India, 309, 315, 418, 427
Ingolstadt, 27
Inn river, 45, 46
Innsbruck, 115, 128
International Commission, 457
Ion Ursu, King, 416
Iranian plateau, 232
Iron Gates, 234, 292, 304-305, 336, 393
"Iron Guard," 434-435, 439, 442
Iron Mask, 98
Isabella of Castile, 310
Ischl, 87, 89
Islam, 4, 236, 290 *et seq.*, 364, 455, 458
Ister river, 10, 11
Istria, 58, 172
Italy, 41, 42, 47, 48, 52, 55, 80, 103, 105, 110, 121, 147, 201, 314, 315, 323 *et seq.*, 398
Ivan the Terrible, 238

Jablonka Pass, 204
Janizaries, 3, 148, 330, 332, 399
Japan, 342
Jassy, 411; prefect of, 435
Jászi, Oscar, 254, 462
Jerusalem, 58, 308
Jewish minorities in Czechoslovakia, 164
Jews, 33, 42-43, 101, 117, 136, 139-140, 223, 256, 269, 291, 407, 428, 449; Hungarian —, 283-286, 376;

Sephardim —, 310; Roumanian —, 366, 377, 378, 434 *et seq.*
John III (Sobieski), King of Poland, 148-149
John the Parricide, 58
John the Saxon of Moldavia, 414
John the Terrible, 413
Jókai, Maurus, 303
Jonescu, N., 435
Joseph II, Emperor, 61, 67, 70-73, 244-245, 416-417
Juarez, Benito, 137
Julia, Daughter of Emperor Augustus, 392
Julia, Princess, of Serbia, 335

Kaerntnerstrasse, 125, 137-138
Kahlenberg, 133
Kaiser Wilhelm II. *See* Wilhelm II.
Kalemegdan, 301, 318, 335, 336, 340
Kara Bogdan, 413
Kara Bagh, 323
Karageorgevich Dynasty. *See* Black George Dynasty
Karl I, Emperor of Austria, 49, 96, 101-103, 253, 261-266, 271
Karl Marx Hof, 138
Károly Király IV of Hungary. *See* Karl I
Károlyi, Count Michael, 224, 254-255
Károlyi family, 223
Karlsbad Program, 193
Karst Mountains, 316
Kaunitz, Prince von, 66
Kazan Narrows, 303
Kecskemét, 260
Kehlheim, 30
Keszthely, 225
Ketterl, Eugene, 85-89
Kiajna of Moldavia, 413-414
Kiajna of Walachia, 399
Kilia river, 367
Kinzing, 43
Kishinev, 366; massacre, 377
Klopstock, F. G., 62

473

Klosterneuburg, 50
Kobenzl Bar, 113
Koeniggraetz, battle of, 55, 154, 250
Kossara, 328
Kossovo, battle of, 329
Kossuth, Louis, 247-250, 461
Kozlany, 178
Kruedner, Baroness de, 73
Kultur vereine, 267
Kumans, the, 395
Kún, Béla, 255 *et seq.*
Kutuzov, Mikhail, 384, 418
Kyburg, 58

Ladislaus V, King of Hungary, 237, 272-273
"Lady King," 63
Laibach, 314
Laibach river, 314
L'Aiglon, Duke of Reichstadt, 136. *See also* Reichstadt, Duke of
Lambrino, Zizi, 431
Landsknechte, 398
Lankowitz, 168
Larisch, Countess, 95, 96
Lauingen, 23
Lausitz, 58
Lazar, Czar, 329
League of Nations, 103, 104, 201
League of Nations of Europe (Habsburgs'), 59
Lee, Lady Vernon, 150
Leipzig, 39, 125
Lehár, Colonel, 263
Leo XI, Pope, 37
Leopold the Habsburg, Flower of Knighthood, 58
Lequeitio, 264
Lhasa, 377
Libussa, Princess, 172
"Limes," the Roman, 5
Linz, 5, 49, 109
Liszt, Franz, 218
Little Entente, 259, 266, 360, 430
Liubica, Princess, 334

Ljubljana, 314-315, 346-347
Lloyd George, David, 185, 186, 347
Lodomeria, 58
Lom Palenka, 364
Lombardy, 53, 63, 64, 132
Longobards, the, 4
Lonyay, Count Elmer, 87
Loretto Chapel, 81
Lorraine, 58, 63
Louis II, King of Hungary, 241-242, 243
Louis XI of France, 238
Louis XV of France, 66
Louis XVI of France, 69, 419
Louis the Severe, Duke of Bavaria, 26
Louis-Philippe, 247
Louvain, University of, 265
Lower Depths, The, Maxim Gorky, 231
Ludwig, Emil, quoted, 185
Ludwig I of Bavaria, "Uncle Ludwig," 25, 39, 456
Ludwigs Kanal, 456
Lueger, Dr. Karl, 135
Lupescu, Magda, 431-432, 434, 437-438, 440, 445
Luther, Martin, 41, 173
Luxembourg, 172
Lyons, 75

Macartney, C. A., quoted, 258
Macedonia, 322-326, 342, 357, 455
Mafia, the Black Hand, 94, 180-181
Magellan, Fernando, 61
Magna Carta, 231, 276
Magyar, 5; —pagans, 24; 38, 52, 63, 68, 83, 142, 159, 160, 168, 232, 233, 292, 314, 374, 375, 442; —army, 95; official language of Hungary, 293; Magyarland, 267, 274, 277
Main river, 456
Mainz, 456
Maniu, Julius, 431, 432-433
Marcomanni, 171
Margaret, Princess, 275
Margareten Island, 275, 293

Index

Maria, Queen of Hungary, 288-289

Maria Theresa, 60, 61-70, 71, 141, 151, 244, 253, 272, 292

Marie, Duchess of Brabant, 24

Marie, Princess, of Roumania, Queen of Yugoslavia, 351, 354

Marie, Queen of Roumania, 354, 380, 429, 445, 452

Marie Antoinette, 61-62, 68-69

Marie Louise, Archduchess, 60-61, 75, 77, 78, 80, 81, 136, 153

Maritza river, 305

Marlborough, Duke of, 24

Marlowe, Christopher, 27

Marne river, 429

Maros valley, 417

Mavrocordato, Constantine, 409

Marseilles, 319, 324, 352, 356

Masařik, Dr. Hubert, 203

Masařyk, Thomas Garrigue, 162, 166, 180-185, 206, 462

Mashin, Draga, 337-338. *See also* Draga, Queen

Matthias the Just, King of Hungary. *See* Hunyadi, Matthias

Maximilian, Archduke, Emperor of Mexico, 137

Maximilian II, Emperor of Germany, 33

Mayerling tragedy, the, 92-98

Mazzini, Giuseppe, 247

Mediterranean, the, 6, 10, 168, 360, 460

Mein Kampf, Adolf Hitler, 135. See also *My Battle*

Meistersinger, 20, 141, 147

Melk monastery, 49

Meran, 114

Metten monastery, 42

Metternich, Prince, 55, 56, 72-73, 76, 77, 78, 103, 111, 132, 134, 145, 153, 177, 243, 246

Mexico, 61

Michael King of Roumania, 432-433; as Grand Voyvoda of Alba Julia, 433

Michael Obrenovich, son of Milosh, 335

Michael the Brave, 397, 402-403

Michelet, Jules, 232

Middle Ages, 18, 21, 109, 221, 280, 396, 397, 449

Mihnea, of Walachia, 399

Milan of Serbia, 336, 340

Military Casino, Bucharest, 432, 437, 451

Mill, John Stuart, 339

Miller, Herbert, 183

Millimetternich. *See* Dollfuss

Milos the Brave, 329

Milosh Obrenovich, 333-335

Minerva, temple of, 28

Minneapolis, Minn., 274

Minnesaenger, the, 21

Mircia, 397

Mitis, Baron O. von, 96

Mitteleuropa, 267

Modena, 58, 77

Moesia, 394

Mohács, 3, 241, 243, 290, 299

Mohammedans, the, 306, 325

Moldau river, 36

Moldavia, 369, 373-377, 381-390, 396, 411-427

Molnár, Ferenc, 279

Mongol Peace, 235

Mongolia, 394

Mongols, 267, 275, 306, 395

Monte Carlo, 224

Montecuccoli, Count Raimondo, 49; quoted, 200

Montenegro, 311, 312, 321-322

Monte Sergio, 315

Montez, Lola, 25, 39

Morand, Paul, quoted, 452

Morava river, 302, 321, 356

Moravec, Colonel Emanuel, 159

Moravia, 58, 159, 160, 203, 233

Moravian Brethren, 176

Moravian Gate, 192

Moreni, 373

Moscow, 350, 418
Mosul, 308
Mozart, Leopold, 68
Mozart, Wolfgang Amadeus, 5, 68-69, 81, 141, 142, 151, 157, 310
Muehlheim, 20
Munich, 26, 108, 202-203
Munich Pact, the, 202-203, 206, 216
Murad I, Sultan, 329
Murad the Unconquerable, 237
Murad III, 413
Murat, Prince, 423
"Murder Stone," 30
Muscovy, Czars of, 238
Mussolini, Benito, 53, 105, 107, 110, 111-112, 113, 117, 118, 119, 123, 201, 202, 356-360, 436, 447, 460
Mustapha, Kara, Grand Vizier, 109, 148-149
Mustapha Kemal, 303
My Austria, by Kurt von Schuschnigg, 117
My Battle, Adolf Hitler, 117. See also *Mein Kampf*

Naples, 67, 243
Napoleon I, 3, 4, 17, 18, 23, 27, 34, 39, 60, 61, 72, 73, 74, 75, 77, 78, 81, 105, 134, 152, 153, 238, 246, 331, 360, 418, 423
Napoleon II. *See* Reichstadt, Duke of
Napoleon III, 339, 421, 422, 423
National Peasant Party (Roumania), 431
National Socialist German Labor Party, 185
Nazis, 146, 157, 267-269, 460; German —, 108-128, 171; Austrian —, 121; — Party Congress, 160, 170; Roumanian —, 435 *et seq.*
Negotin, 305
Negru Voda, 396
Nemanya, Stephen, 328
Netherlands, the, 47, 55, 64
Neue Freie Presse, 94

Neuilly, 432
New York, 325
Nibelungen, 6, 28
Nicaraguan Canal, 447
Nicholas, Grand Duke of Russia, 427
Nicholas, King of Montenegro (Nikita), 321, 339
Nicholas I, Czar of Russia, 249
Niederhaus (the Lower House), 45
Nihilists, 349
Nikita. *See* Nicholas, King of Montenegro
Nile river, 10
No Man's Island, by Maurus Jókai, 303
North Sea, 159, 456
Novi Sad, 300
Nuremberg, 160, 170

Ober-Altaich, 41
Oberhaus, the, 45
Oberhausen, Castle, 26
Oberndorf, 29
Obrenovich Dynasty, 333-335
Ode to Joy, Beethoven, 141
Oder river, 159, 192
Odessa, 419, 431
Oesterreich, 46, 56
Oltenia, 363, 370
Orgovány, 256
On Liberty, by John Stuart Mill, 339
Orleans, Duke of, 16
Orsova, 303
Ortenburg, the Counts of, 43
Orth, John (Archduke Johann), 137
Osmanli Turks, 236, 425
Ostarrichi, the, 56
Ostbahnhof, 129
"Ostmark," 46, 52, 125, 126-128
Otranto, 234, 257
Ottakar II, Duke of Bohemia, 57, 167, 172, 314
Otto, Archduke, 99
Otto, Duc de Bar, 265-266
Otto II, Emperor, 56

Index

Otto the Gay, 58
Otto of Wittlesbach, Count Palatine of Bavaria, 29
Ottoman, the, 4
Ottoman Empire, 426
Ovid, 379, 393

Padover, S. K., quoted, 71
Pamer, Herr, 112
Pamir, 232, 394
Panama Canal, 447
Pannonia, 33, 304
Papen, Franz von, 119
Paris, 3, 55, 61, 69, 349
Parma, 58, 67
Parma, Duchess of. *See* Marie Louise
Pashaliks, Turkish, 407
Pashich, Nicholas, 313, 339-351
Passau, 44-45, 47, 49, 456
Patagonia, 137
Paul, Prince of Yugoslavia, 360
Pavelich, Ante, 356-359
Pázmány, Péter, 243
Peace Conference, the, 22, 104, 159, 186, 340, 345-348, 430, 457
Pelesh, Castle, 372
"Pertinax," 435
Persenbeug, Castle, 49
Persia, 238, 385, 412
Peru, 61
Pesaro, 357
Pest, 28, 247, 271 *et seq.*, 330. *See also* Budapest
Petchenegs, the, 395
Peter II of Yugoslavia, 360
Peter I, King of Serbia, 339, 340, 344, 345, 353
Peter II, Prince of Montenegro, 321
Peter the Ear-ring, 399
Peter the Great, 66, 168, 399, 404, 410
Peter the Lame of Moldavia, 413-414
Peter the Shepherd, 399
Petrograd, 353
Pfahlgraben, 27
Phanariote régime, 407, 409, 414

Philike Hetairia, 419
Philip II, 33
Philippine Islands, 61
Pilsen, 165, 189
Pilsudski, Marshal, 183
Pittsburgh, 183
Pittsburgh Agreement, 205
Pius IV, Pope, 412
Plaisance, 58
Planetta, Sergeant Otto, 108
Plato, 183
Plebiscite, Austrian, 122
Plevna, battle of, 444
Ploesti, 373
Poincaré, Raymond, 101
Poland, 8, 76, 102, 164, 169, 176, 232, 238, 327, 418, 449
Poles, 131, 376
Polzer-Hoditz, Count, 96, 102
Pompadour, Madame de, 66
Popolo d'Italia, 118
Porto Baros, 348
Pozsony, 158, 258
Prague, 36, 123, 161, 163, 170, 173, 175, 176, 195, 201, 254, 349
Prague Castle, Bohemia, 37
Prater, the, 79, 80, 139
Premyslid Dynasty, 172
Pressburg, 158
Princip, 343
Probus, Emperor, 28
Protestants, 243
Prussia, 66, 73, 365, 423
Pruth river, 366, 377, 411
Puszta, 217-218, 259, 271, 293
Pyrenees mountains, 10

"Race-Protecting National Socialist Party," 269
Radich, Ante, 348
Radich, Stephen, 317, 345, 348-352, 354
Ragusa, 58, 272, 315
Rákóczi, Ferenc, 244
Rákóczi March, Berlioz, 244
Rangkórság, 221

477

Ratisbon, 33
Ratispone, 33
Raymond, Count of Toulouse, 328
"Razen," the, 291
Reformation, the, 26, 41, 175, 242
Regat, the, 381
Regensburg, 5, 22, 29, 30-37, 38
Regensburg, Cathedral, 36, 37
Regnitz river, 456
Regina Castra, 31-33
Reichstadt, Duke of, l'Aiglon, 75, 76-81, 136, 153
Reign of Terror, the, 69
Reinhardt, Max, 125
Republic, Plato, 183
Revolution of 1848, 82, 153, 226, 246, 247, 279, 419
Rhine river, 6, 8, 10, 20, 27, 28, 47, 72, 456
Richard the Lion-Hearted, 50
Robinson, Sir Thomas, 65
Rock of the Forty Girls, 379
Romanovs, the, 425
Romans, the Ancient, 19, 52, 300, 304, 331; — in Roumania, 391-394
Rome, 4, 23, 27, 30, 31, 32-33, 52, 55, 103, 242, 243, 458
"Rome pacts," 460
Roosevelt, Franklin D., 202
Roter Turm, 63
Rothenburg 25
Roumania, 6, 11, 213, 231, 257, 298, 302 *et seq.,* 362-442, 456, 463
Roumanian minorities in Czechoslovakia, 164
Rousseau, Jean Jacques, 18
Rudolf the Black, 396
Rudolph I, Count, 57, 60, 147, 167, 172, 314
Rudolph, Crown Prince, Archduke of Austria, 87, 92-98
Rudow, 168
Runciman, Viscount, 195, 199
Rurik the Norseman, 168

Russia, 7, 73, 131, 246, 274, 298, 308, 309, 336, 339, 366, 369, 376, 377, 380 *et seq.,* 455; struggle over Roumania, 410 *et seq.;* conquest of Bucharest, 453
Russian aristocracy, 95
Russian steppes, the, 10, 168, 369
Russo-Turkish War of 1877-1878, 427
Rustchuk, 364
Ruthenia, 216, 376

Sacher Hotel, 137
Sachs, Hans, 20, 21, 147, 155
St. Denys, 37
St. Dionysius, "the Areopagite," 37
St. Emery (Imre), 234
St. Emmeram, 37
St. Gellért, 273, 274, 276
St. Germain, Treaty of, 103
St. George river, 367
St. Helena, 75
St. John de Nepomuc, 36
St. Michael Church, 50
St. Petersburg, 95, 410
St. Sebastian, 41
St. Severinus, 43
St. Stephen, 213, 234, 288
St. Stephen's Cathedral, 77, 81, 136
Saisonstaat, 188
Salonika, 253, 345, 353-354
Salt Route, 364
Salzburg, 58, 87, 119
Salzburg, Archbishop of, 68
Salzburg Festival, 127
Samo, Prince, 171
Samuel, Czar, 328
Sandro. *See* Alexander II, King of Yugoslavia
San Giorgio, Tower of, 364
San Lazarus Archipelago, 61
Sarajevo, 156, 252, 322, 340, 343, 353
Sardinia, 365
Sardinia, King of, 63
Sarmates, 395
Saumur, 75

Index

Sau-Preuss (pig-Prussian), 31
Sava, son of Stephen Nemanya of Serbia, 328
Sava river, 301, 312, 314, 316 *et seq.*, 335, 356
"Savage Diet," 240
Savoia, 359
Savus river, 301
Scharfschuetze, 436
Schlossberg, 314
Schoenbrunn, 80, 87, 89, 156
Schratt, Catherine, 87-88, 102
Schubert, Franz, 141, 153, 157
Schuschnigg, Frau, 116
Schuschnigg, Kurt von, Chancellor, 113-123
Schwarzenberg, Prince, 77
Scythe Cross, 268
Scythians, 233, 377
Season State, the, 188, 196
Second Balkan War, 429
Second Silesian War, 66
Sedgwick, Henry Dwight, quoted, 150
"Seedless," the, 229
Seipel, Chancellor Ignaz, 104, 115
Serbia, 58, 63, 67, 251, 298, 301, 309 *et seq.*, 397, 414, 455
Sereth river, 411
Sesostris the Egyptian, 3
Seton-Watson, R. W., 390, 395, 402-403
Seven Houses, 309
Seven Years' War, 66
Seyss-Inquart, Dr. Arthur, 120, 121, 122
Shakespeare, 218, 247
Sicambria, 287
Siebenbuergische Tageblatt, 436
Siegfried, 19
Sigmaringen, 19
Silesia, 58, 63, 64, 65, 67, 110, 147
Silistra, 361, 365
Simeon, Czar, 327
Simon the Great, Emperor of all the Bulgars and Greeks, 454
Sinaia, 372, 434; — *camarilla*, 437

Sinan Pasha, the Renegade, 403
Singidunum, 320
Sisk, 348
Sixtus, Prince, 101
Skoda, 189, 207
Skoplje, 309
Slavic Wends, 168
Slavonia, 11, 58, 102, 300, 313, 317
Slavs, the, 288, 307, 395
Sljeme peak, 316
Slovakia, 158, 159, 177, 204
Slovenia, 102, 311, 312, 316
Smederovo, 302
Smetana, Friedrich, 162
Social Democrats, the, 110, 111
Socialist Party, the, 104, 105, 111, 112, 117, 126, 138, 144, 165, 255, 257, 349
Society of Germans Abroad, 267
Sofia, 454
Sokols, 163, 170-171, 195, 199
Sommerau ridge, 16
Somme, 200
"Song to Be Whispered," 126
Sonnenberg, 58
Sonnino, Baron Sidney, 347
Sophie, Princess, 342-343
Sorbonne, 422
Sosan, 41
Soutzo, Nicholas, 399
Sozifresser, the, Karl Vaugoin, 111
Spain, 24, 47, 55, 60, 121, 201, 291, 310, 359
Spandau, 168
Sportpalast, 197, 202
Stadtpark, 130, 133
Stalin, 447
Stalingrad, U. S. S. R., 7
Starhemberg, the first Count Ernst Ruediger von, 148
Starhemberg, Prince Ernst Ruediger von, 109-116, 139
"Starvers," the, 229
Steenockerzeel, 265
Stein, von, quoted, 74

Stella Matutina, 114
Stephanie, Crown Princess, 87, 95, 96-97
Stephen the Great, 397, 412, 413
Stephen Tomsa, Prince of Walachia, 403-404
Stuermer, the, 439
Stift Engelszell, 50
Stirbey, Prince, 432
Stock im Eisen, 136
Stone Age, 3, 7, 9
Stoyadinovich, Dr. Milan, 360
Strasbourg, 6
Straubing, 39-40
"Street of Victory." *See* Calea Victoriei
Strauss, Johann, 141, 142, 155, 157
Strauss, Joseph, *Kapellmeister,* 85
Struma river, 305
Sturdza, Prince, "the Calf," 384
Suez, 359
Styria, 58, 64
Sudeten, 160, 164, 173, 186-204, 193
Suleiman the Magnificent, 3, 241, 320, 413
Sulina, 365, 378
Sulina river, 367
Swedes, 38
Switzerland, 103, 181, 264
Swabians, 374
Sylvin, 43
Syrians, 392
Syrovy, Jan, 202
Szálasi, Major Ferenc, 268
Széchényi, Count Stephen, 223, 277, 292-293
Szeged, 218
Székelys, the, 258, 374
Szemere, Herr von, 224
Szeps, Moricz, 96
Szilágyi, Mihaly, 289

Tacitus, 19
Tampeano, Captain, 437
Tankosic, Major, 343
Tard, village of, 229

Targoviste, 453
Tatars, 160, 168, 213
Tatra mountain, 205, 214
Teke, 379
Teleki, Count Paul, 219
Tell, Wilhelm, 58
Teltow, 168
Temes-Kubin, 343-344
Terazye Square, 318-319
Teschen, 58
Teutonic Knights, 169-170, 239, 375
Tharaud Brothers, quoted, 255
Theiss river. *See* Tisza river
Third Reich, 116, 169-170, 266-269, 436, 456
Thirty Years' War, 25, 49, 117, 175-176
Tiber river, 3
Timok river, 363
Timpul, the, 451
Tisa river, 374
Tisza, Count Stephen, 252
Tisza river, 214, 300
Titel, 300
Tolstoy, Leo, 162, 381
Tomis, 379
Tona river, 11
Toscanini, Arturo, 447
Town Hall, Regensburg, 33, 35, 36
Trajan, Emperor, 32, 303, 306, 320, 363, 374, 392, 393
Transdanubia, 215
Transylvania, 9, 58, 102, 214, 216, 369, 374-376, 391, 404, 405, 416, 430, 435
Transylvanian mountains, 364
Treaty of Paris of 1856, 365, 422
Treaty of Versailles, 457
"Tremblers," the, 229
Trente, 58
Trianon Treaty, 258, 277
Trieste, 58, 67, 201, 357
Triple Entente, 428, 429
Tristan, Richard Wagner, 141
Tristes, Ovid, 394
Troy, 10
Trinity Column, 49

Index

Tschuppik, Karl, 83
Tulcea, 367
Tunisia, 359
Turin, 357
Turkey, 31, 301, 364, 410-411, 422, 426, 458; High Porte of, 304, 322; struggle over Roumania, 410 et seq., 443, 446, 447, 453
Turkish Sultans, 396-406
Turks, the, 61, 77, 131, 148-149, 156, 213, 232, 240, 267, 290 et seq., 397 et seq.
Turnu Severin, 304, 425
Tuscany, 58
Tuschl, Henry, 44
Tyrol, 54, 58, 64, 118, 128, 300
Tzintzars, the, 311

Ujvidék, 300
Ukraine, the, 10, 169, 274, 374, 418, 442
Ukrainian minorities in Czechoslovakia, 164
Ulm, 5, 22, 456, 457
U. S. S. R., 169, 170, 192, 197, 298, 377, 378
United States of America, 74, 101, 182, 205, 224, 227, 250, 347, 366
Ural Mountains, 233, 394
Ustasha, 356
Uzhok Pass, 160

Vaclavske Namesti, 195, 202
Vag river, 204
Valkyries, the, 39
Vandals, the, 4, 38, 288
Vardar river, 305, 309, 311, 356
Varna, battle of, 237
Vatha the Cruel, 274
Vaugoin, Karl, 111
Vecchio, Palma, 184
Venetia, 53, 132, 316
Venezuela, 366
Venice, 241, 405, 412
Verdun, 24

Verecke Pass, 233
Versailles, 69; influence on Habsburgs, 60, 84
Vetsera, Baroness Helena, 93
Vetsera, Baroness Marie, 92-94
Victoria, Queen of England, 430
Vidin, Pasha of, 398
Vienna, 11, 18, 23, 45, 47, 50, 51, 54, 55, 62, 63, 65, 67, 72, 74, 75, 78, 85, 89, 92, 93, 103, 107, 111, 112, 121, 124, 125-128, 129-157, 162, 247, 253, 254, 256, 292, 294, 330, 361, 366, 403, 417; Alsergrund, 141; Ballhausplatz, 134; Burg, 134, 151, 156, 157, 240; Burggarten, 134; Congress of Vienna, 72, 74, 129, 135; Court, 142-143; Doeblin, 141; "Gate of ——," 131; Heuriger, 145, 155; Hietzing, 80, 141; Hofburg, the Vienna, 68, 74, 81, 86, 99, 156; Imperial Café, 146; Leopoldstadt, 139-140; Massenmensch, 143; Opera, 134; Rathaus, 135; "Red ——," 144; Ring, the, 125, 133-137, 155; Stattsbeamter, 143; Vieroeckl Cellar, 86; Világos, 249; Vindobona (Latin name of Vienna), 146; Volksgarten, 134; Vienna Woods, 5, 50, 93, 130, 133, 144, 155, 215
Vilna, 449
Vilshofen, 44
Vinca, 7, 8
Virgil, 32
Vitzacu, Michael. See Michael the Brave
Vlachs, the, 311, 416
Vlad the Devil, 237, 398
Vlad the Impaler, 398-399. See also Vlad the Devil
Vlada, 357
Vladimir, King, the Serbian, 328
Voelkerwanderung, 396
Vohburg, 28
Voivodina, 317
Volga river, 6, 10, 395
Voltaire, 18, 34, 70

Vorarlberg, 128
Voronet Monastery, 370
Vutcic, 335

Wachau, the, 5, 49, 107
Wagner, Richard, 141
Wagram, 161
Walachia, 63, 369, 371-372, 381-390,
    396-411, 422-427
Wallenstein, 25
Wandervoegel, the, 29
Waterloo, Battle of, 74, 246
Weisz, Manfred, 285
Wenceslaus I, King of Bohemia, 57
Wendish Marches, 58
Werner the Pious, 58
West Virginia, 204
When Israel Was King, by the Tharaud
    Brothers, 255
White Mountain, battle of, 176
Wieden, 62
Wiener Zeitung, 92
Wilde, Oscar, quoted, 195
Wilhelm I, King of Prussia, 423
Wilhelm II, Kaiser, 90, 94, 101, 169,
    170, 198
Wilson, Woodrow, 182, 347, 350
Wittelsbachs, the, 90

Wittenberg, 243
Wladislaus II of Bohemia, 239
Wolff (father of Magda Lupescu), 437
World War, 4, 24, 54, 82, 84, 98, 100,
    143, 177, 252, 294, 298, 305, 318,
    340 *et seq.,* 350, 354, 366, 369, 374,
    429, 430, 455
Wuerttemberg, 22, 31

Xavier, Prince, 101
Xenopol, 402

Ypres, 200
Yugoslavia, 6, 7, 102, 110, 213, 231,
    259, 297-361, 363, 381, 463

Zagreb, 316, 348, 349-350, 352; —
    Cabinet, 346; — University, 349
Zara, 58, 316, 347
Zator, 58
Zemun, 301, 318
Zernatto, Guido, 120
Zhor, 160, 161
Zinspalaeste, 138
Zita, Empress, 101-103, 261-266
Zizka, John, 174-175
Zlata Praha, 172, 178
Zorka, Princess of Serbia, 339
Zurich, 20, 339, 424

GERMANY
PRAGUE
BOHEMIA
MAEHRISC
-OSTRAU
MORAVIA
FRANCE
REGENSBURG
BLACK FOREST
INGOLSTADT
BAVARIAN WOODS
DONAUWOERTH
PASSAU
ULM
WACHAU
GREIN
Inn
Ilz R.
BRAUNAU
LINZ
MELK
VIENNA
BRATISL
DONAUESCHINGEN
SIGMARINGEN
GERMANY
OSTMARK
GYÖ
River
Lake Balaton
SWITZERLAND
BRENNER PASS
ALPS
HU
Drava River
SLOVENIA
LJUBLJANA
ZAGREB
YUG
CROATIA
Sava
ZARA
DALMATIA
ADRIATIC S
ITALY
STEINBERG